LENIN

COLLECTED WORKS

35

THE RUSSIAN EDITION WAS PRINTED
IN ACCORDANCE WITH A DECISION
OF THE NINTH CONGRESS OE THE R C.P.(B.)
AND THE SECOND CONGRESS OF SOVIETS
OF THE U.S.S.R.

ИНСТИТУТ МАРКСИЗМА-ЛЕНИНИЗМА при ЦК КПСС

В. И. ЛЕНИН

СОЧИНЕНИЯ

Издание четвертое

ГОСУДАРСТВЕННОЕ ИЗДАТЕЛЬСТВО
ПОЛИТИЧЕСКОЙ ЛИТЕРАТУРЫ
МОСКВА

V. I. LENIN

COLLECTED WORKS

VOLUME
35
LETTERS
February 1912 — December 1922

PROGRESS PUBLISHERS
MOSCOW 1966

TRANSLATED FROM THE RUSSIAN
BY ANDREW ROTHSTEIN
EDITED BY ROBERT DAGLISH

PUBLISHERS' NOTE

Translated from the Fourth Russian
Edition of Lenin's *Collected Works*.
Corrections have been made to some
of the letters and notes in accordance
with the Fifth Russian Edition, and
some further editorial comments have
been added.

В. И. ЛЕНИН

СОЧИНЕНИЯ

Том 35

На английском языке

CONTENTS

[1] Letters marked with an asterisk have not been published in previous editions. See Preface, p. 20.—*Ed.*

1915

1917

1918

ILLUSTRATIONS

PREFACE

Volume 35 consists of letters, telegrams and notes written by Lenin between February 1912 and December 1922 inclusive.

The documents in this volume reflect Lenin's activities during the revival of the working-class movement that began in 1910, during the imperialist world war, during the period when the Great October Socialist Revolution was prepared and carried out, and during the first five years of Soviet power.

The letters written in the years of revolutionary revival—to the editorial board of *Pravda*, to Y. M. Sverdlov and others—show Lenin's activity in guiding the Bolshevik legal daily newspaper *Pravda* and the Bolshevik group in the Fourth State Duma, and contain authoritative observations on the problem of nationalities.

A number of letters, to Maxim Gorky, G. K. Orjonikidze and others, throw light on Lenin's efforts to unite the Party on the basis of the decisions of the Prague Conference, and his fight against the anti-Party August bloc, organised by Trotsky.

A large number of letters in this volume reflect Lenin's struggle against the imperialist war and the treacherous policy of the open social-chauvinists, Kautskians and Trotskyists, and expose the anti-Party activity of hidden enemies of the Party—Pyatakov, Bukharin, Zinoviev and their supporters. These letters also show what Lenin did to guide the revolutionary work of the Bolshevik organisations in Russia and unite the Left-wing elements of international Social-Democracy on the principles of proletarian internationalism for the fight against social-chauvinism and for transformation of the imperialist war into civil war.

The volume includes a considerable number of letters from Lenin to Inessa Armand, containing most important propositions on Bolshevik theory and tactics in regard to problems of war, peace and revolution. The Bolshevik attitude to the slogan "defence of the fatherland" receives particular attention.

The letters and telegrams of the years 1918-20 contain directives issued by Lenin on questions of the country's defence, the Red Army's military operations and consolidation of the Soviet rear.

A number of letters sharply criticise the work of the Revolutionary Military Council. These letters, and also the telegrams to the Military Councils of various fronts and armies, expose the suspicious activities of the Trotskyists who had found their way into high military posts and were attempting to frustrate the successes of the Red Army and make more difficult the struggle of the Soviet people against the foreign invaders and the whiteguards.

In the letters covering the years 1921-22 much space is devoted to the strengthening of the Soviet state, economic planning and the electrification of the country. Many documents of this period deal with the problems of improving the work of the machinery of state—the drive against bureaucracy, the proper selection of personnel, systematic checking of the fulfilment of decisions and drawing the mass of working people into state administration.

Lenin's correspondence in these years demonstrates his special concern for scholars and writers, for the development of Soviet culture, science and technology. This can be seen in his letters about the plan for electrification of the country, the importance of radio inventions, the compilation of a dictionary of contemporary Russian, the work of libraries and schools, and in those which point to the necessity for gathering materials on the history of the Civil War and the Soviet Republic.

The volume contains 172 documents that had not been included in previous editions of the *Collected Works* (they are marked with an asterisk in the contents list). Of these 23 appeared in print for the first time in the Fourth Russian Edition.

The letters and telegrams are in chronological order, those sent abroad from Russia being dated in old style, those sent from abroad in new style. Where there is no date in Lenin's original, the editors have added it at the end of the document.

Apart from the reference notes, there is an alphabetical list for identifying the pseudonyms, nicknames and initials used in the text.

1912

1

TO MAXIM GORKY

Dear A. M.,

We shall shortly send you the resolutions of the Conference.[1] We have finally succeeded—in spite of the liquidationist[2] scoundrels—in reviving the Party and its Central Committee. I hope you will be as glad of this as we are.

Won't you write a May Day leaflet for us? Or a little leaflet in a similar May Day spirit? Quite a short one, a "heart-warmer", what do you say? Think of old times, remember 1905, and put down a couple of words, if you have the mind to write. There are two or three illegal printing-presses in Russia, and the Central Committee will republish it, probably, in several tens of thousands of copies. It would be a good thing to get a *revolutionary* manifesto like the *Tales* in *Zvezda*.[3] I am very, very glad that you are helping *Zvezda*. We are having a devilish hard job with it—internal and external and financial difficulties are immense—but still we are managing so far.

All the best,
Lenin

P.S. And *Sovremennik*[4] has had the sense to die, after all! That was a good deed on its part.

Written in February 1912
Sent from Paris to Capri (Italy)

First published in 1925
in *Lenin Miscellany III*

Printed from the original

2

TO MAXIM GORKY

Dear A. M.,

I am very glad you have agreed to try and write a May Day leaflet.

I enclose the Conference resolutions.

I have seen *Zhivoye Dyelo*.[5] A rotten little liquidationist rag with an "approach". Liberal propaganda. They are glad that the police prevent the question of the Party being openly discussed.

Zvezda will continue, either as a weekly *or as a kopek daily*.[6] You helped *Zvezda* very, very much with your splendid *Tales*, and that made me extremely joyful, so that the joy—if I am to talk straight—outweighed my sadness at your "affair" with the Chernovs and Amfiteatrovs[7].... Brr! I am glad, I must confess, that they are "going up the spout".

But as for your having nothing to live on and not being able to get printed anywhere, that's bad. You ought to have got rid of that leech Pyatnitsky long ago and appointed an honest agent, an agent pure and simple, to deal with Znaniye[8] (perhaps it's already too late, I don't know)!!! If only.... It would have been a gold mine....

I see Rozhkov's *Irkutskoye Slovo*[9] very rarely. The man's become a liquidator. And Chuzhak is an old ass, hardened and pretentious.

Yours,
Lenin

Thank M. F.[10] for her letter to Moscow, and a thousand greetings!

Written in February-March 1912
Sent from Paris to Capri

First published
in *Bakinsky Rabochy* No. 17,
January 21, 1927

Printed from the original

3

TO G. L. SHKLOVSKY

Dear Comrade,

I hasten to reply to some of your questions. A report on the Conference is a necessary and most important thing. I hope that, once you have taken it on, you will go round *all* Switzerland, and not only the two cities.[11]

"From the Announcement I cannot make out what steps the Conference took to draw in various trends abroad and national organisations." These are your words.

But the *Announcement* stated clearly and precisely that the *Vperyod* group[12]+*Trotsky*+*Plekhanov*[13] were invited, and the nationals three times. What more was needed?

Lunacharsky at Zinoviev's lecture in Paris had the brass face to say that it was a *"Gaunerkniff"*,* because, he said, the invitations were sent out not by the Conference but by delegates *who had arrived*. Well, isn't this Lunacharsky a scoundrel? 23 sessions=12 days: if the invitations hadn't been sent out *beforehand*, the people who were invited would have missed half (letter has to be sent off, secret addresses given, then they have to arrive—just add it all up!). And from Trotsky's letter you can see that the invitation was from *7 people*=$^1/_2$ of the total of 14.

I was *against* the invitation, but the delegates *invited* the *Vperyod* group and Trotsky and Plekhanov.

The chairman of the credentials committee was the *delegate from Kiev* (a Menshevik). Even Trotsky has admitted (under pressure!) that this is a *bona fide* organisation.

Whom will the worker believe, then? The Kiev *organisation* or ranters abroad?

Don't believe rumours. Neither the Plekhanovites nor the *Vperyod* people, *no one* left the Conference. There were

---

* "Swinder's trick".—*Ed.*

in all *two* pro-Party Mensheviks. The one from Kiev behaved with extreme correctness and on the whole went *with us*. The one from *Ekaterinoslav* behaved with extreme obstructiveness, *but even he did not leave the Conference*, and only moved "protests" in the spirit of Plekhanov.

The Ekaterinoslav delegate moved his *own* draft resolution on the constitution of the Conference, in which he *fully admitted* that *everyone* had been notified, protested that some had not come, but wanted the Conference to constitute itself as representing *Russian* organisations. He remained on this in a minority of *one*.

Now 12 delegates are in Russia, making reports everywhere. *There are already letters* about this from St. Petersburg, Moscow, Kiev, Samara, Nikolayev and Tiflis. The work has begun and will continue.

The Bund[14]+the Letts are trying to fix up a conference with the liquidators. Let them try! It's deeds that are needed, gentlemen, and not words!! You have been impotent (+Trotsky+Vperyodists) since November 26, 1910[15] —when Trotsky proclaimed the calling of a conference— and you will remain impotent.

We have broken with the liquidators, the *Party* has broken with them. Let someone try to set up a different R.S.D.L.P. *with* the liquidators! It would be laughable.

The Duma Social-Democratic group is *directly* neither for us nor for them. But (1) there were *two* deputies at our Conference[16]; (2) *Zvezda* has *nine* Social-Democratic deputies on its list of contributors, while the liquidationist *Zhivoye Dyelo* has *four*. There are facts for you!

Among the Letts the Bolsheviks have declared war on their Central Committee.

Well, I wish you every success! Greetings to all our friends.

Yours,
N. Lenin

Written on March 12, 1912
Sent from Paris to Berne

First published in 1930
in *Lenin Miscellany XIII*

Printed from the original

4

TO G. L. SHKLOVSKY

Dear Comrade,

Nadya sent you my little note today.* I hasten to let you know—so that there should be no misunderstanding and you should not make any mistake in your report— that *yesterday* there was a meeting in Paris of "Social-Democrats" who were enemies of the Conference. They *all* (the Plekhanovites and the *Golos* group,[17] the *Vperyod* group and the conciliators, and *tutti quanti***) adopted a resolution of protest against the Conference, and also something about excluding me from the International Socialist Bureau[18] (this is from hearsay, because, of course, the Bolsheviks and the supporters of the Conference[19] *did not* attend the meeting).

Naturally, all this is laughable. If these gentry proved unable to retain their grip even on the C.C. Bureau Abroad (make fun of it in your report, using Plekhanov's funeral oration in No. 15 of his *Dnevnik*, Supplement 2![20]), now they will be even less able to set up anything. Well, kind friends, not words but deeds: you boast that you have united. Do please unite in *Nasha Zarya* and *Zhivoye Dyelo*, and above all in *Golos Sotsial-Demokrata*.[21]

Comedians!

All the best, and best wishes for success.

Yours,
Lenin

Written on March 13, 1912
Sent from Paris to Berne
First published in 1930
in *Lenin Miscellany XIII*

Printed from the original

* See the previous letter.—*Ed.*
** The like.—*Ed.*

5

TO G. K. ORJONIKIDZE, S. S. SPANDARYAN AND YELENA STASOVA[22]

March 28, 1912

Dear Friends,

I am *terribly* upset and disturbed by the *complete* disorganisation of our (and your) relations and contacts. Truly, it is enough to make one despair! Instead of letters, you send various telegraphically brief exclamations which are quite incomprehensible.

(1) Nothing from Ivanovich. What is he doing? Where is he? How is he getting on? It's devilishly necessary to have someone legal in Petersburg or near Petersburg, because things are bad there. This is a furious and difficult war. We have neither information nor guidance, nor supervision of the paper.

(2) Not one of the Conference delegates gives us any contacts. Not one, and not a single contact. Why, that's complete collapse!

(3) No resolutions from anywhere which are sensible, clear, stating what organisations adopted them, supporting the decisions, confirming that their delegate attended, came back, reported!! Is it really not clear how different such formal resolutions are from letters of an intimate character: "decent", "jolly good", "we won", etc.? There are no resolutions from Kiev or from Savka's town.[23] Nikolai has sent in a letter full of joyful exclamations but absolutely senseless. It is quite unsuitable either for the press or for official use. Were all the resolutions read out? Were they approved? What is the text of resolutions on the

Conference? Are they joining forces with the local liquidators? Not one (not one!) of these fundamental elementary questions is answered. Not a single word of communication with that town (most important!) has been transmitted to us. Is not that collapse? Isn't that a parody of work?

(4) No resolutions from anywhere, not a single one, demanding the money! Simply a disgrace.

(5) Neither from Tiflis nor from Baku (terribly important centres) is there any word of sense about reports having been delivered. Where are the resolutions? Shame and disgrace!

(6) Not a single reprinting from anywhere of the Announcement or even *part* of it, either in print or hectographed! A disgrace.

(7) No precise reply in writing about the platform either. Will it be published? When? Has it been approved completely? We have to print it in the Central Organ, but have no precise information.

(8) They will have to go round all the organisations again and everywhere get resolutions adopted which are precise, formal, detailed, sensible, clear (a) on representation at the Conference and on its substance, (b) on support for the Central Committee, (c) and against the liquidators, specifically against the local ones, and in general, and (d) demanding return of the money.

(9) About the money, things are bad, send us a resolution which gives us the right to bring an action. The Germans have sent a refusal. Unless it is taken to court, we shall have a complete breakdown in three or four months.

(10) If you have *no* financial resources, the budget must immediately be radically reviewed: we have gone beyond all limits, and are approaching bankruptcy.

(11) In *Vorwärts*[24] of March 26, there was a furious and malicious article against the Conference, from the editorial board. Clearly this is Trotsky. There is a great battle over the Conference—but Russia is silent. It is no use putting on a bold show and boasting; everyone knows about *Vorwärts* and the protests, but nothing comes from Russia.

Summing up: this is collapse and disorganisation. A round of visits and contacts. Precise correspondence. Reprinting of the Announcement, even by hectograph. Otherwise it's all boasting.

Lenin

Pass on the letter to S. for further transmission. Greetings.

Sent from Paris to Tiflis

First published in the
magazine *Krasny Arkhiv* No. 1, 1934

Printed from a copy
written by Yelena Stasova

6

TO CAMILLE HUYSMANS[25]

Dear Comrade Huysmans,

I thank you for sending me the Paris "resolution".[26]
As I have already written to you, the Conference of the
R.S.D.L.P. condemned the liquidators and various groups
abroad[27] which are introducing disorganisation into our
Party and represent nothing in Russia. On the one hand,
in Paris at the present time it is groups of this kind that
have voted for the above-mentioned resolution. An old
custom has it that all condemned persons have the right
to inveigh against their judges for 24 hours. The persons
who have signed the resolution have made excessive use of
this right, and perhaps even abused it.

On the other hand, there are groups who *were invited*
to the Conference but refused to take part in it. Now they
are "protesting" and attempting to call another conference,
appealing to the gods to witness that they stand for unity.
A very original way to get unity! We shall see whether they
will make any headway in Russia. It is just as difficult to
carry out anything real in Russia as it is easy to vote for
abusive resolutions in Paris. And, of course, Paris, Vienna,
etc., do not possess the right to speak in the name of Russia.

In any case, the persons who signed the Paris resolution
are in too much of a hurry when they begin to talk about
a "split". In order to establish that a split exists, it must
be established that there exist at least two Central Committees *in Russia*. So far this is not so.

As for Citizen Plekhanov, the C.C. informed him more
than a month ago of the Conference resolutions. He has not

vouchsafed a reply. Consequently, at the present time I am quite ignorant of whether Citizen Plekhanov has (and from *which* C.C.) any powers as a member of the International Socialist Bureau.

If you, dear comrade, are luckier than I, i.e., if you get any reply from Citizen Plekhanov, I hope you will be good enough to inform me.

With fraternal greetings,

              Yours to command,

                     N. Lenin

Written in French earlier
than March 28, 1912

Sent from Paris to Brussels

First published in 1930
in *Lenin Miscellany XIII*

Printed from the original

7

TO G. K. ORJONIKIDZE, S. S. SPANDARYAN AND YELENA STASOVA*

Don't be light-hearted about the campaign of the liquidators abroad. It is a great mistake when people simply dismiss what goes on abroad with a wave of the hand and "send it to hell". The liquidators will cause a lot of confusion if they call their conference with the Bund+the Caucasian Regional Committee[28]+the Letts+liquidationist intellectuals. And they will call it! We must fight stubbornly, seriously and systematically. There must be a round tour and explanation everywhere of the liquidators' deception. Reprint the long article in the last issue of *Rabochaya Gazeta*[29] as a leaflet. I advise you to print a number of leaflets immediately (all the important resolutions of the Conference are a must). With leaflets you will win everything. Be exceptionally careful in setting about *Izvestia*.[30] The paper will be a great pretext for the police. And it is more important than anything else to hold on until the elections. Remember that there are *no* replacements.

Written early in April 1912

Sent from Paris to Tiflis

Published for the first time
in the Fourth (Russian) Edition
of the *Collected Works*

Printed from a copy
written by Yelena Stasova

---

* This letter is a postscript to a letter written by N. K. Krupskaya.—*Ed.*

8

TO THE BUREAU OF THE C.C.
OF THE R.S.D.L.P. IN RUSSIA*

April 16, 1912

Dear Friends,

For God's sake give us more contacts. Contacts, contacts, contacts, that's what we haven't got. Without this everything is unstable. Remember that two have already left the scene, there are no replacements for them. Without contacts everything will fall to pieces after one or two further arrests. You must without fail set up regional committees (or simply groups of trusted *agents*), *linked up* with us, for every region. Without this everything is shaky. As regards publication, you should press on with reprinting the *entire* resolution about the elections,[31] to make it *everywhere* available *in full* and among the masses.

As regards the money, it is time to stop being naïve about the Germans. Trotsky is now in full command there, and carrying on a *furious* struggle. You must send us a mandate to take the matter to the courts, otherwise we shall get nothing. We have already sent the May Day leaflet everywhere. I advise you to publish the appeal to the peasants about the elections as a leaflet (from *Rabochaya Gazeta*: the peasantry and the elections).** Make sure of

---

* This letter was sent via the Kiev Committee of the R.S.D.L.P. —*Ed.*

** See "The Peasantry and the Elections to the Fourth Duma" (present edition, Vol. 17, pp. 529-31).—*Ed.*

republishing the long article from *Rabochaya Gazeta*. This is an essential supplement to the platform, in which a very important paragraph about socialism has been omitted. Write! Contacts, contacts. Greetings.

P.S. *Vorwärts* is printing the most brazen lies, as, for example, that all Russia has already declared in favour of the Bundist-Lettish conference. It's Trotsky and Co. who are writing, and the Germans believe them. Altogether, Trotsky is boss in *Vorwärts*. The foreign department is controlled by Hilferding, Trotsky's friend.

Sent from Paris

Published for the first time
in the Fourth (Russian) Edition
of the *Collected Works*

Printed from a copy
written by Nadezhda Krupskaya

9

TO THE EDITOR OF *ZVEZDA*

Dear Colleague,

I am sending new material today for the *Voter's Handbook*. This is nearly all, there will be another article or two from here in two days' time, and then you will get an article on the budget from Tver.

(1) I very much advise you also to reprint from *Zvezda* No. 34 (December 17, 1911) the article by Frey: "The Role of Worker Electors in the Election Campaign" (it would also be a good thing to reprint his article in No. 36, December 31, 1911, about the role of peasant electors,* as well). Don't go out of your way to cut them down. It is better to publish in full a substantial article which will be of value in giving intelligible guidance for the elections. Don't go out of your way for cheapness and brevity—better publish something solid.

If, after all, it is absolutely impossible to publish all the articles, be certain to return those you don't.

(2) Here it is most essential to make arrangements for regular correspondence. Let your secretary write to me direct here, and not through Arcachon, to avoid any delay. Give us a better address for letters to you.

(3) You are wrong not to reply to the liquidators. This is a great mistake. You can and should reply, without saying a word about the Conference. You should print a brief reply to every lie of *Zhivoye Dyelo*: *Zhivoye Dyelo* in such-and-such a number is lying, as all the liquidators do. It is essential to reply, otherwise you lose.

---

* See present edition, Vol. 17, pp. 372-84.—*Ed.*

(4) If Plekhanov writes, you should send his articles here in proofs. Otherwise it becomes a "privilege" for him, which we cannot tolerate. Be careful. You will force us to leave if Plekhanov is given the privilege of writing against the Conference when we cannot write in favour of it. It would be a mean trick to allow him to abuse it when we cannot praise it.

(5) Be sure to send us in a separate packet, wrapped up in *Novoye Vremya*,[32] these numbers of *Zvezda*: Nos. 24 and 25 of the summer of 1911, No. 18 (54), No. 19 (55), No. 22 (58), No. 23 (59)—we haven't got them—and *Zhivoye Dyelo* No. 11 and No. 12. Please send us confiscated issues separately, wrapping them up in newspapers of the Right.

(6) Let us know as soon as possible about the daily paper.[33] What will be the size? What length of article can be sent?

(7) Try and buy as cheaply as possible the Verbatim Reports of the Third Duma, especially the sessions of 1911-12. Write.

Written on April 22, 1912

Sent from Paris to St. Petersburg

First published in 1923
in the book *Iz epokhi "Zvezdy"
i "Pravdy" (1911-14)*, Part III

Printed from the
typewritten copy found
in police records

10

TO B. N. KNIPOVICH [34]

June 6, 1912

Dear Colleague,

It is terribly annoying that my first letter to you about the book (thank you very much for sending it) has been lost. It is an incredible—but with us, it turns out, a possible—fact that a letter of a purely scientific nature can be lost. I will try and repeat it from memory, because I did not take a copy.

I read your book* with great pleasure, and was very glad to see that you had taken up a serious and large-scale work. This work will certainly enable you to test, deepen and consolidate your Marxist convictions.

I will note some ideas which came into my mind when reading it. It seemed to me that here and there, when studying the results of "differentiation", departures from the countryside are overlooked. I will make clear what I mean by this example, (a) first aspect: out of 100 households 25 have no horse=25 per cent, or have no sowings; (b) second aspect: of 150 households 36 have no sowings=24 per cent. Diminished differentiation, it would seem? But if 30 households or families have left the village for the town, or migrated, etc., then *in fact* proletarisation has increased. I think this is a typical example. The statistics always consider the households in existence, remaining "narrowly statistical" and omitting what is sometimes most important.

Then, the author definitely and more than once confines the subject of his research to the *tillage* aspect. But in

---

* Reference is to B. N. Knipovich's book *K voprosu o differentsiatsii russkogo krestyanstva. Differentsiatsia v sfere zemledelcheskogo khozyaistva* (*A Contribution to the Problem of Differentiation of the Russian Peasantry. Differentiation in the Sphere of Farming*), St. Petersburg, 1912.—*Ed.*

his conclusions he imperceptibly extends the theme, speaking of the whole of *agriculture* and sometimes even of the whole economy. This leads to error, because some aspects of "differentiation", i.e., of the proletarisation of the peasants and the genesis of capital, are, as a consequence, *lost* (for example, commercial stock-breeding in Yaroslavl Gubernia and other forms of penetration of exchange into agriculture, as it becomes specialised).

Furthermore. Do not the rows of figures sometimes obscure the *types*, socio-economic *types* of farmers (substantial bourgeois farmer; middle farmer; semi-proletarian; proletarian)? This danger is *very* great because of the *qualities* of statistical material. The "rows of figures" carry one away. I would advise the author to take this danger into account: our "socialists of the chair" unquestionably in this way *throttle* the living Marxist content of data. They drown the class struggle in rows and rows of figures. This does *not* occur with the author, but in the big work he has undertaken he ought particularly to take account of this danger, this "line" of the socialists of the chair, the liberals and the Narodniks. He should take it into account and *trim it down*, of course.

Lastly, Maslov[35] has appeared as something like a *deus ex machina. Cur? Quomodo? Quibus auxiliis?*[*] After all, his theory is very remote from Marxism. The Narodniks rightly called him a "critic" (=opportunist). Perhaps the author took him on trust more by chance?

Such were my thoughts when reading your interesting and serious book. I shake you by the hand, and wish you success in your work. I take this opportunity to send warm greetings to the whole family, and particularly to the "water-carrying nags"[36]—do you remember?

Yours,

V. Ulyanov

Written in Paris

First published in 1928
in the magazine *Bolshevik* No. 7

Printed from the original

---

[*] Why? How? By what means?—*Ed.*

11

TO THE EDITOR OF *PRAVDA*[37]

Dear Colleague,

I send you one more article by I. Gylka. The author reminds you that he is *expecting an advance*.

It is urgently necessary to reply to him immediately (you can do it through me, but *without fail* on a *separate* sheet). The author lives in Lemberg, makes a special *study* of his subject, and such a contributor should be drawn in. Once again I advise you to pay him an advance, *and in any* case to reply to him *at once*.

N.B. If Gylka's articles are not accepted, return them at once without fail!

We have received the parcel, and cannot help complaining.

Of the books, only *one*! Write and say why. Did other members of the staff take the rest of the books received? Have they taken them for long, or for good? If so, you ought to arrange to send them to us *for a time*. We repeat that without books we *cannot* work.

The office should be more careful about this.

We received the *Voter's Handbook two and a half weeks after publication*! Yet to send it *at once* would have cost 5 *kopeks*....

There has been a delay with the papers, after all. We are stuck here without newspapers, and we shall be without them for another two or three days.

I would very much advise you to send a reporter to the City Council, find out *how many* applications* they are

---

* From what districts? streets? etc., as detailed as possible.

getting from tenants and set about publishing this *systematically* (encouraging successful districts and appealing to the unsuccessful). Very little time is left, and the paper should make itself responsible for the *whole* business.

You should get from the City Council, through any statisticians among your acquaintances (or officially from the editors and the members of the State Duma), *all* the statistical material (if they don't exist, then buy *Rech*[38] for those years and months, or some other paper) about the elections to the *First*, *Second* and Third State Duma+ Petersburg statistics (housing, population, etc.). With such material in your hands, and with an intelligent reporter visiting the City Council daily or 2-3 times a week, you can run a *good* section in the paper about the course of the elections.

Do you send *Pravda* to the Wiener *Arbeiter-Zeitung*[39] in Vienna? Send it, and *send it to us as well by wrapper*.

I advise you to reply to Trotsky through the post: "To Trotsky (Vienna). We shall not reply to disruptive and slanderous letters." Trotsky's dirty campaign against *Pravda* is one mass of lies and slander. The well-known Marxist and follower of Plekhanov, Rothstein (London), has written to us that he received Trotsky's slanders and replied to him: I cannot complain of the Petersburg *Pravda* in any way. But this intriguer and liquidator goes on lying, right and left.

Yours faithfully,

V. Ulyanov

P.S. It would be still better to reply in this way to Trotsky through the post: "*To Trotsky* (Vienna). You are wasting your time sending us disruptive and slanderous letters. They will not be replied to."

Written on July 19, 1912
Sent from Cracow to St. Petersburg

First published in 1933   Printed from the original
in *Lenin Miscellany XXV*

12

TO THE EDITOR OF *NEVSKAYA ZVEZDA*[40]

Dear Colleague,

I have received your long letter, and I see that you and I must most certainly have it out.

First of all, a detail. You won't find correspondents at two kopeks a line. So long as you have no money, you will have to make do with our articles about affairs abroad.

Now for the main thing. You complain of monotony. But this will always be the case if you don't print *polemics*— if, in particular, you cut down *Kamenev* (he writes in a *different* tone)—if you reduce everything to "positive liquidationism". And in addition you will lose all your contributors if you don't print them, and don't even reply and don't send back articles (for example, mine: the reply to Blank—*important!* "Unquenchable Hopes"[41] and *a number of others!!*).

Just look at *Nevsky Golos*: it's more lively. It is not afraid of polemics. It attacks. It boldly makes its point to the bitter end.

By avoiding "painful questions", *Zvezda* and *Pravda make themselves* dry and monotonous, uninteresting, uncombative organs. A socialist paper *must* carry on polemics: our times are times of desperate confusion, and we can't do without polemics. The question is whether they are to be carried on in a lively way, attacking, putting forward questions independently, or only on the defensive, in dry and boring fashion.

For example, the "Supporter of *Zvezda*" in No. 16 gave a good reply. Clearly he is a man of principle. But all the same he did not dissipate the *terrible* fears aroused *everywhere* (I have a *series* of letters) by No. 6 of *Nevsky Golos*.[42] What did happen, after all? *Was* there a conference? Called by whom? What for? None of this is clear! And until this is cleared up *no one* wants to work. Everyone is saying: haven't I the right to know *who* I am working *for*, *whom* I am helping to get elected to the Duma? Maybe it's a liquidator? Maybe it's some muddled Trotskyist conciliator? Perhaps I am taking part (indirectly) in drawing up a "common platform"??

Such questions paralyse energy and introduce demoralisation.

Meanwhile *Nevsky Golos* is attacking briskly and takes a more challenging line. You can't hide differences from the workers (as *Pravda* is doing): it's harmful, fatal, ridiculous. You can't leave it to the *adversary*, to *Nevsky Golos*, to open up discussion of differences. *Pravda* will *perish* if it is *only* a "popular", "positive" organ, that is certain.

It would certainly be victorious if it were not afraid of polemics, talked straight about the liquidators, became lively through argument, by an article against Axelrod,[43] etc. Such articles as Axelrod's attract: *all* the workers hear about the differences and are *attracted* to Axelrod's open explanations, because he *says* things *straight out* a hundred times more boldly than we do. *All* the workers hear the talk about a united platform, all the leading workers know Axelrod's article[44]—and if you are silent, you have fallen behind! And the paper which falls behind is *lost*. A paper must be a step *ahead of everyone*, and that goes for both *Nevskaya Zvezda* and for *Pravda*. Side by side with the two "positive" little articles, *Pravda* must provide *polemics*—Kamenev's literary note—a feature article ridiculing the liquidators—and so forth. Monotony and lateness are incompatible with the newspaper business. And *Pravda* has in addition a special and exceptionally important duty: "whom is it going to *lead*"—this is what *everyone* is asking, what *everyone* is trying to read between the lines. It would be important to have a meeting (once in four years, before the elections)—you can't carry on the paper without even infrequent meetings with your constant contributors. *Think* over this well and quickly, for time won't bear delay.

Best wishes,

Ulyanov

Written on July 24, 1912

Sent from Cracow to St. Petersburg

First published in 1923
in the book *Iz epokhi "Zvezdy" i
"Pravdy" (1911-14)*, Part III   Printed from the original

13

TO THE EDITOR OF *PRAVDA*

Dear Colleague,

I have received your letter about the "pressing matter" and, I confess, read it with a sorrowful feeling. It shows quite clearly that there is between us not enough of the mutual understanding that in a "pressing matter", as in any serious matter, is most essential.

And the matter is really serious and—I agree with you— pressing (not in the sense of a few days, of course). In order to get mutual understanding on this, we ought to meet: this would cost four or five days and $11+11+15+10=47$ rubles all in all....

All that I can do at present to meet your request, I am doing. I am sending you an article "On the Election Platform".[45] You will see clearly, I hope, what my views are from this article.

As regards altering it, I must lay down *special* conditions (usually I don't make any, as you know, relying entirely on a comradely, collective and not pettifogging attitude). But on this occasion these special conditions are essential for me, because the question is one of vast importance, a radical question of principle.

I can agree *only* to (1) eliminating the subhead and (2) minimum corrections for the *censorship* (only!!) in three or four places, correction of *individual* words, *and nothing more at all*. If *even then* you can't print it either in *Pravda* or in *Nevskaya Zvezda*, *return* the article, I need it. To eliminating mention of the liquidators I *cannot* agree.

The essence of the whole question is that the liquidators are setting a trap: "let's have an open platform" (while privately the liquidator thinks: I will sign *anything* in

an open platform). And that is true, the liquidator will
sign *anything* in an open platform!! And it will be not a
platform, not a serious affair, but philistine chatter, a list
of "reforms", a competition with the liberals on *their* own
ground, because every liberal (up to and including Trubets-
koi) will at present, six or eight weeks before the elections, put his name to *anything*!! The liberals and the liquidators will sign anything, if only they can get elected to
the Fourth Duma.

One must grasp the essence of the question, the principle
involved, and not be afraid of somewhat "unusual", "unsuitable" (for *Pravda*) expressions, polemics, etc. The workers in their mass will understand very well the *spirit* of
the thing ("no cutting up")—and that is the whole point.
All will understand why inventing open platforms in Third-
of-June Russia, six or eight weeks before the elections,
is ridiculous, stupid, philistine, even scoundrelly. And
that is the essence.

Such an article printed as a feature in *Pravda*, even in
small type, will at once take up a position, and kill the
adventurism of the inventors of open platforms. It will
kill the demagogy of their "say openly what you believe
in". Used not Katkov in just the same way to ask: "Say
openly that you recognise the autocracy"?

Much has devolved on *Pravda* in the elections, and much
will be required of it. It would be a scandal if *Pravda* were
ridiculed *from the left* for drawing up open platforms.
Pravda has *in practice* the position of leader. That position
must be defended honourably. It should say clearly, calmly
and firmly: against the liquidators. And at once the whole
gang of these petty liberals will be killed. Let them put
forward their *own* list: they won't dare, because they will
be completely disgraced!! I await a *speedy* reply.

With greetings,

Yours,

V. Ulyanov

Written earlier than August 1, 1912
Sent from Cracow to St. Petersburg

Published for the first time   Printed from the original
in the Fourth (Russian) Edition
of the *Collected Works*

14

TO THE EDITOR OF *PRAVDA*

Dear Colleague,

I have your letter, and the letter from Vitimsky. I was very glad to get a word from him. But the contents of his letter gave me great concern.

You write, and as secretary,* evidently, on behalf of the editorial board, that "the editorial board in principle considers my article fully acceptable *including the attitude to the liquidators*". If that is so, why then does *Pravda* stubbornly and systematically cut out any mention of the liquidators, both in my articles and in the articles of other colleagues?? Don't you really know that they already *have* their candidates? We know this *for certain*. We have had official communications about this from a city in the south,** where there is a deputy from the worker curia. Undoubtedly the same applies to other places.

The silence of *Pravda* is more than strange. You write: "The editorial board considers it an *obvious* misunderstanding" that it is being "suspected of striving to legalise the demands contained in the platform". But surely you will agree that this is a fundamental question, one which determines the whole spirit of the publication, and moreover one which is inseparably bound up with the question of the liquidators. I have not the slightest inclination for "suspecting"; you know *from experience* that I show tremendous patience with your corrections for reasons of censorship as

* Reference is to V. M. Molotov.—*Ed.*
** The city referred to is Kharkov.—*Ed.*

well. But a fundamental question requires a *straight answer*. One must not leave a contributor uninformed as to whether the editorial board intends to direct the section of the paper dealing with the elections *against* the liquidators, naming them clearly and precisely, or *not against* them. There is not and cannot be any middle course.

If the article "must be printed anyway" (as the secretary to the editorial board writes), then how am I to understand Vitimsky's "the angry tone is harmful"? Since when has an *angry* tone against what is bad, harmful, untrue (and the editorial board is "in principle" in agreement!) harmed a daily newspaper?? On the contrary, colleagues, really and truly on the contrary. To write without "anger" of what is harmful means to write boringly. And you yourselves refer, and justly so, to monotony!

Furthermore, I have not had any reply for a long time concerning the article about November 9 (the reply of a correspondent).[46] I repeat my request: return what cannot pass the censorship or what you unquestionably reject.

We receive *Pravda irregularly* (yesterday we *didn't* get it *at all*!!). We have not seen *Zvezda*, either No. 14 or No. 17, *at all*. A scandal! Can't you send us the *page proofs* by wrapper, rather than throw them away? That costs two kopeks. It would save time. To send proofs to a contributor is perfectly legitimate. When leaving at night, the night editor would put the wrapper into a post-box—that would be all. (But the wrappers often tear, they should be made larger, the same size as the newspapers. It would be best of all to use long narrow envelopes: in such envelopes—*un*sealed—press material is more likely to arrive, and the envelopes don't cost much.) It is particularly essential to have *Zvezda* No. 17. Today is Thursday: *two days'* delay!!

Finally, please let me know whether it would not be possible to publish in one form or another (like *Nevsky Golos*, which has more than once printed information about the Social-Democrats abroad) the following news. The German *Vorstand** has made an appeal to the 11 (*sic*!) Social-Democratic groups, factions and centres, suggesting a joint conference on the subject of "unity". The so-called "Lenin

---

* Party Executive.—*Ed.*

trend" has replied with the most categorical refusal: what can be more ridiculous and unworthy than this playing at an agreement abroad with "centres and factions" which have demonstrated their absolute impotence in Russia? No negotiations with them, no agreements with the liquidators—such was the reply of the so-called "Lenin trend". Whether anything has come of this arch-stupid idea of Trotsky's, and whether anything will come of it, is not known.

And so I ask you to reply: can a report describing these "Paris novelties", and giving an assessment of them, be published, in one form or another, in the newspaper you edit? Do censorship conditions make this possible, or is it quite impossible?[47] (I ask only about the censorship aspect of the case, since in principle—I venture to think on the basis of the previous letter—the editorial board is *not* in favour of unity with the liquidators, isn't that so?)

With comradely greetings,

V. Ulyanov

Written on August 1, 1912

Sent from Cracow to St. Petersburg

First published in 1930
in the second and third editions
of Lenin's *Collected Works*, Vol. XVI

Printed from the original

15
TO MAXIM GORKY

Cracow, August 1, 1912

Krakau, Oesterreich.
Zwierzyniec. 218.
Wl. Ulijanow

Dear A. M.,

I have received your letter and a letter from the Siberians. My address now is not Paris, but Cracow—see above.

I haven't quite understood what party you have decided to expel me from. From the Socialist-Revolutionary perhaps?

No, joking apart, it's a bad, philistine, bourgeois style you have adopted, to wave us away with a "you're all squabblers". Just have a look at the latest S.R. literature —*Pochin*, *Izvestia zagranichnoi oblastnoi organizatsii*— compare it with *Revolutsionnaya Mysl* and with *Revolutsionnaya Rossiya*[48]—and then again with Ropshin,[49] etc. Remember *Vekhi*[50] and the polemics (quasi-polemics) conducted against it by Milyukov, Gredeskul[51] (who has now discovered that a second revolution in Russia is not necessary), etc., etc.

Compare *all* this as a whole, the sum *total* of ideological trends from 1908 to 1912 among the S.R.s,[52] Trudoviks,[53] Bezzaglavtsi[54] and Cadets,[55] with what existed and exists among the Social-Democrats (somebody, some day—probably a historian—will certainly do this work). You will see that *everyone*, literally everyone outside the Social-Democrats was discussing *the same* questions, literally the very same, on account of which little groups have broken away from our Party in the direction of liquidationism and otzovism.

The bourgeois, the liberals, the S.R.s like to shout about "squabbles" among the Social-Democrats, because they themselves do not take "painful questions" *seriously*, tag along behind others, play the diplomat, and make do with eclecticism. The difference between the Social-Democrats and all of them is that among the Social-Democrats squabbles are the externals of a struggle of groups with *profound* and clear ideological roots, while *among them* squabbles are externally smoothed over, internally empty, petty, trivial. Never and not for anything would I exchange the sharp struggle of currents of opinion among the Social-Democrats for the nicely smoothed emptiness and intellectual poverty of the S.R.s and Co.

All the very ʰest.

Yours,
Lenin

P.S. Greetings to M. F.!
P.S. And in Russia there is a *revolutionary* revival, not just a revival, but a revolutionary one. And we have managed at last to set up a daily *Pravda*—incidentally, thanks precisely to that (January) Conference* which the fools are yapping at.

Sent to Capri

First published in 1924
in *Lenin Miscellany I*   Printed from the original

---

* The Sixth (Prague) All-Russia Conference of the R.S.D.L.P.—*Ed.*

4*

16

TO THE EDITOR OF *PRAVDA*

Dear Colleague,

Kamenev writes to us today that you have informed him that peaceful relations have once again been restored between Plekhanov and yourselves by the elimination of "misunderstandings".

I would very much ask you to let me know the meaning of this dream. We had every reason to believe that the rejection of the articles by Dnevnitsky[56] and Plekhanov regarding a concession to the liquidators (for it was *precisely* about this that they were writing, under the screen of "unity") took place quite deliberately and resolutely. So what "misunderstandings" could there be in this case?

Are there not new misunderstandings in this latest communication?

The last, or more precisely yesterday's, editorial in *Rech* (July 19) is of tremendous importance. It cannot be doubted that the Cadets have done everything in their power (and beyond it) to *"hush up"* *Zvezda* and *Pravda*. And now they have come out with it! It is *clear* that they themselves have thereby admitted the *danger*. They have shown themselves unable to pass it by and hush it up. They have been driven out of their position of silence. And Prokopovich and Blank in *Zaprosy Zhizni*[57] echo them still more crudely, stupidly, tearfully.

Now of all times it is essential, in my opinion, to bring intense pressure to bear on *Rech*, to publish a *number* of articles against it and inflame the struggle still further. This is necessary both from the point of view of principle (since *only* *Zvezda* and *Pravda* are carrying on a campaign on behalf of working-class democracy, while both *Rech* and the Prokopoviches approvingly pat the liquidators on the back), and for practical reasons (since it is just this more lively struggle that must liven up both arguments and talks with the electors and their enrolment in the electoral registers).

Could you not find out how many people are registering, by polling districts, streets and professions? It would be extremely important to *encourage* them by concrete examples, in order to arouse competition between districts, streets and professions.

I hope you'll be kind enough also to inform *Nevskaya Zvezda* that I insist on the return of my article replying to Blank ("Petty Artifices") if it is not printed in No. 18. I will in that case certainly print it in the journal. Now that *all* the liberals+liquidators+non-Party and Co. have turned against us, it would be criminal for us to keep silent.

The election campaign in Petersburg has begun successfully—the leadership has been won by *Zvezda* and *Pravda*—what is necessary is not to lose one's grip on it, and to carry through the fight to a finish. This is in the interests of *the paper itself*, quite apart from everything else, which, of course, I do not mention.

I await news of the "positively decided" question.

With greetings,

V. Ulyanov

P.S. I still *await* a reply about the articles: "The Results of Six Months' Work".*

P.P.S. Couldn't you at least send me a cutting from No. 17 of *Nevskaya Zvezda*—the little article "Unity or Split"?

Written on August 2, 1912

Sent from Cracow to St. Petersburg

Published for the first time
in the Fourth (Russian) Edition
of the *Collected Works*

Printed from the original

---

* See present edition, Vol. 18, pp. 187-202.—*Ed.*

17

TO MAXIM GORKY

Dear A. M.,

If you recognise that "our squabbles are produced by an irreconcilable difference of ideological roots"—that the same applies to the S.R.s (that it is the same with the Cadets—*Vekhi*—this you did not add, but there can be no doubt about it)—that there is being created a *reformist* (apt word!) party—then you *cannot* say both to the liquidator and to his enemy: "Both of you are squabblers."

In that case the business of those who have understood the ideological roots of the "squabble", without taking part in it, is to help the masses to *discover the roots*, and not to justify the masses for regarding the disputes as "a private matter between the generals".

We "leaders have not written a single clear book, not a single sensible pamphlet".... Untrue. We wrote as best we could. No less clearly, no less sensibly, than before. And we have written a lot. There have been cases when we wrote against people without *any* "squabbling" (against *Vekhi*,* against Chernov,[58] against Rozhkov,** etc.). [Do you see all the issues of *Nevskaya Zvezda*?]

... "The result of this: among the workers in Russia there are a great number of good ... young people, but they are so furiously irritated with those abroad".... This is a fact; but it is not the fault of the "leaders", it is the

---

* See "Concerning *Vekhi*" (present edition, Vol. 16, pp. 123-31). —*Ed.*

** See "A Liberal Labour Party Manifesto" (present edition, Vol. 17, pp. 313-24).—*Ed.*

result of the detachment, or, more truly, the *tearing asunder*, of Russia and the emigrant centres. What has been *torn asunder* must be tied together again, and to abuse the leaders is cheap and popular, but of little use ... "that they dissuade the workers from taking part in the conference"....

What conference? The one the liquidators are now calling? Why, we ourselves are dissuading them too! Isn't there some misunderstanding on your part about this?[59]

I have read that Amfiteatrov has written, in some Warsaw paper,[60] if I am not mistaken, in favour of boycotting the Fourth Duma? Do you happen to have this article? Send it me, I will return it.

Things are warming up in the Baltic Fleet! I had a visit in Paris (this is between ourselves) by a special delegate sent by a meeting of the sailors and Social-Democrats. What's lacking is organisation—it's enough to make one weep!! If you have any officer contacts, you should make every effort to arrange something. The sailors are in a fighting mood, but they may all perish again in vain.

Your articles in *Zaprosy Zhizni* were not too good. It's a strange journal, by the way—liquidationist-Trudovik-*Vekhi*. A "classless reformist" party just about sums it up....

You ask why I am in Austria. The C.C. has organised a Bureau here (between ourselves): the frontier is close by, we make use of it, it's nearer to Petersburg, we get the papers from there on the third day, it's become far easier to write to the papers there, co-operation with them goes better. There is less squabbling here, which is an advantage. There isn't a good library, which is a disadvantage. It's hard without books.

All the very best,

Yours,

Lenin

Greetings to M. F.

Written earlier than August 25, 1912

Sent from Cracow to Capri

First published in 1924
in *Lenin Miscellany I*

Printed from the original

18

TO THE EDITOR OF *PRAVDA*

Dear Colleague,

You remind me again about the address of a friend. You have already asked me once for this address, and I sent it to you. It was added by me—I well remember—at the very end of a long letter. Look this up if you can. But perhaps it is simpler to repeat the address: Herrn Kurt Lauschner, Beuthen (Ober-Schlesien). Piekarerstr. 19/III, Germany. Inside it is essential to add: for Herr Hörsing: Für Herrn Hörsing (there are two Beuthens in Germany, therefore it is necessary to specify "Ober-Schlesien")...* has arrived. Many thanks. Dansky's manuscript has also arrived. I am extremely surprised that today, when I had from you both *Pravda* and a packet of reactionary papers, I did not receive Thursday's *Nevsky Golos*. But I, for a number of important reasons, very much need to have *Nevsky Golos* directly it appears. If it does not appear, please don't be too lazy to send me two words about it at once. It is extremely important for me to know as soon as possible whether it appeared on Thursday, August 23 (as *Nevsky Golos* promised on August 17), and, if it did appear, to get a copy. By the way, I sent you a long time ago a list of issues of *Zvezda*, *Nevskaya Zvezda*, *Pravda* and *Zhivoye Dyelo* missing from my files. You still don't reply whether you can send them. Yet one mutual friend told me the other day that you have files of *Zvezda* and *Nevskaya Zvezda*. Let me know, please, whether you have

---

* Some words are missing in the original.—*Ed.*

kept the list I sent, and whether you can send me the missing issues. I take advantage of this opportunity to congratulate Comrade Vitimsky (I hope it will not be difficult for you to pass this letter on to him) on the remarkably fine article in *Pravda* (No. 98)[61] which I received today. The subject chosen was extremely topical, and was splendidly worked out in a brief but clear form. In general it would be useful from time to time to recall, quote and explain in *Pravda* Shchedrin and other writers of the "old" Narodnik democratic movement. For the readers of *Pravda*—for the 25,000—this would be appropriate and interesting, and also it would throw light on present-day questions of working-class democracy from another point of view, and in other words.

What is the circulation of *Pravda*? Don't you think it might be useful to publish monthly statistics, even briefly (circulation, name of town and district)? What could be the arguments against publishing them? If there are no special considerations, it seems to me that you should publish.

I almost forgot. We have had a number of complaints from various places abroad that neither when subscriptions are sent, nor when money is sent for particular issues, does *Pravda* arrive. I don't get it regularly now myself. This means undoubtedly that something is wrong in the dispatch department. Please take the most energetic steps you can. Look yourselves at the letters from abroad about subscriptions, and get the matter cleared up. Send one copy of *Pravda* and *Nevskaya Zvezda* to the following address: Frl. Slutzky: Katherinenstr. 8 g. H.II (bei Worte), Halensee, Berlin.

Written on September 8, 1912

Sent from Cracow to St. Petersburg

First published in 1923
in the book *Iz epokhi "Zvezdy"*
i *"Pravdy" (1911-14)*, Part III

Printed from the typewritten
copy found in police records

19

TO MAXIM GORKY

Dear A. M.,

How is your health? Last time the news you sent me was not good—temperature rising, etc. Are you quite well again? Write a couple of words: I shall be very grateful.

Still nothing from you in *Pravda*. A pity. You ought to support the paper.

We are now "up to the ears" in the elections. Absenteeism is damnably great. In the worker curia likewise. But still everywhere Social-Democrats have been elected. Very much depends on the outcome of the elections for the building up of the Party.[62]

Have you heard anything about the liquidators' conference?

In what journal will you be printed? What's happening about Znaniye?

All the best, and I wish you a speedy and sound recovery. Regards to M. F.

Yours,
Lenin

P.S. My address is not Paris, but Cracow, Ulica Lubomirskiego. 47. Krakau.

P.S. Have you seen *Luch*[63]? Have you heard what sort of an undertaking *Dyen*[64] is? There are rumours that it is the organ of *Witte*[65]....

Written at the beginning of October 1912
Sent to Capri
First published in *Bakinsky Rabochy*
No. 17, January 21, 1927   Printed from the original

20

TO MAXIM GORKY

Dear A. M.,

The other day I had a letter from the editorial board of *Pravda* in Petersburg, in which they ask me to write to you that they would be extremely glad of your regular contributions. "We would like to offer Gorky 25 kopeks a line, but we are afraid of offending him." That's what they write to me.

To my mind, there is nothing at all to be offended at. Nobody could even dream of your contributions depending on considerations of payment. In the same way, everybody knows that the workers' *Pravda*, which usually pays 2 kopeks a line, and still more frequently pays nothing, cannot attract anyone by its fees.

But there is nothing bad about contributors' to a workers' paper receiving regular payment, however small it may be. In fact, it's all to the good. The circulation is now 20-25 thousand. It's time it began thinking of a proper arrangement about payment for contributions. What is bad about *everybody* working on a workers' paper beginning to earn a little? And how can there be anything offensive in this proposal?

I am sure that the fears of the Petersburg editors of *Pravda* are quite without foundation, and that you will not treat their proposal otherwise than in comradely fashion. Write a couple of words, either to them direct at the office, or to me.

Tomorrow is the election of electors in Petersburg (for the worker curia). The struggle with the liquidators has developed. In Moscow and Kharkov the Party people have won.

Have you seen *Luch*, and do you get it at all? There are people who have fiddled the cards and pretend to be "kind-hearted"!

I have seen an advertisement for *Krugozor*.[66] Is this your undertaking, or are you there by invitation?

Every good wish, and above all for your health. Greetings to M. F.

Yours,
Lenin

47. Ulica Lubomirskiego. Krakau.

Written on October 17, 1912
Sent to Capri

First published in 1924
in *Lenin Miscellany I*

Printed from the original

21

TO THE EDITOR OF *PRAVDA*

Dear Colleague,

I read today in *Pravda* and in *Luch* about the result of the elections for the worker curia in Petersburg. I cannot but express to you my congratulations on the leading article in No. 146. At a moment of defeat, inflicted not by the Social-Democrats (analysis of the figures clearly shows that it was not Social-Democrats who got the liquidators in), the editorial board at once took the appropriate, firm and dignified tone in pointing out the significance of a protest in principle against "belittling". Don't misunderstand these lines. Don't think that they are produced by anything except the desire to share my thoughts, so natural for a constant contributor. It was a difficult time. The struggle was hard. Almost everything possible was done, but demoralisation had its effect, and the non-Party workers gave their votes to the opportunists. All the more essential, then, is the strictly principled, insistent and stubborn work of the united whole (the united editorial board, for example, or the general body of contributors, and so forth) to counteract the demoralisation.

It is extremely important not to break off the study of the election results which *Pravda* began, but to continue it. To collect and print the votes of all the candidates (you have only 9 out of 13). To collect and print an enquiry into how the non-Party workers voted, how the Putilov workers voted (7 and 2 liquidators), the Semyannikov workers voted (2 and 1 liquidator), and so on, factory by factory.

Only *Pravda* can do this important job with success. Greetings and best wishes.

Yours,
Lenin

Written on November 2, 1912

Sent from Cracow to St. Petersburg

First published in 1923 in the book
*Iz epokhi "Zvezdy" i "Pravdy"
(1911-14)*, Part III

Printed from the typewritten
copy found in police records

22

TO THE EDITOR OF *SOTSIAL-DEMOKRAT*

WRITTEN ON A COPY OF "MANDATE OF THE ST. PETERSBURG WORKERS TO THEIR WORKERS' DEPUTY"[47]

N.B. *Return* without fail!! Don't dirty. *Extremely important* to preserve this document! *To be set up.*

Written earlier than November 18, 1912
Sent from Cracow to Paris

First published in *Pravda*
No. 123, May 5, 1932

Printed from the original

23

TO THE EDITOR OF *PRAVDA*

Dear Colleague,

I send you the St. Petersburg Mandate which by chance, thanks to an opportunity of very speedy delivery, reached us from Petersburg. Publish this Mandate to the St. Petersburg deputy without fail, in a prominent position and in large type. It is quite intolerable that *Luch*, distorting the Mandate, is already mentioning it and printing reports about it, while *Pravda*, whose supporters drew up the Mandate and got it adopted and put it into action, is silent about it.... What does this mean? Can a workers' newspaper exist if it behaves with such contempt for what interests the workers? (Naturally, if certain expressions and phrases are undesirable from the censorship point of view, partial changes are possible, as usually happens in such cases.) But not to print such a thing means not only to give ground for hundreds of disputes, in which *Pravda* will be the guilty party, but also to inflict the greatest possible damage on it as a newspaper, on the circulation and organisation of the paper as an undertaking. A newspaper, after all, is not just something for the reader to do a bit of reading in and the writer to do a bit of writing in. A newspaper must itself seek out, itself discover in good time and, at the appropriate moment, print certain material. A paper must look for and find the contacts it needs. Yet here suddenly is a Mandate to the St. Petersburg deputy, coming from the supporters of *Pravda*, but not printed in *Pravda*.... Please reply immediately on receiving this letter.

Written on November 24, 1912

Sent from Cracow to St. Petersburg

First published in 1923 in the book
*Iz epokhi "Zvezdy" i "Pravdy"
(1911-14)*, Part III

Printed from the typewritten
copy found in police records

24

TO THE EDITOR OF *PRAVDA*

Dear Colleague,

We were extremely sad to see two blunders in Sunday's *Pravda*. First, there was no article about the Basle Congress, and secondly, you did not print the greetings to the Congress from Badayev and the others.[68] As regards the first point, we are partly to blame as well, because we did not send an article. We were busy with extremely urgent and important affairs. It would not have been at all difficult to write such an article, and the editorial board of *Pravda* knew that the Congress was opening on Sunday. But the second omission is entirely the responsibility of Badayev. It is quite unforgivable that he is not concerned about his paper, that he signs anything that may turn up without at once taking it to his paper. A workers' paper in Petersburg without the co-operation of the workers' deputy for Petersburg (particularly as he is a *Pravda* supporter) is a stupid situation. It is most essential to pay as much attention as possible to this important omission, both on the part of the whole editorial board and on the part of Baturin[69] (to whom, by the way, please pass on this letter, and from whom it would be very pleasant to have a couple of lines), and on the part of the deputy himself.

You asked for the address of Gorky. Here it is: Signor Massimo Gorki. Villa Spinola. *Capri* (Napoli). Italie.

Here is the address of a correspondent in Rome; write to him, he will contribute to *Pravda*: B. Antonoff, Via le Giulio Cesare, 47. Roma. Italy.

Why don't you send the money you owe? This delay is causing us great difficulties. Please don't be late. Why haven't you replied to the request to print a notice in the paper that the editorial board is looking for Nos. 5-10 of *Pravda*?

I wish you all the best.

Yours,

V.

Written on November 26, 1912

Sent from Cracow to St. Petersburg

First published in 1923 in the book
*Iz epokhi "Zvezdy" i "Pravdy"
(1911-14)*, Part III

Printed from the typewritten
copy found in police records

25

TO MAXIM GORKY

Dear Al. M.,

It seems a long time since we have had any word from you. How are you getting on? Are you well?

I received today No. 187 of *Pravda* with the subscriptions for 1913. The paper is having a hard passage: since the summer decline in circulation, the rise has been *very* slow, and a deficit remains. They have even temporarily stopped payment to two permanent contributors, which has made our position exceptionally difficult.

We propose to develop intensive agitation among the workers for *subscriptions*, and to use the money collected to strengthen the paper and expand it, because since the opening of the Duma there has been no room at all for articles.

I hope you too will take part in the agitation for subscriptions, in order to help in "rescuing" the paper. In what form? If you have a tale or something suitable, the announcement of it will make very good agitation. If not, send them a promise to provide one in the near future, and particularly in 1913. Finally, a few simple lines, in a *letter to the workers* from you, about the importance of supporting the workers' paper *actively* (by subscriptions, sales, collections), would also be splendid agitation.

Please drop a line about one or the other—direct to the editor of *Pravda* (2 Yamskaya, St. Petersburg) or to me here (Ulijanow, 47, Lubomirskiego, Krakau).

Probably there will be no war, and we shall remain here for the time being, "taking advantage" of the desperate hatred of the Poles towards tsarism.

The liquidators are now carrying on an attack *against* revolutionary strikes! They've sunk to that. There is talk of a strike and demonstration for January 9.

Among the workers' deputies, for the first time in the three Dumas (2nd, 3rd, 4th), all six deputies from the chief gubernias are on the side of the Party. Things are difficult, but still the cause is going ahead.

Have you seen the "defence" of Ropshin in *Zavety*,[70] in the name of "freedom of thought and criticism" (in reply to the letter to the editor from Natanson and Co.)? That is worse than any liquidationism—renegacy which is muddled, cowardly, evasive and nonetheless systematic!

We are swimming "against the stream".... One has now to fight *for* revolutionary agitation among the masses against very many "would-be revolutionaries".... Among the mass of the workers there is unquestionably a revolutionary mood, but the new democratic intelligentsia (including the workers' intelligentsia) with a revolutionary ideology is growing up slowly, lagging behind, can't yet catch up.

Very warm greetings!

Write me a couple of words.

Yours,

Lenin

P.S. Greetings to M. F.! She has somehow fallen quite, quite silent....

Written on December 22 or 23, 1912

      Sent to Capri

First published in 1924   Printed from the original
   in *Lenin Miscellany I*

1913

26

TO MAXIM GORKY

Dear A. M.,

New Year's greetings to you, too! I wish you all the very best, and above all health! We have Malinovsky,[71] Petrovsky and Badayev staying with us just now. Yesterday I received your letter and read it out to them. They were all extraordinarily pleased. Malinovsky wanted to visit you, but probably the distance will be a barrier. Ah, if only you could be nearer to us.... If your health permitted, you could transfer to the local Galician health resorts like Zakopane, find a healthy place in the mountains, two days nearer to Russia; we could get more frequent visits from the workers, once again organise a workers' school[72]: crossing the frontier is not difficult, the price of the journey from Petersburg is 12 rubles, contacts with the workers of Moscow and the South are also possible.... I've been really day-dreaming in connection with M. F.'s journey.... That was a wonderful idea of hers, really wonderful. Make sure to drop me a line, when you have a chance, whether she has succeeded in getting her legal papers (probably she will succeed). Also let me know how Malinovsky can find her in Petersburg or in Moscow. Through Tikhonov? If we can't find some cash to expand and strengthen *Pravda*, it will perish. The deficit is now 50-60 rubles a day. We have to increase the circulation, reduce costs, expand the paper. We have held out for 200 issues—a record. After all, we are influencing twenty to thirty thousand worker-readers systematically in a Marxist spirit: it is something really big, and we should be damnably sorry if the paper went under. We are discussing with the deputies, from every point of view and in every possible way, how to get *Pravda* out of its difficulties, but fear that without financial help from outside we won't succeed.

Malinovsky, Petrovsky and Badayev send you warm greetings and best wishes. They are good fellows, especially the first. Really, it is possible to build a workers' party with such people, though the difficulties are incredibly great. The base at Cracow has proved to be useful: our move to Cracow has fully "paid for itself" (from the point of view of the cause). The deputies confirm that a revolutionary mood is unquestionably growing among the mass of the workers. If we now create a good proletarian organisation, without obstacles from the treacherous liquidators—the devil knows what victories we can then win when the movement from below develops....

What you write about letters from Russia is remarkably interesting and characteristic. Menshevik workers say that Russia has outlived Marx!! And this is not the only case. The liquidators introduce such corruption, such a spirit of treachery, such desertion, as it is difficult to imagine. And in addition, thousands of intrigues for "uniting" with them: the only way to make a mess of the *whole* cause, to spoil the building of the Party, which has had a difficult start, is once again to begin the intrigues= "unity" with the liquidators. Well, the battle isn't over yet....

I am ready to share with all my heart in your joy at the return of the *Vperyod* group, *if* ... *if* your supposition is justified that "Machism, god-building[73] and all that nonsense has been dumped for ever", as you write. If that is so, if the *Vperyod* people have understood this or will understand it now, then I warmly join in your delight at their return. But I underline *"if"* because this, so far, is still a hope rather than a fact. Do you remember, at Capri in the spring of 1908, our "last meeting" with Bogdanov, Bazarov and Lunacharsky[74]? Do you remember how I said that we should have to part company for two or three years, and how then M. F., in the chair, furiously protested, calling me to order, etc.![75]

It has turned out to be four and a half, nearly five years. And this is not very long, for such a period of the most profound collapse as occurred in 1908-11. I don't know whether Bogdanov, Bazarov, Volsky (a semi-anarchist), Lunacharsky, Alexinsky[76] are *capable of learning* from the painful experience of 1908-11. Have they understood that *Marxism* is a more serious and more profound thing than it seemed to them, that one cannot scoff at it, as Alexinsky used to do, or dismiss it as something dead, as the others did? *If* they have understood this—a thousand greetings to them, and everything personal (inevitably brought in by the sharpness of the struggle) will in one moment be thrown on the scrap-heap. But if they haven't understood it, if they haven't learned anything, then don't hold it against me: friendship is friendship, but duty is duty. Against attempts to abuse Marxism or to confuse the policy of the workers' party we shall fight without sparing our lives.

I am *very* glad it is through *Pravda*, which did not directly attack them, that the *way* has been found for the gradual return of the *Vperyod* people. Very glad. But for the sake of a *lasting* rapprochement, we must now move towards it slowly and *cautiously*. That is what I have written to *Pravda* too. And friends of the reunion of the Vperyodists with us must bend their efforts to this also: a careful, tested *return* of the Vperyodists *from* Machism, otzovism,[77] god-building can yield great results. The least carelessness, any "recurrence of the Machist, otzovist, etc., disease", and the struggle will burst out still more violently.... I have not read the new "Philosophy of Living Experience" by Bogdanov, probably the same old Machism in a new dress....

We have excellent connections with Sergei Moiseyev in Paris. We have known him a long time, and are working together. He is a real Party man and Bolshevik. It is with such people that we are building the Party, but there are damnably few of them left.

Once again I wish you the best: I must finish this letter, which has become indecently long. Good health!

Yours,
Lenin

N. K. sends her warm greetings!

(Some more good workers from Russia have gathered here. We are organising a conference.[78] Alas, we haven't the money, or we could get a devil of a lot done from this base!)

I am writing to *Pravda* today that they, after asking Tikhonov, should print a notice that Tikhonov and you are in charge of the literary department of *Pravda*. Isn't that so? Write to them yourself, if they don't print it.

Written earlier than January 8, 1913

Sent from Cracow to Capri

First published in 1925 in *Lenin Miscellany III*

Printed from the original

27

TO N. A. RUBAKIN

January 25, 1913

Dear Comrade,

In answer to your request, I am sending you as brief an *"exposé"* as possible.[79] If you had not added that "the *history of the polemics"* would not be barred from your book, it would have been *quite* impossible to give an account of Bolshevism.

Moreover, doubt has been aroused in my mind by your sentence: *"I shall try* to make no changes in your account."* I must lay down as a condition for it being printed that there are *to be no changes whatsoever.* (As to purely censorship changes we could, of course, come to a special arrangement.)

If it doesn't suit, please return the sheet.

With fraternal greetings,

N. Lenin

My address is: Wl. Uljanow. 47. Lubomirskiego. *Krakau. Autriche.*

Sent to Clarens (Switzerland)

First published in 1930
in *Lenin Miscellany XIII*   Printed from the original

28

TO MAXIM GORKY

Dear A. M.,

Of course, I have nothing against your sending my letter to Tikhonov.

After your account I have become interested in Lunacharsky's article "Between Fear and Hope". Couldn't you send it to me, if you have a copy? If you want it I shall return it without fail.

The collections for the Moscow paper rejoiced us greatly. *Our* trio of deputies from Moscow Region—Malinovsky, Shagov and Samoilov—will set about this. That has already been agreed. But care is needed: before consolidating *Pravda*, we cannot set about a Moscow paper. We have a plan for organising a *Moskovskaya Pravda*.[80]

Please write to Tikhonov that he should talk *only* to Badayev and *Malinovsky*—but he must talk with them.

I was particularly glad of the following words in your letter: "From all the plans and suppositions of the Russian intelligentsia, it is clear beyond any doubt that socialist thought is interlarded with various currents *radically* hostile to it. They include mysticism, and metaphysics, and opportunism, and reformism, and relapses into Narodism. All these currents are *all the more* hostile because they are *extremely indefinite* and, not having their own platforms, cannot determine themselves with sufficient clarity."

I underline the words which have particularly delighted me. That's just it: "radically hostile", and all the more so because they are indefinite. You ask, for example, about

Stepanov (I. I.).[81] What did he turn out to be in the era of collapse and vacillation, 1908-11 (yet he was a good fellow, a hard worker, well-read, etc.)? He wanted to make peace with the Vperyodists. But then that means that he was wobbling himself.

He wrote letters to me about giving up the democratic revolution in Russia as a bad job, that in our country things would proceed without revolution, on Austrian lines. I branded him as a liquidator for these philistine ideas. He was offended. And then *Larin*[82] blurted out his ideas in print.

Now Stepanov is *demonstratively* writing not for us but for Rozhkov's paper *Novaya Sibir* at Irkutsk.[83] And do you know what "trend" Rozhkov has discovered? Did you read his article in *Nasha Zarya* of 1911 and my reply in *Zvezda*?* And Rozhkov has *dug himself in* as an arch-opportunist. And Stepanov? Allah knows. That's just it: an "extremely indefinite" and muddled position. I should *never* entrust any at all independent department to Stepanov now: he himself doesn't know where he will jump next. But probably he could be a useful contributor. He is one of those who haven't "seen clearly". To commission him to "organise" a department means to kill *both him* and the department for certain.

You write: "It's time we had our journal, but we haven't a sufficient number of people who have come properly to terms with each other for this."

I don't accept the second part of this sentence. The journal would *oblige* a sufficient number of people to *come to terms* with each other, provided there was a journal, provided there was a *nucleus*.

A nucleus does exist, but there is no full-size journal for external reasons—no money. If we had money, I am sure we could manage a full-size journal even now, because in addition to the *nucleus* of contributors we could, for payment, draw in *a lot of people* by giving out subjects and allocating jobs.

---

* See "A Liberal Labour Party Manifesto" (present edition. Vol. 17, pp. 313-24).—*Ed.*

So long as we have no money, we must in my opinion
not only dream but build upon what we've got, in other
words, on *Prosveshcheniye*.[84] Of course, it's a little fish,
but in the first place a big fish, like everything else, grows
from a little one. Secondly, better a little fish than a big
cockroach.

It's time, high time, to *begin* coming to terms, if we want
to have "people who have come to terms" in large numbers.

"It's time we had our journal." The literary nucleus
is there. The correctness of the line has been confirmed
by the experience of 12 years (or even 20), and particularly
by the experience of the last six years. We should gather
around this nucleus, thereby defining it in greater detail,
training it up and expanding. We *had* to begin with the
illegal one and with *Pravda*. But we don't want to *stop*
at that. And therefore, once you have said that "it's time
we had our journal", allow me to call you to account for
these words: *either* to draft out at once a plan of enquiries
for money for a full-size journal with such-and-such a
programme, such-and-such an editorial board and such-
and-such a body of contributors, *or* to begin on the same
plan expanding *Prosveshcheniye*.

Or more truly, not *either—or*, but *both*.

I await your reply. You probably have already had a
letter from Vienna about *Prosveshcheniye*. There is a reliable hope of consolidating it for 1913 in a smaller form.
You want us to "have our journal", then let's push it ahead
together.

I haven't heard anything about the Dashnaks. But I think
it's a nonsensical rumour. It's been started by the government, which wants to swallow up Turkish Armenia.[85]

The P.P.S.* are undoubtedly *for* Austria and will fight
for her. A war between Austria and Russia would be a
very useful thing for the revolution (throughout Eastern
Europe), but it's not very probable that Franz-Josef and
Nicky will give us this pleasure.

You ask me to keep you better informed. With pleasure—
only you must reply. I send you (for the time being confi-

---

* P.P.S. (Polska Partia Socjalistyczna)—Polish Socialist Party
—*Ed.*

dentially) the resolutions of our recent conference (which in my view was very successful and will play its part).[86]

Resolutions, they say, are of all forms of literature the most boring. I am a man who has consumed too many resolutions. Drop me a line about how readable they are for you (especially about revolutionary strikes and about the liquidators).

What bad effect has the rumour about an amnesty had in Russia? I don't know. Drop me a line.

N. K. sends her regards.

All the best,
Yours,
Lenin

Written after January 25, 1913
  Sent from Cracow to Capri
    First published in 1924   Printed from the original
    in Lenin Miscellany I

29

TO Y. M. SVERDLOV[87]

To Comrade Andrei, and if he is not in Petersburg, then to Nos. 3, 6 and others. [88]

Dear Friend,

I was extremely sorry to hear that you consider that Vasily exaggerates the importance of *Dyen*.[89] In reality the *key* to the situation at present is precisely *Dyen* and the way it is run. Unless we secure a reform and proper management in this field, we shall reach bankruptcy, both material and political. *Dyen* is the necessary means of organisation for uniting and lifting up the movement. Only *through* this means can now come the necessary influx of people and resources for what you indicate. Things are bad in Petersburg primarily because *Dyen* is bad, and we are unable to make, or the board of "editors" there prevents us making, use of *Dyen*.

At one kopek a month 25,000 will provide 250 rubles. Remember without fail that there are no other sources at all. The whole situation in general will now depend on the outcome of the struggle with the liquidators in Petersburg. That is clear. And this struggle can be decided only by the proper management of *Dyen*. If it is true that Nos. 1 and 3, or 3 and 6, are for caution in reforming *Dyen*, i.e., for delay in expelling the present editors and office staff, this is very sad. We repeat: this smells of bankruptcy. We must seriously come to agreement and set about reforming *Dyen*. (1) We need accounts made up to the last kopek. (2) Has No. 1 had a letter about this? (3) Have you read this letter?

(4) You must take the cash (revenue and subscriptions) into your own hands. (5) Will this be done, and when will it be done? (6) It is essential to put in our own editorial board of *Dyen* and throw out the present one. Work is thoroughly bad at present, the boosting of the Bundist liquidators (*Zeit*) and the non-Social-Democrat Jagiello is an absolute disgrace. The absence of a campaign for unity from below is stupid and base. They keep silent about unity on Vasilyevsky Island, about the liquidators' refusal, they don't know how to reply to No. 101 of *Luch*[90] or to their reply: are such people editors? They are not people, but wretched wet-rags and wreckers of the cause.

The use made of *Dyen* for keeping the class-conscious workers informed and reporting their work (the Petersburg Committee particularly) is beneath all criticism. You must put an end to the so-called autonomy of these editorial failures. You must set about it before all else. You should install yourself in "sanctuary" with No. 1. Put in a telephone. Take the editorial board into your own hands. Draw in assistants. You on your own—with some of these people as pure executives—given our work from here, can fully cope with the job. If this is well organised, there will also be a revival in the work of the Petersburg Committee, which is ridiculously inept, incapable of saying a word, lets every occasion for a statement go by. And it ought to be making a statement almost daily in legal form (in the name of "influential workers", etc.) and at least once or twice a month illegally. Once again, the key to the *whole* situation is *Dyen*. Here it is possible to conquer, and then (only then) organise the local work as well. Otherwise everything will collapse.

You should wait, so far as a Moscow paper is concerned. But No. 3 and his two colleagues should publish a letter immediately. Their delay is unforgivable. They should come out immediately, take up their position, declare that this is *our* affair—the affair of those three—that they are in charge (otherwise the liquidators will elbow them out). Much has already been lost, hurry.

So a statement must be made. Why shouldn't No. 3, too, be a publisher? What in general is the distribution of duties between Nos. 1, 3, 6 and their immediate friends? Has there been a report? Is there complete agreement?

Written on February 9, 1913

Sent from Cracow to St. Petersburg

First published in 1923 in the book
Iz epokhi "Zvezdy" i "Pravdy"
(1911-14), Part III

Printed from the
typewritten copy found
in police records

30

TO THE EDITORIAL BOARD OF *PRAVDA*

Dear Colleagues,

I cannot but express my indignation at the printing by the editorial board of Mr. Bogdanov's stupid and impudent letter in No. 24, and the senseless note from the editors.[91] It had been precisely and clearly laid down as a condition that such things should not be printed without consultation.

The editorial board is mocking us by infringing the conditions. It is not surprising that for *the same* reasons no confidence *whatever* is aroused by the letter of Mikhalchi, who contradicts himself a hundred times in it.

The enquiry from the Riga workers (No. 24) is dated January *19*.[92] There was every possibility both of linking it up with the article on Narodism in No. 17 (January 22) and of sending it here in good time. I repeat that the editorial board is making a mockery of the conditions laid down. I insistently ask you, after those whom it concerns have read this letter, *immediately* to pass it on to the publisher of the newspaper, Deputy Badayev.

Yours faithfully,
V. Ilyin

Written on February 14, 1913
Sent from Cracow to St. Petersburg

Published for the first time
in the Fourth (Russian) Edition
of the *Collected Works*

Printed from the original

31

TO THE EDITORIAL BOARD OF *PRAVDA*

Today we have learned of the beginning of reform in
Dyen.[93] A thousand greetings, congratulations and wishes
for success. At long last you have managed to begin the
reform. You cannot imagine to what extent we have been
exhausted by working with a sullenly hostile editorial
board. Additional for Nos. 1 and 3[94]: we are surprised that
you could take offence or be displeased at the sharp letter
with the three-rúble note enclosed. All the sharpness was
directed precisely against those editors whom you happily
have begun to throw out. Sharpness against those who
should be thrown out, what is bad about that? Once again
we congratulate you on the beginning of the reform. The
letter by No. 3 in *Dyen* is magnificent, and the other letters
too. Reply whether you have received the draft of the Budget
speech. Send us as much material as possible. One cannot
work without it. The speech on the Budget could be expand-
ed to twice the size, if there were material. The statements
of the numbers[95] are excellent. I congratulate them with
all my heart. Please repeat the second address for letters
to the students: we have some doubt about the name. Please
send us addresses for literature as soon as possible.

How about No. 10[96]? Surely, as a pupil of A., he may
become a number. What is the circulation of *Vechernaya
Pochta*[97]? Did Jan's comrades receive what he sent? Ask
No. 3. Warm greetings.

Written on February 19, 1913

Sent from Cracow to St. Petersburg

First published in 1923 in the book
Iz epokhi "Zvezdy" i "Pravdy"
(1911-14) Part III

Printed from the typewritten
copy found in police records

32

TO MAXIM GORKY

Dear A. M.,

Now, sir, what's the meaning of this bad behaviour of yours? You're overworked, tired, your nerves are out of order. This is all wrong. In Capri of all places, and in the winter when there are probably less "visitors", you ought to have a regular way of life. You have no one to look after you, is that why you have let yourself slide like this? Honestly, it's no good. Pull yourself together and give yourself a stricter régime, really! Falling ill in times like these just isn't allowed. Have you begun working at night? Why, when I was in Capri, I was told that it was only with my coming that things had got out of hand, while before me everyone went to bed at the right time. You must rest and establish a régime, without fail.

I will write to Troyanovsky and his wife about your wish to meet them. This would be a really good thing. They are good people. We haven't seen much of them at work yet, but everything we have heard up to now speaks in their favour. They also have money. They might get into their stride and do a great deal for the journal. Troyanovskaya is going to Russia soon.

It is a great joy to me, and to all of us, that you are *taking up Prosveshcheniye*. I confess that I did have the thought: now as soon as I write about our little journal, A. M. will lose his enthusiasm. I repent, I repent of such thoughts.

Now it really will be splendid if little by little we draw in fiction writers and set *Prosveshcheniye* going! Excellent! The reader is new, proletarian; we shall make the journal cheap; you will let in only democratic fiction, without moaning, without renegade stuff. We shall consolidate the workers. And the workers now are fine. Our six deputies in the Duma from the worker curia have now begun to work *outside the Duma* so energetically that it is a joy to see. This is where people will build up a real workers' party! We were never able to bring this off in the Third Duma. Have you seen the letter in *Luch* (No. 24) from the four deputies about their resignation?[98] A good letter, wasn't it?

And have you seen in *Pravda* how mildly Alexinsky is writing, and so far not making a row? Wonderful! He sent one "Manifesto" (why he entered *Pravda*). They didn't print it. And still, *so far*, he is not making a row. Wonder-ful! But Bogdanov is making a row: a piece of exceptional stupidity in *Pravda* No. 24. No, we shall never get anywhere with him! I have read his *Engineer Mannie*. It's the same old Machism=idealism, so concealed that neither the workers nor the stupid editors of *Pravda* understood it. No, this Machist is as hopeless as Lunacharsky (thanks for his article). If only Lunacharsky could be separated from Bogdanov in aesthetics, as Alexinsky has begun to draw apart from him in politics ... if only....

As regards the theory of matter and its structure, I am fully in agreement with you that one should write about it, and that it is a good remedy against "the poison which the shapeless Russian soul is sucking". Only you are wrong to call this poison "metaphysics". It ought to be called *idealism* and agnosticism.

For the Machists call materialism metaphysics! And it so happens that a *host* of the most prominent present-day physicists, *on the occasion* of the "wonders" of radium, electrons, etc., are smuggling in the *God business*—both the crudest and the most subtle—in the shape of philosophical idealism.

As regards nationalism I am fully in agreement with you that we ought to take this up more seriously. We have a marvellous Georgian who has sat down to write a big arti-cle for *Prosveshcheniye*, for which he has collected *all* the Austrian and other materials.[99] We shall go at this hard. But that our resolutions (I am sending them in printed form) "are formalities, bureaucracy", there your abuse is off target. No. It's not a formality. In Russia and in the Caucasus the Georgian+Armenian+Tartar+Russian Social-Democrats have worked *together*, in a *single* Social-Democratic organisation *for more than ten years*. This is not a phrase, but the proletarian solution of the problem of nationalities. The only solution. So it was in Riga too: Russians+Letts+Lithuanians. *Only the separatists*—the Bund—used to stand aloof. The same at Vilna.

There are two good Social-Democratic pamphlets on the nationalities problem: Strasser and Pannekoek. Would you like me to send them to you? Will you find anyone to translate them from the German for you?

No, the disgusting situation that exists in Austria *won't happen* here. We won't allow it! And there are more of our Great Russians here. With the workers on our side we won't let in any of the "Austrian spirit".

As regards Pyatnitsky,[100] I am *for* prosecution. There is no need to stand on ceremony. Sentimentalism would be unforgivable. Socialists are not at all against use of the state court. We are *for* making use of legality. Marx and Bebel made use of the state court *even* against their socialist opponents. One must know *how* to do it, but it must be done.

Pyatnitsky must be prosecuted, and no nonsense. If you hear reproaches against you for this—spit in the mugs of those who make them. It is the hypocrites who will reproach you. To give way to Pyatnitsky, to let him off for fear of going to court, would be *unforgivable*.

Well, I have chattered more than enough. Write and tell me about your health.

Yours,
Lenin

P.S. We know *Foma*-Piterets. He is now at Narym. Foma from the Urals? We don't seem to remember him. At the Congress of 1907 there was a Foma-Piterets.

Written between February 15 and 25, 1913

Sent from Cracow to Capri

First published in 1924   Printed from the original
in *Lenin Miscellany I*

33

TO THE EDITORIAL BOARD OF *PRAVDA*

Dear Colleagues,

Let me first of all congratulate you on the vast improvement in the whole conduct of the paper which has become apparent during the last few days. I want to congratulate you and to wish you further successes in the same direction. The day before yesterday I sent the first two short articles entitled "An Increasing Discrepancy".* From No. 234 of *Pravda* I see clearly that these articles will not be suitable. Therefore please pass them over without delay to *Prosveshcheniye*, to which I am sending the final section. Please pass over to them also the other articles which have not been printed (the reply to Mayevsky; on morality; Bulgakov on the peasants[101]—Bulgakov's articles from *Russkaya Mysl*, etc.). Please be sure to reply as soon as possible whether you have done this. Send me Nos. 7, 8, 21 and 24 of *Luch* and No. 25 of *Pravda*. I had always been getting *Pravda* until lately in the mornings, as I do *Rech* and *Novoye Vremya*. But for the last week *Pravda* has begun to come late, and arrives only in the evenings. Clearly the dispatch department is working carelessly. I earnestly request you to take steps to see that they display greater care with the daily post.

I receive no new books at all. Steps must be taken (a) to get them from the publishers on a deposit account, (b) to get the Duma and official publications through the deputies. It is absolutely impossible to work without books .... I don't receive either *Zavety* or *Russkaya Molva*.[102] I can't get on

---

* See present edition, Vol. 18, pp. 562-79.—*Ed.*

without them. I particularly need the issue of *Russkaya Molva* where they wrote about *Luch* and explained that the Mensheviks are against underground work.

March 1 (14) will be the 30th anniversary of the death of Marx. You ought to publish a supplement for two or three kopeks, four pages in *Pravda* format with a big portrait of Marx and a number of small articles.[103] There should also be detailed advertisements Loth for *Pravda* and *Prosveshcheniye*. Probably it would pay for itself with a circulation of 25-30 thousand, and make a profit. If you agree, cable me: "Draw up" (we shall then sit down to write), then, in addition, send a more detailed reply. Reply please, two or three times a week in a few lines, about what articles you have received and which will be printed.

In my opinion you were quite right to publish Dnevnitsky in full, as a first step. But for the future it would be better to hold up such long (and bad) articles, and to begin correspondence about passing them over to *Prosveshcheniye*.

Yours,

I.

Written on February 21, 1913

Sent from Cracow to St. Petersburg

First published in 1923 in the book
*Iz epokhi "Zvezdy" i "Pravdy"
(1911-14)*, Part III

Printed from the typewritten
copy found in police records

34

TO M. A. SAVELYEV

For Vetrov
Urgent

Dear Colleague,

It is extremely sad that our correspondence is still not properly organised, that I still have no special address for you personally, that you don't reply to my questions for so long. (1) I wrote to you a very, very long time ago that *Zvezda* still had, in addition to the article "Debates in Britain on Liberal Labour Policy", the articles "Two Utopias"* and a criticism of the boycott policy (against Amfiteatrov, I don't remember the title[104]). I repeat what I asked: get hold of them and send them to me. I hope to make use of them. (2) At *Pravda* there are also a number of articles which have not been used there. I very much want you to find them and make them into notes of a publicist signed, say, T.... The approximate arrangement would be: I. Reply to Mayevsky (in *Luch*, about liquidationism). (This subject is the more necessary because Dnevnitsky and Plekhanov, in No. 234 of *Pravda*, have struck false notes.) II. Bulgakov in *Russkaya Mysl* on the peasants (I don't remember the title). III. On morality (two short articles). IV. "An Increasing Discrepancy" (on the February 1913 conference of the Cadets. We must react to this. Two short articles were sent to *Pravda* the day before yesterday; the remaining four are small, I am sending them today). The titles for these paragraphs should

---

* See present edition, Vol. 18, pp. 360-65, 355-59.—*Ed.*

not be in large type (as was done in the article "Results of the Elections"* in No. 1 of *Prosveshcheniye*) but in small point.

There are an awful lot of misprints in No. 1 of *Prosveshcheniye*.... I enclose the corrected proofs of the article "Debates in Britain on Liberal Labour Policy". It should be printed. Have you really not managed to get rid yet of Mikhalchi.... This is essential, I assure you, essential. I have seen a misprint on page 26 of *Prosveshcheniye* No. 1. A correction in print is absolutely necessary. I enclose the correction.

V. Il.

Misprint

Many misprints occurred in the January number of *Prosveshcheniye* (1913, No. 1). We correct one which distorts the sense. On page 26, line 23 from the top, it reads: "25 per cent in the workers' party", but should read "52 per cent".

Written on February 22, 1913

Sent from Cracow to St. Petersburg

First published in 1923 in the book
*Iz epokhi "Zvezdy" i "Pravdy"
(1911-14)*, Part III

Printed from the typewritten copy found in police records

---

* See present edition, Vol. 18, pp. 493-518.—*Ed.*

35

TO L. B. KAMENEV

Dear L. B.,

I am sending you Poletayev's letter (*return it immediately*) and a short article (also to be returned)....*

I have read *Current Topics*. What scoundrels! But we don't know whether to attack or *keep silent* about these young pigs. Is it really worth pitching into them now? What is your opinion?

My view is that they ought to be hammered a little, but not too much, in the next issue of the C.O.[105]

Your report seems to have turned out wonderfully well....

A thousand greetings!

Yours,
Lenin

P.S. *Good* news from Petersburg, Moscow Region and the South. The *workers'* illegal organisation is growing and taking shape. A reform of *Pravda* has *begun*.

Troyanovsky is starting something like an intrigue on account of Koba's article for *Prosveshcheniye*: "The Problem of Nationalities and Social-Democracy". He wants it to be stated that the article is for discussion, because Galina is for cultural-national autonomy!!

Of course we are absolutely against. The article is a *very good one*. It's a burning question, and we shall not give up one iota of our attitude in principle against the Bundist rabble.

It may "blow over", but ... *tenez vous pour averti!***

---

* The manuscript is damaged in places. Several words here and below are illegible.—*Ed.*
** Bear it in mind.—*Ed.*

We have decided to attack the Vperyodists. Get Miron to write whether there is enough money for four pages of the C.O.

Have you read "The Meteor" in *Russkoye Bogatstvo*? What is it? A lampoon?

Written on February 25, 1913
Sent from Cracow to Paris
First published in
full in the Fifth (Russian)
Edition of the *Collected Works*

Printed from the original

36

TO MAXIM GORKY

Dear A. M.,

I have read the "Manifesto"[106] today....

It seems there is a complete amnesty for writers. You should try to get back—*having first found out, of course, whether they won't play you a dirty trick on account of the "school"*,[107] etc. Probably they won't be able to prosecute you for this.

I hope you don't take the view that one mustn't "accept" an amnesty? This would be wrong. A revolutionary, as things are today, will do *more* from inside Russia, and our deputies even sign "the solemn oath".

But you don't have to sign anything, only to make use of the amnesty. Drop me a line about your opinion and your *plans*. Perhaps you will call here if you do move— after all, it's on your way!

And for a revolutionary writer to have the possibility of roaming around Russia (the new Russia) means that he is afterwards able to hit a hundred times harder at the Romanovs and Co....

Did you get my last letter? Somehow we haven't had news from you for a long time. Are you well?

Yours,
Lenin

P.S. Did you get the letter from N. K. with the *material*?

Written after March 6, 1913

Sent from Cracow to Capri

First published in 1924
in *Lenin Miscellany I*

Printed from the original

37

TO L. B. KAMENEV

Dear L. B.,

I received your letter today and ...* from the report on the Third Duma group. Thanks. I passed it on today to Malinovsky, who is here; ... is leaving today ....

It's strange, very strange indeed, about Dan! He lives quite freely, goes to the group, is the editor of *Luch*, etc.!! The secret police are playing some *big* game here!

There are heavy arrests at home. Koba has been arrested. We have discussed with Malinovsky what measures to take. The circulation of *Pravda* is 30-32 thousand on week-days and 40-42 thousand on holidays. There is a general·cry that we haven't the people. The liquidators have a mass of intellectuals, while all ours get arrested.

It's been decided "in principle" to abolish the extra sheets and to publish weekly supplements to *Pravda*, for an extra payment, of 4-8-12 pages (in place of *Zvezda*); it would be a good thing if successful—but the lack of people is a hindrance.

The Six get on very well together, but complain that it's hard going....

All the "intelligentsia" are with the liquidators. The mass of the workers are with us (40,000 *Pravda*, against 12,000 *Luch*) but the workers are producing their *own* intelligentsia with the greatest difficulty. Slowly and with difficulty.

Party affairs in Russia in general are obviously improving. Workers' circles, groups and organisations are obviously developing everywhere and growing stronger. Expanding. And the Urals and the South and Moscow

---

* The manuscript is damaged in places. Several words here and below are illegible.—*Ed.*

Region (particularly). In the Caucasus there is an improvement (latest information is that there are arrests again)....

There is an undoubted revival in the Social-Democratic movement. Once again people have begun to give (a little) money. News! There are signs of a revival of revolutionary organisations in the forces. But the tempo of the movement is different somehow, new in some way.

You have, of course, noticed Plekhanov in *Pravda*? Had his fling and ... returned. What a wobbler he is! Helped Mayevsky[108] (after January 1912)—then abandoned him (August 1912) — was mercilessly attacked by him—now attacks him in turn!! Kiselyov has sent me a long letter, reproaching me for keeping down the pro-Party Mensheviks, of whom I am supposed to be unwarrantedly demanding that they should be "Leninists". The man's a crank! But Gr—y thinks this is a "move" by Plekhanov....

Something new in the history of intrigue: K. Radek has put out a pamphlet *Meine Abrechnung*, against Tyszka, gave him a terrific lambasting. They have promised to send you a copy too.

I have read Rosa's new book *Die Akkumulation des Kapitals*. She has got into a shocking muddle. She has distorted Marx. I am very glad that Pannekoek and Eckstein and O. Bauer have all with one accord condemned her, and said against her what I said in 1899 against the Narodniks. I intend to write about Rosa for No. 4 of *Prosveshcheniye*.[109]

Koba had time to write a big article on the nationalities problem (for three issues of *Prosveshcheniye*). Good! We must fight for the truth against the separatists and opportunists of the Bund and among the liquidators.

There is a certain moving of the waters towards Russia: there are more leaving foreign parts to work at home than before.

Trotsky, they say, is offended with *Luch*.

But I must close. Warm regards from Malinovsky and us all. All the best.

Yours, *Lenin*

Written before March 29, 1913
  Sent from Cracow to Paris
  Published for the first time
in the Fourth (Russian) Edition
  of the *Collected Works*

Printed from the original

38

TO THE EDITORIAL BOARD OF *PRAVDA*

For Iv. Iv.

Dear Comrades,

Many thanks for your detailed letter and very valuable information. Write more often, and give us contacts with the districts.

It is very important that the liquidators are giving a "hostile" reception to the rapprochement of the pro-Party Mensheviks with the Party. A resolution about this ought to be adopted in the districts. This fact proves for the 1,000th time that the liquidators have finally become a non-Party and anti-Party element, that unity is possible only against them (against *Luch*) and by no means with them. You are quite right, in my belief, in attributing great importance to this fact. One can't in any way talk about unity with the liquidators: one cannot unite the Party with the destroyers of the Party. The resolution of the February Conference of 1913 about unity from below, it seems to me, should be hectographed (if there are not enough copies), adding the resolution against *Luch* with the precise list of the five points.[110]

Furthermore, I fully share your opinion about the importance of a campaign against the Seven,[111] and of the workers displaying initiative in this respect. The Seven are wavering and near-Party, but to a very little extent Party people. One can enter into agreements with them within the Duma, in order to direct them and drag them after oneself, but it would be a crime to gloss over their liquidationism, their

lack of character and principle. We must support and
develop the campaign against the Seven. Now that the liquidators' *Luch* is expanding (obviously on liberals' money,
because its deficit is 1,000 rubles a month, and its circulation is only 12,000) we must strengthen tenfold the campaign to support the six workers' deputies, to increase
Pravda's readership, to extend *Pravda*. We must take the
struggle for *Pravda* direct into the factories, pressing them
to subscribe for more copies, winning away every factory
from *Luch*, so that there is a competition between the factories for the largest number of subscribers to *Pravda*. A victory of Party principles is a victory for *Pravda* and vice
versa. We should start this kind of campaign: to increase
the circulation of *Pravda* from 30,000 to 50,000-60,000,
and the number of subscribers from 5,000 to 20,000, and
proceed unfalteringly in this direction. Then we shall
extend and improve *Pravda*.

Your remarks about the lack of intellectuals are very
true. And we won't have them. *Pravda* and the illegal publications will replace them. You should publish at least
hectographed resolutions and leaflets until more is technically possible. There should be a weekly publication of 30-60
copies of hectographed resolutions of the Petersburg Committee by way of directives. We could always come to an
agreement by correspondence about these resolutions. Think
this over. It will strengthen the illegal work, reduce the
number of victims, make the propaganda more general,
etc.

The resolution of the Petersburg Committee for the Six
against the Seven is excellent.[112] Haven't you even hectographed it? This is absolutely essential. Now this is just
the kind of campaign that is necessary. We shall try to
send you articles for *Izvestia*.[113] Let us know the dates.
Tell us what the size will be, and what the length of the
articles should be.

L.

Written on April 5, 1913
Sent from Cracow to St. Petersburg

First published in 1923 in the book
Iz epokhi "Zvezdy" i "Pravdy"
(1911-14), Part III

Printed from the typewritten
copy found in police records

39

TO MAXIM GORKY

Dear A. M.,

How do you stand about a little article or a story for the *May* issue of *Prosveshcheniye*? They write to me from there that they could publish *10-15 thousand* (that's how we are marching ahead!), if there were something from you. Drop me a line whether there will be.[114] Then *Pravda* reprints it, and we get 40,000 readers. Yes ... the affairs of *Prosveshcheniye* could begin to prosper; otherwise there *does not exist*, devil take it, a single consistent journal for the workers, for the *Social-Democrats*, for revolutionary democracy; nothing but rotten sour-pusses of one kind or another.

How is your health? Have you rested, and will you be taking a rest in the summer? It is essential, my word on it, that you should have a *good* rest!

Things are not too well with me. The wife is down with goitre. Nerves! My nerves are also playing me up a little. We are spending the summer in the village of Poronin, near Zakopane. (My address is: Herrn Wl. Ulianow, *Poronin, Galizien*, Austria.) It's a good place, and healthy. Height about 700 metres. Suppose you took it into your head to pay us a visit? There will be interesting workers from Russia. Zakopane (seven versts from us) is a well-known health resort.

Have you seen Demyan Bedny's *Fables*?[115] I will send them if you haven't. If you have, write and say what you think of them.

Do you get *Pravda* and *Luch* regularly? Our cause is going ahead—in spite of everything—and the workers' party is being built up as a *revolutionary* Social-Democratic party, against the liberal renegades, the liquidators. We shall have cause to celebrate one day. We are rejoicing just now at the victory of the workers in Petersburg over the liquidators when the Board of the new Metalworkers' Union[116] was elected.

And "your" Lunacharsky is a fine one!! Oh, what a fine fellow! Maeterlinck, he says, has "scientific mysticism".... Or Lunacharsky and Bogdanov are perhaps no longer yours?

Joking apart. *Keep well.* Send me a couple of words. *Rest* as well as you can.

Yours,
Lenin

Ulianow, Austria. *Poronin* (Galizien).
How did you find the jubilee number of *Pravda*?[117]

Written not earlier than May 9-10, 1913

Sent to Capri

First published in 1924
in *Lenin Miscellany I*

Printed from the original

40

TO THE EDITORIAL BOARD OF *PRAVDA*

Dear Colleagues,

Today at last I have received the file of *Pravda* for the last few days or, more precisely, for the last week. My best thanks and best congratulations on your success: in my opinion the paper has now undoubtedly *found* its feet. The improvement is a tremendous one and a serious one, and, let us hope, firm and for good. The length of Plekhanov's articles and the abundance of anti-liquidationism (about which one of the workers' deputies writes to me) are now questions of detail; it won't be difficult to correct matters in this respect, now that the paper has taken a firm stand, and I think that the workers on the spot will see at once how to make the necessary correction. We have also received the detailed letter of a member of the staff (who unfortunately has not the pleasant "deputy" quality), and we were very glad of it, congratulating him on every kind of success. It seems as though now (and only now, after the St—v* adventure) the period of wavering has ended ... touch wood! ...

I don't advise you to present Plekhanov with ultimatums: it is too early, it may do harm!! If you do write to him, write as kindly and mildly as possible. He is valuable now because he is fighting the enemies of the working-class movement.

As regards Demyan Bedny, I continue *to be for*. Don't find fault, friends, with human failings! Talent is rare. It should be systematically and carefully supported. It will be a sin on your conscience, a great sin (a hundred

---

* Who this refers to has not been established.—*Ed.*

7*

times bigger than various personal "sins", if such occur...)
against the democratic working-class movement, if you
don't draw in this talented contributor and *don't help*
him. The disputes were petty, the cause is a serious one.
Think over this!

As regards expansion, I have recently written in detail
to one of the *Prosveshcheniye* people; I hope you also *have*
seen the letter. I, too, am in favour of financial caution:
to provide the same six pages (the present extra sheets) *in
another form*, with a different sauce and title and content:
4 pages of Sunday supplement for the advanced workers+2
pages of a "workers' kopek" for 1 kopek, for the *masses*,
to win a hundred thousand readers, with an especially
popular content. You shouldn't imitate *Luch* but go your
own road, the proletarian road: 4 pages for the advanced
workers and *2* pages (and *later* even 4) for the *masses*, for a
long and stubborn battle for 100,000 readers. We must go
wide and deep, into the masses, and not follow intellectual
patterns like *Luch*.

Once again greetings, congratulations and best wishes.

Yours,

V. I.

Another special greeting to Vitimsky: his article about
the workers' press and workers' democracy against the
liberals[118] was *very successful*!! And the Bogdanov "Ideology" is *certain* to be heresy: I promise you that I will prove
this exactly!![119]

Marxists are glad of an increase in circulation when it
is increased by *Marxist* articles, and not by articles
against Marxism. We want a principled paper—all the
contributors and readers of *Pravda* want it—a Marxist,
not Machist paper? Isn't that so?

P.S. The address is not Paronen, but *Poronin* (Galizien),
and be sure to *add* on the wrapper: *via Warsaw-Frontier-
Zakopane*.

Written not earlier than May 25, 1913

Sent to St. Petersburg

First published in 1933
in *Lenin Miscellany XXV*

Printed from the original

41

TO THE BOLSHEVIK DEPUTIES
IN THE FOURTH STATE DUMA

Dear Friends,

In our opinion you made a mistake in tying yourselves up with Fyodor.[120] Probably nothing but squabbles will come of it. You should have published your own report.[121] But now we have to start from what has already been done. In the present situation it is essential to insist above all *on complete equality*, and at the very outset to move a formal resolution, approximately in this form: "The co-operative [122] resolves that in drawing up the report no majority decision of one wing over another is allowed, and both wings (the Six and the Seven) enjoy complete equality in all respects, i.e., the commission is set up on a parity basis, and disputed passages are edited by agreement, and not by a majority decision. If speeches of the deputies are printed at the end of the report, the selection of the speeches also is to be by agreement." This resolution is essential. Otherwise they will set up a commission on the basis of equality, and then the co-operative, by a majority of one, will endorse what the liquidator proposes. If Feodora rejects such a resolution, we recommend you officially to declare that, in view of their unwillingness to agree to equality, you reserve complete freedom of action. Even so, you can still put forward your own candidate.

We append the first rough draft of the theses:

1) The election campaign. The circumstances in which it takes place. Its results for the Social-Democrats. The platform of the Social-Democrats: the 8-hour day, confiscation of the land, complete democratisation.

2) The composition of the Social-Democratic group. How it was set up. The Jagiello case.[123] (Exposition of the points of view of the Six and the Seven. Indication of protests made.)

3) The political platform of the group and its first speeches. The declaration. Indicate that the Six reject cultural-national autonomy. Indicate that wide sections of the workers have approved precisely ... the watchwords in the declaration. An outline of the political position of the Social-Democrats.

The main watchwords are still: the 8-hour day, transfer of the land, complete democratisation.

4) Questions put down by the group.

5) The group and the Budget.

6) The bourgeois groups in the Duma and sharp criticism of them and of the liberals (the speeches by Maklakov, the Octobrists,[124] the Black Hundreds[125]).

7) The workers and the group. Their instructions, appeals, reactions, material for questions, mutual aid in cash, etc.

8) Immunity of the deputies (the case of Petrovsky[126]).

Internal differences: each side puts forward its own point of view, with an equal number of pages to each. Statements made by each side to the press are reprinted. A list of workers' resolutions, as many as there are. The supplement. Most important tasks.

We await your news. Apartments have been taken.[127]

Written on June 17, 1913

Sent from Poronin to St. Petersburg

First published in 1924 in the
magazine *Krasnaya Letopis* No. 1

Printed from the typewritten
copy found in police records

42

TO G. V. PLEKHANOV

Dear Georgy Valentinovich,

At the request of the six Social-Democratic deputies I invite you to come for a few weeks to Zakopane in the summer to deliver lectures on such questions of Marxism and the Social-Democratic movement as you may select. We have heard today from Petersburg that it is also possible that four deputies may come who support the liquidators or who are wavering (Buryanov, Tulyakov, Khaustov and *maybe* even Mankov). As Mensheviks, they naturally attribute particular importance to the question of your participation.

On our part, we should think it very useful that Party people of various views should take part in an enterprise which seems to us extremely important for strengthening connections with the workers and reinforcing Party work.

In view of the conspirative nature of the case, we have decided not to tell a single group abroad about the plan to organise these lectures—all the more so because the deputies would probably be in peril of particularly severe penalties.

Poronin, where it is proposed to hold the lectures, is seven kilometres by rail from Zakopane—one of the best mountain health resorts in Galicia. As to the financial

side (travelling expenses), we can come to a special arrangement by correspondence, if required.

Please write whether you agree to this proposition.

Yours faithfully,

N. Lenin

My address is: Herrn Wl. Ulianow.
            Poronin (Galizien). Autriche.

Written not later than June 22, 1913

Sent to Geneva

First published in 1930   Printed from the original
in *Lenin Miscellany XIII*

43

TO MAXIM GORKY

Dear Al. Max.,

We have had a letter today from Petersburg that our plan for a visit of the Social-Democratic deputies here is close to fulfilment (*extra-conspiratively*: it has been decided not to say a word to anyone except you). In addition to the six supporters of *Pravda* it is possible, they write, that Tulyakov, Buryanov, Khaustov and even, maybe, Mankov may come. Probably they will manage to draw in some of the workers as well (non-deputies). Write, please, whether you could come (for a number of lectures, or talks, or classes, just as you please). It would be a fine thing! Seven kilometres from here by rail is Zakopane, a very good health resort. As regards money for the journey, we shall raise it, in all probability (so they write). We can collect and send you all the information about Zakopane as a health resort.

If your health permits, do come for a short time! You would meet more workers, after the ones at London[128] and the Capri school.

Malinovsky wanted to visit you but didn't manage it, he was short of time. He and all the deputies send you warm greetings.

I await your reply.

Yours,
Lenin

The newspapers are full of reports about the "conflict".[129] think they are going to stifle *Pravda* for us. Maklakov will bring this off one way or another—by-passing the Duma, against the Duma or in some other way, but bring it off he will![130]

In that case we shall turn again to illegal literature—but we have no money.

Hasn't the "merchant" begun to contribute yet? It is time, just the right time.

Address: Herrn Wl. Ulianow. *Poronin* (Galizien). Autriche.

Written not later than June 22, 1913

Sent to Capri

First published in 1924   Printed from the origin l
in *Lenin Miscellany I*

44

TO MAXIM GORKY

July 25, 1913

Dear A. M.,

I have kept on intending to write to you, and then putting it off on account of my wife's operation. The other day at last the operation took place, and things are now on the mend. The operation proved a rather difficult one: I am very glad indeed that we managed to get Kocher to operate.

Now to business. You wrote that you would be in Berlin in August. When in August? At the beginning or at the end? We intend to leave here on August 4. Our tickets take us through Zurich, Munich and Vienna, and we shall break the journey in each of these cities. (Possibly the doctor will not let us leave so soon as the 4th: in that case we shall postpone it again.)

Couldn't we see each other somewhere? In all probability it would suit you to travel through Berne, or through Zurich, or through Munich, wouldn't it?

There is *great* need for us to meet. The closing down of *Pravda* creates a devilishly difficult situation. Perhaps we could think of something. Then in Berlin you could do a very great deal for us, i.e., for *Pravda*.

Therefore I beg you to write *immediately*, be it only two words, whether our meeting is possible, either here or in the places mentioned, at the beginning of August? If it is *im*possible, I will write to you about everything in greater detail, particularly about the school (the arrest of the

organiser* has spoilt things for us damnably; we are looking
for another).

I shake your hand warmly and wish you the best of luck,
and most of all health for the journey. So reply *at once*!

Yours,
Lenin

Address: Herrn Ulianoff. 4. Gesellschaftsstraße, 4. (Sviz-
zera). *Bern.*

Sent to Capri

First published in 1924   Printed from the original
in *Lenin Miscellany I*

---

* E. F. Rozmirovich.—*Ed.*

45

TO THE GERMAN SOCIAL-DEMOCRATIC PARTY ON THE DEATH OF AUGUST BEBEL

We share your grief at the loss of one of the most prominent leaders of international revolutionary Social-Democracy.

By instruction of the Central Committee of the Russian Social-Democratic Labour Party,

Lenin

Written in German
between August 13 and 17, 1913

Sent from Poronin to Berlin

Published in *Vorwärts* No. 211,
August 17, 1913

Printed from the
newspaper text

46

TO S. G. SHAHUMYAN[131]

Dear Comrade,

I found your letter on my return home. Be sure and send as much material as you can about the nationalities problem in the Caucasus (since you, *unfortunately*, cannot write yourself), send us both the article by *Kostrov* and his booklets, reports by the delegates translated into Russian (I hope you will find someone to do this), *statistics of nationalities* in the Caucasus and material on the relations between the nationalities in the Caucasus, in Persia, Turkey and Russia. In a word, send everything there is and that you can collect. Don't forget also to *look for* comrades in the Caucasus who could write articles about the problem of nationalities there.

Greetings and wishes for success.[132]

Yours,

V. Ilyich

Written on August 24, 1913
Sent from Poronin to Astrakhan

First published in 1925
in *Lenin Miscellany III*

Printed from the handwritten
copy found in police records

47

TO THE EDITORIAL BOARD OF *PRAVDA TRUDA* [133]

P.S. I have not received No. *5* of *Pravda Truda*. Thank you very much for sending me *Novaya Rabochaya Gazeta*: only No. *7* is missing, and also Nos. *7* and *9* of *Nash Put*.[134] Please send them.

It seems to me that you are making a gigantic mistake in drifting unconsciously with the stream *and not changing* the tone of the paper. Everything suggests that both the tone *and the content* of the news section must be *changed*. It is essential to *achieve* legality, ability to pass the censor. This can and must be achieved. Otherwise you are destroying, for no reason at all, the work you have undertaken. Think this over more seriously.

Written not earlier than September 30, 1913
Sent from Poronin to St. Petersburg

First published in 1933
in *Lenin Miscellany XXV*

Printed from the original

48

TO MAXIM GORKY

September 30, 1913

Dear A. M.,

This reply has been delayed a little. Sorry. How devilishly furious I was in Berne, and later!! I thought: if you were in Verona (the telegram from you about Bebel was from Verona)—or in some Rom...[135]?? Why, I *could* have come to Verona from Berne!! But from you at that time there was not a sound for *months*....

What you write about your illness worries me terribly. Are you doing the right thing in living without treatment at Capri? The Germans have excellent sanatoria (for example, at St. Blasien, near Switzerland) where they treat and *completely* cure lung diseases, achieve *complete* healing, feed you up, then systematically accustom you to cold, harden you against catching cold, and turn out fit people, able to work.

While you, after Capri, and in winter, want to go to Russia???? I am terribly afraid that this will injure your health and undermine your working capacity. Are there *first-class* doctors in that Italy of yours??

Really, go and visit some first-class doctor in Switzerland* or Germany, and set about a couple of months of *serious* treatment in a *good* sanatorium. Because to squander official property, i.e., to go on being ill and undermining your working capacity, is something quite intolerable in every respect.

---

* I can find out names and addresses.

I have heard (from the editor of *Prosveshcheniye*, who saw Ladyzhnikov) that you are dissatisfied with *Pravda*. Because it's dry? That is true. But it's not easy to correct this defect all at once. We haven't the people. With *great* difficulty, one year after it started, we secured a merely *tolerable* editorial board in Petersburg.

(I have forwarded your letter to *Prosveshcheniye*.)

Write what your plans are, and what your *health* is like. I earnestly ask you to *set about your treatment seriously*— really, it is *quite possible* to be cured, and to let it go on is simply outrageous and criminal.

Yours,
Lenin

P.S. Some of the people we have had here, and some we shall have, are good. *And have you seen "Nash Put"*? What a success, eh? Our second paper. We shall start a third, too, in the South.

Address: Ulianow. *Poronin* (Galizien). *Austria*. (During the winter I shall be in Cracow: Lubomirskiego. 51.)

Sent to Capri

First published in 1924
in *Lenin Miscellany* I

Printed from the original

49

TO THE EDITORIAL BOARD OF *ZA PRAVDU* [136]

Dear Colleagues,

Thank you very much for *twice* sending the newspaper *in time*, i.e., *simultaneously* with all the bourgeois papers. But apart from these two occasions, *Za Pravdu* always comes *half a day* later than the bourgeois papers. Can't this be altered, and the paper *always* be sent at the proper time, so that it comes *at the same time* as the bourgeois press?

Best greetings!

Yours,
Lenin

P.S. What is the circulation now? Will there ever be (at last!!) a financial report? As regards legality, your secretary is wrong in his last letter: *much* can and should still be done in the sense of increasing the paper's legality.

How many subscribers are there *now*?

Written earlier than October 26, 1913

Sent from Cracow to St. Petersburg

First published in *Pravda*
No. 99, May 5, 1927

Printed from the original

50

TO THE EDITORIAL BOARD OF *ZA PRAVDU*

To the Editor

For the Editorial Board

Dear Colleagues,

Welcoming the excellent beginning of the struggle by the six deputies for proper respect of the will of the majority of the workers, and the excellent campaign of your paper,[137] I would ask you also to take notice of the following:

If the Seven begin impudently proclaiming *themselves* the Social-Democratic group (as they have done at the end of their article in No. 60[138]), then the Six must without fail declare calmly, briefly and firmly: "We are the Social-Democratic Labour group, since we act in keeping with the will of the majority of the class-conscious workers, put it into effect and represent the majority. The seven non-Party deputies have not refuted a single fact, a single figure, out of the mass quoted in our paper and demonstrating this truth. Here is our address; write to us, worker comrades, and do not imagine that we shall insult you by thinking you capable of believing the theory that 'seven deputies are higher than the Party, higher than the will of the majority of the workers'. Even 77 deputies could not be higher than that will. We are strictly fulfilling it."

Such a brief declaration is essential. Then you should send a formal statement to Senior Conventus (i.e., to the State Duma). *Then* the Seven will very rapidly, at once lose their arrogance: very, very rapidly they will *agree* to equality (which *all* of them have recognised in writing). *Neither* they *nor* anyone else will have any other way out.

Once you have begun a job, you can't back out. The Six have made a *splendid* beginning, and their victory is *assured, if* they carry on *correctly*—in a week or two their victory is inevitable.

Best greetings and wishes,

V. I.

Written between November 2 and 7, 1913

Sent from Cracow to St. Petersburg

First published in *Pravda*   Printed from the original
No. 123, May 5, 1932

51

TO THE EDITORIAL BOARD OF *ZA PRAVDU*

Dear Colleagues,

I congratulate you on the excellent beginning of your campaign for the rights of the worker deputies.

After reading the dirty intrigue in *Novaya Rabochaya Gazeta*, I earnestly advise you to think matters over and accept my plan of yesterday.* Such things *must not* be left without an *organisational* solution.

It is not enough for the workers to send resolutions: it is essential that the workers should organise *deputations* to the Duma group.

Greetings and best wishes!

Yours,

V. I.

Written not earlier than
November 3, 1913

Sent from Cracow to St. Petersburg

First published in 1933
in *Lenin Miscellany XXV*

Printed from the original

---

* See the previous letter.—*Ed.*

52

TO THE EDITORIAL BOARD OF *ZA PRAVDU*

In view of the importance of the campaign against the Seven, it is extremely important for us, as contributors, to have daily information. But *Za Pravdu* is late every day. We earnestly ask you to take steps to see that the paper is sent daily in good time, and without delay.

That the majority is for the Six is clear. But the conduct of the Six is inconsistent. Victory is within their grasp, if they take the logically (and politically) inevitable step and proclaim themselves a separate group.

Once this is done, and a statement handed in to the Duma, the Seven will be obliged (by the very technique of work in the Duma) to enter into an agreement with the Six.

It would be ridiculous to let victory slip from their hands when it is completely assured. The more resolutely they separate, the more speedily will federation be restored.

The campaign against the Seven began excellently, but is now being carried on with insufficient determination. In reply to the most shameless insolence of the liquidators, the newspaper needs not to complain but to attack, stressing the *infringement of the will* of the proletariat by the Seven, and their *anti-Party character*. The watchword should be: "Resign your seats, gentlemen of the Seven, if you don't want to reckon with the will of the majority of the workers, if you want to go against the Party." This watchword should be made quite clear and precise, repeating it daily.

Written on November 7, 1913

Sent from Cracow to St. Petersburg

First published in 1924
in *Krasnaya Letopis* No. 1

Printed from the typewritten
copy found in police records

53

TO THE EDITORIAL BOARD OF *ZA PRAVDU*

Dear Colleagues,

It is essential to insert a loose sheet on Sunday, devoted *entirely* to the campaign for the Six.

One big article, with *subheads.*

We send you the text.* Put in the resolution of the *Conference*[139] (was it *on account of that resolution* that that issue of *Za Pravdu* was confiscated?).

You should demand that the Seven resign their seats.

Add the results of the Petersburg resolutions, if they are clearly in our favour.[140]

Drop us a line, or telegraph: "Supplement in hand."

Best greetings,

Yours,

V. I.

Written not later than
November 7, 1913

Sent from Cracow to St. Petersburg

First published in 1933   Printed from the original
in *Lenin Miscellany XXV*

---

* See "Material on the Conflict Within the Social-Democratic Duma Group" (present edition, Vol. 19, pp. 458-74).—*Ed.*

54

TO THE EDITORIAL BOARD OF *ZA PRAVDU*

Dear Colleagues,

I hasten to congratulate with all my heart all Marxist workers on the victory of the cause of the majority against the disorganisers, on the setting up of a group which does not wish to thwart the will of the majority.[141] I have just received the Sunday issue of *Za Pravdu*. The calculations are particularly good—they should be continued.

Once again, greetings to all from all.

Yours,
Lenin

Written not earlier than
November 13, 1913

Sent from Cracow to St. Petersburg

First published in 1933
in *Lenin Miscellany XXV*

Printed from the original

55

TO MAXIM GORKY

Dear A. M.,

Whatever are you doing? This is simply terrible, it really is!

Yesterday I read your reply in *Rech* to the "howling" over Dostoyevsky,[142] and was preparing to rejoice, but today the liquidators' paper arrives, and *in it there is a paragraph of your article* which was not in *Rech.*

This paragraph runs as follows:

"And 'god-seeking' should be *for the time being*" (only for the time being?) "put aside—it is a useless occupation: it's no use seeking where there is nothing to be found. Unless you sow, you cannot reap. You have no God, you have not *yet*" (yet!) "created him. Gods are not sought—*they are created*; people do not invent life, they create it."

So it turns out that you are against "god-seeking" only "for the time being"!! It turns out that you are against god-seeking *only* in order to replace it by god-building!!

Well, isn't it horrible that such a thing should *appear* in your article?

God-seeking differs from god-building or god-creating or god-making, etc., no more than a yellow devil differs from a blue devil. To talk about god-seeking, not in order to declare against *all* devils and gods, against every ideological necrophily (all worship of a divinity is necrophily— be it the cleanest, most ideal, not sought-out but built-up divinity, it's all the same), but to prefer a blue devil to a yellow one is a hundred times worse than not saying anything about it at all.

In the freest countries, in countries where it is *quite* out of place to appeal "to democracy, to the people, to public opinion and science", in such countries (America, Switzerland and so forth) particular zeal is applied to render the people and the workers obtuse with just this very idea of a clean, spiritual, built-up god. Just because any religious idea, any idea of any god at all, any flirtation even with a god, is the most inexpressible foulness, particularly tolerantly (and often even favourably) accepted by the *democratic* bourgeoisie—for that very reason it is the most dangerous foulness, the most shameful "infection". A million *physical* sins, dirty tricks, acts of violence and infections are much more easily discovered by the crowd, and therefore are much less dangerous, than the *subtle*, spiritual idea of god, dressed up in the most attractive "ideological" costumes. The Catholic priest corrupting young girls (about whom I have just read by chance in a German newspaper) is *much less* dangerous, precisely to "democracy", than a priest without his robes, a priest without crude religion, an ideologically equipped and democratic priest preaching the creation and the invention of a god. For it is *easy* to expose, condemn and expel the first priest, while the second *cannot* be expelled so simply; to expose the latter is 1,000 times more difficult, and not a single "frail and pitifully wavering" philistine will agree to "condemn" him.

And you, knowing the "frailty and pitiful wavering" of the (Russian: why Russian? Is the Italian any better??) *philistine* soul, confuse that soul with the sweetest of poisons, most effectively disguised in lollipops and all kinds of gaily-coloured wrappings!!

Really, it is terrible.

"Enough of self-humiliation, which is our substitute for self-criticism."

And isn't god-building the *worst* form of self-humiliation?? Everyone who sets about building up a *God*, or who even merely tolerates such activity, *humiliates* himself in the worst possible way, because instead of "deeds" he is *actually* engaged in self-contemplation, self-admiration and, moreover, such a man "contemplates" the dirtiest, most stupid, most slavish features or traits of his "ego", deified by god-building.

From the point of view, not of the individual, but of
society, *all* god-building is precisely the *fond self-contemplation* of the thick-witted philistine, the frail man in the
street, the dreamy "self-humiliation" of the vulgar petty
bourgeois, "exhausted and in despair" (as you condescended
to say very truly about the *soul*: only you should have said,
not "the Russian", but the *petty-bourgeois*, for the Jewish,
the Italian, the English varieties are all *one and the same
devil*; stinking philistinism everywhere is equally disgusting—but "democratic philistinism", occupied in ideological necrophily, is particularly disgusting).

Reading your article over and over again, and *trying
to discover* where this *slip* of your tongue could come from,
I am at a loss. What does it mean? A relic of the "Confession", which *you yourself* did not approve?? Or its echo??

Or something different: for example, an unsuccessful
attempt to *bend back* to the viewpoint of *democracy in general*, instead of the viewpoint of the *proletariat*? Perhaps
it was in order to talk with "democracy in general" that
you decided (excuse the expression) to indulge in baby-talk? Perhaps it was "for a popular exposition" to the
philistines that you decided to accept for a moment *their*,
the philistines', prejudices??

But then that is a *wrong* approach, in all senses and in
all respects!

I wrote above that in *democratic* countries it would be
quite out of place for a proletarian writer to appeal "to
democracy, to the people, to public opinion and science".
Well, but what about us in Russia?? Such an appeal is *not
quite* appropriate, because it also in some ways flatters
the prejudices of the philistines. A kind of general appeal,
general to the point of vagueness—even Izgoyev of *Russkaya
Mysl*[143] will sign it with *both hands*. Why then select watchwords which *you* distinguish perfectly well from those of
Izgoyev, but which the *reader* will not be able to distinguish?? Why throw a democratic veil over the question
for the reader, instead of *clearly* distinguishing the *petty
bourgeois* (frail, pitifully wavering, exhausted, despairing,
self-contemplating, god-contemplating, god-building, god-indulging, self-humiliating, *uncomprehendingly-anarchistic*—
wonderful word!!—et cetera, et cetera)

— from the *proletarians* (who know how to be of good cheer not only in words, and who are able to distinguish the "science and public opinion" of the *bourgeoisie* from their own, bourgeois democracy from proletarian democracy)?

Why do you do this?

It's damnably disappointing.

Yours,

V. I.

P.S. We sent you the novel by registered book post. Did you receive it?

P.P.S. Get as good *medical* treatment as you can, please, so that you can travel in the winter, *without colds* (it's dangerous in the winter).

Yours,

V. Ulyanov

Written on November 13 or 14, 1913

Sent from Cracow to Capri

First published in *Pravda* No. 51, March 2, 1924

Printed from the original

56

TO THE EDITORIAL BOARD OF *ZA PRAVDU*

To the Editor:

It is essential to reprint the "Material",[144] even if in parts, since the issue was confiscated *not* on that account. Legality, legality without fail!!

If you can't reprint it at once, announce immediately in print, for those who didn't see the issue of October 29 that it *will be* reprinted.

Written not earlier than
November 14, 1913

Sent from Cracow to St. Petersburg

First published in 1933
in *Lenin Miscellany XXV*

Printed from the original

57

TO THE EDITORIAL BOARD OF *ZA PRAVDU**

To the Editor: The article by "Friend" in No. *25* is bad. Sharp, and nothing more. For God's sake, less sharpness. Analyse the arguments more calmly, repeat the *truth* as circumstantially and simply as possible. That, and only that, is the way to ensure definite victory.

Written not earlier than November 16, 1913

Sent from Cracow to St. Petersburg

First published in 1933
in *Lenin Miscellany XXV*

Printed from the original

---

* This letter was attached to an unidentified article.—*Ed.*

58

TO MAXIM GORKY

...* On the question of god, the god-like and everything connected with it, there is a contradiction in your position—the same, I think, which I used to point out in our talks when we last met in Capri. You broke (or appeared to break) with the *Vperyod* people, without having noticed the ideological basis of "Vperyodism".

The same has happened now. You are "most vexed", you "cannot understand how the words 'for the time being' crept in"—that is how you write—and yet at the same time you defend the idea of God and god-building.

"God is the complex of those ideas, worked out by the tribe, the nation, mankind, which awaken and organise social feelings, having as their object to link the individual with society and to bridle zoological individualism."

This theory is obviously connected with the theory or theories of Bogdanov and Lunacharsky.

And it is clearly wrong and clearly reactionary. Like the Christian socialists (the worst variety of "socialism", and its worst distortion), you make use of a method which (despite your best intentions) repeats the hocus-pocus of the priests: you eliminate from the idea of God everything about it that is *historical and drawn from real life* (filth, prejudices, sanctified ignorance and degradation, on the one hand, serfdom and monarchy, on the other), and instead of the reality of history and life there is substituted in the idea of God a gentle petty-bourgeois phrase (God= "ideas which awaken and organise social feelings").

---

* The beginning of the letter has never been found.- *Ed.*

Your wish in so doing is to say something "good and kind", to point out "truth and justice" and the like. But your good wish remains your personal affair, a subjective "innocent desire". Once you have written it down, it goes out among the *masses*, and its *significance* is determined not by your good wishes, but by the *relationship of social forces*, the objective relationship of classes. By virtue of that relationship *it turns out* (irrespective of your will and independently of your consciousness) that you have put a good colour and a sugary coating on the idea of the clericals, the Purishkeviches, Nicholas II and the Struves,[145] since *in practice* the idea of God helps *them* keep the people in slavery. By beautifying the idea of god, you have beautified the chains with which they fetter ignorant workers and peasants. There—the priests and Co. will say—what a good and profound idea this is (the idea of God), as even "*your*" leaders recognise, Messrs. democrats: and we (the priests and Co.) serve that idea.

It is untrue that god is the complex of ideas which awaken and organise social feelings. That is Bogdanov *idealism*, which suppresses the material origin of ideas. God is (in history and in real life) first of all the complex of ideas generated by the brutish subjection of man both by external nature and by the class yoke—ideas which *consolidate* that subjection, *lull to sleep* the class struggle. There was a time in history when, in spite of such an origin and such a real meaning of the idea of God, the struggle of democracy and of the proletariat went on in the form of a struggle of *one religious* idea against another.

But that time, too, is long past.

Nowadays both in Europe and in Russia *any*, even the most refined and best-intentioned defence or justification of the idea of God is a justification of reaction.

Your entire definition is reactionary and bourgeois, through and through. God = the complex of ideas which "awaken and organise social feelings, having as their object to link the individual with society and to bridle zoological individualism".

Why is this reactionary? Because it falsely colours the idea of "bridling" zoology preached by priests and feudals. In reality, "zoological individualism" was bridled not by the idea of God, it was bridled both by the primitive herd and the primitive community. The idea of God *always* put to sleep and blunted the "social feelings", replacing the living by the dead, being *always* the idea of slavery (the worst, hopeless slavery). Never has the idea of God "linked the individual with society": it has always *tied* the oppressed *classes hand and foot* with faith in the *divinity* of the oppressors.

Your definition is bourgeois (and not scientific, not historical) because it operates with sweeping, general, "Robinson Crusoe" conceptions in general, not with definite *classes* in a definite historical epoch.

The idea of God among the Zyrian savages, etc. (including semi-savages) is one thing. With Struve and Co. it is something quite different. In both cases class domination supports this idea (and this idea supports it). The "popular" conception of God and the divine is "popular" ignorance, degradation, darkness, just like the "popular conception" of the tsar, the devil and dragging wives by the hair. I completely fail to understand how you can call the "popular conception" of God "democratic".

It is untrue that philosophical idealism "always has in view only the interests of the individual". Did Descartes have the interests of the individual more in mind than Gassendi? Or Fichte and Hegel as compared with Feuerbach?

That "god-building is the process of the further development and accumulation of social elements in the individual and society" is simply terrible!! If there were freedom in Russia, the entire bourgeoisie would praise you to the skies for such things, for such sociology and theology of a purely bourgeois type and character.

Well, that's enough for the time being: this letter is too long as it is. Once again, I shake your hand and wish you good health.

Yours,

V. I.

Written in the second half
of November 1913

Sent from Cracow to Capri

First published in 1924
in *Lenin Miscellany 1*

Printed from the original

59

TO INESSA ARMAND[146]

I have just had the telegram, and changed the envelope, which had been marked for A....

What's happening to the Central Organ?? This is a disgrace and a scandal!! No sign of it yet, and not even the proofs. Enquire and get an explanation, please.

The issue of *Vorwärts* where Kautsky used the rotten phrase that there is no Party (*die alte Partei sei verschwunden* literally) is No. 333 of December 18, 1913. You should get hold of it (rue de Bretagne. 49 or somewhere else) and organise a protest campaign. We are *for* an exchange of opinion, *for* the resolution of the I.S.B.—*this N.B.*—but are absolutely against Kautsky's *scoundrelly* phrase.[147] He should be beaten unmercifully for this, with the reservation that we are *for* Aussprache (exchange of opinion), etc.

Written after December 18, 1913

Sent from Cracow to Paris

Published for the first time
in the Fourth (Russian) Edition
of the *Collected Works*

Printed from the original

60

TO INESSA ARMAND

...* Idiotically stupid are the people who have "taken fright" at trusted agents,[148] as something allegedly "insulting" to the Party cells. That means, the argument runs, that there are no Party cells if *they want* trusted agents!

Comedians! They chase *words*, without thinking about how devilishly complicated and subtle life is, producing *entirely new* forms, which we only partly "catch on" to.

People for the most part (99 per cent of the bourgeoisie, 98 per cent of the liquidators, about 60-70 per cent of the Bolsheviks) don't know how to *think*, they only *learn words by heart*. They've learnt the word "underground". Firmly. They can repeat it. They know it by heart.

But *how* to change *its forms* in a new situation, how to learn and think *anew* for this purpose, this we do not understand.

The summer conference of 1913 (abroad) decided to overcome the Seven. The campaign of the working *masses* in the autumn of 1913 in Russia—the *majority* are for us!! A "circle" of "trusted agents" (without election by the Party cells!! Alarm!!—shout Antonov, Isaac and Co.) decided—and the *masses* carried it out.

How can that be done? Well, that is where one must learn to understand such a "cunning" mechanism. It *could not* have been done, were there no underground and no Party cells. *And it could not have been done*, if there were no new and *cunning* forms of the underground and the Party cells.

---

* The beginning of the letter has never been found.—*Ed.*

9*

I am very interested in whether you will succeed in making our people understand this. Write in as much detail as you can.

We have received *one* copy of *Sputnik Rabochego*.[149] 5,000 copies have *already* been sold!! Hurrah!! *Set about* the women's journal[150] super-energetically!

Written at the end of December 1913

Sent from Cracow to Paris

Published for the first time
in the Fourth (Russian) Edition
of the *Collected Works*

Printed from the original

1914

61

TO DAVID WIJNKOOP

Cracow, January 12, 1914

Dear Comrade Wijnkoop,

Thank you most cordially for your kind letter. I hope you have read in the German Social-Democratic papers (*Vorwärts* and *Leipziger Volkszeitung*) the articles of our opponents (for example, *J. K.* of the Rosa Luxemburg group, and *Z. L.*, who represents *no* group in Russia, in *Leipziger Volkszeitung*). The German Social-Democratic press is boycotting us, particularly *Vorwärts*, and only *Leipziger Volkszeitung* has printed *one* article from us (signed by the editorial board of *Sotsial-Demokrat*, Central Organ of the Russian Social-Democratic Labour Party*).

In *Bremer Bürger-Zeitung*[151] Radek writes about Russian affairs. Yet Radek also represents *no* group whatever in Russia! It is ridiculous to print articles by emigrants who represent nothing, and not accept articles from the representatives of organisations which exist in Russia!

And the attitude of Kautsky—can anything be more idiotic? In relation to all other countries he studies the history of the movement, criticises documents, tries to understand the *true sense* of the differences, the political significance of splits. In relation to Russia, history does not exist for him. Today he repeats what he has heard from

---

* See "The Split in the Russian Social-Democratic Duma Group" (present edition, Vol. 19, pp. 480-84).—*Ed.*

Rosa Luxemburg, yesterday he repeated what he had heard
from Trotsky, Ryazanov and other writers who only represent
their own "pious wishes", tomorrow he will begin to repeat
what other Russian students or emigrants are kind enough to
tell him, and so on. While in *Neue Zeit* (!!) only common-
places, declamations, no facts, no understanding of the
essence of the questions on which we differ!! Pure childish-
ness!!

We are being lectured on unity with the liquidators of
our Party—an absurdity. It is we who are bringing unity
into being, by rallying the workers of Russia *against* the
liquidators of our Party. I attach a document which we
circulated to members of the International Socialist Bureau.
You will find there *facts* and *figures* which prove that we
are the ones who represent the unity of the Party (and
the vast majority of the workers) in Russia *against* groups
of liquidators who are without workers.

Unfortunately even Pannekoek in *Bremer Bürger-Zeitung*
refuses to understand that you have to print the articles
of the two wings of Social-Democracy in Russia, and not
the articles of Radek who represents only his own personal
ignorance and fantasy, and who *does not wish* to provide
precise facts.

Once again I thank you, dear Comrade Wijnkoop, you
personally and the Executive Committee of the Social-
Democratic Party, for your kind letter, and please pass on
my greetings to Comrade Gorter.

I hope you will forgive my bad French.

Yours,

Vl. Ulyanov (*N. Lenin*)

Wl. Uljanow. 51. Ulica Lubomirskiego, *Krakau* (Cra-
covie).

Written in French
Sent to Amsterdam

First published in *Pravda* No. 21,   Printed from   the   original
    January 21, 1934

62

TO INESSA ARMAND

Dear Friend,

I send you the draft Ukrainian appeal for *Shakhtyorsky Listok*,[152] and particularly ask you to be tactful in getting it adopted (not on my behalf, of course, and better not in your name either) *through* Lola[153] and two or three Ukrainians (of course, *against* Yurkevich and, *if possible*, without the knowledge of this disgusting, rotten nationalist philistine, who under the flag of Marxism is preaching the *division* of the workers by nationalities, a *special* national organisation of the Ukrainian workers).

You will understand why it is inconvenient for *me* to send such a draft in my own name. Lola wrote to me that he agrees with me *against* Yurkevich, but Lola is naïve. The matter, however, must not drag on. It is terribly important that a voice should be heard from *amongst the Ukrainian Social-Democrats* for unity *against* dividing up the workers by nations. And now *Shakhtyorsky Listok* (received by me only today, Wednesday, April 1, as a supplement to the Sunday *Put Pravdy*) should *immediately* be made use of for this purpose.

Rewrite my draft (I agree to *all* changes, of course, if only there remains the direct protest against the division by nations); let Lola *alone* or with someone else, etc., *accept and translate it into Ukrainian*, and then send it *through me* to *Put Pravdy* in his name or (better) on behalf of a group (though it be of two or three people) of Ukrainian Marxists (still better, Ukrainian workers).

This should be done tactfully, quickly, against Yurkevich and *without his knowledge*, because this twister will
make trouble.

(I have received your story of Stepanyuk's report and
the speech by Yurkevich; frankly speaking, I was angry
with you—you didn't understand what the *essence* of
Yurkevich's position was. And I again—I'm sorry—called
you the Holy Virgin. Please don't be angry, it was because
I'm fond of you, because we're friends, but I can't help
being angry when I see "something that recalls the Holy
Virgin".)

Reply as quickly as possible and say whether you can
carry out this assignment properly, and how soon.

On Monday I sent you the collection and a note attached
to Nadya's letter. Have you received them?

All the best,
Yours,
V. U.

If my draft could be retold by a Ukrainian voice, and
with a couple of vivid Ukrainian examples, that would be
best of all!! I will bring pressure to bear on *Put Pravdy*.

Written on April 1, 1914

Sent from Cracow to Paris

Published for the first time   Printed from the original
in the Fourth (Russian) Edition
    of the *Collected Works*

63

TO INESSA ARMAND

Dear Friend,

I enclose Lola's letter.[154] Return it *at once* after reading it. (He is obviously twisting, but all the same we shall make a small *step* forward through him. I beg you very much, if you go to Zurich, do your utmost to see the Ukrainian Social-Democrats, ascertain their attitude on the question of a separate national-Ukrainian Social-Democratic organisation, and try and organise even a little group of anti-separatists.)

If Nik. Vas. has not yet been at our printing-press, let him ask them:

1) to stick *both* leaflets on paper with the printed heading of the press;

2) to write out *in German* (or, if they don't know the language, then in French) an exact estimate of the cost of (α) setting, (β) the *same* paper 5,000+1,000, (γ) printing and *everything else*.

As regards an intensive effort to discover contacts (in order to prepare for "the important affair"[155])—and especially for correspondence—both in Paris and in Switzerland, I hope you will do your best.

Yours,

V. U.

P.S. Would it not be possible before your departure to concentrate all our books (and those which Kamsky has from Orlovsky's library) with *Nik. Vas.*, and make him *swear an oath not to allow them to be plundered.* If brother*

---

* This word was written by Lenin in English.—*Ed.*

has written about his books, do the same with them. From
this library (Orlovsky's, Kamsky has it) please get, or have
procured, the *Minutes of the Second Congress* of the
R.S.D.L.P., and send them to me as quickly as possible.

One more thing *s.v. pl.*:

It is essential to republish the Party Programme and
Rules (with the changes of January 1912).[156] Please let the
Committee of Organisations Abroad have them set up
(*after ascertaining the exact cost*) and send us the *page* proof:
we shall say *then* how many should be printed.

["Programme and Rules of the R.S.D.L.P."]

Is there in Paris No. *11* of *Sotsial-Demokrat* (February
or March 1910)? If there is, send us *all* the copies.

Written on April 24, 1914

Sent from Cracow to Paris

Published for the first time   Printed from the original
in the Fourth (Russian) Edition
of the *Collected Works*

64

TO THE EDITORIAL BOARD OF *DZVIN*[157]

P.S. I have not spoken with Yurkevich, but I must say that I am profoundly indignant at the preaching of *separation* of the Ukrainian workers into a special Social-Democratic organisation.

With Social-Democratic greetings,
Lenin

Written on April 26, 1914 in Cracow

First published in 1937
in *Lenin Miscellany XXX*

Printed from the original

65

TO N. N. NAKORYAKOV[158]

May 18, 1914

Dear Comrade Nazar,

Many thanks to you for the bulletins of the 13th Census and for the fifth volume of the 12th (1900) Census.

I have been expecting any day the *same* volume (Agriculture) of the 13th Census (Census of 19*10*), but for some reason it does not arrive. Probably the Statistical Bureau has sent it to you, because Hourwich wrote to me that this volume had been published. Please drop me a line whether you have this volume (Agriculture. Census of 19*10*), .whether you can get it and send it me. I will immediately send you the cost of postage.

Please note my new address: Poronin (Galizien).

Congratulations on the splendid May Day in Russia: 250,000 in Petersburg alone!! *Put Pravdy* for May 1 has been confiscated, but I have learned from *Novy Mir*[159] that you often get confiscated issues as well. Altogether the news from Russia is evidence that revolutionary feelings are developing not only among the working class.

On May 15 Sima is leaving Cracow (Zakład Kąpielowy D-ra Kadena w *Rabce*. Galizien) for the summer to take a post in a village between Cracow and Poronin; she is very glad to have got this post.

N. K. sends her greetings. With all my heart I hope you will get better and have a good rest in the summer.

Yours,
V. I.

P.S. We have lately had news from the organisation in the Urals: things are not at all bad there. They're alive and growing!

Sent to New York

First published in 1930   Printed from the original
in *Lenin Miscellany XIII*

66

TO S. G. SHAHUMYAN

May 19, 1914[160]

Dear Suren,

I have received your letter of April 17. I hope you will reply when you have read the end of the article on self-determination of nations (I am writing it just now) in *Prosveshcheniye.**

Regarding your pamphlet against An, *be sure* to send a *Selbstanzeige*, or exposition, to *Prosveshcheniye.*[161]

I propose the following plan to you in addition. In order to combat the stupidity of the "cultural-national autonomists", it is necessary for the Russian Social-Democratic Labour group to bring in a Bill in the Duma for the equality of nations and the defence of the rights of national minorities.

Let's draft such a Bill.[162] The general principles of equality—the division of the country into autonomous and self-governing territorial units according to, among other things, nationality (the local population indicates the boundaries, the State Parliament endorses them)—the limits of powers of autonomous regions and areas, as well as of self-governing local units—illegality of any departure from the equality of nations in the decisions of the autonomous regions, Zemstvos, etc.; common school councils, democratically elected, etc., freedom and equality of language—choice of languages by municipal institutions, etc.—defence of minorities: the right to a proportional share of

---

* See "The Right of Nations to Self-Determination" (present edition, Vol. 20, pp. 393-454).—*Ed.*

expenditure, to school premises (free) for pupils of "alien" nationalities, to have "alien" teachers, "alien" departments in museums and libraries, theatres, etc.—the right of every citizen to seek cancellation (by the courts) of every departure from equality in respect of any "infringement" of the rights of national minorities (five-year censuses of the population in mixed regions, ten-year censuses in the state as a whole), etc.

I have a feeling that by this means we could give a popular explanation of the stupidity of cultural-national autonomy and *kill* the supporters of this stupidity for good.

The Bill might be drafted by the Marxists of *all*, or of very many, nations of Russia.

Write immediately whether you agree to help in this. In general, write *more frequently*, not less than once a week. It is unforgivable to put off replying for a long time: have this in mind, especially now!!

All the best,

Yours,

V. I.

Sent from Poronin to Baku

First published in 1930
in *Lenin Miscellany XIII*   Printed from the original

67

TO INESSA ARMAND

I have just read, my dear friend,* Vinnichenko's new novel which you sent me.[163] There's balderdash and stupidity! To combine together as much as possible of every kind of "horror", to collect in one story "vice" and "syphilis" and romantic crime, with extortion of money by means of blackmail (with the sister of the blackmailed person turned into a mistress), and the trial of the doctor! All this with hysterical outbursts, eccentricities, claims of having one's "own" theory of organising prostitutes. This organisation represents nothing bad in itself; but it is the *author*, Vinnichenko himself, who makes nonsense of it, *smacks his lips* over it, makes it his "hobby horse".

The review in *Rech* says that it is an imitation of Dostoyevsky and that there are good parts in it. There is an imitation, in my opinion, and a supremely bad imitation of the supremely bad in Dostoyevsky. Of course, in real life there are individual cases of all the "horrors" which Vinnichenko describes. But to lump them all together, and in *such* a way, means laying on the horrors *with a trowel*, frightening both one's own imagination and the reader's, "stunning" both oneself and the reader.

Once I had to spend a night with a sick comrade (delirium tremens), and once I had to "talk round" a comrade who had attempted suicide (after the attempt), and who some years later did commit suicide. Both recollections *à la* Vinnichen-

---

* The words "my dear friend" were written by Lenin in English.—*Ed.*

V. I. Lenin in Zakopane
1914

ko. But in both cases these were small fragments of the lives of both comrades. But this pretentious, crass idiot Vinnichenko, in self-admiration, has from such things compiled a collection that is nothing but horrors—a kind of "twopenny dreadful". Brrr.... Muck, nonsense, pity I spent so much time reading it.

P.S. How are things going with your arrangements for the summer?

Yours,
V. I.

*Franchement, continuez vous à vous fâcher ou non?**

Written earlier than June 5, 1914

Sent from Poronin to Lovran
(Austria-Hungary, now Yugoslavia)

Published for the first time
in the Fourth (Russian) Edition
of the *Collected Works*

Printed from the original

---

* Tell me frankly, are you still angry, or not?—*Ed.*

68

TO INESSA ARMAND

*My dear friend!

The precedent letter I've sent in too much hurry. Now I can more quietly speak about our "business".*

I hope you've grasped what is in the report?[164] The most important part is the conditions *1-13* (and then 14—slanderous, less important). They should be presented as vividly as possible.

N.B.: The addendum about the demonstration on April 4, 1914 goes *into the report*, under the question of *closing* the liquidationist paper. The addendum about the Plekhanov *Yedinstvo*[165] goes into the report under the question of the *groups abroad*.

I am sure that you are one of those people who develop, grow stronger, become more vigorous and bold when they are alone in a responsible position—and therefore I obstinately *do not believe* the pessimists, i.e., those who say that you ... can hardly.... Stuff and nonsense! I don't believe it! You will manage splendidly! With your excellent French you'll lay them all flat, and you won't allow Vandervelde to interrupt and shout. (In the event of anything like that, a formal protest to the *whole* Executive Committee and a threat to leave the meeting+the written protest of the whole delegation.)

They must give you the right to make a report. You will say that you ask for the opportunity, and that you *have*

---

* The passage between the asterisks was written by Lenin in English.—*Ed.*

precise and practical *proposals*. What could be more business-like and practical? We put ours forward, you put yours, and then we shall see. Either we adopt common decisions, or let us each report to our congresses, *to the Congress of our Party*. (But in practice, clearly, we shall adopt *absolutely nothing*.)

The essential thing, in my opinion, is to prove that only we are the Party (the other side are a fictitious bloc or tiny groups), only we are a workers' party (on the other side are the bourgeoisie, who provide money and approval), only we are the *majority*, four-fifths.

This is the first thing. And the second is to explain in *as popular language as possible* (I should absolutely fail in this, not knowing the language, while you will succeed) that the Organising Committee = a fiction. The reality which it conceals is *merely* a group of liquidationist writers in St. Petersburg. Proof? The literature....

Collapse of the August bloc.	(Cf. *Prosveshcheniye* No. 5,
(N.B. Departure of the Letts.)	I am sending my article*
	to Popov.)

The argument may be: your (i.e., Bolshevik) advantage among the Letts is small, your majority is a small one. Reply: "Yes, it is small. If you like to wait, it will soon be *écrasante*."

We excluded the liquidators' group from the Party in January 1912. The result? Have they set up a *better* party?? *None at all*. What they have is the complete break-up of the August bloc—aid to them by the bourgeoisie, desertion of them by the workers. Either accept our conditions, or no *rapprochement*, not to speak of *unité*!!

Arguments against Jagiello: an *alien* party. We don't trust it. Let the Poles unite.

Argument against Rosa Luxemburg: *what is real is not her* party, but the "opposition". Proof: there were *three electors* from Warsaw for the worker curia: *Zalewski, Bronowski* and *Jagiello. The first two* belong to the opposition. (If Rosa evades this, make her talk. If she denies it, demand that it be entered in the minutes, promising that we shall

---

* See "Disruption of Unity under Cover of Outcries for Unity" (present edition, Vol. 20, pp. 325-47).—*Ed.*

expose Rosa L.'s *untruth*.) And so *all the Social-Democratic* electors from Warsaw=opposition (the elections to the Fourth Duma). And in the rest of Poland? *Unknown*!! Give us the *names* of the electors!!

> Kautsky's letter against Rosa and for the opposition was in *Pravda*.[166]
> I am sending this No. to Popov. It can be *quoted*.

In general, I think I have sent you rather *too* many of the "most detailed" kind (as you asked), than too few.

In any case, the three of you will always find arguments and reasons and facts, and you always have the right to have a separate consultation—as to appointing a speaker from the delegation, etc.

The O.C. and the Bund will *lie* impudently:

... "They too, they will say, have an underground. It was recognised by the August Conference...."

Untrue! Literature published abroad. Newspapers? The departure of the Letts? Their verdict?

Quotations from "Nasha Zarya" and "Luch" against the underground!! (These were "slips of the tongue"?? Untrue! This is being said *below* by a bunch, a· *handful* of liquidationist workers, and it is a crying act of disorganisation.)

Or: you haven't an underground either.

> But is *Pravda* with 40,000 copies ranting about the underground? Or are the workers letting themselves be deceived??
>
> And what about the conference of the summer of 1913 and its *decision*: that the 6 deputies should make a statement? And then 6,722 votes for us, 2,985 against. A majority of 70 per cent!!

Lay as much *stress* as possible on the trade unions and the insurance committees: this has exceptional influence with the Europeans. We shall not allow the liquidators' to disorganise our firm majority in the trade unions and insurance committees!!

* I've forgotten the money question. We will pay for letters, *telegrams* (please wire oftener) & railway expenses, hotel expenses & so on. Mind it!

If possible try to be on Wednesday evening already in Brussels in order to arrange, *prepare* the delegation, come to agreement & so on.

If you succeed to receive the first report, for 1-2 hours,— it is almost all.* Afterwards it will only be a matter of "hitting back", worming out "their" counter-propositions (on all 14 questions) and declaring that we are *not in agreement*, and will report to the Congress of our Party. (We shall not accept a single one of their propositions.)

Very truly. Yours,**

V. I.

If there is talk of the money held by the former trustee, refer to the resolution of January 1912,[167] and refuse to say any more. We, that is, don't renounce our right!!

I am sending Popov Plekhanov's articles (from *Pravda*) about the *liquidators*.[168] Quote them, and say that *Pravda* remains of *the same* opinion.

Written between July 10 and 16, 1914
        at Poronin

    Published for the first time
 in the Fourth (Russian) Edition
     of the *Collected Works*

                                    Printed from the original

---

* The whole of this passage between asterisks, except for the words "come to agreement" (in Russian, "spetsya"), was written by Lenin in English.—*Ed.*

** This line was written by Lenin in English.—*Ed.*

69

TO I. E. HERMAN

Dear Comrade Herman,

It seems to me that an *important* moment is approaching in the attitude of the Lettish Social-Democrats to the Russian Social-Democratic Labour Party (in the person of the Central Committee—to our *part* of the R.S.D.L.P.—if that suits your legitimists, who want to "consider" the liquidators a little).

Here clarity and honesty are necessary.

In 1911-14 the Letts (their C.C.) were liquidators.

At the Congress of 1914[169] they became opponents of liquidationism, but *neutral* as between the O.C. and the C.C.

Now, after Brussels, after the resolution in No. 32 of *Trudovaya Pravda*,[170] the Letts want to enter our Party and conclude an agreement with the C.C.

Is this a good thing?

It is good, if what is being done is clearly understood and there is an honest attitude towards it.

It is bad, if it is being done without clear understanding, without firm resolution and reckoning with the consequences.

Those who want legitimacy in the sense of restoring the Stockholm-London (1906-07) R.S.D.L.P., had better not join our Party: there will be no result except squabbles, disappointments, offence taken and mutual hindrance. That was "a federation of the worst type" (as was stated in the resolution of the January 1912 Conference of the R.S.D.L.P.).[171] It was *rottenness*. Away with that rottenness!

If it is a question of defending the relics of federalism (for example, the Stockholm agreement and *delegation* from the Lettish C.C. to the Russian C.C.[172]), then it's a waste of time! In my belief we shall not accept it. It is play-acting, diplomacy *à la* Tyszka (which is now being imitated by the scoundrels in the Polish opposition, who went over at Brussels to the liquidators), not team work. Are we agreed in *principle*? Yes or no? If the answer is yes, then we must march together *against* (1) liquidationism, (2) "nationalism" (=(a) "cultural-national autonomy" and (b) the separatism of the Bund), (3) against federalism.

We have clearly, openly, before all the workers of Russia, unfurled these banners *since January 1912*. That is not a short time. You could and should have realised what was involved.

So let's come to an agreement—if we are to agree— clearly and honestly. To play at hide-and-seek, in my opinion, is out of place and unworthy. We are waging a *serious war*: against us are all the bourgeois intellectuals, the liquidators, the nationalists and the separatists of the Bund, the federalists overt and covert. Either we conclude an agreement *against* all these enemies, or *it would be better put off*.

It is better to confine ourselves to engagement than to tie ourselves up with marriage, if there is no complete certainty that the union will endure!!

All this is my personal opinion.

But I should very much like to come to an understanding with you and to reach clarity. If we came to an agreement on fundamentals at Brussels, we can and must ask ourselves *without diplomacy* whether we can agree on a stable treaty.

I am *very* worried that part of the Letts are

for cultural-national autonomy, or wavering,

for Bundist federalism, or wavering,

hesitating to attack the nationalism and separatism of the Bund,

hesitating to support our demand that the liquidationist paper of a group of disorganisers in Petersburg[173] should be closed, etc.

Is it a great part? in general and among members of the Central Committee? among the workers and among the intellectuals?

Is it influential?

After all, it is *we* who are waging the battle against the liquidators in Petersburg and throughout Russia. What is to be done if you *cannot conscientiously* help us fight the liquidators and the Bundists?? To conclude a *lasting* agreement in that case would be dishonest, and simply unrealistic!

And now, in addition, there is this disgusting manoeuvre of the Polish opposition *in favour* of the liquidators (voting *for* the Brussels resolution),[174] *for* nationalism (recognition of cultural-national autonomy as "an arguable proposition"), *for* federalism (the demand for the *old*, Tyszka, agreement of 1906 with the P.S.D.*).

Clarity, clarity before everything else! Anyone who has not realised the state and the circumstances of the war of proletarian democracy against bourgeois democracy (=the liquidators and the nationalists) *had better wait.*

I would like to know your opinion!

Yours,

Lenin

I should be very glad to hear the opinion of "Paragraph" on these questions. Show him this letter!

(Please give the "14 points" of our C.C.[175] to Rude for a day to read through.)

Written later than July 18, 1914

Sent from Poronin to Berlin

First published in 1935
in the magazine *Proletarskaya
Revolutsia* No. 5   Printed from the original

---

* Polish Social-Democracy.—*Ed.*

70

TO THE SECRETARY, EDITORIAL BOARD
OF THE GRANAT BROS. ENCYCLOPAEDIC DICTIONARY

July 21, 1914

Dear Colleague,

To my greatest regret, a number of quite exceptional and unforeseen circumstances (beginning with the resignation of Malinovsky) obliged me at the very beginning to interrupt the article on Marx[176] which I had begun, and after several unsuccessful attempts to find time to continue it, I have been forced to the conclusion that I shall not be able to do this work before the autumn.

I offer you my profound apologies, and express the hope that the editorial board of your so valuable publication will have time to find another Marxist and get the article from him by the time appointed.

Yours to command,

V. Ilyin

Sent from Poronin to Moscow

First published in 1930
in *Lenin Miscellany XIII*

Printed from the original

71

TO THE SECRETARY, EDITORIAL BOARD
OF THE GRANAT BROS. ENCYCLOPAEDIC DICTIONARY

Dear Colleague,

Some days ago, despairing of any opportunity to finish the work, I sent you a letter giving it up, with my apologies.* But now the political circumstances on which I am so extremely dependent are suddenly changing again in radical fashion. First of all, the exceptional security measures in St. Petersburg, about which I read today in the Russian papers, are to remain in force until September 4, 1914, evidently meaning that the paper for which I was writing is stopped until then. Secondly, the war will, it seems, interrupt a number of *urgent* political affairs with which I was burdened. Therefore I could now set about continuing the article on Marx which I have begun, and could probably finish it soon. If you have not yet placed the order with someone else, and commissioned another author, please reply by cable to me (at my expense): Uljanow. Poronin. Rabotaite.**

If you have already commissioned someone else, please reply by postcard.

With assurances of my deep respect,

V. *Ilyin*

Absender: Wl. Uljanow, Poronin (Galizien), Austria.

Written on July 28, 1914

Sent to Moscow

Published for the first time
in the Fourth (Russian) Edition
of the *Collected Works*

Printed from the original

---

* See the previous letter.—*Ed.*
** Work.—*Ed.*

72

TO V. A. KARPINSKY

Dear K.,

I have had your postcard, and hasten to reply. Wait a little: we shall let you know about what can and should be done regarding what you (and we) desire.[177] Don't forget, by the way, that legality here is now of a special kind: have you spoken about this with the friends at Lausanne? Be sure to have a talk with them.

We remain at Berne. The address is Donnerbühlweg 11a. Uljanow.

As regards a lecture, I don't know yet. I shall have to think it over, and consult in greater detail. How many people could be counted on where you are?[178]

All the best. Greetings from all.

Yours,
Lenin

P.S. It might, perhaps, be better to give a talk about the critique and my anti-critique. Two words nevertheless: one cannot on formal grounds defend the scoundrelly chauvinism of the Germans. There were bad resolutions, there were some that were not bad; there were declarations of both types. But there is a limit to everything! *And it has been overstepped.* We cannot be patient, we cannot be diplomatic, we must revolt against shameful chauvinism with all our strength!!

Written later than September 27, 1914

Sent from Berne to Geneva

First published in 1929
in *Lenin Miscellany XI*

Printed from the original

73

TO V. A. KARPINSKY

Dear Karpinsky,

I am taking advantage of this messenger to speak openly.

There is *every* ground for expecting that the Swiss police and military authorities (at the *first signal* from the Russian or French Ambassador, etc.) will bring us before a military tribunal or expel us for breach of neutrality, etc. Therefore don't write anything openly in your letters. If you have to communicate anything, write in chemicals (the sign of chemicals is the date on the letter underlined).

We have decided to publish the *attached* manifesto, instead of the not very readable theses.[179] Let us know when you get it, calling the manifesto "The Development of Capitalism".

It ought to be published. But we advise you to do this only on condition that you take (are *able* to take) the maximum precautions!!

No one should know *where* and by whom it was published. All rough copies should be burned!! The copies printed should be kept *only* by some influential Swiss citizen, deputy and so forth.

If this is impossible, *don't* print it.

If it cannot be printed, do it on a mimeograph (also with the greatest precautions). Reply: I have received the development of capitalism (*in so many*) copies=I shall reprint it in so many copies.

If it cannot be published, either in print or mimeographed, write immediately. We shall think of something else. Reply in as much detail as possible.

(If you succeed in publishing it, send us here *by hand*
3/4 of the copies; we shall find somewhere to keep them.)
I await a reply!

Yours,
Lenin

N.B

P.S. We shall find the money for the publication.
Only write beforehand, *how much* will be needed, because there is *very* little money. Could not the 170
francs from the Committee of Organisations Abroad[180]
be used for this purpose?

Written earlier than October 11, 1914
    Sent from Berne to Geneva
        First published in 1929   Printed from the original
        in *Lenin Miscellany XI*

74

TO V. A. KARPINSKY

Dear Friend,

I spoke here today at Plekhanov's lecture, against his chauvinism.[181] I intend to deliver a lecture here on Tuesday. I should like to lecture at Geneva (the European war and European socialism) on Wednesday.[182] Arrange it, after proper discussion—as conspiratively as possible, i.e., so that no permission will be required (of course, it is also desirable that there should be a maximum audience). You are the best judge of how to do this. It should combine the maximum audience with the minimum of police publicity and police interference (or police threats). At Berne I lectured to members of the groups and guests whom they recommended (about 120-130 persons), without notices, etc. Would not this method be best?

Reply immediately to Mr. Ryvline. Villa Rougemont. Chailly sur Lausanne. For me. On Tuesday I am lecturing here at Lausanne, and your reply should be here by Tuesday afternoon. When we meet, we can have a more detailed talk about our affairs. And so, if permission is required at Geneva, then think it over ten times, whether a closed meeting would not be best. In general, of course, you decide. If it is all right for Wednesday (to arrange the lecture for Wednesday evening), I will arrive on Wednesday morning.

All the best,

Yours,

Lenin

Written on October 11, 1914
Sent from Lausanne to Geneva

First published in 1929
in *Lenin Miscellany XI*

Printed from the original

75

TO V. A. KARPINSKY

Dear K.,

Just while I was staying in Geneva *joyful* news arrived from Russia. There also arrived the text of the reply of the Russian Social-Democrats to Vandervelde.[183] We therefore decided to publish, instead of a separate manifesto, the next issue of the Central Organ, *Sotsial-Demokrat*.[184] Today this decision will be finally shaped, so to speak.

And so, please take all the necessary steps as soon as possible to find a Frenchman, i.e., a Swiss citizen, as a responsible editor, and to determine the costs. We think of two pages as the size, with a format something like that of the Paris *Golos*.[185] The dates of publication will be *indefinite*—hardly more often than two or three times *a month* at first. The printing will be small, because with our orientation we cannot reckon on the man in the street (500 copies?). The price is to be about 10 centimes. All this is still *assumption*, but you need to know it for the discussion with the compositor.

And so, the price?

How long is needed for the publication (setting, etc.) of an issue of that size?

Then the type? Is there only one large size, or is there also a small size, brevier? How many thousand letters and spaces will go into two pages of *Golos* format of (1) large type and (2) small type, brevier?

You should not distribute the type of the manifesto which has already been set: we shall fit it into the paper. By Monday we shall send you some small amendments to the manifesto, and a *different* signature (because after contact with Russia we are now acting *more officially*).

A thousand greetings!

Yours,
Lenin

P.S. Please check up whether my letters to you arrive absolutely to time (without any delay).

Written on October 17, 1914

Sent from Berne to Geneva

First published, but not in full, in *Pravda* No. 92, April 22, 1926

Published in full in 1929 in *Lenin Miscellany XI*

Printed from the original

76

TO A. G. SHLYAPNIKOV[186]

October 17, 1914

Dear Friend,

I arrived home last night.after my lecture tour and found your letters. Heartiest greetings to you, and, through you, to all Russian friends. The reply to Vandervelde was given to a translator yesterday, and I have not yet seen the text. I will write about it as soon as I see it.

In my view the most important thing now is a consistent and organised struggle against the chauvinism which has seized upon the whole bourgeoisie and the majority of the opportunist socialists (and those making their peace with opportunism—like Mr. Kautsky!). And to perform the tasks imposed by this struggle it is first of all necessary to combat the chauvinism of one's *own* country—specifically, in Russia the gentry *à la* Maslov and Smirnov (see *Russkiye Vedomosti* and *Russkoye Slovo*) whose "works" I have read,[187] or Messrs. Sokolov, Meshkovsky, Nikitin and others whom you have seen or heard. Plekhanov, as I think you have already been told, has become a French chauvinist. Among the liquidators there is evidently confusion.* Alexinsky, *they say*, is a Francophil. Kosovsky (the Bundist, a Right-winger, I heard his lecture) is a Germanophil.** It seems

---

* Our intellectuals in Paris (outvoted in the section by the workers) have gone as volunteers (Nik. Vas., Antonov and others) and have issued a stupid non-Party appeal[188] jointly with the S.R.s. It has been sent to you.
** Martov is behaving most decently of all in *Golos*. But will Martov hold out? *I don't believe it.*

as though the middle course of the whole "Brussels bloc"[189] of the liquidator gentry with Alexinsky and Plekhanov will be adapting themselves to Kautsky, who now is *more harmful than anyone else*. How dangerous and scoundrelly his sophistry is, covering up the dirty tricks of the opportunists with the most smooth and facile phrases (in *Neue Zeit*[190]). The opportunists are an obvious evil. The German "Centre" headed by Kautsky is a concealed evil, diplomatically coloured over, contaminating the eyes, the mind and the conscience of the workers, and more dangerous than anything else. Our task now is the unconditional and open struggle against international opportunism and those who screen it (Kautsky). And this is what we shall do in the Central Organ, which we shall shortly issue (probably two little pages). We must with all our strength now support the legitimate hatred of the class-conscious workers for the rotten behaviour of the Germans, and draw from this hatred a political conclusion *against* opportunism and any concession to it. This is an international task. It devolves on us, there is no one else. We must not retreat from it. It is wrong to put forward the watchword of the "simple" restoration of the International (for the danger of a rotten conciliatory resolution on the Kautsky-Vandervelde line is very, very great!). The watchword of "peace" is wrong: the watchword should be transformation of the national war into a civil war. (This transformation may be a long job, it may require and will require a number of preliminary conditions, but all the work should be carried on *in the direction* of precisely *such* a transformation, in that spirit and on that line.) Not sabotage of the war, not separate, individual actions in that spirit, but mass propaganda (not only among "civilians") leading to the transformation of the war into a civil war.

In Russia chauvinism hides behind phrases about "*la belle* France" and unfortunate Belgium (and what about the Ukraine, etc.?) or behind "popular" hatred of the Germans (and of "Kaiserism"). Therefore our unquestionable duty is to combat these sophistries. And in order that the struggle should proceed along precise and clear lines we need a watchword which generalises it. That watchword is: for us *Russians*, from the point of view of the interests of the working masses and the working class of *Russia*, there cannot be the smallest doubt, absolutely any doubt, that the *lesser* evil would be now, at once the *defeat* of tsarism in this war. For tsarism is a hundred times worse than Kaiserism. Not sabotage of the war, but the struggle against chauvinism and the concentration of all propaganda and agitation on the international rallying (rapprochement, solidarity, agreement, *selon les circonstances**) of the proletariat for the purpose of civil war. It would be a mistake both to call for *individual* acts of shooting officers, etc., and to tolerate arguments like the one that "we don't want to help Kaiserism". The first is a deviation towards anarchism, the second towards opportunism. We, on the contrary, must prepare mass (or at the very least collective) action among the troops—not only of one nation—and carry on *all* propaganda and agitation work in that direction. The direction of our work (stubborn, systematic, maybe protracted) in the spirit of turning the national war into a civil war—there is the crux of the matter. The time for this transformation is a different question, at present still unclear. We must allow this moment to mature, and systematically "make it mature".

This is all for the time being. I will write frequently. You write more often too.

Set forth in greater detail the leaflet of the Petersburg Committee.

More details about the views and reactions of the workers.

The balance of *forces* among the "groups" in St. Petersburg? That is, have the liquidators grown stronger as regards ourselves? To what extent?

Is Dan at liberty? His position? And that of Chirkin, Bulkin and Co.?

More details.

To whom precisely, and in whose name, did you send a hundred rubles?

All the very best,

Yours,

Lenin

---

* According to circumstances.—*Ed.*

11*

The watchword of peace, in my opinion, is incorrect at the present moment. It is a philistine, parson's watchword. The proletarian watchword must be civil war.

Objectively, from the radical change in the situation in Europe, such a watchword follows for the epoch of a mass war. The same watchword follows from the Basle resolution.[191]

We can neither "promise" civil war nor "decree" it, but to go on working—if necessary for a very long time—in *that direction*, we are in duty bound. You will see the details in the Central Organ article.* Meanwhile I am only indicating the main points of our position, so that we can reach a really good understanding.

Sent from Berne to Stockholm

First published in 1924   Printed from the original
in *Lenin Miscellany II*

---

* See "The Position and Tasks of the Socialist International" (present edition, Vol. 21, pp. 35-41).—*Ed.*

77

TO A. G. SHLYAPNIKOV

October 17, 1914

Dear Friend,

I have read the reply to Vandervelde, and attach my ideas on the subject of that reply.

It would be extremely desirable that in the event of the Duma being convened (*is it true* that it is being summoned in a month's time?)[192] our group should make a statement independent of the bloc, and should set forth a *consistent* point of view. Reply at once (1) whether there will be a session of the Duma, (2) whether you have good contacts with the Duma group,[193] and how many days this will require.

October 21, 1914

I continue my interrupted letter. My criticism of the reply, of course, is a private affair, intended *only for friends* with the object of reaching complete mutual understanding. The Central Organ will appear in a day or two, and we shall send it to you.

About the International, don't be an optimist, and beware of the intrigues of the liquidators and opportunists. Although Martov is going left today, this is because he is alone. But what will happen tomorrow? Tomorrow he will descend to their common plan: to stop the mouths (and the mind and the conscience) of the workers with an indiarubber resolution in the spirit of Kautsky, who justifies all and sundry. Kautsky is the most hypocritical, most revolting and most harmful of all! It is internationalism, if you please, for the workers of every country to shoot at the workers of another country under the guise of "defence of the fatherland"!!!

Let them intrigue—it is after all no more than a petty intrigue today, at such a moment in world history, to think of playing diplomacy with opportunism and setting up a "German" International Socialist Bureau![194] We must today maintain our principles. The workers of Petersburg are imbued with the best feelings of enmity to the traitors among the German Social-Democrats. With all our strength we must support and consolidate that feeling and consciousness into firm resolution to fight international opportunism. Up till now German Social-Democracy was the main authority—today *it is a model of what not to do*!

You are needed in Stockholm. Organise the correspondence with Russia as well as you can. Send my letters (is that possible?) to the one who gave you a note in pencil: we must reach an understanding with him in as much detail as possible.[195] This is extremely important. We are beginning publication of the Central Organ.

Write more often!

Yours,
Lenin

Sent from Berne to Stockholm

First published in 1924   Printed from the original
in *Lenin Miscellany II*

78

TO A. G. SHLYAPNIKOV

October 27, 1914

Dear Friend,

I have just received your second letter, and sit down to have a talk with you.

Many thanks for the letter about events in St. Petersburg.[196] It will make an excellent report for the Central Organ. An issue of the Central Organ will be published in a few days, and we shall send it to you. Wait for it. Wait also for the next issue. You must stay for the time being in Stockholm until transport *through* Stockholm (1) of letters, (2) of people and (3) of literature has been *completely* organised. For this you should systematically train and *test* a good transmitting agent in Stockholm. Is Comrade Skovno suitable for this? What's good about her is that she is a Bolshevik. She won't go over to the other side. But is she business-like, is she alert, does she attend to details?

I am delighted if Comrade Kollontai[197] has taken up our position, and I am also glad at the excellent (on the whole) management of *Golos* by Martov in Paris. But I am in deadly fear that Martov (and others akin to him) will go over ... to the position taken up by Kautsky and Troelstra. I hate and despise Kautsky now more than anyone, with his vile, dirty self-satisfied hypocrisy. Nothing has happened, so he says, principles have not been abandoned, everyone was entitled to defend his fatherland. It is internationalism, if you please, for the workers of all countries to shoot one another "in order to defend their fatherland".

Rosa Luxemburg was right when she wrote, long ago, that Kautsky has the "subservience of a theoretician"—

servility, in plainer language, servility to the majority of the Party, to opportunism. Just now there is *nothing* in the world more harmful and dangerous for the *ideological* independence of the proletariat than this rotten self-satisfaction and disgusting hypocrisy of Kautsky, who wants to smother and cover up everything, to tranquillise the awakened conscience of the workers by sophistries and pseudo-scientific chatter. If Kautsky succeeds in this, he will become the main representative of bourgeois corruption in the working-class movement. And Troelstra will be for him —oh, that Troelstra is a more skilful opportunist than the "kind" little old man Kautsky! How that Troelstra manoeuvred in order to drive honest men and Marxists out of the Dutch Party (Gorter, Pannekoek, Wijnkoop)!! I shall never forget how Roland-Holst, when she once visited me in Paris, said about Troelstra: *"ein hundsgemeiner Kerl" (gredin*, in French)*.... I am sorry that you cast pearls before him....[198] Troelstra+the opportunist scoundrels in the *Vorstand*** of the German Social-Democrats are carrying on a dirty little intrigue in order to cover everything up. Be on your guard, don't become the unwilling victim of that intrigue!! Don't accidentally give any help to these worst enemies of the working-class movement, who in an epoch of crisis are defending chauvinism "theoretically", and carrying on a petty and revolting diplomacy. The only one who has told the workers the truth—although not loudly enough, and sometimes not quite skilfully—is Pannekoek, whose article we have sent to you (pass on a translation to the Russians).[199] His words, that if now the "leaders" of the International that was murdered by the opportunists. and Kautsky come together and begin "papering over" the cracks, this "will be of no significance whatever"— these are the *only* socialist words. They are the *truth*. Bitter, but the truth. And now the workers need the truth, the whole truth, more than at any other time, not rotten diplomacy, not playing at "papering over", not smearing over the evil with indiarubber resolutions.

---

* "A scoundrelly son of a bitch."—*Ed.*
** Executive or C.C.—*Ed.*

It is clear to me that Kautsky, Troelstra plus Vandervelde (it may be plus $X+Y+Z$ or minus X, Y, Z—this is not important) are now busy with an intrigue for that purpose. The transfer of the International Bureau to Holland is a similar intrigue by the same scoundrels.

I shall keep away from them and from it—and will give the same advice to our representative in the International Socialist Bureau (Litvinoff, 76. High Street. Hampstead, London, N. W.)—and I advise you to do the same.

"Don't attend the counsels of the impious",[200] don't put any faith in Troelstra, and the like, etc., etc., just present them with a brief ultimatum: here is the manifesto (a revision of the theses; we shall send it to you in print in a few days) of our C.C. on the war: do you want to publish it in your language?? No? Well, then *adieu*, our roads diverge!

If Kollontai is on our side, let her help to "push" this manifesto in the other languages. Make the acquaintance of *Höglund*, a young Swedish Social-Democrat, leader of the "opposition", read him our manifesto (refer to me: we became acquainted at Copenhagen). Sound out whether he is *ideologically* close to us (he is only a naïve, sentimental anti-militarist: these are the very people who should be told—either the watchword of civil war, or remain with the opportunists and the chauvinists).

The essence of the whole problem in Russia now is to organise an ideological rebuff to the opportunists of the International and to Kautsky. This is the key question. Won't Martov go over at this point??... I fear so!...

All the best,

Yours,

Lenin

Sent from Berne to Stockholm

First published in 1924
in *Lenin Miscellany II*

Printed from the original

79

TO A. G. SHLYAPNIKOV

Für Alexander

Dear Friend,

In two or three days you will receive our Central Organ, and then I hope there will be complete "harmony" of our views. Frankly speaking, I am a little afraid whether some of the steps you have taken may not be interpreted in the sense that you are ignoring our legitimate representative in the International Socialist Bureau—Mr. Litvinoff, 76. High Street. Hampstead. London, N. W. Of course, such an interpretation will be a malicious distortion, but all the same be more careful.

Troelstra has deceived you, or led you into error. He is an arch-opportunist, and an agent of the intrigues of the most scoundrelly centre of the most scoundrelly opportunists—the German Social-Democrats (headed by Kautsky, who basely defends the opportunists), with their most foul *Vorstand*. We shall not attend any conferences or join in any steps, taken on the initiative of scoundrels like them. We will stand aside: let them disgrace themselves! For they, having disgraced themselves once, will disgrace themselves again. The French have already rejected their intrigues, and without the French there can be only a dirty comedy acted by dirty blackguards.

Larin, to all appearances, is swindling you without scruple. If he expresses his "confidence" in the German *Vorstand*, I can well understand that Troelstra has "taken note of it". Of course he would!! Confidence in the rottenest opportunists!! For God's sake correct what can be corrected, and don't express the least confidence, direct or indirect, in any of the opportunists, either German or French. Pannekoek is right: the Second International is dead for ever. It was killed by the opportunists (and not by "parliamentarism", as the slow-witted Pannekoek put it). "Papering over" the differences is only a petty intrigue, and *we* must take *no* part in it, either direct or indirect.

We shall try to send you a couple of leaflets shortly. Don't go away, have patience. Arrange everything I wrote to you about, wait until the Central Organ has reached Russia, wait until we reach a *complete* understanding with the Russian colleagues too (both with Kamenev and with others), after they have received the Central Organ. Before all this has been done there can be no thought of your departure. It would be premature for us as yet to leave.[201] Find out, by the way, whether Social-Democratic things can be printed in Sweden (as for example, our Central Organ).

Poor Gorky! What a pity that he has disgraced himself by putting his signature under that rotten little paper of the Russian liberal gentry.[202] Both Meshkovsky and Plekhanov and others (including Maslov and Smirnov) have sunk to the same level.

Make sure of getting and rereading (or get someone to translate to you) Kautsky's *Weg zur Macht**—what he wrote there about the revolution of our times!!

And what a scoundrel he has become now, renouncing all this!

Our job now is a merciless war on chauvinism, covered up by chatter about defence of the "fatherland", etc., especially on the "socialist chauvinism" of Plekhanov, Guesde, Kautsky (the worst of the lot, the hypocrite!) and Co. Defending the revolution (bourgeois in Russia and socialist in the West), we preach it in wartime too. Our watchword is civil war. It is all purest sophistry that this watchword is unsuitable, etc.; and so forth. We cannot "make" it, but we preach it and we work in that direction. In every country preference should be given to the struggle against the chauvinism of the *particular* country, to awakening of hatred of one's *own* government, to appeals (repeated,

* *Path to Power.—Ed.*

insistent, numerous, tireless) to the solidarity of the workers of the warring countries, to their *joint* civil war against the bourgeoisie.

No one will venture to *guarantee* when and to what extent this preaching will be "justified" in practice: *that is not the point* (only base sophists renounce revolutionary agitation because they don't know when the revolution will take place). The point is to work on those *lines. Only* that work is socialist, not chauvinist. And it *alone* will bear socialist fruit, revolutionary fruit.

The watchword of peace now is absurd and mistaken (*especially* after the *betrayal* by almost all the leaders up to and including Guesde, Plekhanov, Vandervelde, Kautsky). In practice it would mean petty-bourgeois moaning. But we must remain revolutionaries *in war conditions too.* And must preach the *class struggle* among the troops also.

All the best. Write more often.

Yours,
Lenin

Written on October 31, 1914
Sent from Berne to Stockholm

First published in 1924   Printed from the original
in *Lenin Miscellany II*

80

TO THE SECRETARY, EDITORIAL BOARD
OF THE GRANAT PUBLISHING HOUSE

Berne, November 17, 1914

Dear Colleague,

I have sent you today by registered post the article on Marx and Marxism[203] for the dictionary. It is not for me to judge how far I have succeeded in solving the difficult problem of squeezing the exposition into a framework of about 75,000 letters and spaces. I will observe that I had to compress the literature very intensively (15,000 was the ultimatum), and I had to select the *essence* of various tendencies (of course, with the majority *for* Marx). It was difficult to make up my mind to renounce many *quotations* from Marx. In my view, quotations are very important for a dictionary (especially on the most controversial questions of Marxism, which include philosophy and the agrarian problem first and foremost). Readers of the dictionary should have available *all* the most important statements by Marx, otherwise the purpose of the dictionary would not be achieved. That is how it seemed to me. I don't know either whether you will be satisfied from the point of view of censorship: if not, perhaps we could manage to agree on the *rewording* of some passages, having in mind passing the censor. For my part, without ultimative demands from the editorial board, I could not make up my mind to "correct" a number of quotations and propositions of Marxism for reasons of censorship.

I hope you will be kind enough to let me know immediately (a postcard will do) that you have received the article.

I would ask you particularly to send the fee due to me as soon as possible to Gospodin Mark Timofeyevich *Yeliza-rov*, 17 Grechesky Prosp., Flat 18, *Petrograd* (sending it to me here in wartime would involve the expense of an exchange operation and would be most inconvenient for me).

With assurances that I am at your service,

V. Ilyin

P.S. On account of the war, my library has been held up in Galicia,[204] and I could not find some quotations from Marx's works in the Russian translations. If you think it *necessary*, perhaps you could request someone in Moscow to do it? (In my view, it is not.) Incidentally, I should be very glad if you found it possible to send me a proof of the article, and to let me know whether *partial* corrections of the proof are possible or not. If you cannot send the proof, I hope you will be kind enough to send me an off-print.

My address: Wl. Uljanow. 11. Distelweg. 11. Bern.

Sent to Moscow

First published in 1923
in *Proletarskaya Revolutsia*
No. 6-7

Printed from the original

81

TO A. G. SHLYAPNIKOV

November 28, 1914

Dear Friend,

I have had a telegram from Branting[205] today that "the newspapers *confirm* the arrest of five deputies".[206] I fear that now we cannot doubt the fact of the arrest.

This is terrible. The government has evidently decided to have its revenge on the Russian Social-Democratic Labour group, and will stick at nothing. We must be ready for the very worst: falsification of documents, forgeries, planting of "evidence", false witness, trial behind closed doors, etc., etc.

I think that without such methods the government would not succeed in getting a sentence.

Could you not try to find out the names of the six who have been arrested?

Is K. all right?

At all events, the work of our Party has now become 100 times more difficult. And still we shall carry it on! *Pravda* has trained up thousands of class-conscious workers out of whom, in spite of all difficulties, a new collective of leaders—the Russian C.C. of the Party—will be formed. It is now particularly important that you should remain in Stockholm (or *near* Stockholm), and put all your energy into establishing contacts with Petersburg. (Write whether you have received any money as a loan: in my last letter I put in a little note for you about this. If you have not had any and cannot get any, we shall probably be able to send you something; write in as much detail as possible.)

In Zurich a newspaper *Otkliki* is promised (probably the liquidators+Trotsky) in December. In Paris a daily S.R. *Mysl* (*arch-philistine* phrase-making, playing at "Leftism")[207] has begun to appear. An abundance of papers, phrases from the intelligentsia, today r-r-revolutionary, tomorrow...? (tomorrow they will *make peace* with Kautsky, Plekhanov, the liquidationist "patriotic-chauvinist-opportunist intelligentsia" in Russia)....

Among the *working* class in Russia they never had anything, and have nothing. You cannot trust them in the slightest.

I shake you warmly by the hand, and wish you *courage*. Times are difficult, but ... we shall get through!

Yours,
Lenin

Sent from Berne to Stockholm

First published in 1924   Printed from the original
in *Lenin Miscellany II*

82

TO ALEXANDRA KOLLONTAI

Dear Comrade,

I have received your letter and the English enclosure.[208] Many thanks!

I send you both the things you wrote about. Let us know— if you translate them and send them off—what happens to them.

It is said that in *Hamburger Echo* there was a leading article "Über unseren Verrat an der Internationale",* which stated that the Germans (i.e., the German opportunist scoundrels) are all in it, and that Plekhanov, Maslov and Chkheidze are *for them*.[209]

Is it true? And what do you think about it?

Greetings and best wishes,

V. Ilyin

P.S. Ask Alexander to make the acquaintance of Kobetsky (Kobezky. Kapelwej. 51⁴. Kjobenhavn VI) and to take from him my letter to himself (Alexander).

It is useless to advocate a well-meaning programme of noble wishes for peace, if we do not at the same time and in the first place advocate the preaching of illegal organisation and civil war of the proletariat against the bourgeoisie.

N. Lenin

The European war has brought this great benefit to international socialism, that it has exposed for all to see

---

* "On Our Betrayal of the International."—*Ed.*

the utter rottenness, baseness and meanness of opportunism, thereby giving a splendid impetus to the cleansing
of the working-class movement from the dung accumulated during decades of peace.

N. Lenin

Written earlier than
December 16, 1914

Sent from Berne to Copenhagen

First published in 1924   Printed from the original
in *Lenin Miscellany II*

1915

83

TO BASOK[210]

Copy of a reply handed to Tria on January 12, 1915

Dear Citizen,

Tria has passed on to me your letter of December 28, 1914. You are obviously mistaken. We take the stand of international revolutionary Social-Democracy, and you of the national bourgeoisie. We are working to bring together the *workers* of various (and particularly the *warring*) countries, while you evidently are moving nearer to the bourgeoisie and the government of "your" nation. We are on different roads.

N. Lenin

Berne, January 12, 1915
Bern. Uljanow. Distelweg. 11.

Sent to Constantinople

First published in 1924
in *Proletarskaya Revolutsia* No. 3

Printed from the original

84

TO INESSA ARMAND

Dear Friend,

I very much advise you to write the plan of the pamphlet in as much detail as possible.²¹¹ Otherwise too much is unclear.

One opinion I must express here and now:

I advise you to throw out altogether § 3—the "demand (women's) for freedom of love".

That is not really a proletarian but a bourgeois demand.

After all, what do you understand by that phrase? What *can* be understood by it?

1. Freedom *from* material (financial) calculations in affairs of love?

2. The same, *from* material worries?

3. From religious prejudices?

4. From prohibitions by Papa, etc.?

5. From the prejudices of "society"?

6. From the narrow circumstances of one's environment (peasant or petty-bourgeois or bourgeois intellectual)?

7. From the fetters of the law, the courts and the police?

8. From the serious element in love?

9. From child-birth?

10. Freedom of adultery? Etc.

I have enumerated many shades (not all, of course). You have in mind, of course, not nos. 8-10, but either nos. 1-7 or something *similar* to nos. 1-7.

But then for nos. 1-7 you must choose a different wording, because freedom of love does not express this idea exactly.

And the public, the readers of the pamphlet, will *inevitably* understand by "freedom of love", in general, something like nos. 8-10, even *without your wishing it*.

Just because in modern society the most talkative, noisy and "top-prominent" classes understand by "freedom of love" nos. 8-10, just for that very reason this is not a proletarian but a bourgeois demand.

For the proletariat nos. 1-2 are the most important, and then nos. 1-7, and those, in fact, are not "freedom of love".

The thing is not what you *subjectively* "mean" by this. The thing is the *objective logic* of class relations in affairs of love.

Friendly shake hands!*
W. I.

Written on January 17, 1915
Sent from Berne

First published in 1939
in the magazine *Bolshevik* No. 13

Printed from the original

---

* These words, like "Dear Friend" at the beginning, were written by Lenin in English.—*Ed.*

85

TO INESSA ARMAND

Dear Friend,

I apologise for my delay in replying: I wanted to do it yesterday, but was prevented, and I had no time to sit down and write.

As regards your plan for the pamphlet, my opinion was that "the demand for freedom of love" was unclear and—independently of your will and your wish (I emphasised this when I said that what mattered was the objective, class relations, and not your subjective wishes)—would, in present social conditions, turn out to be a bourgeois, not a proletarian demand.

You do not agree.

Very well. Let us look at the thing again.

In order to make the unclear clear, I enumerated approximately ten *possible* (and, in conditions of class discord, inevitable) different interpretations, and in doing so remarked that interpretations 1-7, in my opinion, would be typical or characteristic of proletarian women, and 8-10 of bourgeois women.

If you are to refute this, you have to show (1) that these interpretations are wrong (and then replace them by others, or indicate which are wrong), or (2) incomplete (then you should add those which are missing), or (3) are not divided into proletarian and bourgeois in that way.

You don't do either one, or the other, or the third.

You don't touch on points 1-7 at all. Does this mean that you admit them to be true (on the whole)? (What you write about the prostitution of proletarian women and their dependence: "impossibility of saying no" fully comes under points 1-7. No difference at all can be detected between us" here.)

Nor do you deny that this is a *proletarian* interpretation. There remain points 8-10.

These you "don't quite understand" and "object" to: "I don't understand how it is *possible*" (that is what you have written!) "to *identify*" (!!??) "freedom of love with" point 10....

So it appears that *I* am "identifying", while you have undertaken to refute and demolish *me*?

How so?

Bourgeois women understand by freedom of love points 8-10—that is my thesis.

Do you deny this? Will you say what *bourgeois* ladies understand by freedom of love?

You don't say that. Do not literature and life really *prove* that that is just how bourgeois women understand it? They prove it completely! You tacitly admit this.

And if that is so, the point is their class position, and it is hardly possible and almost naïve to "refute" *them*.

What you must do is *separate* from them clearly, *contrast* with them, the proletarian point of view. One must take into account the objective fact that otherwise *they* will snatch the appropriate passages from your pamphlet, interpret them in their own way, make your pamphlet into water pouring on their mill, distort your ideas in the workers' eyes, "*confuse*" the workers (sowing in their minds the fear that *you* may be bringing them *alien* ideas). And in their hands are a host of newspapers, etc.

While you, completely forgetting the objective and class point of view, go over to the "offensive" against *me*, as though I am "identifying" freedom of love with points 8-10.... Marvellous, really marvellous....

"Even a fleeting passion and intimacy" are "more poetic and cleaner" than "kisses without love" of a (vulgar and shallow) married couple. That is what you write. And that is what you intend to write in your pamphlet. Very good.

Is the contrast logical? Kisses without love between a vulgar couple are *dirty*. I agree. To them one should contrast ... what?... One would think: kisses *with* love? While you contrast them with "fleeting" (why fleeting?) "passion" (why not love?)—so, logically, it turns out that kisses without love (fleeting) are contrasted with kisses without love by married people.... Strange. For a popular pamphlet, would it not be better to contrast philistine-intellectual-peasant (I think they're in my point 6 or point 5) vulgar and dirty marriage without love to proletarian civil marriage with love (adding, *if you absolutely insist*, that fleeting intimacy and passion, too, may be dirty and may be clean). What you have arrived at is, not the contrast of class *types*, but something like an "incident", which of course is possible. But is it a question of particular incidents? If you take the theme of an incident, an individual case of dirty kisses in marriage and pure ones in a fleeting intimacy, that is a theme to be worked out in a novel (because there the whole *essence* is in the *individual* circumstances, the analysis of the *characters* and psychology of *particular* types). But in a pamphlet?

You understood my idea very well about the unsuitable quotation from Key,[212] when you said it is "stupid" to appear in the role of "professors of love". Quite so. Well, and what about the role of professors of fleeting, etc.?

Really, I don't want to engage in polemics at all. I would willingly throw aside this letter and postpone matters until we can talk about it. But I want the pamphlet to be a good one, so that *no* one *could* tear out of it phrases which would cause you unpleasantness (sometimes *one single* phrase is enough to be the spoonful of tar in a barrel of honey), *could* *mis*interpret you. I am sure that here, too, you wrote "without wishing it", and the only reason why I am sending you this letter is that you may examine the plan in greater detail as a result of the letters than you would after a talk—and the plan, you know, is a very important thing.

Have you not some French socialist friend? Translate my points 1-10 to her (as though it were from English), together with your remarks about "fleeting", etc., and watch her, listen to her as attentively as possible: a little experiment as to what *outside* people will say, what their impressions will be, what they will expect of the pamphlet.

I shake you by the hand, and wish you fewer headaches and to get better soon.

V. U.

P.S. About Baugy [213] I don't know.... Possibly my friend* promised too much.... But what? I don't know. The thing has been postponed, i.e., the conflict has been postponed, *not* eliminated. We shall have to fight. and fight!! Shall we succeed in dissuading them? What is your opinion?

Written on January 24, 1915

Sent from Berne

First published in 1939
in *Bolshevik* No. 13   Printed from the original

----

* These two words were written by Lenin in English.—*Ed.*

86

TO A. G. SHLYAPNIKOV

February 11

Dear Friend,

I have received your two letters, of February 4 and 5. Many thanks. As regards sending *Sotsial-Demokrat*, we have given your letter to the secretary of the dispatch committee to read. Tomorrow I shall remind him personally, and I hope that they will do everything.

The Parisians promised to send you Plekhanov's little pamphlet, and we are very surprised that you have not received it. We shall order it once more, and get one ourselves to send you.[214]

The two Plekhanovites of whom you wrote were here. We chatted with them. Take notice of the little fair one (they are going back the same way): apparently Plekhanov repelled him even more than the little dark one. The latter, I think, is a hopeless chatterbox. But the former keeps very quiet, and you can't find out what is going on in his head.

From *Nashe Slovo* (which is appearing in Paris in place of *Golos*) we have had a letter today with a plan for a common protest against "official social-patriotism" (on the subject of the scheme for a London conference of socialists *de la* Triple Entente[215]). Whether the conference will take place, we don't know; we had the other day from Litvinov a letter he transmitted from Huysmans, who is planning something strange, calling together the Executive Committee of the International Socialist Bureau on February 20 at The Hague, and on February 20-25 organising in the same place personal negotiations (!!) with the delegates from Britain, France and Russia!! Astonishing!! It looks like preparations of some kind for something Francophil and patriotic (by the way, you are absolutely right that there are now many "phils" and few socialists. For us both Franco- phils and Germanophils are one and the same=patriots, bourgeois or their lackeys, and not socialists. The Bundists, for example, are for the most part Germanophils and glad of the defeat of Russia. But in what way are they any better than Plekhanov? Both are opportunists, social-chauvinists, only of different colours. And Axelrod too).

We have replied to *Nashe Slovo* that we are glad of their proposal, and have sent them our draft declaration.* Hopes of an agreement with them are not great, because Axelrod, it is said, is in Paris—and Axelrod (see Nos. 86 and 87 of *Golos* and No. 37 of *Sotsial-Demokrat*) is a social-chau- vinist, who wants to reconcile Francophils and Germano- phils on the basis of social-chauvinism. Let us see what is dearer to *Nashe Slovo*—anti-chauvinism or the good will of Axelrod.

I think that both in Russia and throughout the world a new basic grouping is coming into existence within Social- Democracy: the chauvinists ("social-patriots") and their friends, their defenders—and the anti-chauvinists. In the main, this division corresponds to the division between the opportunists and the revolutionary Social-Democrats. But it *plus précis* represents, so to speak, a higher stage of development, nearer to the socialist revolution. And among us the old grouping (liquidators and Pravdists) is becoming out of date, and being replaced by a new, more sensible division: social-patriots and anti-patriots. By the way. They say that Dan[216]=a *German* "social-patriot", i.e., a Germano- phil, i.e., *for Kautsky*. Is this true? It looks very much like the truth. It's an odd thing that in the Organising Committee[217] the split is along *bourgeois* lines: Francophils (Plekhanov + Alexinsky + Maslov+*Nasha Zarya*) and Germanophils (Bund+Axelrod+Dan?? etc.).

If you don't get any money from the Swedes, let us know:

---

* See "To the Editors of *Nashe Slovo*" (present edition, Vol. 21, pp. 125-28).—*Ed.*

we shall send you 100 francs. Think over very thoroughly where it is best (i.e., most useful for the cause and safest for you: this is very important: you must protect yourself!!) to lie low, in London or in Norway, etc. It is of the greatest importance to organise transport, even little by little. You ought to have an interview with the Plekhanovites who in two or three weeks will be in your place, and come to an arrangement about all this.

All the best; I wish you courage and all good things.

Yours,
Lenin

Sent from Berne to Stockholm

First published in 1924
in *Lenin Miscellany II*

Printed from the original

87

TO ALEXANDRA KOLLONTAI

Dear Comrade,

Many thanks for all your trouble and assistance, about which you write in your last letter.

Your articles in *Nashe Slovo* and for *Kommunist*[218] on Scandinavian affairs have raised the following question in my mind:

Can one praise and find correct the position of the Left Scandinavian Social-Democrats who reject the arming of the people? I argued about this with Höglund in 1910 and tried to prove to him that this was not Leftism, nor revolutionism, but simply the philistinism of petty-bourgeois provincials.[219] These Scandinavian petty-bourgeois have tucked themselves away in their little countries, almost at the North Pole, and are proud of the fact that you can't get to them in a month of Sundays! How can one allow that a revolutionary class on the eve of the social revolution should be *against* the arming of the people? This is not struggle against militarism, but a cowardly attempt to retire from the great questions of the capitalist world. How can one "recognise" the class struggle, without understanding its inevitable transformation at certain moments into civil war?

It seems to me that you ought to collect material on this, and come out resolutely *against* in *Kommunist*, and then, for the instruction of the Scandinavians, print it afterwards in Swedish, etc.

I should like to know your opinion about this in more detail.

Bruce Glasier, in my belief, is an unsuitable contributor: although he has a proletarian strain in him, still he is an unbearable opportunist. You will hardly be able to go along with him: he will start crying after two days, and saying that he was "trapped", that he doesn't want and doesn't recognise anything of the kind.

Have you seen the book by David, and his opinion about our manifesto?[220]

Is there not in the Scandinavian countries any material on the struggle of *the two currents of opinion* concerning the attitude to the war? Could not one gather precise material (reactions, assessments, resolutions) with a precise contrasting of *facts* regarding the tendencies of the two currents? Do facts confirm (in my opinion, they do) that the opportunists—taken as a *current of opinion*—are, on the whole,>chauvinists than the revolutionary Social-Democrats? What do you think, would it not be possible to gather and work up such material for *Kommunist*?

I shake your hand, and wish you all the best,

N. Lenin

P.S. Who is this Shaw Desmond who has been giving a lecture in the Scandinavian countries? Is the text of his lecture available in English? Is he a conscious revolutionary, or *à la* Hervé?

Written later than May 22, 1915

Sent from Berne to Christiania (Oslo)

First published in 1924   Printed from the original
in *Lenin Miscellany II*

88

TO DAVID WIJNKOOP

Dear Comrade,

The weathercock (*Drehscheibe*) Kautsky and Co. want now, with the help of Left phrases and a purely verbal departure from "the policy of August 4", [221] to "stifle" the revolutionary ferment which is beginning. We are now for peace, these gentlemen will be saying together with Renaudel and Co., striving thereby to satisfy the revolutionary masses.

There is talk of a conference of the Lefts—and it is *more than likely* that dirty little souls of the Bernstein-Kautsky type will make use of such a conference in order, once again, to deceive the masses with the help of "passive radicalism".

It is quite possible that sensible statesmen of *both belligerent groups* now have *nothing* against the incipient revolutionary ferment being stifled by an idiotic "peace programme".

I don't know whether the German Lefts are already strong enough to upset the manoeuvre of these passive (and hypocritical) "radicals". But you and we are *independent parties*. We must do something: work out a programme of revolution, expose the idiotic and hypocritical watchword of peace, denounce and refute it, talk with utter frankness to the workers—in order to tell the *truth* (without the base diplomacy of the leaders of the Second International). And the truth is this: either one supports the revolutionary ferment which is beginning, and assists it (for this one needs the watchword of revolution, of civil war, of illegal organisation, etc.), or one stifles it (for this one needs the watchword of peace, the "condemnation" of "annexations", maybe disarmament, etc., etc.).

History will show that it is we who were right, i.e., the revolutionaries in general, not necessarily *A* or *B*.

I should like to know whether you (your Party) are able to send your representative (knowing *one* of the three main languages). And do you think it possible that both our *parties* officially (in writing or verbally, better: *and verbally*) should propose a joint declaration (or resolution)?

If there are *only* money difficulties, let us know exactly how much is needed. Perhaps we will be able to help.

Best greetings.

Yours,

N. Lenin

My address:
Wl. Uljanow,
Hotel Marienthal in *Sörenberg*
(Kanton Luzern). Schweiz.

Written in German
between June 19 and July 13, 1915

Sent to Zwolle (Holland)

First published in *Pravda* No. 21,
January 21, 1949

Printed from the original

89

TO ALEXANDRA KOLLONTAI

Dear Comrade,

The question of a conference of the "Left" is going ahead. There has already been a first *Vorkonferenz*,[222] and a second, decisive one, will be held *shortly*. It is extremely important to draw in the Left Swedes (*Höglund*) and the Norwegians.

Be kind enough to write (1) whether we are in agreement with you (or you with the C.C.), if not, wherein we differ, and (2) whether you will undertake to draw in the "Left" Scandinavians.

Ad 1. You know our position from *Sotsial-Demokrat*. In Russian affairs we shall *not* be for unity with the Chkheidze group[223] (which Trotsky, and the O.C., and Plekhanov, and Co. want: see *The War*), because this is a cover-up and defence of *Nashe Dyelo*. In international affairs we shall *not* be for rapprochement with Haase-Bernstein-Kautsky (for *in practice* they want unity with the Südekums and to shield them, they want to get away with Left phrases and to change nothing in the old rotten party). We cannot stand for the *watchword* of peace, because we consider it supremely muddled, pacifist, petty-bourgeois, helping the governments (they now want to be with one hand "for peace", in order to climb out of their difficulties) and obstructing the revolutionary struggle.

In our opinion, the Left should make a common declaration *of principle* (1) unquestionably condemning the social-chauvinists and opportunists, (2) giving a programme of revolutionary action (whether to say civil war or revolu-

tionary mass action, is not so important), (3) against the
watchword of "defence of the fatherland", etc. A declaration of principle by the "Left", in the name of several countries, would have a *gigantic* significance (of course, not in
the spirit of the Zetkin philistinism which she got adopted
at the Women's Conference [224] at Berne; Zetkin *evaded* the
question of condemning social-chauvinism!! out of a desire
for "peace" with the Südekums+Kautsky??).

If you are not in agreement with these tactics, drop us
a line straightaway.

If you are in agreement, do take on the translation of
(1) the manifesto of the Central Committee (No. 33 of
Sotsial-Demokrat)* and (2) the Berne resolutions (No. 40 of
Sotsial-Demokrat)** into Swedish and Norwegian, and get
in touch with Höglund—do they agree to prepare a *common*
declaration (or resolution) on such a basis (naturally we
shall not quarrel over details)? *Particular* speed with this
is necessary.

And so I await your reply.

Every good wish,

Yours,

Lenin

Written later than July 11, 1915

Sent from Sörenberg (Switzerland)
    to Christiania (Oslo)

First published in 1924   Printed from the original
in *Lenin Miscellany II*

---

* See present edition, Vol. 21, pp. 25-34.—*Ed.*
** Ibid., pp. 158-64.—*Ed.*

90

TO DAVID WIJNKOOP

Dear Comrade Wijnkoop,

The scheme with which we are now occupied, the plan for an international declaration of principle by the Marxist Left, is so important that we have no right to delay, and must carry it through successfully to its conclusion, moreover as quickly as possible. The fact that we are late with it presents a great danger!

The article by A. P. in *Berner Tagwacht* (July 24) on the Congress of the S.D.P. of Holland is extremely important for our mutual understanding.[225] I welcome with the greatest joy the position taken up by you, Gorter and Ravesteyn on the question of a people's militia (we have that in our programme too). An exploited class which did not *strive* to possess arms, to know how to use them and to master the military art would be a class of lackeys. The defenders of disarmament as against a people's militia (there are "Lefts" of this kind in Scandinavia too: I argued about this with Höglund in 1910) are taking up the position of petty bourgeois, pacifists, opportunists in the small states. But for us it is the point of view of the *great states* and the *revolutionary struggle* (i.e., *also of civil war*) which must be decisive. Anarchists may be against a people's militia, from the point of view of the social revolution (conceived of without relation to time and space). But our *most important* task now is to draw a sharp line of demarcation between the Marxist Left on the one hand and the opportunists (and Kautskians) and anarchists on the other.

One passage in the article by A. P. really revolted me, namely the one where he says that the declaration of principle by Mme. Roland-Holst "completely corresponds to the point of view of the S.D.P."!!

From that declaration of principle, in the form in which it was printed in *Berner Tagwacht* and in *Internationale Korrespondenz*, [226] I see that we cannot *in any circumstances* accept solidarity with Mme. Roland-Holst. Mme. Roland-Holst, in my opinion, is a Dutch Kautsky or a Dutch Trotsky. These people *in principle* "firmly disagree" with the opportunists, but *in practice*, on all important questions, they *agree*!! Mme. Roland-Holst rejects the principle of defence of the fatherland, i.e., she rejects social-chauvinism. That is good. *But she does not reject opportunism!!* In a most lengthy declaration there is not one word against opportunism! There is not one clear, unambiguous word about *revolutionary* means of struggle (but in return, all the more phrases about "idealism", self-sacrifice, etc., which every scoundrel, including Troelstra and Kautsky, can very willingly accept)! Not one word about a *rupture* with the opportunists! The watchword of "peace" is quite *à la* Kautsky! Instead of this (and quite consistently, from the point of view of the unprincipled "declaration of principle" of Mme. Roland-Holst) the advice to co-operate *both* with the S.D.P. and the S.D.L.P.!! This means unity with the opportunists.

Quite like our Mr. Trotsky: "in principle *firmly* against defence of the fatherland", in practice *for* unity with the Chkheidze group in the Russian Duma (i.e., with the opponents of our group which has been exiled to Siberia, with the *best friends* of the Russian social-chauvinists).

No. No. Never and in no circumstances shall we agree in principle with the declaration of Mme. Roland-Holst. It is a quite thoughtless, purely platonic and hypocritical internationalism. Just one long compromise. It is suited (speaking politically) only to the task of forming a "Left wing" (i.e., a "harmless minority", a "decorative Marxist signboard") in the old, rotten and scoundrelly lackey parties (the Liberal Labour parties).

Of course, we do not demand an *immediate* split in this or that party, for example, in Sweden, Germany or France. It is very possible that the time for this will be more favourable (for example, in Germany) somewhat later. But *in principle* we must unquestionably demand a complete break with opportunism. The *whole* struggle of our Party (and of the working-class movement in Europe generally) must be directed against opportunism. The latter is not a current of opinion, not a tendency; it (opportunism) has now become the organised tool of the bourgeoisie within the working-class movement. And furthermore: questions of the revolutionary struggle (tactics, means, propaganda in the army, fraternisation in the trenches, *etc.*) must undoubtedly be analysed *in detail*, discussed, thought out, tested, explained to the masses in the illegal press. Without this any "recognition" of revolution remains only an empty phrase. We have no common road with phrase-mongering (in Dutch: "passive") radicals.

I hope, dear Comrade Wijnkoop, that you will not take offence at these remarks of mine. After all, we must come to a proper agreement, in order to carry on jointly this *difficult* struggle.

Please show this letter to Comrade Pannekoek and other Dutch friends.

Yours,

N. Lenin

P.S. I will shortly send you the official resolution of our Party (of 19*13*) on the question of the right of all nations to self-determination.[227] We are *for this*. Now, in the struggle against the social-chauvinists, we must be more for this than ever before.

Written in German
later than July 24, 1915

Sent from Sörenberg (Switzerland)
to Zwolle (Holland)

First published in *Pravda* No. 21,   Printed from the original
January 21, 1949

91

TO ALEXANDRA KOLLONTAI

Dear A. M.,

We are sending you the money tomorrow. Many thanks for the news from Russia. In principle we have nothing against an agreement; we hope that you will be extra careful.

As regards armament of the people versus disarmament, it seems to me all the same that we cannot alter the programme.[228] If the words about the class struggle are not an empty phrase in the liberal sense (as they have become with the opportunists, Kautsky and Plekhanov), how can one object to a fact of history—the transformation of this struggle, under certain conditions, into civil war? How moreover can an oppressed class in general be against the armament of the people?

To reject this means to fall into a semi-anarchist attitude to imperialism—in my belief, this can be seen in certain Left-wingers even among ourselves. Once there is imperialism, they say, then we don't need either self-determination of nations or the armament of the people! That is a crying error. It is precisely for the socialist revolution against imperialism that we need both one and the other.

Is it "realisable"? Such a criterion is incorrect. Without revolution almost the entire minimum programme is unrealisable. Put in that way, realisability declines into philistinism.

It seems to me that this question (like *all* questions of Social-Democratic tactics today) can be put *only* in connection with the evaluation of (and reckoning with) opportunism. And it is clear that "disarmament", as a tactical watchword, is opportunism. Moreover it is a provincial one, it stinks of a little state, detachment from the struggle, poverty of ideas: "it's no business of mine"....

We are sending you the draft (individual) of a declaration of the international Left.* We urge you to translate it and to pass it on to the Left in Sweden and Norway, in order to make a *business-like* advance to a *Verständigung*** with them. Send us your observations, *resp.* your counterdraft. if you wish, and *secure* the same from the Left in Scandinavia.

*Beste Grüsse.****

Yours,
Lenin

Written on July 26, 1915

Sent from Sörenberg (Switzerland)
   to Christiania (Oslo)

First published in 1924   Printed from the original
in *Lenin Miscellany II*

---

* Reference is to "The Draft Resolution Proposed by the Left Wing at Zimmerwald" (see present edition, Vol. 21, pp. 345-48).—*Ed.*
   ** Understanding.—*Ed.*
   *** Best greetings.—*Ed.*

92

TO ALEXANDRA KOLLONTAI

Dear A. M.,

We were very glad about the statement by the Norwegians and your efforts with the Swedes.[229] It would be devilishly important to have a joint international statement by the *Left* Marxists! (A statement of principle is the main thing, and so far the only thing possible.)

Roland-Holst, like Rakovsky (have you seen his French pamphlet?), like Trotsky, in my opinion, are *all* the most harmful "Kautskians", in the sense that all of them in various forms are for unity with the opportunists, all in various forms *embellish* opportunism, all of them (in various ways) preach eclecticism instead of revolutionary Marxism.

I think your criticism of the draft declaration does not show (unless I am mistaken) any serious differences between us. I think it mistaken in theory and harmful in practice *not* to distinguish types of wars. We cannot be against wars of national liberation. You quote the example of Serbia. But if the Serbs were *alone* against Austria, would we not be *for* the Serbs?

The essence of the thing today is the struggle *between* the Great Powers for the redivision of the colonies and the subjugation of the smaller powers.

A war of India, Persia, China and so forth with Britain or Russia? Would we not be *for* India against Britain, etc.? To call *that* "a civil war" is inexact, an obvious exaggeration. It is extremely harmful to stretch the conception of civil war beyond measure, because that *blurs* the essence of the question: a war of hired workers against the capitalists of a *particular* state.

It is the Scandinavians, apparently, who are falling into a petty-bourgeois (and provincial, *kleinstaatisch*) pacifism, repudiating "war" in general. That is not Marxist. One has to combat this, like their rejection of the militia.

Once again greetings, and congratulations on the Norwegian declaration!

Yours,
Lenin

Written not earlier than
August 4, 1915

Sent from Sörenberg (Switzerland)
to Christiania (Oslo)

First published in 1924   Printed from the original
in *Lenin Miscellany II*

93

TO K. B. RADEK

Dear Comrade Radek,

I return your draft.[230] Not a word about social-chauvinism and (=) opportunism and the struggle against them!! Why such an embellishing of the evil and concealment from the working masses of their main enemy in the Social-Democratic parties?

Will you make an ultimatum of insisting that not a word should be said openly about a ruthless struggle against opportunism?

I hope to *arrive two days earlier* (i.e., September 2-3) if you inform me that the Germans will also come earlier (otherwise Zinoviev will come alone).

(Your draft is too "academic", not a militant appeal, not a fighting manifesto.)

Will you be sending your draft to Wijnkoop? *Are you insisting* that they (the Dutch) should come?

Please send me at once the (German) translation of *my draft* (about which you wrote to Wijnkoop) and the translation of our resolution of 1913 (the nationalities question). That makes *two things*.

We must make *every* effort to publish our pamphlet (in German) before September 5. I am writing today to Kasparov that he should help you and find another translator (in Berne—Comrade Kinkel). Can you (with Kasparov) work at "extra speed" and translate this pamphlet in the course of a week? And what about the printing? Can it be printed in three or four days? We must make *every* effort and do this!

I beg you to reply immediately.

Yours,

N . Lenin

Written in German
on August 19, 1915

Sent from Sörenberg to Berne

First published in 1930   Printed from the original
in *Lenin Miscellany XIV*

94

TO A. G. SHLYAPNIKOV

August 23, 1915

Dear Alexander,

As regards the plan of your journey, it is very hard for me to give you definite advice from so far off.[231] Our financial affairs are known to you. Nadezhda Konstantinovna has written to you in detail (in addition to what was sent, 600 francs were promised before October 10+400 francs one month later. In all, 1,000 francs. *For the time being* there is no hope of more).

On the one hand, extreme care is essential. Have you completely reliable papers? And all the rest?

On the other hand, it would be unquestionably useful for the cause just now, if a fully-informed and independent person travelled round two or three centres, made contacts, established relations and *immediately* returned to Sweden, to pass on all the contacts to us and to discuss the further situation. This would be most important.

Kommunist No. 1 will appear in 8-10 days; then, after as many more, No. 2 (or Nos. 1-2 together). No. 44 of the Central Organ will appear in a day or two. A pamphlet about the war *with all documents* will come out in a fortnight. It is already being set.

Events in Russia have completely endorsed our position, which the social-patriot donkeys (from Alexinsky to Chkheidze) have christened defeatism. The facts have proved that we are right!! The military reverses are helping to shake the foundations of tsarism, and facilitating an alliance of the revolutionary workers of Russia and other countries. People say: what will "you" do, if "you", the revolutionaries, defeat tsarism? I reply: (1) our victory will fan the flames of the "Left" movement in Germany a hundredfold; (2) if "we" defeated tsarism completely, we would propose peace to all the belligerent powers on democratic terms and, if this were rejected, we would conduct a *revolutionary* war.

It is clear that the advanced section of Pravdist workers, that bulwark of our Party, has survived, in spite of terrible devastations in its ranks. It would be extremely important for leading groups to come together in two or three centres (*most conspiratively*), establish contact with us, restore a Bureau of the Central Committee (one exists, I think, in Petersburg already) and the C.C. itself in Russia. They should establish firm ties with us (*if necessary*, one or two persons should be brought to Sweden for this purpose). We would send news-sheets, leaflets, etc. The most important thing is firm and constant relations.

Chkheidze and Co. are obviously shuffling: they are true friends of *Nashe Dyelo*, Alexinsky is pleased with them (I hope you have seen *The War* by Plekhanov + Alexinsky+Co. There's a disgrace!!) and yet they "play" at Leftism with the help of Trotsky!! I don't think they will succeed in deceiving the class-conscious Pravdists.

Write what you decide. Greetings.

Yours,
Lenin

P.S. Will A. Kollontai agree to help us arrange in the U.S.A. for an edition of our pamphlet in English*?

Sent from Sörenberg (Switzerland)
to Stockholm

First published in 1924   Printed from the original
in *Lenin Miscellany II*

---

* Reference is to the pamphlet *Socialism and War* (*The Attitude of the R.S.D.L.P. towards the War*) (see present edition, Vol. 21, pp. 295-338).—*Ed.*

95

TO A. G. SHLYAPNIKOV

Für Alexander

Dear Friend,

Try and see Belenin and tell him, please, that he has been co-opted a member of the Central Committee of the Russian Social-Democratic Labour Party. You understand, of course, that the maximum secrecy must be observed in this matter, and that you must "forget" about it after passing on the information to Belenin (I am not writing to him direct for obvious reasons). His function during the journey is very important: Trotsky and the company of lackeys of opportunism abroad are straining every effort to "gloss over" the differences, and "save" the opportunism of *Nasha Zarya*, by whitewashing and lauding the Chkheidze group (=the most faithful friends of *Nasha Zarya*). It is necessary to set up groups in Russia (of old, experienced, sensible Pravdist workers who have *fully* mastered the question of the war) and take the best of them (2-3) into the C.C. If there are difficulties, or if doubts arise, then he could limit himself to setting up *analogous* bodies (for example, "the leading All-Russia Workers' Group" or "Committee", etc.; it's not the name that counts, of course).

Your connections and your knowledge of old and experienced workers will help you to give advice to Belenin, who, of course, will treat this work with exceptional seriousness and caution. And the most important thing is that he should now be extremely careful, making *a short trip* and bringing back *all the contacts*.

Best greetings! Drop me a line directly you receive this letter.

Yours,
Lenin

P.S. The pamphlet will appear earlier than I thought. I have already received part of the proofs. Probably in a week or ten days we shall have both the pamphlet and No. 1-2 of *Kommunist*.

There *will* now *be* three members of the C.C. abroad. In Russia there are a number of candidate members (workers) and arrested members of the C.C. (also workers, leading Pravdists).

P. P. S. Tomorrow you will get a more detailed letter from Nadezhda Konstantinovna. Treat it with the utmost attention.

Written earlier than
September 13, 1915

Sent from Sörenberg (Switzerland)
to Stockholm

First published in 1924
in *Lenin Miscellany II*

Printed from the original

96

TO A. G. SHLYAPNIKOV

October 10, 1915

Dear Friend,

Tomorrow we are publishing two issues of the Central Organ at the same time—No. 45-46 (devoted to the Zimmerwald Conference) and No. 47, containing news from Russia and the "theses" on tactics.* These theses consist partly of replies to the questions which we touched on in our correspondence, and you in your talks with N. I., etc. I shall await your comments.

Have you received the *Russian* text of the pamphlet *Socialism and War*?

(In parenthesis: A. M. has sent in a criticism of the German text, and I replied to her in a detailed letter to America. If you are interested, ask her to send it to you. About her leaflet I wrote to her at Bergen, asking permission to make corrections. There is no reply. I am afraid I shall have to write to America, and that means a big delay.)

News from Russia testifies to the growing revolutionary mood and movement, though to all appearances this is not yet the beginning of revolution.

The most important thing for us now is to establish contacts and make them regular (this is quite possible by correspondence; consider whether one copy of the paper and manifestos cannot be sent in a thin binding). Let us hope that Belenin will succeed in organising this. Otherwise one cannot dream of any systematic, connected work.

---

* Reference is to Lenin's article "Several Theses" (see present edition, Vol. 21, pp. 401-04).—*Ed.*

Pay special attention to the thesis about the Soviet of Workers' Deputies. One must be careful with this thing: 200 or 300 leaders might be arrested!! Except in connection with an insurrection, the "strength" of a Soviet of Workers' Deputies is an *illusion*. One should not give way to it.

All the best.

Yours,
Lenin

Could not one organise the transcribing of such articles in the Central Organ as "Eleven Theses" in chemical ink, for rapid delivery to Petersburg? Think it over well.

Sent from Berne to Stockholm

First published in 1924
in *Lenin Miscellany II*

Printed from the original

97

TO ALEXANDRA KOLLONTAI

November 9, 1915

Dear A. M.,

Only yesterday did we get your letter of October 18 from Milwaukee. Letters take a terribly long time! You have not yet received my letter (and Nos. 45-46 and 47 of *Sotsial-Demokrat*) about Zimmerwald, and containing all the replies to your questions; yet that letter was written more than a month ago. Try at any rate to calculate where you will be (approximately, in six weeks' time) and give us addresses (for letters to you), so that they arrive nearer.

As regards the New York *Volkszeitung*, Grimm assured me today that they are quite Kautskian! Is that the case? I think our *German* pamphlet* might help you to determine the "strength" of their internationalism. Have you had it? (500 copies were sent to you.)

In a few days we are publishing here (in German, and then *we hope* to put it out in French and, if we can manage the money, in Italian) a little pamphlet on behalf of the *Zimmerwald Left*. Under this name we should like to launch into international circulation, as widely as possible, our Left group at Zimmerwald (the C.C.+the Polish Social-Democrats+ the Letts+the Swedes+the Norwegians+1 German+1 Swiss) with its *draft resolution* and *manifesto* (printed in No. 45-46 of *Sotsial-Demokrat*). The little pamphlet (20-30-35 thousand letters and spaces) will contain these two documents and a small introduction.[232] We rely on you to publish it in America *in English too* (for it is hopeless to do this

---

* Reference is to the pamphlet *Socialism and War (The Attitude of the R.S.D.L.P. towards the War)* (see present edition, Vol. 21, pp. 295-338).—*Ed.*

in England: it has to be brought there *from* America) and, if possible, in other languages. This is to be the first publication by the *nucleus of Left* Social-Democrats of *all* countries, who have a clear, exact and full *reply* to the question of what is to be done and in which direction to go. It would be most important if you could succeed in publishing this in America, circulating it as widely as possible and *establishing firm publishing links* (*Charles Kerr* (N.B.) at Chicago; the *Appeal to Reason** at *Kansas, etc.*), for it is generally most important for us to come out in various languages (you could do *a great deal* in this respect).

·As regards money, I see with distress from your letter that so far you have not managed to collect anything for the Central Committee. Perhaps this "Manifesto of the Left" will help....

I never doubted that Hillquit would be for Kautsky and even *to the right* of him, because I saw him at Stuttgart (1907) and *heard* how *afterwards* he defended the prohibition against bringing yellow people into America (an "internationalist")....

The Zimmerwald Manifesto itself is *inadequate*; Kautsky and Co. are ready to put up with it, on *condition* that there is "not a step further". We *don't* accept this, because it is *complete hypocrisy*. So that if there are people in America who are afraid *even* of the Zimmerwald Manifesto, you can brush them aside, and bring in only those who are *more Left than the Zimmerwald Manifesto*.

I shake you by the hand and wish you every success!

Yours,
Lenin

(Ulianow. Seidenweg. 4ª. III. *Bern*)

Sent from Berne to New York

First published in 1924   Printed from the original
in *Lenin Miscellany II*

---

*Try establishing contact with them—if only in writing, should you not get to Kansas. Their little paper is sometimes *not bad*. Be sure to sound them out with our resolution of the "Zimmerwald Left". And what is Eugene *Debs*? He sometimes writes in a revolutionary way. Or is he also a wet-rag *à la* Kautsky?

Write *when* you will *again* be in New York, and for *how many* days. Try *everywhere* to see (if only for 5 minutes) the local *Bolsheviks*, to "refresh" them and *get them in touch with us*.

1916

98

TO MAXIM GORKY

January 11, 1916

Dear Alexei Maximovich,

I am sending you at the *Letopis* address, not for *Letopis* but for the publishing house, the manuscript of a pamphlet and request you to publish it.[233]

I have tried in as popular a form as possible to set forth new data about America which, I am convinced, are particularly suitable for popularising Marxism and substantiating it by means of facts. I hope I have succeeded in setting out these important data clearly and comprehensibly for the new sections of the reading public which are multiplying in Russia and need an explanation of the world's economic evolution.

I should like to continue, and subsequently also to publish, a second part—about Germany.

I am setting to work on a pamphlet about imperialism.*

Owing to war-time conditions I am in extreme need of earnings, and would therefore ask, if it is possible and will not embarrass you too much, to speed up publication of the pamphlet.

Yours with respect,

V. Ilyin

The address is Mr. Wl. Oulianoff, Seidenweg, *4-a, Berne*, (Suisse).

Sent to Petrograd

First published in 1925 in *Lenin Miscellany III*

Printed from the original

* Reference is to *Imperialism, the Highest Stage of Capitalism* (see present edition, Vol. 22, pp. 185-304).—*Ed.*

99

TO A. G. SHLYAPNIKOV

Dear Friend,

As regards your letter and its mention of the current reproach that I am "uncompromising", I should like to discuss the subject with you in greater detail.

As regards James, he never understood politics and was always against the split. James is a wonderful person, but *on these subjects* his judgements are profoundly wrong.

In Russia (and now in the new International too) the question of a split is the *basic* one. Any compromise *here* would be a crime. I know well how many good people (James, Galyorka, the Petrograd "friends" among the intellectuals) were *against* the split in the Duma group. All of them were 1,000 times wrong. The split was essential. And the split with *Chkheidze and Co.* now, too, is *absolutely* essential. All who waver on this subject are *enemies* of the proletariat, and we must be *un*compromising with them.

But who is wavering? Not only Trotsky and Co. but also *Yuri*+Eug. B. (as late as last summer they were "creating scenes" on account of Chkheidze!!). Then the *Poles* (the opposition). In their *Gazeta Robotnicza* No. 25, there is their resolution: once again *for manoeuvring*, as in Brussels on July 3 (16), 1914.

With them an *un*compromising attitude is obligatory.

Radek is the best of them; it was useful to work *with* him (for the Zimmerwald Left as well, by the way), and we did work. But *Radek* is also *wavering*. And our tactics here are *two-sided* (this Yuri+Nik. Iv. *absolutely* could not or would not understand): on the one hand, to *help* Radek to move

left, to *unite* all who could be united for the Zimmerwald
Left. On the other hand, not to allow *one iota* of wavering on
the basic issue.

The basic issue is the break with the O.C., with Chkheidze
and Co.

The Poles are *wavering*, and published a most black-
guardly resolution *after* No. 1 of *Kommunist.*

The conclusion?

Either to hang on to the title of *Kommunist*, and *open
the door to squabbling and wavering*, to letters to the editor
(from Radek, Bronski, perhaps Pannekoek and others),
complaints, whining, gossip, etc.

Not on any account.

This would be harmful to the cause.

It means helping the scoundrels of the O.C., Chkheidze
and Co.

Not on any account.

Kommunist was a temporary bloc to achieve a definite
object. The object has been achieved: the journal was published, the rapprochement attained (*then* it was possible,
before Zimmerwald). Now we have to go by *another* road,
to go further.

Kommunist has become *harmful*. It has to be *stopped*,
and replaced by a *different* title: *Sbornik Sotsial-Demokrata*
(edited by the *editorial board of "Sotsial-Demokrat"*).[234]

Only in this way will we avoid squabbling, avoid wavering.

In Russia, is there also discord? Oh, of course! *But it is
not our business to increase it.* Let Chkheidze and Co., Trotsky and Co. busy themselves with increasing the discord
(that is their "profession"). Our job is to pursue *our own* line.
The fruits of *such* work are manifest: the Petrograd workers
are 100 times better than the Petrograd intellectuals (even
the "sympathisers"...).

We had to make *temporary* concessions to the "trio" (Yuri
+Eug. Bosh+Nik. Iv.), because *at that time* it was impossible to bring out the journal otherwise (now it is possible);
and the main thing was that we had not yet seen Eug. Bosh+
Yuri *at work*, and could hope that the *work* would lead
them *upwards.*

But they went downwards.

And the temporary alliance *must* be dissolved. Only in that way will *the cause* not suffer. Only in that way will *they too* learn.

For we are not against *discussion*. We are against *editorial* rights for those who displayed unforgivable vacillation (perhaps owing to their youth? then we shall wait: perhaps in five years' time they will straighten themselves out).

Nik. Iv. is an economist who studies seriously, and *in this* we have always supported him. But he is (1) credulous where gossip is concerned and (2) devilishly *unstable* in politics.

The war pushed him towards semi-anarchist ideas. At the conference which adopted the Berne resolutions (the spring of 1915)[235] he produced *theses* (I have them!) which were the height of stupidity, a disgrace, semi-anarchism.

I attacked sharply. Yuri and Eug. Bosh listened and remained satisfied that I did not allow any falling away to the left (they declared at the time their complete disagreement with N. Iv.).

Six months passed. Nik. Iv. studies economics. He *doesn't* occupy himself with politics.

And lo and behold, on the question of self-determination, *he* serves us up *the same* nonsense. Eug. Bosh+Yuri sign it!! (Take their "theses" from N. Iv., and my reply to him.[236])

Yet the question is an important one. It is an essential question. It is inextricably bound up with the question of *annexations*—a most topical question.

They didn't think it out. They didn't read. They didn't study. They listened two or three times to Radek (he has the old "Polish" disease: he is confused on this)—and *signed*.

That is a scandal. It is a disgrace. These are not editors. We must refute such people, expose them, give them time to study and think, and be in no hurry to humour them: "Here are editorial rights for you, distribute your nonsense among the workers!!"

If that is allowed, they will *bring* matters to polemics in the press—and then I will be *obliged* to call them "imperialist Economists", and demonstrate their complete emptiness, the *completely* unserious and unthought-out character of their ideas. Polemics in the press will drive them away *for years*.

But if we stop *Kommunist* now, they will think it over and drop their nonsense: they will read and become convinced. Come on, dear friends, write a serious *pamphlet*, if you proclaim that you have "differences" on policy (which you have never studied or worked on), let's have it! They will think it over, and *not* produce it. And in a few months they will be "cured".

That's how it has been in the past. So it will be in the future.

On the question of annexations (and of self-determination) our position (the resolution of 1913)* has been *completely* confirmed by the war. And this question has become a topical one. While Radek+the Dutchmen (Gorter and Pannekoek) have obviously got muddled on this. In *Sbornik Sotsial-Demokrata* we shall explain this affair again and again.

We must conduct matters so as to:

(1) stop *Kommunist*;

(2) in publishing the miscellany about the Jews,[237] give Yuri+Eug. Bosh as *much* humouring, rights and privileges as possible (it won't harm *the cause* in *this case*). Detailed conditions in a written agreement;

(3) the same as regards their transport group (take their regulations and our amendments to them);

(4) publish *Sbornik Sotsial-Demokrata* under the editorship of the editorial board of *Sotsial-Demokrat*.

We shall invite them to contribute. We shall say to them: you have differences? Prepare a serious pamphlet! *We shall undertake to print it.* (They won't write it, because they haven't even begun to think seriously about the question; they haven't even studied it!!)

Now that will be a *business-like* policy.

Eug. Bosh has long been intending to go to Russia. There she could be useful. Here *she has nothing to do*, and she will *invent* something to do.

Do you know that *affliction* of life abroad: "inventing" things to do for people stranded abroad? A terrible affliction.

---

* See present edition, Vol. 19, pp 427-29.—*Ed.*

Well, that's all for the time being. Gather all the documents and put yourself abreast of the facts. We shall talk about it again and again.

Yours,
Lenin

P. S. I attach a copy of my reply to N. I. Bukharin on the subject of what the new "differences" mean.

Written later than March 11, 1916
Sent from Zurich to Stockholm

First published in 1929   Printed from the original
in *Proletarskaya Revolutsia* No. 7

100

TO G. Y. ZINOVIEV

May 21, 1916

Dear Grigory,

I don't want to turn our correspondence into an altercation. The question is a serious one and, although I have discussed it more than once, I will repeat my views since it is a necessity.

After more than six months' work with the "publishers" (from Kiev) and several months of thinking over this experience from every point of view, the editorial board of the Central Organ sent them in the winter of 1915 a letter which you also signed. In this letter the editorial board stated that it was giving up participation in *Kommunist*, on account of a number of considerations which were set forth in exceptional detail, took up a great deal of space in our letter, and amounted to this: that we could not assume Party responsibility for such co-editors, that their attitude to the cause was a non-Party one, and that we must regard the temporary attempt to reach understanding as unsuccessful.

We decided to publish *Sbornik Sotsial-Demokrata*.

Then you began to have hesitations, which led to our last talk at Kienthal. I made a concession to you by agreeing to an attempt to restore relations, on the condition that (1) there should be an agreement between the *editorial board* of the Central Organ and the publishers for each issue; (2) they should give up their group position of an "imperialist Economic" character, their "playing" on the differences with Radek, etc.

These conditions were not written down, and you now dispute them. But that dispute has become unimportant, since you *yourself* have set forth in writing, in your draft letter to A., *your* conditions, and the publishers have *not* accepted *even these*! (and you had been assuring me that the question was settled, that they would not insist on equal rights!).

The fact is, consequently, that if, even after our meeting at Kienthal, one were to accept your "interpretation", i.e., that I had laid down more extensive conditions than you, even so, *your* lesser conditions have also been rejected by the publishers.

It is obvious that your direct and unquestionable duty after this was to attack the publishers with all your strength, to break with them for good, and to use every effort to prove to Alexander that it was impossible to have any dealings with these gentry as editors of a leading journal.

Instead of this you propose to surrender to them, to renounce all conditions and to withdraw the letter written by the editorial board of the Central Organ which you yourself signed! And this on the pretext that "they should not be taken seriously". In reality, what you are proposing is that *your* policy should *not* be taken seriously. You reduce the letter from the editorial board to devil knows what, abjure your own point of view and give the *right* to the publishers to draw the conclusion that the editorial board of the Central Organ was merely throwing its weight about!

These are no longer hesitations, these are hesitations cubed, which are turning into something much worse.

It remains for me only to repeat for the last time why I don't enter *Kommunist*, why I consider it anti-Party and harmful, why I maintain the position of the letter from the editorial board of the Central Organ breaking with the publishers.

We concluded a temporary "federation" with the publishers, and called it a "federation" in so many words, quite definitely making a reservation about its temporary character, "as an experiment". When we concluded this temporary alliance, the publishers were *opposing* the wobblings of Bukharin (at the Conference in Berne in March 1915); and there *was not* a single fact pointing to any rapprochement of this group of three (the publishers+Bukharin) with special views of their own.

But after the very first number of the journal they did come together in this way, and when, after a long preliminary correspondence, I called their trend "imperialist Economism", you wrote to me that you agreed. This was in March 1916. It confirmed once more the most detailed letter from the editorial board of the Central Organ written during the winter.

The Party—and international—situation now is such that the Central Committee must continue to go ahead independently, *not tying its hands* either in Russian or in international affairs. The "publishers", good for nothing as writers and as politicians (which the editorial board of the Central Organ was obliged to recognise in its winter letter), want to *tie us down* with an agreement about *equal rights*, i.e., we must agree to grant equal rights to a lady who hasn't written a single line and doesn't understand a single thing, and to a "young man" who is entirely under her influence. And they will make use of this equality to *play* on our differences with Radek, with Bukharin and others!

It is simply madness to agree to equal rights on such conditions, it means ruining all the work.

It is not true that they want "only a discussion". They have every opportunity for a discussion. They have money. Nearly a year has gone by. Why don't they write, why don't they publish discussion pamphlets? Because they don't want to take responsibility *themselves*! That is clear. And it is this that constitutes their mockery of Party principles, because anyone who proclaims that he has differences must think out his case, come forward openly, face his responsibility, and not "play" and not aspire to "equality" when the Party does not even know the position they take up (and when *they* have no position).

It is a fact that Bukharin stumbles at every step into the views which he set forth in writing in March 1915 (at the Conference), and which you *also* rejected. You admitted this fact by agreeing in March 1916 (a year later) with my assessment of "imperialist Economism".

By granting "equality", you grant equality in face of the Party to the wobblings of Bukharin! You tie our hands and encourage these wobblings. That is an insane policy.

You know that Radek, in the first place, was so "offend-

ed" (at our insistence on the printing of our theses in Pannekoek's journal[238]) that—as you yourself wrote to me in
March 1916—he carries on "no team work" with you! And
the differences with him have not disappeared; on the contrary, you yourself agreed with me that his estimate of the
Irish insurrection was a philistine one. And you propose to
give "equality" to publishers who hide behind Radek,
playing (for 2,000 francs!) on our differences with him!!
This is an insane policy.

Secondly, Radek is one thing and the editorial board of
his paper (*Gazeta Robotnicza*) is another. That this paper
has also started a game (using the Chkheidze group, Trotsky,
etc.) you yourself have admitted. Remember that this
paper appeared in February 1916, and that the letter of
the Committee of Organisations Abroad* *against* it was
worked out with your participation. Well then, is it serious
politics if we now in our leading journal grant "equality"
to people who want to make their career by "utilising" our
struggle with the Poles, who betrayed us to Vandervelde
and Kautsky on July 3 (16), 1914??

Thirdly, you know that at Kienthal Radek wanted to
build up a majority against us among the Left, at the meeting of the Left, making use of Fröhlich, the Robmann woman, etc., and that an *ultimatum* was required to force him
to recognise the *independence* of our Central Committee.
What *new* "game" will these people make of this when the
question arises of the attitude to Junius (the question has
already arisen), or of a "mechanical separation" from the
Kautskians and others! Do you *guarantee* that there will
be none?? If you do, this would amount on your part to
renouncing all our policy. If you don't, then it is insane to
tie our hands after this in the editorial board of our leading
journal.

In no circumstances do I accept this insane policy. This
is my final decision. I continue to think that only the publication of *Sbornik Sotsial-Demokrata* disentangles the affair
(which you want to put in a hopeless tangle). *Sbornik Sotsial-
Demokrata* groups around us a number of most useful
workers (Varin, Safarov, the Letts, etc.), detaches Bukharin

---

* See present edition, Vol. 22, pp. 157-60.—*Ed.*

from the publishers to us, enables us to *lead* the Party (and the international Left) and not to march at the tail of ... Madam Publisher.

Write to me precisely what your decision is. Formally the matters now stand in this way, that the editorial board of the Central Organ has broken with *Kommunist*, and its final attempt (even your *lesser* conditions) has been rejected. That means that we must announce in print that *Kommunist* has stopped, and that *Sbornik Sotsial-Demokrata* is going to appear.

I shake your hand and send you *salut*.

V. U.

Sent from Zurich to Berne

First published in 1934
in *Proletarskaya Revolutsia* No. 4

Printed from the original

101

TO A. G. SHLYAPNIKOV

Dear A.,

Evidently there has been an interruption in our correspondence, and *quite a number* of misunderstandings have been caused by your not receiving our second letter sent to Stockholm. Otherwise I cannot understand *how* you can write that we don't answer your questions. We replied to *everything* in the greatest detail; it was *you* who *didn't* reply to us. N. K. is writing very often; we will have to be patient and repeat some things in order to achieve results. It is essential to maintain regular correspondence.

About *Kommunist* you write to me that the split with Chkheidze arouses no doubts. In whom? In Bukharin and Co.! But what I wrote was that this relates *not* to Bukharin and Co. but to *Radek and Co.*

Kommunist was our temporary bloc with two groups or elements—(1) Bukharin and Co., (2) Radek and Co. While it was possible to march together with them, this· *was* the right thing *to do.* Now it *is not*—and we must *temporarily* part or, more correctly, move away.

The Poles adopted in the *summer* of 1915 (*after* No. 1-2 of *Kommunist*) and printed *only in 1916* a resolution which once again showed their wobblings on the question of Chkheidze. Is it reasonable *now* to afford them the *possibility* and *right* (they are, after all, staff members of *Kommunist*!!) to muscle in and spoil the journal with their squabbling??

In my belief, it is not reasonable. It is much more useful for the cause to take another title (*Sbornik Sotsial-Demokrata*) and *wait a while*, until the Poles have learned better (or until they come under Germany) or until the situation changes.

Further. About Bukharin and Co. I will certainly send you
(though not very soon, because it depends on a journey
to Berne) Bukharin's "theses" of the *spring* of 1915. Then
you will see what it is all about:

1) In the spring of 1915 Bukharin (at the Conference!)
writes theses in which he is visibly rolling down into the
swamp. The Japanese[239] are *against* him. (Therefore we
temporarily accept the maximum of concessions in *Kommunist*, in order to create a form convenient for *clearing up* the
affair: shall we succeed in overcoming Bukharin's waverings "in comradely fashion"? will E. B., who calls herself a
Bolshevik, help in this or not?)

2) In the summer of 1915 (or approaching the autumn)
Bukharin + *the Japanese*, now as a group of three, sign the
theses about self-determination. *Utterly wrong*, in our
opinion, and a *repetition* of Bukharin's mistakes.

3) At the beginning of 1916 Bukharin on the question of
the "Dutch Programme" (from No. 3 of the *Bulletin* of the
I.S.C.) *again* returns to the ideas of his spring theses of
1915!!!

The conclusion? A bloc is impossible in this case *also*.
We must *wait* until Bukharin's waverings have ceased. A
journal which would be an organ of Polish-Bukharin waverings would be *harmful*. It would be harmful in such a situation to cling to the old title, and not to be capable of selecting
another (*Sbornik Sotsial-Demokrata*).

The non-Party and dishonest behaviour of the Japanese
lies in this, that they want to throw the responsibility for
their wobblings *on us*. Excuse us, kind friends, we shall not
allow you to do this! If you want to be Party people, you
will help us partly in money to publish *Sbornik Sotsial-
Demokrata*, where we (after all, we are not wobbling) will
analyse your mistakes in comradely fashion *without* naming
you, *not giving* the enemy the chance to rejoice and gloat.

Moreover, if the Japanese took seriously the most serious
question of differences (abroad *il n'y a qu'un pas**** to a
separate faction!! You can believe me, I've been seeing this
happen for about **20** years!!), they would force themselves
to study the difference, think it over, work at it (they did

---

* There is but one step. —*Ed.*

not think and did *not* study, but simply *blurted out the first thing that came into their heads*). They would have given a full statement of *their* differences, either in a manuscript for an intimate circle of leading comrades (who could have helped in *not* giving publicity to the question in the press), or in a pamphlet if *they* wanted to "go into print" (they've got the money).

Then *they themselves* would be answering for their "ideas" That is essential. If you want to teach the workers new truths —*answer for them*, and don't throw responsibility on us, don't hide behind us (we are nobodies, let Lenin and Co. answer to the Party for the "discussion", i.e., for the gloating of our enemies).

No, kind friends!! That won't wash!! *I* am not going to answer for *your* wobblings. We shall publish *Sbornik Sotsial-Demokrata* even without your help, Messrs. Japanese. We shall grant you a *postponement*: think it over, clear up your ideas, *decide* finally whether you want to assume responsibility for a new muddle or not. If all you want is to "match" *us* against the Poles and the Dutch in the Russian press, that we *won't* allow you to do.

This is the situation, these are my views; and I repeat that I will certainly send you Bukharin's spring theses, so that you can judge the whole situation *according to the documents*.

N. K. is writing today about self-determination. We are *not* for fragmentation. But what about the question of *annexations*? Bukharin and Co. (just like Radek with Rosa Luxemburg and Pannekoek) have not thought over what it means to be "against old and new annexations" (the formula *in the press* drawn up by Radek)?? Why, that *is* "self-determination of nations", only expressed in *other* words!

Well, so long until next time.

Yours,
Lenin

Written earlier than June 17, 1916
Sent from Zurich to Christiania (Oslo)

First published in 1929   Printed from the original
in *Proletarskaya Revolutsia* No. 1

102

TO M. N. POKPOVSKY[240]

July 2, 1916

Dear M. N.,

I am sending you the manuscript* today by registered post. All the material, the plan and the greater part of the work were already completed on the plan as ordered, 5 signatures (200 manuscript pages), so that to cut it down once more to 3 signatures was absolutely impossible. It will be terribly disappointing if they don't publish it! Wouldn't it be possible at least to get it printed in the journal of the same publisher?[241] Unfortunately, for some reason my correspondence with him has lapsed.... As regards the name of the author, I would, of course, prefer my usual pseudonym. If that is inconvenient, I suggest another: N. Lenivtsyn. Or if you want to, take any other. As regards the notes, I would earnestly ask you to retain them; you will see from No. 101 that they are exceptionally important for me. And then in Russia the students, etc., are also readers: they need to have the literature indicated to them. I deliberately selected a most economical system (in the sense of space and *paper*). Using small type, 7 manuscript pages mean something like two pages of print. I particularly ask you to leave in the notes, or to appeal to the publisher to leave them. As regards the title: if the one given is inconvenient, if it is desirable to avoid the word imperialism, then put in: "The Basic Peculiarities of Contemporary Capitalism." (The

---

* This was the MS. of Lenin's book *Imperialism, the Highest Stage of Capitalism* (see present edition, Vol. 22, pp. 185-304).—*Ed.*

subheading, "A Popular Outline", is unquestionably necessary, because a number of important matters are set forth in that style.) The first sheet with a list of chapters, some of which have headings that are perhaps not quite convenient from the point of view of the restrictions, I am sending for you. If you find it more convenient and safer, retain it and don't send it further. Altogether it would be very pleasant if both could be printed in the journal of the same publisher. If you see nothing inconvenient in this, drop them a line about it. I shall be very grateful to you. I shake your hand and send my best greetings.

Yours,

V. Ulyanov

P.S. I strove with all my might to adapt myself to the "restrictions". It's terribly difficult for me and I feel there is a great deal of unevenness on account of this. But it can't be helped!

Sent from Zurich to Sceaux (Seine),
France

First published in full in 1932   Printed from the original
in the second edition of Lenin's
Collected Works, Vol. XXIX

103

TO G. Y. ZINOVIEV

Bukharin's article is beyond question unsuitable.[242]
There is *not* any shadow of a "theory of the imperialist state".
There is a summary of data about the growth of state capitalism, and nothing else. To fill an illegal journal with this
most legal material would be absurd. It must be rejected
(with supreme politeness, promising every assistance in
getting it published legally).*

But perhaps we had better wait for Yuri's article, and
not write to Bukharin for the time being.

We should wait, too, with the letter to Bukharin about
their "faction", otherwise he will think that we have
rejected it out of "factionalism".

To pose the question of the "epoch" and the *"present
war"*, as though they were "extremes", is just what is meant
by falling into eclecticism. Just as though our aim were to
strike the "happy mean" between "extremes"!!!

The problem is to give a *correct* definition of the relationship of the *epoch* to the *present* war. This has been done
both in the resolutions and in my articles: "the *present* imperialist war is *not an exception*, but a typical phenomenon in
the imperialist *epoch*." [The typical is not the unique.]

One cannot understand the present war without understanding the epoch.

When people say this about the epoch, this is not just a
phrase. It is correct. And your quotations from my old
articles say *only* that. *They are correct.*

---

* Privately, in my own name, I will advise Bukharin to change
the title and retain *only* the economic part. For the political part is
quite incomplete, not thought out, useless.

But when people draw from this the conclusion, *as they have begun to do*, that "in the epoch of imperialism there *cannot* be national wars", that is nonsense. It is an obvious error—historical and political and *logical* (for an epoch is a sum of varied phenomena, in which in addition to the typical there is *always* something else).

And you *repeat this error*, when you write in your remarks:

"Small countries cannot in the present epoch defend their fatherland."

[=the vulgarisers]

Untrue!! This is just the error of Junius, Radek, the "disarmers" and the Japanese!!

One should say: "Small countries, *too*, cannot *in imperialist wars*, which are most typical of the current imperialist epoch, defend their fatherland."

That is quite different.

In this difference lies the *whole essence* of the case against the *vulgarisers*. And it's just the *essence* which you haven't noticed.

Grimm repeats the error of the vulgarisers, and you *indulge* him by providing a wrong formulation. On the contrary, it is just now that we must (both in talks and in articles) refute the vulgarisers for Grimm's benefit.

We are not at all against "defence of the fatherland" *in general*, not against "defensive wars" *in general*. You will *never* find that nonsense in a single resolution (or in any of my articles). We are against defence of the fatherland and a defensive position in the *imperialist war* of 1914-16 and in other *imperialist* wars, typical of the imperialist *epoch*. But in the imperialist *epoch* there *may* be also "just", "defensive", revolutionary wars ‖⌐namely (1) national, (2) civil, (3) socialist *and suchlike*⌐‖.

Written in August 1916

Sent from Flums to Hertenstein
(Switzerland)

First published in 1932   Printed from the original
in *Bolshevik* No. 22

104

TO N. I. BUKHARIN

Dear Com.,

Unfortunately we cannot print the article "On the Theory of the Imperialist State". As it turns out, so much space is occupied with material from Russia that all other subjects are restricted, and there is not enough money. Things are difficult.

But the main thing is not that. The main thing is some defects in the article.

The title does not correspond to the contents. The article consists of two parts, the combination of which has been insufficiently thought out: (1) about the state in general, and (2) about state capitalism and its growth (especially in Germany). The second part is good and useful, but nine-tenths legal. We would advise you to print it in one of the legal reviews (if not in *Letopis*), after *very* little alteration, and would be ready to do everything we can to help such publication.

The first part touches on a subject of tremendous importance in principle, but that's just it—it only *touches* on it. We cannot, when publishing a review once a year, print on such a basic question of theory an article which has been insufficiently thought out. Leaving aside the polemic against Gumplowicz, etc. (that would also be better worked over and *developed* into a legal article), we must point out a number of extremely inexact formulations by the author.

Marxism is a "sociological" (???) "theory of the state"; the state = the "general" (?) organisation of the ruling classes; the quotations from Engels are *broken off* just at those points which are *particularly* important, if you are discussing this subject. The distinction between the Marxists and the anarchists on the question of the state (pp. 15-16) has been defined *absolutely incorrectly*: if you are to deal with this subject, you must speak *not* in that way; you *must not* speak in that way. The conclusion (the author gives it in italics): "Social-Democracy must intensively underline its hostility in principle to the state power" (p. 53)— [compare: the proletariat creates "its provisional state organisation of power" (p. 54) ("state organisation of power"!?)]—is also either supremely inexact, or incorrect.

Our advice is to work up into legal articles (α) the section about state capitalism and (β) the polemic with Gumplowicz and Co. Leave the rest *to mature*. That is our conviction.

Written at the end of August
and beginning of September 1916

Sent from Flums (Switzerland)
     to Christiania (Oslo)

First published in 1932   Printed from the original
in *Bolshevik* No. 22

105

TO A. G. SHLYAPNIKOV

Dear Friend,

Evidently Belenin's decision about his "trip" has already been taken, judging by the letter which Grigory has sent me today. And the time is quite short! Yet we have particular reason to exchange letters and come to an understanding with him: this is now incredibly important. Therefore I most earnestly request you to take all possible steps to see Belenin *personally*, to pass on to him all that follows, and *frankly* and also in detail write to me (without fail!) how matters stand, i.e., whether or not there are differences, divergencies, etc., between us and Belenin, and what they are (and how to eliminate them, if they exist).

The elimination of James[243] (I earnestly ask you *not* to say one word about this elimination to a *single* person abroad: you cannot imagine how dangerous in *all* respects is chatter abroad on these subjects, and *in connection* with such events)—the elimination of James makes the position critical and once again raises the question of the general plan of work.

In my convinced opinion, this plan is composed, first, of the *theoretical* line, secondly, of the most immediate *tactical* tasks and, thirdly, of direct organisational tasks.

(1) On the first point, the order of the day now is not only the *continuation* of the line we have endorsed (against tsarism, etc.) in our resolutions and pamphlet* (this line has

---

* The resolutions of the Conference of the R.S.D.L.P. Groups Abroad and the pamphlet *Socialism and War* (see present edition, Vol. 21, pp. 158-64, 295-338).—*Ed.*

been remarkably confirmed by events, by the split in Britain,[244] etc.), but also cleansing it of the stupidities which have accumulated, and the muddle about rejecting democracy (this includes disarmament, repudiation of self-determination, the theoretically wrong rejection "in general" of defence of the fatherland, the wobblings on the question of the role and significance of the state in general, etc.).

It will be an extreme pity if Belenin does not receive my article in reply to Kievsky (just yesterday it was sent to be transcribed, and will be ready only in a few days). What are we to do? Don't neglect the necessity of coming to an understanding on theoretical questions: really and truly, it is essential for work in such difficult times. Think over whether we could not put into effect the following plan (or something similar): I am beginning to realise that Belenin's wife is not in America, as I thought, but in Spain, through which Belenin will of course travel now. Could we not organise the copying and passing on of manuscripts to his wife in Spain? In that case perhaps my article, too, even if sent in a week from now, would reach Belenin in time, because he will certainly spend a few days in Spain.

Think it over; apart from this special case, regular correspondence with Belenin's wife, and with Spain in general, is extremely important. Spain is a supremely important point just now, because it is still more convenient to work there than in Britain and elsewhere.

I cannot dwell more fully on theoretical agreement. The enemy has already seized on the stupid repudiation of the significance of democracy (Potresov[245] in No. 1 of *Dyelo*). Bazarov has made a fool of himself in *Letopis*. Bogdanov is talking *another kind* of balderdash, but *also* balderdash in *Letopis*. An exceptionally suspicious bloc of the Machists and the O.C.-ists has come into being there. A shameful bloc! It's hardly likely that we can break it up.... Should we perhaps try a bloc with the Machists against the O.C.-ists? Hardly likely to succeed!! Gorky is always supremely spineless in politics, a prey to emotion and passing moods.

The legal press in Russia is acquiring exceptional importance, and therefore the question of the correct line, too, becomes still more and more important, because it is easier for the enemy to "bombard" us in this field.

The best thing would be, probably, if Belenin could have a "base" in Spain and receive our letters and manuscripts there: we could continue our discussion, exchange letters, Belenin could return there soon after his short trip further on (for the danger is very great, and it would be much more useful for our cause if Belenin made *brief* trips round a few cities and then returned to Spain, or to where he is now, or to a neighbouring country to *consolidate* contacts, etc.).

On the second point. The main thing now, I think, is to publish popular leaflets and manifestos against tsarism. Consider whether this could be organised in Spain? If not, we shall prepare them here and send them on. For this *the most efficient* transport contacts are essential. You were quite right: the Japanese have proved *absolutely* useless. Best of all would be foreigners, with whom we could correspond in English or some other foreign language. I will not dwell on the question of transport, because you yourself realise and know this. The trouble is that there is no money, but they should collect some in Petersburg.

The main Party question in Russia has been *and remains* the question of "unity". Trotsky in the 500 or 600 issues of his paper has not managed to speak out, or to think out, fully whether there is to be unity with Chkheidze, Skobelev and Co., or not. I think there are still some "unifiers" in Petersburg as well, though very weak (was it not they who published *Rabochiye Vedomosti* in Petersburg?).[246] "Makar", they say, is in Moscow and also playing the conciliator. Conciliationism and unificationism is the most harmful thing for the workers' party in Russia—not just idiocy, but the *destruction* of the Party. For *in practice* "unification" (or conciliation and the like) with Chkheidze and Skobelev (they are the key point, because they give themselves out to be "internationalists") is "unity" with the O.C., and through it with Potresov and Co., i.e., in practice it is *playing the lackey* to the social-chauvinists. If Trotsky and Co. have not understood this, so much the worse for them. *Dyelo* No. 1 and—especially—the participation of the workers in the war industries committees, *prove* that this is so.

Not only in elections to the Duma the day after peace is signed, but in general on *all* questions of Party practice, "unity" with Chkheidze and Co. is the *essential question* today. We can rely only on those who have understood just how deceptive the idea of unity is and how necessary it is to break with that fraternity (Chkheidze and Co.) in Russia. Belenin ought to rally *only* such people as leaders.

By the way, a split on the international scale is also due. I consider it quite timely now that *all* class-conscious leading workers in Russia should understand this, and should adopt resolutions in favour of an organisational break with the Second International, with the International Bureau of Huysmans, Vandervelde and Co., in favour of building a Third International *only* against the Kautskians of all countries (Chkheidze and Co., also Martov and Axelrod = the Russian Kautskians), *only* in rapprochement with people who take the stand of the Zimmerwald Left.

On the third point. The most pressing question now is the weakness of contacts between us and leading workers in Russia!! No correspondence!! No one but James, and now he has gone!! We can't go on like that. We *cannot* organise either the publication of leaflets or transport, either agreement about manifestos or sending over their drafts, etc., etc., without *regular* secret correspondence. That is the key question!

This Belenin did not do on his first visit (probably he couldn't at the time). Convince him, for Christ's sake, that this must be done on the second visit! It must be done!! The immediate success of the visit, really and truly, must be measured by the number of contacts!! (Of course the personal influence of Belenin is still more important, but he *will not be able* to stop anywhere for long without destroying himself and harming the cause.) The number of contacts in each city will be the measure of the success of his visit!!

Two-thirds of the contacts, as a minimum, in each city, should be with leading *workers*, i.e., they should *write* themselves, *themselves* master secret correspondence (artists are made, not born), should themselves each train up 1-2 "heirs" in case of arrest. This should not be entrusted to the intelligentsia alone. Certainly not. It can and must be done by the leading workers. Without this it is *impossible* to establish continuity and purpose in our work—and that is the main thing.

That's all, I think.

As regards legal literature, I will also add:

it is important to ascertain whether they will accept my articles in *Letopis* (if the O.C.-ists cannot be thrown out by means of a bloc with the Machists). With restrictions? Which?

We must find out in greater detail about Volna. [247]

As regards myself personally, I will say that I need to earn. Otherwise we shall simply die of hunger, really and truly!! The cost of living is devilishly high, and there is nothing to live on. The cash must be dragged *by force** out of the publisher of *Letopis*, to whom my two pamphlets*** have been sent (let him pay *at once* and as much as possible!). The same with Bonch. The same as regards *translations*. If this is not organised I really will not be able to hold out, this is absolutely serious, absolutely, absolutely.

I shake you firmly by the hand and send a thousand best wishes to Belenin. Drop me a line that you have received this *immediately*, just two words.

Yours,

Lenin

P.S. Write *frankly*, in what state of mind Bukharin is leaving? Will he write to us or not? Will he carry out our requests or not? Correspondence (with America) is possible *only* through Norway. Tell him this and arrange it.

Written later than October 3, 1916

Sent from Zurich to Stockholm

First published in 1924   Printed from the original
in *Lenin Miscellany II*

---

* About cash Belenin will have a talk with Katin, and with Gorky himself, of course *if it is not* inconvenient.

** Reference is to *New Data on the Laws Governing the Development of Capitalism in Agriculture* and *Imperialism, the Highest Stage of Capitalism* (see present edition, Vol. 22, pp. 13-102, 185-304).—*Ed.*

106

TO FRANZ KORITSCHONER[248]

October 25, 1916

Dear Friend,

We regret very much that you haven't written a single line to us so far. One must hope that the big events in Vienna will stimulate you at long last to write to us in detail.

Berner Tagwacht (and then other papers) printed a report that at a war factory in Speyer (Austria) there was a strike of 24,000 workers, that Czech soldiers opened fire, and that 700 (seven hundred!) workers were killed! How much truth is there in this? Please let us know about it in as much detail as you can.

As regards the act of Friedrich Adler,[249] I would beg you to let us know the details.

The papers here (*Berner Tagwacht* and *Volksrecht*—do you get them both, or neither?) extol this act. *Avanti!* (does *Avanti!* reach you?) states that Friedrich Adler was the author of the famous manifesto of the Austrian internationalists. Is that true? And is it now convenient to speak about this openly?

(1) Did Friedrich Adler tell anyone about his plan? (2) Did he give any friend any documents, letters, statements to be published later? (3) Is it true, as the Vienna *Arbeiter Zeitung* writes, that *everywhere* (both in the railway club and in other places) he was in a minority (and how big was that minority?), (4)——that his position in the organisation had become "unbearable" (?)—(5)—that at the last party conference he received only *seven* votes?—(6) that at the last two meetings of trusted agents he attacked the

party extremely sharply and demanded "demonstrations"? (What kind precisely?)

Please write us in as much detail as possible about all these questions, and in general give us more information and details about Friedrich Adler. Unless you give us special instructions to the contrary, *we shall print* in our papers everything that we get from you (and will also publish them—as material from our editorial office—in the local German-language press).

As regards the political assessment of the act, we maintain, of course, our old conviction, confirmed by decades of experience, that individual terrorist acts are *inexpedient* methods of political struggle.

"Killing is no murder,"* wrote our old *Iskra* about terrorist acts; we are *not at all opposed* to political killing (in this sense the servile writings of the opportunists in *Vorwärts* and the Vienna *Arbeiter Zeitung* are simply revolting), but as revolutionary tactics individual attacks are inexpedient and harmful. Only the mass movement can be considered genuine political struggle. Only in direct, immediate connection with the mass movement can and must individual terrorist acts be of value. In Russia the terrorists (against whom we always struggled) carried out a number of individual attacks; but in December 1905, when matters at last reached the stage of a mass movement, insurrection—when it was necessary to help the *masses* to use violence—then just at that moment the "terrorists" were *missing*. That is where the terrorists make their mistake.

Adler would have been of much greater help to the revolutionary movement if, without being afraid of a split, he had systematically gone over to illegal propaganda and agitation. It would be very good if some Left group were found to publish a leaflet in Vienna which would inform the workers of its view; if it branded in the sharpest possible way the servile behaviour of the Vienna *Arbeiter Zeitung* and *Vorwärts*, morally justified Adler's act ("killing is no murder"), but as a *lesson* for the workers declared: not terrorism but systematic, prolonged, self-sacrificing activity in revolutionary propaganda and agitation, demon-

---

* These words were written by Lenin in English.—*Ed.*

strations, etc., etc., *against* the lackey-like opportunist party, *against* the imperialists, *against* one's own governments, *against* the war—that is what is needed.

Tell us also, please, how right it would be to regard Adler's act as a gesture of *despair*? I think that politically it is so. He had lost his faith in the party, he could not bear the fact that it was impossible to work with this party, that it was impossible to work with Victor Adler, he could not accept the idea of a split and take upon himself the burdensome task of a struggle against the party. And as a result of his despair came this attempt.

An act of despair of a Kautskian (*Volksrecht* writes that Adler was not a supporter of the Zimmerwald Left, but rather a Kautskian).

But we revolutionaries cannot fall into despair. We are not afraid of a split. On the contrary, we recognise the necessity of a split, we explain to the masses why a split is inevitable and necessary, we call for work against the old party and for revolutionary mass struggle.

What trends (*resp.* what individual shades of opinion) exist in Vienna and in Austria in assessing Adler's act?

I am afraid that the Vienna Government will declare Friedrich Adler insane, and not let matters come to a trial. But if they do, it will certainly be essential to organise the distribution of leaflets.

Write more and in greater detail, and observe exactly all technical precautions.

Best greetings!

Yours,

N. Lenin

Written in German

Sent from Zurich to Vienna

First published in *Pravda* No. 60,
March 1, 1932

Printed from the original

107

TO N. D. KIKNADZE[250]

Dear Comrade,

Thank you very much for your story of the Geneva arguments.[251] It is very important for us to have reactions from our readers. It's a pity that we rarely get to know them.

Lunacharsky, Bezrabotny and Co. are people without heads.

I advise you to put the question to them squarely: let them produce *written* theses (and afterwards in the press), brief and clear (like our resolutions)—(1) about self-determination (§ 9 of our Party Programme). Do they agree or not with the resolution of 1913?

If they don't, why have they kept silent? Why haven't they produced their own?

(2) *Why* do they reject defence of the fatherland in the *present* war?

(3) *How* do they pose the question of "defence of the fatherland"?

(4) What is their attitude to national wars, and (5)—to national insurrections?

Let them reply!

They will muddle themselves up like children, I'll take a bet. They haven't understood *anything whatever* on the question of the historical character of the "nation" and of "defence of the fatherland".

Since you want to argue with them, I send you my article from No. 3 (or 4) of *Sbornik* on this subject.[252] *This is private, i.e., only for you*: after reading it, return it to me or give it to the Karpinskys, *to return to me with their next packet*. I cannot as yet show it to everyone.

I thought that you had left, and therefore sent my letter about Swiss affairs only to Noah. But the letter is *intended* for you *too*. *Read it*. Noah does not send *a word* in reply. Strange! Very strange!

Best greetings. Get better!

Yours,
Lenin

Written at the end of October
and beginning of November 1916

Sent from Zurich to Geneva

First published in 1925   Printed from the original
in *Lenin Miscellany III*

108

TO N. D. KIKNADZE

Dear Comrade,

You question my remark as to the *possibility* of transforming the present imperialist war, *too*, into a national war.

Your argument? "We shall have to defend an imperialist fatherland"....

Is that logical? If the fatherland remains "imperialist", how can the war then be national??

The talk about "possibilities", in my opinion, has been theoretically wrongly introduced by Radek, and by § 5 of the theses of the *Internationale*.[253]

Marxism takes its stand on the facts, and not on possibilities.

A Marxist must, as the foundation of his policy, put *only* precisely and unquestionably demonstrated *facts*.

That is what our (Party) resolution does.*

When *instead* of it we are presented with "impossibility", I reply: untrue, un-Marxist, a cliché. All kinds of transformation are *possible*.

And I quote a historical fact (the wars of 1792-1815). I take this example to illustrate the possibility of something like that nowadays (if there is a development *backwards*).

In my opinion, *you* are confusing the possible (about which it was *not* I who began talking!!) with the real, when you think that the recognition of a possibility allows us to alter our tactics. That is the height of illogicality.

---

* See present edition, Vol. 21. pp. 158-64.—*Ed.*

I recognise the possibility that a Social-Democrat may be transformed into a bourgeois, *and the reverse*.

An indubitable truth. Does it follow from this that I will now recognise a *particular* bourgeois, Plekhanov, as a Social-Democrat? No, it does not follow. But what about the possibility? Let's wait for it to be transformed into reality.

That's all. It is precisely in "methodology" (about which you write) that one must distinguish the possible from the real.

All kinds of transformation are possible, even of a fool into a wise man, but such a transformation rarely becomes *actual*. And merely because of the "possibility" of such a transformation I shall not cease to consider the fool to be a fool.

Your perplexities about "dualistic" training are not clear to me. For I *concretely* gave the example (Norway) both in *Prosveshcheniye** and in my article against Kievsky.**

You *don't* reply to that!! You choose the quite unclear example of Poland.

This is not "dualistic" training, but *reducing* different things to a common denominator, bringing Nizhni and Smolensk to a *common* Moscow.

A Swedish Social-Democrat who does not stand for the *freedom* of secession for Norway is a scoundrel. This you do not challenge. A Norwegian Social-Democrat may be either *for* secession or *against* it. Is unity on such a question obligatory for all Social-Democrats of all countries? No. That would be a cliché, a ridiculous cliché, a ridiculous pretension.

We never blamed the Polish Social-Democrats (I wrote this in *Prosveshcheniye*) because *they* were against the independence of Poland.

Instead of a simple, clear, theoretically unchallengeable argument: we cannot now be for the *kind* of democratic

---

* See "The Right of Nations to Self-Determination" (present edition, Vol. 20, pp. 425-30).—*Ed.*
** See "A Caricature of Marxism and Imperialist Economism" (ibid., Vol. 23, pp. 48-55).—*Ed.*

demand (for an independent Poland) that *in practice* subor-
dinates us *completely* to one of the imperialist powers
or coalitions

(this is unquestionable, this is enough; it is essential and
sufficient)

—instead of this they talked themselves into an absurdity: "It is unrealisable."

We laughed this out of court in 1903 and in April 1916.

The good Polish Social-Democrats almost, almost proved
the unrealisability of a new Polish state, only ... only
the imperialist Hindenburg interfered: he went and
realised it.[254]

To what ridiculous pedantry people descend when they
desire (from the Cracow point of view[255]) to make more
profound (or more foolish?) the "economic" aspect!!

The P.S.D. have got themselves into the position of
repudiating *"Staatenbau"**!! But is not all democracy
Staatenbau? And the independence for the Dutch Indies
which Gorter demands, is *not* that the *Staatenbau*?

We are for freedom of secession for the Dutch Indies.
But is a Social-Democrat of the Dutch Indies *bound* to
be for secession? There is another example for you of what
you call "dualistic" training!!

War is the continuation of politics. Belgium is a colonial-
ist country, you argue. Nevertheless, shall we really be
unable to determine *which* politics the *present* war continues,
the politics of Belgian slave-owning or of Belgian liberation??

I think we shall be able to.

And if anyone loses his way, that will be a question
of *fact*.

One cannot, after all, "prohibit" national wars (as Radek
wants) out of fear that brainless people or swindlers *again*
pretend that the imperialist war is a national one!! That is
ridiculous, yet that is the conclusion from what Radek is
saying.

---

* "Building of a state."—*Ed.*

We are not against a *national* insurrection, we are *for* it. That is clear. And we cannot go further than that: we shall consider each case concretely, and I don't think we shall take the rebellion of the South in the United States in 1863 as a "national insurrection"....

I had Engels's article from the Grünberg Archives,[256] but sent it away to Grigory. I shall get it back from him and *send it to you.*

Very best greetings,
Yours,
Lenin

N. K. asks me very much to send her greetings too.

Written later than November 5, 1916

Sent from Zurich to Geneva

First published in 1925
in *Lenin Miscellany III*

Printed from the original

109

TO INESSA ARMAND

Dear Friend,

Of course, I also want to correspond. Let's continue our correspondence.

How I laughed over your postcard, I really had to hold my sides, as they say. "In France there is no such measure as the ha, but there is the acre, and you don't know how big an acre is...."

That really is funny!

It was *France—imaginez-vous*?—that introduced the metric system. According to the metric system, adopted in most countries of the world, a ha=hectare=100 ares. An acre is *not* a French measure but an English one, about 4/10 of a hectare.

You mustn't be offended over my laughing. I didn't mean any harm. After all, is it so surprising that you do not often come across the words hectare, ha, etc.? They are dull, technical words.

Many thanks for translating the theses.[257] I will send them to Abramovich and Guilbeaux.

Alter them for France? It's hardly worth the while, much is different there.

Today there was a meeting of the Lefts here: *not* everyone came, only 2 Swiss+2 foreigners (Germans)+3 Russ. Jew. Polish* ... *Schwach*! I think it will be almost a failure: the second meeting will be in ten days' time.... It's difficult for them, because what it *actually* amounts to is a war

---

* And the lecture did not come off, only a talk.

with Grimm, and their forces are too small. Well, we'll see.

As regards women, I agree with your addendum.

You are being captious about the thesis that Social-Democrats (1) in *Switzerland* (2) now should not vote in any circumstances for war credits. After all, the beginning goes on *all the time* about the *present*, imperialist war. Nothing else but that.

"The working men have no country"—this means that (α) his economic position (*le salariat**) is not national but international, (β) his class enemy is international, (γ) the conditions of his emancipation also, (δ) the international unity of the workers is *more important* than the national.

Does this mean, does it follow from this, that we *should not* fight *when it is a question* of throwing off a foreign yoke?? Yes or no?

A war of colonies for emancipation?
   —of Ireland against England?
And an insurrection (national), is not that defence of the fatherland?

I will send you my article against Kievsky about this.**

If you need more books, *write*. One can get a lot here, and all the same I am often in the libraries.

All the best.

Lenin

Written on November 20, 1916

Sent from Zurich to Sörenberg
       (Switzerland)

First published in 1949   Printed from the original
   in *Bolshevik* No. 1

---

* Wages system.—*Ed.*
** See "A Caricature of Marxism and Imperialist Economism" (present edition, Vol. 23, pp. 28-76).—*Ed.*

110

TO INESSA ARMAND

Dear Friend,

As regards rewording for the French, I would not undertake it.* Perhaps you will try?

They were written for the Swiss: the "military part" here is a special one (for a small state), the inner-party situation is different, etc., etc. Besides, I would not be able to find *concrete* material about France.

I should be heartily glad to do something for the French Left, but somehow contacts don't get established. Grisha writes long but exceptionally meaningless letters, full of water, chews old stuff, nothing business-like, tells us nothing precise about the French *Left*, and establishes no, absolutely no contact with them.

As regards the fatherland, you evidently want to establish a contradiction between my writings previously (when? 1913? where precisely? what precisely?) and now. I don't think there are any contradictions. Find the exact texts, then we shall look at it again.

Of course, there were always differences between the orthodox and the opportunists as to the conception of fatherland (cf. Plekhanov 1907 or 1910, Kautsky 1905 and 1907, and Jaurès: *L'armée nouvelle*). I entirely agree with this: here the divergence was a radical one. I don't think I have ever said anything against that.

---

* Lenin refers to his theses "Tasks of the Left Zimmerwaldists in the Swiss Social-Democratic Party" (see present edition, Vol. 23, pp. 137-48).—*Ed.*

That the defence of the fatherland is admissible (when it is admissible) only as the defence of democracy (in the appropriate epoch), is my opinion too.

Of course, proletarians should never "merge" with the general democratic movement. Marx and Engels did not "merge" with the bourgeois-democratic movement in Germany in 1848. We Bolsheviks did not "merge" with the bourgeois-democratic movement in 1905.

We Social-Democrats always stand for democracy, not "in the name of capitalism", but in the name of clearing the path for *our* movement, which clearing is impossible without the development of capitalism.

Best greetings.

Yours,
Lenin

P.S. If you need books, write.

Written on November 25, 1916

Sent from Zurich to Sörenberg
      (Switzerland)

First published in 1949   Printed from the original
  in *Bolshevik* No. 1

111

TO INESSA ARMAND

Dear Friend,

As regards "defence of the fatherland" I don't know whether we differ or not. You find a contradiction between my article in the collection of articles *To the Memory of Marx*** and my present statements, *without quoting* either precisely. I cannot reply to this. I haven't got the collection *To the Memory of Marx*. Of course, I cannot remember word for word what I wrote in it. Without *precise* quotations, then and now, I am not able to reply to *such* an argument on your part.

But *generally* speaking, it seems to me that you argue somehow in a somewhat one-sided and formalist manner. You have taken *one* quotation from the *Communist Manifesto* (the working men have no country) and you seem to want to apply it without any reservations, *up to and including the repudiation of national wars*.

The whole spirit of Marxism, its whole system, demands that each proposition should be considered (α) only historically, (β) only in connection with others, (γ) only in connection with the concrete experience of history.

The fatherland is an historical concept. The fatherland in an epoch or, more precisely, at the *moment* of struggle for the overthrow of national oppression, is one thing. At the moment when national movements have been left far behind, it is another thing. For the "three types of countries" (§ 6 of our theses on self-determination****) there *cannot*

---

* See "Marxism and Revisionism" (present edition, Vol. 15, pp. 29-39).—*Ed.*
** See "The Socialist Revolution and the Right of Nations to Self-Determination" (present edition, Vol. 22, pp. 150-52).—*Ed.*

be a proposition about the fatherland, and its defence, identically applicable in all conditions.

In the *Communist Manifesto* it is said that the working men have no country.

Correct. But *not only* this is stated there. It is stated there also that when national states are being formed the role of the proletariat is somewhat special. To take the first proposition (the working men have no country) and *forget* its *connection* with the second (the workers are constituted as a class nationally, though not in the same sense as the bourgeoisie) will be exceptionally incorrect.

Where, then, does the connection lie? In my opinion, precisely in the fact that in the *democratic* movement (at such a moment, in such concrete circumstances) the proletariat cannot refuse to support it (and, consequently, support defence of the fatherland in a national war).

Marx and Engels said in the *Communist Manifesto* that the working men have no country. But the same Marx *called* for a *national* war more than once: Marx in 1848, Engels in 1859 (the end of his pamphlet *Po and Rhine*, where the *national* feeling of the Germans is directly inflamed, where they are directly called upon to wage a national *war*). Engels in *1891*, in view of the then threatening and advancing war of France (Boulanger)+Alexander III against Germany, *directly* recognised "defence of the fatherland".[258]

Were Marx and Engels muddlers who said one thing today and another thing tomorrow? No. In my view, admission of "defence of the fatherland" in a national war *fully* answers the requirements of Marxism. In 1891 the German *Social-Democrats* really *should have* defended their fatherland in a war against Boulanger + Alexander III. This would have been a peculiar variety of *national* war.

Incidentally, in saying this, I am *repeating* what I said in my article against Yuri.* For some reason you don't mention it. It seems to me that on the question raised here there are *precisely* in that article a number of propositions which make clear completely (or nearly so) my understanding of Marxism.

---

* See "A Caricature of Marxism and Imperialist Economism" (present edition, Vol. 23, pp. 28-76).—*Ed.*

As to Radek—my "quarrel" (???!!!) with Radek. I had
an argument last spring with Grigory, who had no understanding at all of the political situation at that time, and
reproached me for breaking with the Zimmerwald Left.
That is nonsense.

The connection with the Zimmerwald Left is also a
conditional thing. First of all, Radek is not=the Zimmerwald Left. Secondly, there was no "break" with Radek in
general, but only in a particular *sphere*. Thirdly, it is stupid
to conceive of the connection with Radek in such a way
that *our* hands should be tied in the *necessary* theoretical
and practical struggle.

Ad 1 (to point 1). I never, anywhere, took a single step,
not a suspicion of it, not merely towards a break, but even
towards weakening the ties with the "Zimmerwald Left".
Nobody has ever pointed one out to me, or will be able to
point it out. Neither with Borchardt, nor with the Swedes,
nor with Knief, etc., etc.

(Radek very meanly threw us out of the editorial board
of *Vorbote*. Radek behaves in politics like a Tyszka huckster, impudent, insolent, stupid. *Grigory* wrote to me in
the spring of 1916, when I was already in Zurich, that *he*
had *no* "team work" with Radek. Radek has *moved away*—
that is the *fact*. He moved away *on account* of *Vorbote*,
both from me *and from Grigory*. On account of the impudence
and huckster-like meanness of one person, the Zimmerwald Left does not cease to be Left, and there is no purpose
in dragging *it* into the affair: it's not sensible, not correct.

Gazeta Robotnicza, in the number for February 1916,
is a pattern of such a Tyszka-like rotten servile "game"
(Radek follows in his footsteps). Anyone who *forgives*
such things in politics I consider a donkey or a scoundrel.
I shall never forgive them. For such things you punch men's
faces or turn away.

Of course I did the second. And I don't repent. We did
not lose a *single hair* of our ties with the *Left* Germans.
When the problem arose of marching together with Radek
in practice (the Zurich Congress of November 4-5, 1916[259]),
we went ahead together. All Grigory's silly phrases about
my break with the Zimmerwald Left proved to be a stupidity, which they always were.)

Ad 2—the "sphere" of the break with Radek, therefore, were (α) Russian and Polish affairs. The resolution of the Committee of Organisations Abroad confirmed this. (β) The affair with Yuri and Co. Radek even now is writing (I can send you them if you wish) the most impudent letters to me (and Grigory) on the theme that, "we" (he $+$ Bukharin $+$ Yuri and Co.) "see things" in such-and-such a way!! Only a donkey and a scoundrel, who wants to invent an *"intrigue"*, *squeezing through the crack* of differences between us and Yuri and Co., can write in this way. If Radek did *not* understand *what* he was doing, then he is a donkey. If he did understand, then he is a scoundrel.

The political task of our Party was clear: *we could not tie* our hands by equality in the editorial board with N. I.$+$ Yuri$+$E. B. (Grigory did not understand this, and drove me to a direct ultimatum: I declared that I would *resign* from *Kommunist* if we did not break with it. *Kommunist* was a good thing, *so long as* there was *no* separate programme of the trio who composed 1/2 the editorial board). To grant *equality* to a group consisting of Bukharin$+$Yuri$+$ E. B. would be idiocy and the ruin of all the work. Neither Yuri, quite a little pig, nor E. B. has a drop of brains, and if they had allowed themselves to descend to *group* stupidity with Bukharin, then we had to break with them, more precisely with *Kommunist*. And that was done.

The polemics over self-determination are only beginning as yet. Here they are in complete confusion—as *in the whole question* about the attitude to democracy. To grant "equality" to little pigs and fools—never! They didn't want to learn peaceably and in comradely fashion, so let them blame themselves. (I *pestered* them, provoking conversations about it in Berne: they turned up their noses! I wrote them letters, tens of pages long, to Stockholm—they turned up their noses! Well, if that's how it is, let them go to the devil. I did everything possible for a *peaceable* outcome. If you don't want it, I will punch your faces and expose you as idiots before the whole world. That, and only that, is the way to treat them.) But where does Radek come in, you may ask.

Because he was the "heavy artillery" of this "group", artillery hidden in the bushes on one side. Yuri and Co.

were quite skilful in their calculations (E. B. is capable as an intriguer, it turned out that she was not *leading Yuri to us*, but setting up a group against us). Their calculation was: we shall start the war, but it's Radek who will fight for us!! Radek will fight *for us*, while Lenin will have his hands *tied*.

But it didn't come off, my dear little pigs! I will not let my hands be tied in politics. If you want to fight, come out openly. But the role of Radek—secretly inciting young pigs, but himself hiding behind the "Zimmerwald Left"— is the height of scoundrelism. The most lousy ... of the Tyszka swamp could not have been playing the huckster, the lackey and the intriguer behind one's back in dirtier fashion.

Ad 3—I have already stated clearly. The question of the relationship of imperialism to democracy and the minimum programme is arising on an *ever wider* scale (see the Dutch programme in No. 3 of the *Bulletin*[260]; the American S.L.P. have thrown out the *whole* minimum programme. *Entwaffnungsfrage**). On this Radek has *absolute confusion* in his head (this is clear from his theses; it was also shown by the question of indirect and direct taxes raised in my theses). I will never let my hands be tied in explaining this most important and fundamental question. I cannot. The question has to be cleared up. There will be *dozens* of "falls" over it yet (they will stumble for certain).

Anyone who understands the "connection" with the Zimmerwald Left in such a way that we should let *our* hands be tied in the theoretical struggle against "imperialist Economism" (that *international* disease; Dutch-American-Russian, etc.), understands nothing. To learn by heart the words "Zimmerwald Left" and to kowtow before the utter theoretical confusion in Radek's head, that I don't accept.

The results: after Zimmerwald *manoeuvres* were *more difficult*. It was necessary to *take the essential* from Radek, E. B. and *Co.*, *without allowing one's hands to be tied*. I consider that I was successful in this. After Bukharin's departure to America and, *above all*, after Yuri had sent us his article and after *he had accepted* (he accepted! *he had*

---

* The question of disarmament.—*Ed.*

to accept) my reply, their affairs, as a "group", were *finished*. (Yet Grigory wanted to *perpetuate* that group, granting it *equality*: *we* would give it equality!!)

With Radek we *parted company* on the Russo-Polish arena, and *did not invite* him into our *Sbornik*.[261] *It had to be that way.*

And now he can do nothing which could *spoil* the work. He was obliged at the Zurich Congress (November 5, 1916) to go *together* with me, as now, *against Grimm*.

What does this mean? It means that I succeeded in *dividing** the questions: *not in one iota* is the international-ist pressure on the Kautskians (Grimm *y compris***) weak-ened, and at the same time I am not subjected to "equal-ity" with Radek's stupidity!

Strategically I now consider the cause to have been won. It is possible that Yuri + *Co.* + Radek + Co. will *abuse me*. *A llez-y, mes amis!**** *Now* the *odium* will fall on *you*, not on us. But you will *now* not injure the cause, and for us the road has been cleared. We have disentangled our-selves from the *dirty* (in all senses) muddle with Yuri and Radek, *without in one iota weakening* the "Zimmerwald Left", and possessing the *requisites* for the struggle against stupidity on the question of the attitude to democracy.

Voilà. I apologise for this long letter and for the abun-dance of sharp words: I can't write otherwise when I am speaking frankly. Well, after all, this is all *entre nous*, and perhaps the unnecessary bad language will pass.

Best greetings.

Yours,
Lenin

In general, both Radek and Pannekoek are *incorrect* in the way they approach the question of the struggle against Kautskianism. This *N.B.!!*

Written on November 30, 1916

Sent from Zurich to Clarens
(Switzerland)

First published in 1949   Printed from the original
in *Bolshevik* No. 1

---

* This was *very* difficult!!
** Included.—*Ed.*
*** Go ahead, my friends!—*Ed.*

112

TO ARTHUR SCHMID[262]

Dear Comrade,

Will you allow me to suggest an amicable agreement?

I must admit that yesterday I paid insufficient attention to one very important point in your arguments.[263] Namely, the idea that the peculiarity of Switzerland lies, among other things, in her greater degree of democracy (the referendum), and that this peculiarity should be made use of *also* for propaganda purposes. This idea is very important and, in my opinion, completely correct.

Could we not apply this idea in such a way that our differences (which are probably very insignificant) should disappear? For example:

If we put the question for the referendum *only* in this way—for complete elimination or against?—we shall get a mixture of pacifist (bourgeois-pacifist, etc.) and socialist votes for it, i.e., we shall get not a clarification of a socialist consciousness but a darkening of it, not the application of the idea and the policy of *class struggle* to this particular question (namely, the question of militarism) but the renunciation of the point of view of the class struggle on the question of militarism.

But if we put the question for the referendum in this way—for the expropriation of large capitalist enterprises in industry and agriculture, *as the only way* of completely eliminating militarism, or against expropriation?

If we put it like that, we shall be saying in our practical policy the same thing that we all recognise theoretically, namely, that the complete elimination of militarism is thinkable and realisable only in connection with the elimination of capitalism.

Consequently there should be approximately the following formulation: (1) we demand the *immediate* expropriation of large enterprises, perhaps in the form of a direct Federal property and income tax, with such high, revolutionarily-high, rates for large properties that the capitalists will, in fact, be expropriated.

(2) We declare that such a socialist transformation of Switzerland is economically possible already today, directly, and, in consequence of the unbearably high cost of living, is urgently necessary as well, and that for the political effecting of such a transformation Switzerland needs not a bourgeois but a proletarian government, which would rely not on the bourgeoisie but on the broad masses of hired workers and small people, and that the revolutionary mass struggle which we see beginning, for example, in the mass strikes and street demonstrations in Zurich, and which is recognised by the Aarau decision,[264] pursues *exactly* that purpose—to put a *real* end in that way to the intolerable position of the masses.

(3) We declare that such a transformation of Switzerland *will quite inevitably arouse* imitation and the most resolute enthusiastic support on the part of the working class and the mass of the exploited in *all* civilised countries, and that *only* in connection with such a transformation will *the complete elimination of militarism* for which we strive, and for which at present particularly wide masses in Europe are instinctively thirsting, become not an empty phrase, not an amiable wish, but a genuine, practically achievable and politically self-explanatory measure.

What do you think of this?

Do you not consider that, if the question is put in this way (both in practical agitation and in parliamentary speeches and proposals for a legislative initiative and for a referendum), we shall avoid *the* danger that bourgeois and "socialist" pacifists will falsely understand and misinterpret our anti-militarist slogan in the sense that we suppose it possible to completely abolish militarism in *bourgeois Switzerland*, in her *imperialist* environment, *without* a socialist revolution (which, of course, is nonsense that we all unanimously repudiate).

With Party greetings,
                                                           N. Lenin

Wl. Uljanow.
Spiegelgasse 14^{II} (bei Kammerer). Zürich I.

Written in German
on December 1, 1916

Sent to Winterthur (Switzerland)

First published in 1931   Printed from a typewritten copy
in *Lenin Miscellany XVII*

113

TO INESSA ARMAND

Dear Friend,

Another letter has arrived today from St. Petersburg—they have been attentive in their writing lately.

Apart from the letter from Guchkov,[265] which is going into No. 57 of the Central Organ (being set), and which probably Grigory showed you in Berne, letters from Lvov and Chelnokov[266] have been received, all on the same subject, the country's bitter indignation (against the traitors carrying on negotiations for a separate peace), etc.

The mood, they write, is supremely revolutionary.

My manuscript about imperialism has reached Petersburg, and now they write today that the publisher (and this is Gorky! oh the calf!) is dissatisfied with the sharp passages against ... who do you think? ... Kautsky! He wants to get in touch with me about it!!! Both laughable and disappointing.

There it is, my fate. One fighting campaign after another—against political stupidities, philistinism, opportunism and so forth.

It has been going on since 1893. And so has the hatred of the philistines on account of it. But still, I would not exchange this fate for "peace" with the philistines.

Now there is Radek as well. No. 6 of *Jugend-Internationale* (have you seen it?) contains the article by Nota Bene. We (Grigory and I) at once recognised Bukharin. I replied to his exceptional stupidities in No. 2 of *Sbornik.** (You haven't seen it? It was ready a few days ago.)

---

* The reply was in the article "The Youth International" (see present edition, Vol. 23, pp. 163-66).—*Ed.*

Today Grigory sends me No. 25 of *Arbeiterpolitik*. There is the *same* article in it (with cuts, obviously made by the censors), signed by Bukharin. (We have received one more number of *Novy Mir*, from New York, containing a criticism—alas, alas! *A correct one*: that is the tragedy, that a Menshevik is *right* against Bukharin!!—a criticism *evidently of the same* article (in a number which we haven't got) by Bukharin in *Novy Mir*.)

And Radek—"Tyszka's methods", Grigory writes to me today—publishes in No. 25 of *Arbeiterpolitik* praise of Bukharin ("a young force") and a little note, in passing, about the "three editors of *Kommunist*"!

He squeezes into the crack of the differences between us: the time-honoured policy of riffraff and scoundrels, incapable of arguing with *us* straightforwardly and resorting to intrigues, double-dealing, baseness.

There is a picture for you of *what is*, and of *what* Radek *does* (a man is judged not by what he says or thinks about himself, but by what he does—do you remember that Marxist truth?).

Voilà.

This is the kind of *"environment"* one has to fight with!!

And what theoretical disgrace and nonsense in Radek's "theses"....

I have been reading the *Plaidoirie*[267] by Humbert-Droz. My God, what a philistine of Tolstoyism!! I have written again to Abramovich. Is he really hopeless after all? I am wondering whether there are not in Switzerland bacilli of petty-bourgeois (and petty-state) thick-wittedness, Tolstoyism, and pacifism, which destroy the best people? I am sure there must be!

I have read the *second* pamphlet by P. Golay (*L'Antimilitarisme*)—what a gigantic step back in comparison with the first (*Le Socialisme qui meurt*), and into *the same* swamp....

All the very best,
Yours,
Lenin

P.S. Do you ski? You really should! Learn the trick, get yourself skis and go off to the mountains—you must. It's good in the mountains in winter! It's delightful, and smells of Russia.

Written on December 18, 1916

Sent from Zurich to Clarens
(Switzerland)

First published in 1949   Printed from the original
in *Bolshevik* No. 1

114

TO M. N. POKROVSKY

December 21, 1916

Dear M. N.,

I have received your postcard of December 14, 1916. If they write to you that the publisher owes me "in addition to the 500 rubles another 300 rubles", I must say that I consider he owes me *more*, because he accepted (1) my work on the agrarian question, Part I* and (2) my wife's booklet on an educational subject.[268] And I consider that there is an obligation to pay for what has been accepted, once the manuscript has been delivered.

I wrote about this to Petersburg, but my contacts with Petersburg are exceptionally weak and intolerably slow.

You "thought it possible" to throw out the criticism of Kautsky in my pamphlet[269].... Sad! Really, really sad. Why? Would it not be better to ask the publishers: print outright, gentlemen, that *we*—the publishers—have eliminated criticism of Kautsky. Really, that is how it should have been done.... Of course, I am obliged to submit to the publisher, but let the publisher not be afraid to say what he wants and what he doesn't want; let the publisher answer for the cuts, not I.

You write: "You won't thrash me, will you?", i.e., for agreeing to throw out this criticism?? Alas, alas, we live in too civilised an age to settle questions so simply....

---

* The work was *New Data on the Laws Governing the Development of Capitalism in Agriculture*. Part I (see present edition, Vol. 22, pp. 13-102).—*Ed.*

Joking aside, it is sad, devil take it…. Well, I shall settle accounts with Kautsky in another place.

I shake your hand and send my best greetings.

V. Ulyanov

Sent from Zurich to Sceaux
(Seine) (France)

First published in full in 1932
in the second edition of Lenin's
Collected Works, Vol. XXIX

Printed from the original

115

TO INESSA ARMAND

Dear Friend,

About Radek. You write: "I told him at Kienthal that he had behaved badly."

Is that all? Only that! What about the political conclusion?? Or was his action only an accident?? Only his personal affair?? Nothing of the kind! There is the source of your political mistake. You do not assess what is going on politically. Yet really this is a question of politics, however strange it might seem at first sight.

As regards defence of the fatherland. It would be most unpleasant for me if we differed on this. Let us try once more to come to agreement.

Here is some "material for reflection":

War is the continuation of politics.

Everything depends on the *system* of political relations before the war and during the war.

The main types of these systems are (a) the relation of the oppressed nation to the oppressing, (b) the relation between two oppressing nations on account of the loot, its division, etc., (c) the relation of a national state which does not oppress others to one which oppresses, to a particularly reactionary state.

Think over this.

Caesarism in France + tsarism in Russia against *non-imperialist* Germany in 1891—that was the historical situation in 1891.

Think over that! And I was writing of *1891* in No. 1 of *Sbornik* as well.*

---

* See "The Discussion on Self-Determination Summed Up" (present edition, Vol. 22, pp. 320-60).—*Ed.*

How glad I am that you have had a talk with Guilbeaux and Levi! It would be a good thing to do this more frequently, or at any rate from time to time. As for the Italian, he is lying! Turati's speech is a model of *rotten* Kautskianism (he has dragged *"droits nationaux"* into the *imperialist* war!!). And the article by *bb* about this speech in *Volksrecht* is rotten too.

Oh, how I would like to write about this, or to have a talk with the Italian!!

How stupid that Levi is attacking parliamentarism!! Stupid!! And a "Left", too!! God, how much muddle there is in people's heads.

Yours,
Lenin

Written later than December 23, 1916

Sent from Zurich to Clarens

First published in 1949   Printed from the original
in *Bolshevik* No. 1

116

TO INESSA ARMAND

Dear Friend,

About Radek you,. following Grigory, seem to have got confused between personal impressions and sadness over the "dark" political picture in general and politics. You are sorry, you regret, you sigh—and nothing more. *No* other policy than that which was followed *could* have been pursued. We could not renounce correct views and surrender to "Tyszka's methods". The picture is "dark" not because of this, and the Lefts are weak not because of this, and *Vorbote* is not appearing not because of this—but because the revolutionary movement grows extremely slowly and with difficulty. This has to be put up with; rotten blocs with a certain person (or with E. B. + *Kii*) would only interfere with performing the difficult task of standing fast in difficult times.

As regards "imperialist Economism", it somehow turns out that we are "talking past each other". You *evade* the definition I gave, *pass it by* and put the question again.

The "Economists" did not "renounce" political struggle (as you write)—that is inaccurate. They defined it *wrongly*. The "imperialist Economists" do the same.

You write: "Would even the complete rejection of democratic demands mean rejecting the political struggle? Is not the *direct struggle* for the conquest of power political struggle?"

The whole point is that with Bukharin (and partly with Radek as well) this is just the kind of thing you get, and it is wrong. "The direct struggle for

the conquest of power" while "completely rejecting democratic demands" is something unclear, unthought-out,
confused. This is just what Bukharin is confused about.

More precisely, you approach the question from rather
a different point of view, when you see a contradiction
between §§ 2 and 8.

In § 2 there is a *general* statement: the socialist revolution
is *impossible* without the struggle for democracy. This is
unquestionable, and this is just the weakness of Radek +
Bukharin that they, *while disagreeing* (like you), don't
venture to challenge it!!

But further, in a certain sense for a certain period, *all*
democratic aims (not only self-determination! Note that!
You have forgotten that!) are capable of hindering the
socialist revolution. In what sense? At what moment?
When? How? For example, if the movement has already
developed, *the revolution has already begun*, we have to
seize the banks, and we are being appealed to: wait, *first*
consolidate, legitimise the republic, etc.!

An example: in August 1905, the boycott of the Duma
was correct, and was not rejection of political struggle.

((§ 2=*in general*, refusal to participate in representative
institutions is an absurdity; § 8=there are cases when we
have to refuse; there is a visual comparison for you which
makes clear that there is *no* contradiction between § 2
and § 8.))

Against Junius. The situation is the imperialist war.
The remedy for it? Only a socialist revolution in Germany.
Junius did not draw this conclusion, and took democracy
without the socialist revolution.

One should know how to *combine* the struggle for democracy and the struggle for the socialist revolution, *subordinating* the first to the second. In this lies the whole
difficulty; in this is the whole essence.

The Tolstoyans and the anarchists throw out the first.
Bukharin and Radek have become confused, failing to combine the first with the second.

But I say: don't lose sight of the *main* thing (the socialist
revolution); put it first (Junius has not done this); put *all*
the democratic demands, but subordinating them to it,
co-ordinating them with it (Radek + Bukharin unwisely

eliminate *one* of them), and bear in mind that the struggle for the main thing may blaze up even though it has begun with the struggle for something partial. In my opinion, only this conception of the matter is the right one.

A war of France + Russia against Germany in 1891. You take "my criterion", and apply it *only* to France and Russia!!!! For pity's sake, where is the logic here? That's just what I say, that *on the part of France and Russia* it would have been a reactionary war (a war in order to turn back the development of Germany, to return her from national unity to dismemberment). *But on the part of Germany?* You are silent. Yet that is the chief thing. For Germany in 1891, the war did not, and could not, have an imperialist character.

You have forgotten the main thing—that in 1891 no imperialism existed at all (I have tried to show in my pamphlet that it was born in 1898-1900, not earlier), and there was no imperialist war, there could not be, on the part of Germany. (By the way, there was no revolutionary Russia then either; that is very important.)

Furthermore, you write: "The 'possibility' of the dismemberment of Germany is not excluded in the 1914-17 war either", simply sliding away from the assessment of what exists to what is *possible*.

That is not historical. It is not political.

What *exists* today is an *imperialist* war on *both* sides. This we have said 1,000 times. This is the essence.

And the "possible"!!?? All kinds of things are "possible"!

It is ridiculous to deny the *"possibility"* of transforming the imperialist war into a national war (though Usiyevich was horrified at the idea!). What is not "possible" on this earth! But *so far* it has not been transformed. Marxism buttresses its policy on the *actual*, not on the "possible". It is possible that one phenomenon will change into another—and our tactics are not fossilised. *Parlez-moi de la réalité et non pas des possibilités!**

Engels was right. In my day I have seen an awful lot of hasty charges that Engels was an opportunist, and my attitude to them is supremely distrustful. Try, I say,

---

* Talk to me of reality and not of possibilities!—*Ed.*

and prove first that Engels was wrong!! You won't prove it!

Engels's foreword to *The Class Struggles in France*[270]? Don't you know that it was distorted in Berlin *against* his will? Is that serious criticism?

His statement about the Belgian strike[271]? When? Where? What? I don't know it.

No. No. Engels was *not* infallible. Marx was *not* infallible. But if you want to point out their "fallibility" you have to set about it differently, really, quite differently. Otherwise you are 1,000 times wrong.

Very, very best greetings.

Yours,
Lenin

Written on December 25, 1916
Sent from Zurich to Clarens

First published in 1949
in *Bolshevik* No. 1

Printed from the original

1917

117

TO INESSA ARMAND

A meeting of the C.C. of the Swiss party was held here on Sunday (January 7).

The scoundrel Grimm *at the head of all the Rights* got carried (against Nobs, Platten, Münzenberg *and Naine*) a decision to *postpone*, for an indefinite period, the party congress which had been fixed for February 11, 1917 specially on the question of the war. The reasons were false. In reality it was his desire for a bloc with the Rights, with the social-patriots, who threatened to resign if defence of the fatherland were rejected!! They don't want to allow the Swiss workers to decide the question of defence of the fatherland!!!

Naine, they say, told Grimm excellently that he was cutting his own throat as international secretary.

Chairman of Zimmerwald, etc.—yet such a scoundrel in politics!

I have a mind to write an open letter to Charles Naine,* a member of the International Socialist Commission, to publish it, to call Grimm a blackguard in it, and to say that I don't want to be in the Zimmerwald organisation with such a type, and am sending a reasoned statement on this to my Central Committee.

It's important to "catch" Grimm immediately, *en flagrant délit***—to expose him (since "they" will not let anything get into the press), to tear off his mask.

---

* See present edition, Vol. 23, pp. 220-28.—*Ed.*
** Red-handed.—*Ed.*

I think this will make Radek + Roland-Holst also say *something* to Grimm.

Of course, *such* a leaflet is not suitable for publishing under our imprint, it must be published separately, outside our firm.

Very, very best greetings.

Yours,
Lenin

Written on January 8, 1917

Sent from Zurich to Clarens

Published for the first time
in the Fourth (Russian) Edition
of the *Collected Works*

Printed from the original

118

TO INESSA ARMAND

Dear Friend,

About Engels. If you have run across the issue of *Neue Zeit* with Kautsky's story (and Engels's letters) about how they distorted Engels's preface to *Klassenkämpfe*, it would be a good thing if you copied it out in full detail in a special notebook. If you can't, then send me the exact number of *Neue Zeit*, the year, volume and page.[272]

Your attacks on Engels, I am convinced, are totally groundless. Excuse my frankness. One must prepare much more seriously before writing like that! Otherwise it's easy to disgrace oneself—I warn you *entre nous*, as a friend, between ourselves, in case you begin talking *in this way* some day in the press or at a meeting.

The Belgian strike? First of all it is possible that on this question of fact, an individual question, Engels was mistaken. Of course, that is possible. One must collect everything he wrote on this question. Secondly, events in *recent* times *in general*, 1905 definitely, have provided something *new* about general strikes, which Engels did not know. Engels had been accustomed for decades to hear about the "general strike" *only* the empty phrases of the anarchists, whom he *legitimately* hated and despised. But later events have *demonstrated* a *new* type of "mass strike", a *political* one, i.e., a particularly non-anarchist one. This new feature Engels did not know *yet*, and could not know.

This must not be forgotten.

Was not the Belgian strike a *transition* from the old to the new? Could Engels *at that time* (1891-92?? He was already 71-72; dying) see that this was not the old Belgian belch (the Belgians for a long time were Proudhonists), but the transition to something new? This must be thought over.

As regards "defence of the fatherland", in my opinion, you are falling into abstraction and unhistoricalness. I repeat what I said in the article against Yuri*: defence of the fatherland=justification for taking part in the *war*. Nothing more. To generalise this, to make it a "general principle", is *ridiculous*, supremely unscientific. (I will send you the American programme of the S.L.P., with this ridiculous generalisation.) Wars are a supremely varied, diverse, complex thing. One cannot approach them with a general pattern.

(I) Three main types: the relation of an oppressed nation to the oppressor (every war is the continuation of politics; politics is the *relationship* between nations, classes, etc.). As a general rule, war is legitimate on the part of the oppressed (irrespective of whether it is defensive or offensive in the military sense).

(II) The relation between two oppressor nations. The struggle for colonies, for markets, etc. (Rome and Carthage; Britain and Germany 1914-17). As a general rule, a war of that kind is robbery on *both* sides; and the attitude of democracy (and socialism) to it comes under the rule: "Two thieves are fighting, may they both perish"....

(III) The third type. A *system* of nations with equal rights. This question is *much more complex*!!!! Especially if side by side with civilised, comparatively democratic nations there stands tsarism. That's how it was (approximately) in Europe from 1815 to 1905.

1891. The colonial policy of France and Germany was *insignificant*. Italy, Japan, the United States *had no* colonies *at all* (now they have). In Western Europe a *system* had come into being (N.B. this!! Think over this!! Don't forget this!! We live not only in separate states, but also in a certain *system* of states; it is permissible for the anarchists to ignore this; we are not anarchists), a *system* of states, on the whole constitutional and national. *Side by side* with them was powerful, unshaken, pre-revolutionary tsarism, which had plundered and oppressed everyone for hundreds of years, which crushed the revolutions of 1849 and 1863.

---

* See present edition, Vol. 23, pp. 28-76.—*Ed.*

Germany (in 1891) was the country of *advanced* socialism. And this country was menaced by tsarism in alliance with Boulangism!

The situation was quite, quite different from what it is in 1914-17, when tsarism has been undermined by 1905, while Germany is waging a war to dominate the world. A *different* pair of shoes!!

To identify, even to compare the international situations of 1891 and 1914, is the *height* of unhistoricalness.

Stupid Radek wrote recently in the Polish manifesto (*"Befreiung Polens"*) that *"Staatenbau"* is not the aim of the Social-Democratic struggle. This is arch-stupidity! It is half-anarchism, half-idiocy! No, no, we are not at all indifferent to the *Staatenbau*, to the *system* of states, to their *mutual relations*.

Engels was the father of "passive radicalism"?? Untrue! Nothing of the kind. You will never be able to prove this. (Bogdanov and Co. tried, but only disgraced themselves.)

In the *imperialist* war of 1914-17, between *two* imperialist coalitions, we must be against "defence of the fatherland", since (1) imperialism is the eve of socialism, (2) imperialist war is a war of thieves over their booty, (3) in *both* coalitions there is an *advanced* proletariat, (4) in both a socialist revolution is *ripe*. *Only* for these reasons are we against "defence of the fatherland", *only* for these reasons!!

Best greetings and wishes.

Yours,
Lenin

I have sent for the addresses of the youth organisations. They have been promised me.

And so, as regards the plan of publication: *push ahead* with the affair. And your lecture *on pacifism*?[273]

P.S. I got both your last two letters at once, but it must have been my own fault.

Written on January 19, 1917
Sent from Zurich to Clarens

First published in 1949   Printed from the original
in *Bolshevik* No. 1

119

TO INESSA ARMAND

Dear Friend,

Your lecture was yesterday, and I am impatiently waiting for news of how it went off. When I got your express letter on Thursday, I hurried to Radek at the other end of the town and collected some cuttings from him. I wanted very much to write you a long letter on pacifism (an extremely important subject in general, a basic one from the point of view of the whole international situation today, about which I wrote in the article*—I have received it, *merci!*— and lastly a particularly important subject *for Switzerland*). But I did not manage it: both on Thursday and on Friday we had meetings of the Lefts.

Things have gone badly for the Lefts here, because Nobs and Platten have become frightened of a war against Grimm, who *furiously attacked* the referendum[274] and frightened our young friends!! Sad!! In Berne, judging from Grigory's letters, things are better. Radek, at my insistence, has written a little pamphlet against the "Centre" here and Grimm, but yesterday the "Lefts" defeated (!!) the plan that it should be published by the Lefts: they have been frightened by the fright of Nobs and Platten. What warriors! What Lefts!

I think you should consider your lecture last night a *rehearsal*, and make ready to repeat it in Geneva and La Chaux-de-Fonds. It is worth working up this subject,

---

* Reference is apparently to the article "Bourgeois Pacifism and Socialist Pacifism" (see present edition, Vol. 23, pp. 175-94).—*Ed.*

and lecturing on it *more* than once. It will do the Swiss a tremendous lot of good. Write in as much *detail* as possible *how* you put the question, *what* arguments you advanced, what objections you met, etc.

Have the draft resolutions for the Swiss Congress on defence of the fatherland and the question of the war been translated into French? I mean translation in the *press*: *Grütlianer*, *Sentinelle*, etc. Or not?

It would be well to arrange for their translation, if it has not been done, and to think about agitation and propaganda.

Probably this question will go ahead in connection with your visit to Chaux-de-Fonds. I shall await news from you.

Abramovich is working wonderfully, and he should be supported in every possible way.

All possible greetings.

Yours,
Lenin

P.S. Trotsky has sent in a silly letter. We shall neither print it nor reply to him.

Has any campaign begun in the press of French Switzerland about (1) the referendum and (2) the resolutions on the war question for the Congress? Or is there *no* campaign? Do you see, and regularly, *Volksrecht* and *Berner Tagwacht*? This is essential now; we have to help the Swiss Lefts.

Did I write to you that Guilbeaux refused to sign the resolution against Grimm? (Or maybe you have heard this already from Grigory?) He's not up to much, our Guilbeaux; he's afraid of a war with Grimm, he's *afraid* of Sokolnikov, who is *afraid* of a split; he's afraid of Merrheim, who is afraid of "Monsieur" Jouhaux!! Well, what warriors!! I want to write about this to Olga.

Written on January 22, 1917
Sent from Zurich to Clarens

Published for the first time
in the Fourth (Russian) Edition
of the *Collected Works*

Printed from the original

120

TO INESSA ARMAND

Dear Friend,

I send you the cuttings I have taken from Radek (only up to Saturday: return them (to me) *immediately* after the lecture).

Note the paragraph in the resolution of the *Internationale* which declares against pacifism (against "persuasion").

The conference at The Hague and similar pacifist declarations and measures undertaken by the governments and the bourgeoisie are produced

(1) by hypocrisy

(2) by deception of the people

(3) by the *trend* of bourgeois pacifism, possessing "big" names and dreaming of *peace* without a social revolution. This trend has a *vast* literature (aristocratic, not for the people)

(4) by calculation: it is convenient sometimes for one, sometimes for another power to "show itself" peaceful, to gain time, etc.

This is in general. Concretely, one must study each particular case, and each power.

I *haven't* got the figures you ask for.

(The addresses have been sent: Abramovich and his friends are the best people to give a recommendation, *if required*.)

The key to the question of pacifism (a question most important for Switzerland): the idea that war is *not* connected with capitalism, is *not the continuation* of the politics of *peace*time. In this lies the theoretical falsity; the practical one is evasion of the social *revolution*.

In great haste. Greetings.

Yours,
Lenin

Written between January 22 and 30, 1917

Sent from Zurich to Clarens

First published in 1949
ı *Bolshevik* No. 1

Printed from the original

121

TO INESSA ARMAND

Dear Friend,

I have received the cuttings. *Merci*!

We were recently visited by two escaped prisoners of war. It was interesting to see "live" people, not corroded by emigrant life. As types: one is a Jew from Bessarabia, who has seen life, a Social-Democrat or nearly a Social-Democrat, has a brother who is a Bundist, etc. He has knocked about, but is uninteresting as an individual because commonplace. The second is a Voronezh peasant, a man of the soil, from an Old Believers' family. A breath from the Black Earth. It was extremely interesting to watch him and listen. He spent a year in a German prison camp (a mass of horrors) with 27,000 *Ukrainians*. The Germans build up camps according to nations, and do their utmost to break them away from Russia; for the Ukrainians they sent in skilful lecturers from Galicia. The results? Only 2,000, according to him, were for "self-rule" (independence in the sense more of autonomy than of separation) after months of effort by the agitators!! The remainder, he says, were furious at the thought of separation from Russia and going over to the Germans or Austrians.

A notable fact! One cannot but believe him. 27,000 is a big number. A year is ample time. The conditions for the Galician propaganda were exceptionally favourable. And yet closeness to the Great Russians got the upper hand! This does *not* imply, of course, that "freedom of separation" is in any way wrong. On the contrary. But it follows from this that, maybe, fate will free Russia from the "Austrian type" of development.

As regards defence of the fatherland our Voronezh man is like Troyanovsky and Plekhanov. He sympathises with socialism, but "if the Germans are pushing on, why shouldn't we defend ourselves?" He doesn't understand. He is deeply hurt (both he *and the Jew*!!) that the Germans are so mercilessly beating "our people". As regards the tsar and God, all the 27,000, he says, have finished with them completely, as regards the big landowners too. They will return to Russia embittered and enlightened.

All the yearning of the Voronezh man is to get back home, to the land, to his farm. He traipsed around the German villages working, kept his eyes open and learned a lot.

They praise the French (in the prison camps) as good comrades. "The Germans also curse their Kaiser." They hate the English: "Swelled heads; won't give you a piece of bread if you won't wash the floor for them" (that's the kind of swine you get, perverted by imperialism!).

To change the subject, what a splendid row has arisen over the referendum, especially its preamble! Delightful! You should have seen the articles by Grimm and Co. in *Berner Tagwacht* and the "provincial" Social-Democratic press! One continuous howl and groan! We've hit the scoundrels just where it hurt. I did my utmost to incite Radek (he is still here, and we are maintaining—you didn't expect it?— the *utmost* friendship, as always against the "Centre", when there is *no* ground for Radekite twisting, diplomacy about "rights", etc.) to write a little pamphlet: we walked about Zurich for hours with me "nagging" him. He sat down and wrote it. Our "Lefts", frightened by Nobs and Platten (those heroes were *frightened* by Grimm, who himself was frightened by Greulich and Co.!!), heard it read and *turned* it *down* (!!): it must not be printed, or they would be expelled from the Party (!!). We shall print it separately.

The situation is such that interest has been heightened, and that all who are *internationalists* not merely in words *must* help the Swiss workers and the Left. And we shall help them!

And yet another subject. I have been rereading Engels's *Zur Wohnungsfrage*[275] with his preface of 1887. Do you know it? Wonderful! I am still "in love" with Marx and Engels, and cannot calmly stand any abuse of them. No, these were real people! We must learn from them. We must not leave that basis. It was from *that* basis that both the social-chauvinists and the Kautskians departed. (By the way, have you seen the Loriot-Rappoport, Saumoneau resolution?[276] Also ³/₄ Kautskian. I want to write something for the French, to demolish it and pacifism as a whole. I will ask Grisha whether he will publish it. He did *not* reply about my answer to Souvarine!*). Well, each and every good wish, I've chattered three bags full.

All the best.

Yours,
Lenin

P.S. I hope that the referendum will bring much benefit in French Switzerland as well. I await news from Abramovich, Olga, etc.

Written on January 30, 1917
Sent from Zurich to Clarens

First published in 1949   Printed from the original
in *Bolshevik* No. 1

---

* See "An Open Letter to Boris Souvarine" (present edition, Vol. 23, pp. 195-204).—*Ed.*

122

TO INESSA ARMAND

Dear Friend,

I was very glad to have your letter. I like the plan of your lecture* very much. I advise you to be sure to repeat it, to challenge H. Droz to battle, to supplement the lecture with a section on the revolution (only perhaps the size of the lecture will not permit it?), i.e., *how* can the revolution take place, what is the dictatorship of the proletariat, why is it necessary, why is it *impossible* without arming the proletariat, why is it fully compatible with complete, all-round democracy (in spite of the vulgar opinion)?

Droz and the other Swiss social-pacifists do *not* understand it; they have *not* thought it out; and the Swiss conditions *d'un petit État et de la petite bourgeoisie d'un petit État*** *generate* in every possible way precisely pḅs (=petty-bourgeois) pacifism.

If you receive *Volksrecht* and *Berner Tagwacht* (it is *essential* to read these two papers), that is, in my opinion, enough for judging the position of the *Centre*, which is exactly the position of Grimm (the scoundrel! How fraudulently he "fights" the social-patriot Huber-Rohrschach!!), and to which both Nobs and Platten have ($^3/_4$) descended. You are terribly mistaken if you are not joking, when you write of my "influence" on Platten. This is how matters

---

* A lecture on pacifism.—*Ed.*
** of a little state and of the petty bourgeoisie of a little state.— *Ed.*

stand: he and Nobs "put themselves down" as Lefts at Zimmerwald and Kienthal. I made dozens of attempts to draw them into discussions, a study circle, talks. All in vain!! They are *afraid* of Grimm and of a struggle against him. They are $^3/_4$ in the "Centre". They are *almost* hopeless. Perhaps a strong movement of the Left will straighten them out, but even that is hardly likely!

Today we have not yet received the corrected resolution. We hope for it tomorrow.

Münzenberg told me yesterday that on Tuesday they are having a conference of the Young from German- and French-speaking Switzerland. By that time we must have *our* resolution on the question of the war. (Radek undertook to draft one, but so far has *not* produced it.) My opinion is that you should set to work as hard as you can, so as *before* Tuesday to be able (1) to write to Geneva and Ch.-de-F.* that for the time being they should take *my* theses (the paragraphs on the question of the war, section I) as a basis; (2) to discover who will be at the meeting of the Young from French Switzerland; (3) to "work them over", "instruct" them, so that they understand what really distinguishes us from (α) social-pacifism and (β) the "Centre" (=Grimm and Co.). (Platten has understood absolutely nothing, and doesn't want to learn.) Our position, in general, =Karl Liebknecht, the struggle against social-patriotism and the Centre of *one's own* country; the inseparable connection between the struggle against the war and the struggle against opportunism, and *all-round* and *immediate revolutionary* work *for* the socialist revolution.

The preamble to the referendum, by the way, =the first step to a platform of the *Left* in Switzerland. *N.B.* this.

On Tuesday the Young from French Switzerland will definitely put forward a draft Left resolution and fight for it. I have not yet seen the corrections, but I am sure that he is *injuring* the cause (reconciling and muddling the differences between the Left and the Swiss social-patriots, not opening them up. In this lies the whole essence and the whole foulness of Grimm's articles in *Berner Tagwacht* and *Neues Leben* about the majority and the minority).

* La Chaux-de-Fonds. —Ed.

Try to make friends with the French internees, start corresponding with them, make contacts, *found* (a secret and informal) group of *Lefts* among them. *Most* important!

The slogan of "a mass movement" is not bad, but it is *not* completely correct. Because it forgets the *revolution*, the *conquest of power*, the *dictatorship of the proletariat*. N.B. this!! Or more correctly: the support and development (at once) of every kind of *revolutionary* mass actions, *with the object* of bringing nearer the *revolution, etc.*

Platten = a muddlehead. With Scheidemann or with Liebknecht? he asks, not understanding that the very thing Grimm is doing is "reconciling", uniting, *confusing* the Swiss social-patriots (Greulich and Co.) and the Swiss "Left", who are *quite politically unconscious*!!!

You are right: revolutionary struggle against the high cost of living, strikes, demonstrations, etc., *at once*. At once "go to the people", i.e., to the *masses*, to the *majority* of the oppressed, preaching the *socialist revolution* (i.e., taking over the banks and *all* large-scale enterprises).

Very best wishes.

Yours,
Lenin

Written on February 3, 1917

Sent from Zurich to Clarens

Published for the first time
in the Fourth (Russian) Edition
of the *Collected Works*

Printed from the original

123

TO ALEXANDRA KOLLONTAI

February 17, 1917

Dear A. M.,

We had your letter today, and were very glad to get it. For a long time we did not know that you were in America, and had no letters from you except one, telling us that you were leaving America.

I wrote to you on January 7-8 (the day the letter was forwarded from Stockholm—all the letters direct from here to America are intercepted by the French!), but evidently this letter (with an article for *Novy Mir*) did not reach you while you were still in New York.

Pleasant as it was to learn from you of the victory of N. Iv. and Pavlov in *Novy Mir* (I get this newspaper devilishly irregularly; it must be the fault of the post and not the dispatch department of the paper itself), it was just as sad to read about the bloc between Trotsky and the Right for the struggle against N. Iv. What a swine this Trotsky is—Left phrases, and a bloc with the Right against the Zimmerwald Left!! He ought to be exposed (by you) if only in a brief letter to *Sotsial-Demokrat*!

I have already received No. 1 of *The Internationalist*, and am very glad of it. I have inadequate information about the conference of the S.L.P. and the S.P. on January 6-7, 1917. It appears that the S.L.P. is throwing out all its minimum programme (there is a temptation and a danger for Bukharin, who has been stumbling "at that there spot" since 1915!!). It is a great pity that I cannot collect all the documents about the S.L.P. (I asked Bukharin about it, but letters clearly get lost). Have you any material? I could return it after reading.

I am preparing (have almost got the material ready) an article on the question of the attitude of Marxism to the state.[277] I have come to conclusions which are even sharper against Kautsky than against Bukharin (have you seen his "Nota Bene" in No. 6 of *Jugend-Internationale?* and *Sbornik Sotsial-Demokrata* No. 2*?). The question is exceptionally important. Bukharin is far better than Kautsky, but Bukharin's mistakes may *destroy* this "just cause" in the struggle with Kautskianism.

I will send you my article about self-determination against P. Kievsky.** What a pity we have no money! We would publish *Sbornik Sotsial-Demokrata* No. 3 (all the material is *ready and waiting*) and No. 4 (Bukharin's article about the state, which we rejected at first, and my article on the state)!

The Zimmerwald Right, in my opinion, has ideologically buried Zimmerwald: Bourderon+Merrheim in Paris voted for *pacifism*, Kautsky also on January 7, 1917 in Berlin, Turati (December 17, 1916!!) and the whole Italian party also. This is the death of Zimmerwald!! In words they *condemned* "social-pacifism" (see the Kienthal resolution), while in practice they have turned towards it!!

Grimm has basely turned towards the social-patriots within the Swiss party (our friend in Stockholm will send you material about it), entering into a bloc with them on January 7, 1917 (*Parteivorstandssitzung***) *against the Left* for postponement of the Congress!! And now he has even more basely attacked the Left for the *Begründung des Referendums**** (we shall send it to you) and drawn up a "mid-way", "Centrist" resolution. Have you got the Zurich *Volksrecht*, or can you get it?? If not, we shall send you something, or try to.

---

* See "The Youth International" (present edition, Vol. 23, pp. 163-66).—*Ed.*
** See present edition, Vol. 23, pp. 28-76.—*Ed.*
*** The session of the Party Executive.—*Ed.*
**** The preamble to the referendum.—*Ed.*

Tomorrow (February 18) is the Congress of the Swedish party. Probably a split? It seems as though there are *devilish* dissension and confusion among the Young.[278] Do you know Swedish? Could you arrange contributions (by me and other Lefts) to the newspaper of the Swedish Young?

Please reply, if only briefly, but *quickly* and regularly, because it's terribly important for us to organise *good* correspondence with you.

Best greetings.

Yours,
Lenin

Sent from Zurich to Christiania (Oslo)

First published in 1924
in *Lenin Miscellany II*

Printed from the original

124

TO INESSA ARMAND

Dear Friend,

The other day we had a gratifying letter from Moscow (we shall soon send you a copy, although the text is uninteresting). They write that the mood of the masses is a good one, that chauvinism is clearly declining and that probably our day will come. The organisation, they say, is suffering from the fact that the adults are at the front, while in the factories there are young people and women. But the fighting spirit, they say, is not any the less. They send us the copy of a leaflet (a good one) issued by the Moscow Bureau of the Central Committee.[279] We shall print it in the next issue of the Central Organ.

Richard is himself again! It's difficult for people to live, and for our Party in particular. But still they do live.

There is also a letter from Kollontai, who (let this be *entre nous* for the time being) has returned to Norway from America. N. Iv. and Pavlov (the Lett who was in Brussels: Pavel Vasilyevich) had *won Novy Mir*, she says (I get this paper very irregularly), but ... Trotsky arrived, and this scoundrel at once ganged up with the *Right* wing of *Novy Mir* against the Left Zimmerwaldists!! That's it!! That's Trotsky for you!! Always true to himself =twists, swindles, poses as a Left, *helps* the Right, so long as he can....

Among the Left in America, she says, things are not going badly, though Kollontai is afraid of anarcho-syndicalist tendencies in the S.L.P. (N. Iv., she says, is not afraid of this). I have read in the S.L.P. organ (*The Weekly People*)[280] that they are throwing overboard their minimum

programme.... N. Iv. has been stumbling "at that there
spot" since 1915. I fear for him! But the post to America
is *not* working.

I have been putting in a lot of study recently on the
question of the attitude of Marxism to the *state*; I have
collected a lot of material and arrived, it seems to me,
at very interesting and important conclusions, *much more*
against Kautsky than against N. Iv. Bukharin (who, however, is not right all the same, though *nearer* to the truth
than Kautsky). I would terribly much like to write about this:
perhaps publish No. *4* of *Sbornik Sotsial-Demokrata* with
Bukharin's article, and with my discussion of his little
mistakes and Kautsky's big lying and vulgarisation of
Marxism.

Nadya is ill: she has caught bronchitis and has a temperature. It looks as though she will be in bed for some time.
I called in the doctor today.

Well, and what about your visit to La Chaux-de-Fonds?
Have you given up this idea altogether, and all your plans
about work in French Switzerland? You should not let that
drop. Things here, as I wrote, are not very good, yet today
we have finished *leaflet No. 1*[281] ("the Swiss group of
Zimmerwald Lefts"). We shall see what happens!

If not now, then in general (i.e., a little later) we shall
succeed (I am sure)—if not we, then our successors—in
building up a Left *trend* in Switzerland. The *ground* for
this exists!

Have you read the propositions of the Left at the Congress of the Zurich cantonal party at Töss,[282] February 11,
1917? in *Volksrecht*? Not bad all the same, eh?

All the very best greetings and handshakes. Excuse the
scribble on the last page: I am being hurried.

Yours,
Lenin

Written on February 19, 1917

Sent from Zurich to Clarens

First published in 1949   Printed from the original
in *Bolshevik* No. 1

125

TO ALEXANDRA KOLLONTAI

March 5, 1917

Dear A. M.,

Newspaper reports speak of a congress of the Young being called in Sweden on May 12 to found a new party "on Zimmerwald principles".

I must admit that this news particularly disturbs and angers me. For "Zimmerwald" is clearly bankrupt, and a good word is once again serving to cover up decay! The Zimmerwald majority—Turati and Co., Kautsky and Ledebour, Merrheim—have *all* gone over to the position of social-pacifism, condemned so solemnly (and so fruitlessly!) at Kienthal. The manifesto of Kautsky and Co. of January 7, 1917, a number of resolutions of the Italian Socialist Party, the resolutions of Merrheim—Jouhaux and Longuet—Bourderon (+Raffin-Dugens in *unity* with Renaudel), is not this the bankruptcy of Zimmerwald? And the Zimmerwald "Centre"—R. Grimm, who on January 7, 1917 entered into an *alliance* with the social-patriots of Switzerland to fight the Left!! Grimm, who abuses the social-patriots of *all* countries *except* the Swiss, whom he *covers up*! *C'est dégoûtant!** I am beside myself with fury at these scoundrels; it is revolting to listen to them and to hear about them; it is even more revolting to think of working with them. Buffoonery!

We intend to collect material for you about this bankruptcy of R. Grimm. Write whether you can get the Zurich *Volksrecht*. You will find the *principal* material there in

---

* It is disgusting!—*Ed.*

the *preamble* to the referendum, in the resolution of the *Left* at Töss (February 11, 1917), etc., etc.

But the majority of the Swedish Left, *I am sure*, are sincere. This is clear. And it is necessary at all costs to help them before May 12 to understand *beforehand* the utter banality of social-pacifism and Kautskianism, all the vileness of the Zimmerwald majority, to help them work out a good programme and tactics for themselves, for the new party.

Really, we must (all of us, the Left in Sweden and those who can get into touch with them) unite, bend every effort, help—for the moment in the life of the Swedish party, the Swedish *and Scandinavian* labour movement, is a *decisive* one.

Since you read Swedish (and speak it too), a considerable share of responsibility falls on you, if we understand "internationalism" not in the sense of "it's no concern of mine".

I am sure you are doing a great deal. One would like to rally and unite the Lefts to help the Swedes at such a difficult moment in their life. Could not one organise in Christiania, Copenhagen and Stockholm for this purpose a group of Russian Bolsheviks and Lefts who know Swedish and can help? The work could be divided: to collect the main documents and articles (I was sent the polemic between Nerman and Mauritz Västberg in *Politiken* of November 28, 1916 on the theme, "first a programme, then a new party"— but I could not understand it); to work out one's own theses to help them; to print a number of articles to aid them. Swedes able to *write* in German, French or English could also enter such a group.*

What is your opinion, is this possible or not? Is it worth while worrying with it?

My opinion is that it is worth while, but of course I am not in a position to judge from far away, outside. I only see and *know* in the firmest way possible that the question of the programme and tactics of a *new* socialism, genuinely revolutionary Marxism and not rotten Kautskianism, *is*

---

* What sort of a figure is Lindhagen? "S.R."? "Narodnik"? "Radical-socialist"? Hervé?

on the agenda *everywhere*. This is clear both from the S.L.P.
and *The Internationalist* in America, and from the data
about Germany (the resolutions of the Lefts, January 7,
1917) and about France (the pamphlet of the Lefts in Paris,
Les socialistes de Zimmerwald et la guerre*), *and so on*.

In Denmark *Trier* and others would, I am sure, join in
the cause of setting up a new, *Marxist*, party in Scandinavia; part of the Norwegian Lefts also. The struggle with
Branting and Co. is a serious business: necessity *must* force
them to take a more serious attitude to questions of the
theory and tactics of revolutionary Marxism.

In my opinion, the work of preparing for May 12 should
be pushed *intensively*, and from *three* sides simultaneously:
(1) the assistance group mentioned earlier; (2) groups of
the Scandinavian Lefts: write an article (in the Swedish
papers) about the necessity of founding *at once* such groups
to prepare a programme and tactics for May 12.

(3)—the third interests me particularly, *not* because it
is the most important (initiative from within is more
important), but because *we* can help here. If, for example,
you were *immediately*, after looking through the main
literature of the Left and Right in Sweden, to rough out
on the basis of it theses on these lines:

theoretical (programme) and practical (tactical) differences

> defence of the fatherland;
> conception of imperialism;
> character of the war;
> disarmament;
> social-pacifism;

+ dicta-
torship
of the
prole-
tariat
{
> the nationalities question;
> revolution;
> "mass actions";
> civil war;
> attitude to trade unions;
> opportunism and struggle against it,
> *etc.*

Every thesis should include (a) what has been said about
it ("the *essence*") by the Left in Sweden; (b) by the Right
there.

---

* *The Socialists of Zimmerwald and the War.—Ed.*

On this basis, taking account of the position of the Left in Russia, Germany and America (the main countries in this respect), we could work out our own theses and, by publishing them in Swedish, *help* the Swedes to make preparations for May 12.

Some of the *main* points from the *most important* resolutions and articles of the Right and the Left wing in Sweden ought for this purpose to be translated into Russian or German or French or English.

In essence, morally and politically, we are all responsible for the Swedish Young and must help them.

You are in an exceptionally favourable position to give such aid. Write at once what you think about it.

It would be useful, probably, to send this letter on to Lyudmila also, together with your views.

All the very best. I wish you every success.

Yours,
Lenin

Sent from Zurich to Christiania (Oslo)

First published in 1924   Printed from the original
in *Lenin Miscellany II*

126

TO INESSA ARMAND

Dear Friend,

I enclose the leaflet and my best congratulations on it.

Don't give it to anyone as yet: it would be a good thing if no one knew that it comes *partly* from the Russians. May not Usiyevich or someone *near* him have blabbed?

Let the distribution be made by the *Swiss* groups.

We here in Zurich are in a state of agitation today: there is a telegram in *Zürcher Post* and in *Neue Zürcher Zeitung* of March 15 that in Russia the revolution *was victorious* in Petrograd on March 14 after three days of struggle, that 12 members of the Duma are in power and the ministers *have all been arrested*.

If the Germans are not lying, then it's true.

That Russia has for the last few days been *on the eve* of revolution is beyond doubt.

I am *beside* myself that I cannot go to Scandinavia!! I will not forgive myself for not risking the journey in 1915!

Best greetings.

Yours,
Lenin

Written on March 15, 1917

Sent from Zurich to Clarens

Published for the first time
in the Fourth (Russian) Edition
of the *Collected Works*

Printed from the original

127

TO ALEXANDRA KOLLONTAI

March 16, 1917

Dear A. M.,

We have just received the second set of government telegrams about the revolution of March 1 (14) in Petrograd. A week of bloody battles by the workers—and Milyukov+ Guchkov+Kerensky[283] in power!! On the "old" European pattern....

Well, what of it! This "first stage of the first revolution (among those engendered by the war)" will not be the last, nor will it be only Russian. Of course, we shall continue to be against defence of the fatherland, against the imperialist slaughter controlled by Shingaryov[284]+Kerensky and Co.

All our watchwords remain the same. In the last issue of *Sotsial-Demokrat* we actually spoke of the possibility of a government "of Milyukov and Guchkov, if not of Milyukov and Kerensky".* It turned out that it was *both ... and*: all three together. Lovely! We shall see how the party of people's freedom (after all, it's in a majority in the new ministry, since Konovalov[285] is even just a little "more Left", while Kerensky is certainly more Left!) will give the people freedom, bread and peace.... We shall see!

The main thing now is the press and the organisation of the workers in a *revolutionary* Social-Democratic party. Chkhenkeli[286] must now (he promised!) provide funds for "defence of the fatherland". While Mr. Chkheidze, although he did utter ultra-Left speeches *during* the revolution or on its eve (when Yefremov, too, spoke in no less

---

* See "A Turn in World Politics" (present edition, Vol. 23, pp. 262-70).—*Ed.*

rrrevolutionary fashion), of course, does not deserve
one atom of confidence after all his "politics" with Potresov
and Co., with Chkhenkeli, etc. It would be the greatest
misfortune if the Cadets were now to promise a legal
workers' party, and if our people accepted "unity" with
Chkheidze and Co.!!

But this will not happen. First, the Cadets will not allow
anyone a legal workers' party except the Potresovs and
Co. Secondly, if they do allow it, we shall set up as before
our *own* separate party and *without fail* combine legal work
with illegal.

On no account a repetition of something like the Second
International! *On no account* with Kautsky! Definitely a
more revolutionary programme and tactics (there are elements of it in K. Liebknecht, the S.L.P. in America, the
Dutch Marxists, etc.) and definitely the combination of
legal and illegal work. Republican propaganda, the struggle
against imperialism, *as before* revolutionary propaganda,
agitation and struggle with the aim of an *international* proletarian revolution and the conquest of power by
the "Soviets of Workers' Deputies" (and not the Cadet
swindlers).

... After the "great rebellion" of 1905—the "glorious
revolution"* of 1917!...

Be so kind as to forward this letter to Lyudmila, and
drop me a line as to how far we are in agreement, or how
far we differ, and also as to the plans of A. M., etc. If our
deputies[287] are allowed to return, one must definitely be
brought for a couple of weeks to Scandinavia. All the best.

Yours,
Lenin

Sent from Zurich to Christiania (Oslo)

First published in *Pravda*   Printed from the original
. No. 169, July 27, 1924

----

* "great rebellion" and "glorious revolution" were written by
Lenin in English.—*Ed.*

128

TO ALEXANDRA KOLLONTAI

March 17, 1917

Dear A. M.,

I have just had your telegram, worded so that it sounds almost ironical (just imagine thinking about "directives" from here, when news is exceptionally meagre, while in Petersburg there are probably not only effectively leading comrades of our Party, but also formally commissioned representatives of the Central Committee!).

Only just this minute I have read the telegram of the Petersburg Telegraph Agency of the 17th giving the programme of the new government, and the news about Bonar Law's statement that the tsar has not yet abdicated and that no one knows where he is.

Yesterday it seemed that the Guchkov-Milyukov government was already completely victorious and had already come to an agreement with the dynasty. Today the situation is that the dynasty does not exist and the tsar has fled, clearly preparing for a counter-revolution!...

We have begun working out theses which we shall perhaps finish this evening and then, naturally, will immediately forward to you. If possible, wait for these theses, which correct (*resp.* cancel) what I am writing now in my own name only, so far.

—Zinoviev and I have just managed to draw up a first draft of the theses, *a rough one*, very unsatisfactory in the editorial sense (of course, we shall not print it *in this form*). but giving, I hope, an idea of the main point.

We earnestly ask you to acquaint Yuri and Eug. B. with it, and also Lyudmila, and likewise to drop us at least a

line or two before you leave*—and also *make certain* to
arrange with someone who is *staying* in Norway to forward
our material to Russia and *Russian* material to us. Please
do this, and ask this comrade remaining behind (or a Norwegian comrade who knows German, French or English) to
be *exceptionally* efficient. We shall send money for the
expenses.

In my opinion, the main thing now is not to let oneself
get entangled in stupid "unification" attempts with the
social-patriots (or, what is still more dangerous, with the
wobblers like the Organising Committee, Trotsky and Co.)
and to continue the work of *our* Party in a consistently
internationalist spirit.

What is now on the agenda is expansion of the work,
organisation of the masses, awakening of new sections—the
backward, the rural, domestic servants—Party cells in the
forces for systematic and detailed *Entlarvung*** of the new
government, and preparation for the conquest of power by
the *Soviets of Workers' Deputies*. Only such a power *can*
give bread, *peace* and liberty.

What is needed today is to finish off the reactionaries,
not a shadow of confidence or support for the new
government (not a shadow of confidence in Kerensky,
Gvozdyov,[288] Chkhenkeli, Chkheidze[289] and Co.) and
armed temporising, *armed preparation* of a *wider* base for
a *higher* stage.

If there is freedom of the press, republish (as material
for the history of the recent past) our writings here, and
inform us by cable whether we can help by writing from
here through Scandinavia. We are afraid that it will be
some time before we succeed in leaving accursed Switzerland.

All the best.

Yours,
Lenin

I wish you every kind of success!

---

* Alexandra Kollontai and other Bolsheviks were leaving for
Russia.—*Ed.*
** Exposure.—*Ed.*

P .S. I am afraid that there will now be an *epidemic* in Petersburg "simply" of excitement, without systematic work on a party of a *new* type. It *must not* be à *la* "Second International". Wider! Raise up new elements! Awaken a new initiative, new organisations in all sections, and *prove* to them that *peace* will be brought only by an armed Soviet of Workers' Deputies, if it takes power.

Sent from Zurich to Christiania (Oslo)

First published in *Pravda* No. 169, July 27, 1924

Printed from the original

129

TO V. A. KARPINSKY

Dear Vyach. Al.,

I am considering every possible way of travelling.* The following is an absolute secret. Please reply to me immediately and, perhaps, best by express (I think we won't ruin the Party by a dozen extra express letters), so that I can be sure no one has read the letter.

Take out papers in your own name for travelling to France and England, and I will *use them* to travel through England (and *Holland*) to Russia.

I can put on a wig.

The photograph will be taken of *me* with the wig on, and *I* shall go to the Consulate in Berne with your papers and wearing the wig.

You must then disappear from Geneva for a minimum of a few weeks (until my telegram arrives from Scandinavia): for this period you must hide yourself well away in the mountains, where, *we shall, of course, pay* for your board and lodging.

If you agree, begin *preparations immediately* in the most energetic (and most secret) fashion, and drop me a line at once in any case.

Yours,
Lenin

Think over all the practical steps *involved* and write to me in detail. I am writing to you because I am convinced that between us everything will remain *absolutely* secret.

Written on March 19, 1917
Sent from Zurich to Geneva

First published in *Pravda* No. 92,
April 22, 1926

Printed from the original

* Of returning to Russia.—*Ed.*

130

TO V. A. KARPINSKY

Dear Comrade,

I have sent you (through Inessa) copies of two of my articles for *Pravda*—for information, to co-ordinate our views.

I need them back on *Monday*: if necessary, send them express and take them to the station.

Be careful about blocs with the *Nachalo*[290] people: we are against rapprochement with other parties, are *for* warning the workers *against* Chkheidze. Essential! Chkheidze is clearly wobbling: cf. how he is being praised in the *Temps* of March 22 and in many other papers. We are *for* the C.C. in Russia, *for Pravda*, *for* our Party, *for* a proletarian militia preparing the way for peace and socialism.

Greetings!

Yours,
Lenin

Written on March 24, 1917

Sent from Zurich to Geneva

First published in 1930
in *Lenin Miscellany XIII*

Printed from the original

131

TO A. V. LUNACHARSKY[291]

Dear Comrade Anatoly Vasilyevich,

As regards a conference, my *personal* opinion (I am sending on your letter to Zinoviev) is that it is expedient now only between people who are ready to warn the proletariat not only against the Gvozdyov supporters,[292] but also against the *waverings of Chkheidze*.

In this, I believe, is the essence of our inner-Party and, if one may use the term, near-Party situation.

It is just for this reason that I am *not* wasting time on a single conference with Martov and Co.

Independence and separateness of our Party, *no rapprochement with other parties*, are indispensable conditions for me. Without this one cannot help the proletariat to move through the *democratic* revolution to the *commune*, and I would not serve any other ends.

I personally would be *for* a conference with people and groups who agree on this basic point.

I should be very glad to have a talk with you, without any formal conferences, and should consider it *valuable* for myself personally (and for the cause).

With all my heart I congratulate you, too, and shake your hand, and send greetings as well from N. K. to you both.

With fraternal greetings,
Lenin

My address:
Wl. Uljanow. Spiegelgasse. 14^{II} (bei Kammerer). Zürich. I.

Written earlier than March 25, 1917
Sent from Zurich to Geneva
First published in 1934
in *Lenin Miscellany XXVI*

Printed from the original

132

TO V. A. KARPINSKY

Dear Comrade,

I have sent you through Inessa copies of my two letters to *Pravda*. I hope you have done what I asked, and today (Sunday) or tomorrow have sent them back to me *by express*.

After Tuesday (I am lecturing here on Tuesday evening) I will send you a copy of letter No. 3.* Then, I think, it will be easy for us to *come to an agreement* about tactics.

Lunacharsky has written to me proposing a "conference". I have replied: I am agreeable to having a talk with you (Lunacharsky) personally.** (He will be coming to Zurich.) I am agreeable to a conference, however, *only* on condition that the workers are warned *against* the waverings of Chkheidze. He (Lunacharsky) *has said nothing*.

So it means that we shall confine ourselves to a *personal* talk.

Chkheidze is obviously *wobbling*: cf. *Le Temps* of March 22 *praises* Chkheidze, while on March 24 it *abuses* him.

The picture is clear!!

Therefore I am a little afraid that you have been in too much of a hurry to draw up a general resolution[293] (I have sent it to *Pravda* today, together with my article, addressed to Herrn Fürstenberg, Boulevard Hotel, *Kristiania*. You can send articles there, with a note that the articles are for *Pravda*, and that I supplied the address; as to articles on questions of *principle*, it would be useful for us to reach preliminary agreement).

---

* See present edition, Vol. 23, pp. 320-32.—*Ed.*
** See the previous letter.—*Ed.*

Pravda, probably, *needs* articles. At any rate I am writing, and *I am advising all friends to write*.

I fear that you are too much in a hurry also to unite with the *Vperyod* group.

In your resolution the ending is good (I had time only to look through it *rapidly*: it had to go off), but the beginning (about democracy in general) seemed to me very bad.

As regards unity with *Vperyod*. I sent a telegram to Scandinavia to the members of our Party who are leaving:

" Notre tactique: méfiance absolue, aucun soutien nouveau gouvernement, Kerensky surtout soupçonnons, armement prolétariat seule garantie, élection immédiate douma de Petrograd *aucun rapprochement autres partis.*"*

The last is *conditio sine qua non*.

We don't trust Chkheidze.

Our deputies and Kamenev are *already* in Petersburg, *or* will be there in a few days. There is a *Central Committee* in Petersburg (*Frankfurter Zeitung* printed extracts from its manifesto, *lovely!*), *Pravda* exists. We are for preservation of *this* party *absolutely*, against all fusions with the Organising Committee.

(Probably there is *no* O.C. in Petersburg, since *Frankfurter Zeitung* and *Vossische Zeitung* gave a detailed account of the *manifesto* of Chkheidze and Co. of March 16,[294] and there is *not a word* about the O.C. there.)

It is precisely for the elections to the Constituent Assembly (or for the overthrow of the government of Guchkov and Milyukov) that we *must have* a separate party, ours, which has in my opinion *completely* justified itself during the years 1914-17.

That means? Do the Vperyodists want *honestly* to join this party?

Bon!

They don't want to? I won't agree to "concessions" and "bargaining".

---

* "Our tactics: absolute distrust, no support for the new government, suspect Kerensky above all, arming of the proletariat the only guarantee, immediate elections to the Petrograd Duma, *no rapprochement with other parties.*"—*Ed.*

Have a talk with them, *as man to man* and *more than once*, and drop me a line, so that I have your reply by Tuesday (or at latest Wednesday morning).

Will you undertake to type in two copies (or in one copy) my manuscript* of 500 pages (written on octavo), *for payment not less than last time*? I would then publish it at once in Petersburg.

You will oblige me greatly!

Reply.

All the best.

Yours,
Lenin

P.S. Lyudmila has *left* Stockholm. Don't use Stockholm as an address!

P.P.S. Will you and Olga go to Russia, if there is an opportunity, and when? Who else would go from Geneva?

Written on March 25, 1917

Sent from Zurich to Geneva

First published in full in 1930
in *Lenin Miscellany XIII*

Printed from the original

---

* Reference is to Lenin's *The Agrarian Programme of Social-Democracy in the First Russian Revolution, 1905-1907* (see present edition, Vol. 13, pp. 217-431).—*Ed.*

133

TO INESSA ARMAND

Dear Friend,

You must be in an excessively nervous state. This is my explanation for a number of theoretical "oddities" in your letters.

We should not distinguish the first and the second revolution, or the first and the second stage??

That's just what we have to do. Marxism requires that we should distinguish the *classes* which are in action. In Russia *it is not the same* class as before that is in power. Consequently, the revolution which lies ahead is quite, quite *different*.

My phrase about support of the workers by the Milyukovs has (it seemed to me) a clear sense; *if* the Milyukovs really wanted to finish off the monarchy, they *should have* supported the workers. Only that!

One must not make a "fetish" out of revolution. Kerensky is a revolutionary, but a chatterbox, a petty liar, a deceiver of the workers. It is almost certain that *even* in the Petrograd "Soviet of Workers' and Soldiers' Deputies" the *majority* has been fooled by him (with the help of the wobbling and muddling Chkheidze). And what will happen to the countryside?

It is *quite* possible that *for a time* the majority both of the workers and of the peasants will really be *for* the imperialist war (which the Guchkovs+Milyukovs are representing as "defence of the Republic").

It would be a good thing if someone with free time (better still a group, but if one doesn't exist, then at least an individual) undertook to *collect all* the telegrams (and articles if possible) in *all* the foreign newspapers about the Russian revolution.

There are mountains of material. It is impossible to follow it all.

Probably we *won't* manage to get to Russia!! Britain *will not let us through*. It can't be done through Germany.

Greetings!

Lenin

Written between March 25 and 31, 1917

Sent from Zurich to Clarens

Published for the first time   Printed from the original
in the Fourth (Russian) Edition
of the *Collected Works*

134

TO J. S. HANECKI[295]

March 30, 1917

Dear Comrade,

I thank you with all my heart for the trouble you are taking and for your help. I cannot, of course, make use of the services of people who are connected with the publisher of *Die Glocke*.[296] I cabled you today that the only hope of breaking out of here is by an exchange of emigrants in Switzerland for German internees. Britain will on no account let me through, or any internationalists at all, neither Martov and his friends nor Natanson and his friends. The British sent Chernov back to France, although he had all his papers for transit!! It is clear that the Russian *proletarian* revolution has no more malignant enemy than the British imperialists. It is clear that Milyukov (and Co.), agents of Anglo-French imperialist capital, and Russian imperialists themselves, are capable of *everything*—deception, treachery, and everything else—in order to prevent the internationalists returning to Russia. The least confidence in this respect either in Milyukov or in Kerensky (an empty chatterer, an agent of the Russian imperialist bourgeoisie in his objective role) would be simply ruinous for the working-class movement and for our Party, and would border on betrayal of internationalism. The only—without exaggeration, the only—hope for us to get to Russia is to send as soon as possible a reliable person to Russia, to secure from the government, by pressure from the "Soviet of Workers' Deputies", an *exchange* of all the emigrants in Switzerland for interned Germans. It is necessary to act with the maximum energy, making a record of every step, not sparing expense on telegrams, and collecting documents against Milyukov and Co., who are capable of dragging matters out, feeding us with promises, swindling, etc. You can imagine what torture it is for all of us to be sitting here at such a time.

Furthermore, the dispatch of a reliable person to Russia is *still more necessary* for reasons of principle. The latest information in the foreign press gives clearer and clearer indications that the government, with the direct help of Kerensky and thanks to the (putting it mildly) unforgivable wobblings of Chkheidze, is swindling—and swindling *not without success*—the working class, representing the imperialist war as a "defensive" one. Judging from the telegram of the St. Petersburg Telegraph Agency of March 30, 1917. Chkheidze has allowed himself to be completely deceived by this slogan, adopted also by the Soviet of Workers' Deputies —if this source, generally unreliable of course, is to be believed. At all events, even if the report is untrue, the *danger* of such a deception is all the same undoubtedly *vast*. All the efforts of our Party must be concentrated on fighting it. Our Party would disgrace itself for ever, commit political suicide, if it tolerated such a deception. To judge from one report, Muranov returned from Kronstadt *together with Skobelev*. If Muranov went there *on behalf* of the Provisional Government of the Guchkovs and Milyukovs, I very much ask you to pass on (through someone reliable), *and to print*, that I *absolutely condemn this*, that any rapprochement with those who are wobbling in the direction of social-patriotism and have taken up the profoundly mistaken, profoundly harmful social-pacifist, Kautskian, position of Chkheidze and Co. is, I am deeply convinced, *harmful* for the working class, *dangerous*, *inadmissible*.

I hope you have received my "Letters from Afar" Nos. 1-4,* in which I developed the theoretical and political foundation for these views. If these letters have been lost, or did not reach Petrograd, please cable me, and I will send you copies.

---

* See present edition, Vol. 23, pp. 295-342.—*Ed.*

There is no doubt that in the Petrograd Soviet of Workers' and Soldiers' Deputies there are numerous, even, it seems, a majority of, (1) supporters of Kerensky, a most dangerous agent of the imperialist bourgeoisie, pursuing imperialism, i.e., the defence and justification of a plundering war of conquest *on Russia's part*, under cover of an ocean of sounding phrases and empty promises, (2) supporters of Chkheidze, who is wobbling hopelessly in the direction of social-patriotism and sharing all the philistinism and stupidity of Kautskianism. Our Party is obliged to carry on the most stubborn, the most highly principled, the most pressing and most merciless struggle against *both*-currents. And I personally will not hesitate for a second to declare, and to declare in print, that I shall prefer even an immediate split with anyone in our Party, whoever it may be, to making concessions to the social-patriotism of Kerensky and Co. or the social-pacifism and Kautskianism of Chkheidze and Co.

I must at all costs demand the republication in Petrograd —if only under the title: *From the History of the Last Years of Tsarism*—of the *Sotsial-Demokrat* published here, of the pamphlet by Lenin and Zinoviev on the war and socialism,[297] of *Kommunist* and *Sbornik Sotsial-Demokrata*. But most of all, and first of all, the theses in No. 47 of *Sotsial-Demokrat* (of October 13, 1915).* These theses are now exceptionally important.

These theses say directly, clearly, precisely how we should act in a revolution in Russia, and they do it $1\frac{1}{2}$ years before the revolution.

These theses have been remarkably, literally confirmed by the revolution.

The war has *not* ceased, *and cannot cease*, to be imperialist on the part of Russia, so long as (1) the landowners and capitalists, representatives of the bourgeois *class*, are in power; (2) so long as such direct agents and servants of that bourgeoisie as Kerensky and the other social-patriots are in power; (3) so long as the treaties between tsarism and the Anglo-French imperialists remain in force (the Guchkov-Milyukov government has *openly* declared *abroad*—I don't

---

* Reference is to Lenin's article "Several Theses" (see present edition, Vol. 21, pp. 401-04).—*Ed.*

know whether it has done so in Russia—that it is *loyal* to these treaties). They are robber treaties, for the seizure of Galicia, Armenia, Constantinople, etc., etc.; (4) so long as these treaties have *not* been published and *not* annulled; (5) so long as the whole alliance between Russia and the Anglo-French bourgeois, imperialist governments has *not* been broken off altogether; (6) so long as state power in Russia has *not* passed *from* the imperialist bourgeoisie (mere promises and "pacifist" declarations, however much the stupid Kautsky, Chkheidze and Co. believe in them, do *not* transform the bourgeoisie into a *non*-bourgeoisie) *into the hands* of the proletariat, which *alone* is capable, on condition that it is supported by the poorer section of the peasantry, of breaking *not merely in words* but in deeds with the interests of capital, with imperialist policy, with the plundering of other countries, of emancipating the peoples oppressed by the Great Russians *completely*, withdrawing the troops from Armenia and Galicia *at once*, etc.; (7) only the proletariat is capable, if it rids itself of the influence of its national bourgeoisie, of winning the *genuine* confidence of the proletarians of *all* the belligerent countries, and entering into peace negotiations *with them*; (8) these proletarian peace terms are set forth precisely and clearly both in No. 47 of *Sotsial-Demokrat* and in my letter *No. 4*.

Hence it is clear that the watchword: "We are *now* defending the Republic in Russia, we are *now* carrying on a 'defensive war', we shall fight *Wilhelm*, we are fighting *for* the overthrow of Wilhelm" is the greatest deception, the greatest swindling of the workers!! For Guchkov-Lvov-Milyukov and Co. are landowners and capitalists, representatives of the *class* of landowners and capitalists, *imperialists* who are fighting for the *same* robber ends, on the basis of the same robber treaties concluded by tsarism, in alliance with the *same* imperialist robber bourgeoisie of Britain, France and Italy.

The appeal to the Germans by the bourgeois and *imperialist* republic in Russia—"Overthrow Wilhelm"—is a repetition of the lying slogan of the French social-chauvinists, traitors to socialism, Jules Guesde, Sembat and Co.

In a very popular way, very clearly, without learned words, it must be explained to the workers and soldiers that it is not only Wilhelm who has to be overthrown, but also the kings of Great Britain and Italy. That is first of all. And secondly, and *most important*, the *bourgeois* governments must be overthrown, *beginning with Russia*—for otherwise peace cannot be won. It may be that *we cannot* immediately "overthrow" the government of Guchkov-Milyukov. That may be so. But that is not an argument for *telling an untruth!!* The workers must be told the *truth*. We have to say that the government of Guchkov-Milyukov and Co. is an imperialist government, that the workers and peasants must *first of all* (now or after elections to the Constituent Assembly, if it is not used to deceive the people, if the elections are not postponed until after the war—the question of choice of moment cannot be decided from here), first of all must transfer *all* state power into the hands of the working class, the enemy of capital, the enemy of imperialist war, and only then will they have the *right* to appeal for the overthrow of *all* kings and *all* bourgeois governments.

For God's sake try and deliver all this to Petrograd and to *Pravda*, to Muranov and Kamenev and the others. For God's sake make every effort to send this with a most reliable person. It would be best of all if a reliable sensible chap like Kuba went (he would perform a great service to the whole world working-class movement) and helped our friends in Petrograd!! I hope you will do this!! Do everything in your power.

Conditions in Petrograd are exceptionally difficult. The republican patriots are straining *every* effort. They are trying to drown our Party in slander and dirt (the Chernomazov "affair": I am sending a document about it*), etc., etc.

There *cannot* be any confidence in Chkheidze and Co., or Sukhanov or Steklov and the like. No rapprochement with other parties, any of them! Not a shadow of confidence in or support for the government of Guchkov-Milyukov and Co.!! The most irreconcilable propaganda of internationalism and of struggle with republican chauvinism and social-chauvinism everywhere, both in the press and within the Soviet of Workers' Deputies; the organisation of *our* Party: this is

---

* Reference is to Lenin's article "Tricks of the Republican Chauvinists" (see present edition, Vol. 23, pp. 362-64).—*Ed.*

the essential. Kamenev must realise that he bears a *world*-historic responsibility.[298]

Don't grudge money on communications between Stockholm and Petrograd!!

I beg you very much, dear comrade, to cable me on receipt of this letter, and generally to keep me *au courant* in every respect. I hope the Swedish friends will also help in this.

All the best.

Yours,
Lenin

Sent from Zurich to Stockholm

First published in 1921
in *Proletarskaya Revolutsia* No. 2

Printed from the original

135

TO V. A. KARPINSKY

Dear Friends,

And so we are leaving through Germany *on Wednesday*. Tomorrow this will be finally decided.

We shall send you a mass of packages containing our books, *papers* and things, requesting you to forward them in turn to Stockholm for transhipment to us in Petrograd.

We shall also send you money and credentials from the Central Committee authorising you to carry on all correspondence and manage affairs.

We are thinking of publishing a leaflet, "Farewell Letter to the Swiss Workers"* in German, *in French* and in Italian.

Inessa will not have time to do the French translation: I hope you will do it and publish it (with Guilbeaux).

A comrade here (who knows German and Italian), Julius *Mimiola*, has promised me he will do the Italian translation and publish it.

(Krummgasse. 2.)

Zürich. 4.

I have given him *your* address. When you have the German pamphlet, send it to him (and a letter in *German*) and money for publication.

((Here is another address for you of a *Left-wing* German here, who published leaflet No. 1 of the Zimmerwald Left, and may be useful again for publications: Herrn Karl *Schnepf*. Thurwiesenstrasse. 8. *Zürich. I will give him your address*.))

Very best greetings and thousands of wishes.

All the best.

Yours,
Lenin

---

* See present edition, Vol. 23, pp. 367-73.—*Ed.*

P.S. We hope to collect the journey money *for about 12 persons*, because the comrades in Stockholm have helped us *very much*.

P.S. Please take 2-3 copies, on the thinnest possible paper, of my letters No. 1 and No. 2 to *Pravda* ("Letters from Afar"), to send (for the information of comrades) to Paris and elsewhere in Switzerland.

We shall hand over correspondence with Paris to you. You will have to find a bookbinder (a most reliable one) for sending letters to Paris in bindings (and to learn chemical writing).

P.P.S. Come to a *detailed* agreement about correspondence with Chaux-de-Fonds, and about publishing my speech,[299] with Abramovich (notify him that he should hurry up with his preparations for travelling: we are going on Wednesday).

Written on April 2, 1917
Sent from Zurich to Geneva

First published in 1930   Printed from the original
in *Lenin Miscellany XIII*

136

TO V. A. KARPINSKY

April 12, 1917

Dear Friend,

I hope that this letter will all the same reach you, and also the newspapers which are being sent to you. I say "all the same" because the difficulties of communication with foreign countries are incredibly great. We were allowed in, and received here with furious attacks, but up till now we have received no books, manuscripts or letters. Evidently the military censorship is working wonderfully—even with excessive zeal, since you know, of course, that we had not even the slightest mention of the war, and could not have.

Please stop typing the agrarian manuscript, because I *have found* one copy here, already set. What is missing in it is the end, the end of the "Conclusion",[300] beginning with the words:

"The whole of the peasantry and the proletariat are opposed to the private ownership of the land. The reformative path of creating a Junker-bourgeois Russia necessarily presupposes the preservation of the foundations of the old system of landownership and the slow...."

Now, from these words the end of the Conclusion is missing.

You will oblige me very much if *from these words*, and to the end of the Conclusion, you take 4-5 copies and send them (1) to me personally; (2) to *Pravda*, 32 Moika; (3) to Stockholm, to the address given to you. I ought to receive at least one of these copies.

Drop me a postcard, addressed to *Pravda*, or better still to M. T. Yelizarov (for V. I.), 48/9 Shirokaya, Flat 24,

Petrograd, whether you have received this letter, and when you sent the copies of the end of the Conclusion.

Our journey was wonderful. Platten was not admitted by Milyukov.

The atmosphere here is a furious campaign of the bourgeoisie against us. Among the workers and *soldiers*—sympathy.

Among the Social-Democrats, victory of "revolutionary defencism" (now, they say, there is something to defend—the Republic, against Wilhelm). Chkheidze and Co., Steklov (leaders of the Soviet of Workers' and Soldiers' Deputies in Petrograd) have completely descended into revolutionary defencism. Chkheidze is in a bloc with Potresov. All are howling and screaming for "unity" of the whole Russian Social-Democratic Labour Party. We, of course, are against.

On April 22, 1917 there will be an All-Russia Conference of the Bolsheviks (of our Party) in Petrograd.[301]

Write me whether our "Farewell Letter" has been published, in what languages and how sales are going.

Write whether you have received the papers (I am sending you a file of *Pravda* and cuttings from various papers). Keep Paris and all Switzerland as well informed as possible. All the best.

Yours,

V. Ulyanov

Written on April 12 (25), 1917

Sent from Petrograd to Geneva

First published in 1923
in *Proletarskaya Revolutsia* No. 9

Printed from the typewritten
copy found in police records

137

TO THE BUREAU
OF THE CENTRAL COMMITTEE ABROAD

August 17 (30), 1917

Dear Friends,

With great difficulty, after long weeks of forced interruption, it seems as though we are successfully resuming our correspondence. Of course, to make this completely successful you will have to go to a lot of pains and effort to organise it at your end.

The shameful campaign of slander launched by the bourgeoisie about the alleged espionage, or connection therewith, of Hanecki, Kollontai and many others is, of course, a scoundrelly cover for the crusade against the internationalists on the part of our bold "republicans", who want to "compare favourably" with tsarism in their slander-mongering.

(1) I have read somewhere in the Russian papers that Hanecki and Radek have been publishing a denial.[302] I don't know whether this is true. But it is essential. The first thing to do is for Radek to write to Paris and get the minutes of the last Paris trial of himself (by various factions of the R.S.D.L.P.). Lunacharsky, denouncing these base slanderers, long ago described this trial in *Novaya Zhizn*.[303] But that is not enough. Someone should try to get the minutes or at least the full sentence of the court, and, if it cannot be printed, take several typed copies and send them here. If it is impossible to get the minutes or the sentence, it would be desirable to procure at least a written account of the trial by one of the Parisians who took part in it, and to publish

at least a small pamphlet in Russian (there is a Russian print-ing-press in Christiania), in order to give a documentary refutation of these disgusting slanders. It will be possible to send us at least some copies of the pamphlet, and extracts from it should appear in .*Arbeiterpolitik*, *Politiken*, *Demain*, etc.

(2) It is equally essential that Hanecki should give a docu-mentary refutation of the slanderers, by publishing as rapidly as possible the financial accounts of his trading and his "business deals" with Sumenson (who is this lady? It's the first time I have heard of her!) and with Kozlovsky (it is desirable that the accounts should be audited and signed by a Swedish notary or Swedish socialists, several of them, mem-bers of Parliament). It is also necessary to publish the text of the telegrams (there has already been something in the Russian papers, in *Russkaya Volya*, *Bez Lishnikh Slov*[304] and others, but probably not in full), and to analyse and explain each.

We must fight against this shameful Dreyfus campaign, against this slandering, by publishing the pamphlet, and as quickly as possible, not sparing toil, trouble or money, in order to brand the slanderers and, as far as possible, to help those who have been arrested on this base and slan-derous charge.

(3) How are the financial affairs of the Bureau Abroad, which was appointed by our Central Committee? After the July persecutions it is clear that our C.C. cannot help (I think so at any rate). Write whether you have succeeded in collecting anything through the Swedish Left, and will the Bureau manage to exist? What about the *Bulletin*? How many issues have been published, and in what languages?[305] Has Guilbeaux had all the issues? Have you a file of *Demain*? Was the *Bulletin* sent to America, North and South? Write about all this in as much detail as you can.

(4) By the way. I don't remember who informed us, but it seems that after Grimm, and independently of him, Moor appeared in Stockholm. That the scoundrel Grimm, as a Kautskian "Centrist", proved capable of a scoundrelly understanding with "his" minister does not surprise me: anyone who does not break resolutely with the social-chau-vinists always risks falling into this scoundrelly situation.

But what kind of man is Moor? Has it been fully and absolutely proved that he is an honest man? That he never had,
and has not now, any direct or indirect dealings with
the German social-imperialists? If it is true that Moor
is in Stockholm, and if you know him, I would very, very
much ask you, earnestly ask you, insistently ask you to
take every step to check this up in the most strict and the
most documented fashion. There is not, or rather, should
not be, any room even for a shadow of suspicion, reproach,
rumour, etc. I very much regret that the "Zimmerwald
Commission" did not condemn Grimm more severely![306]
It should have been done more severely!

(5) I have been, and remain, unquestionably against participation in the Stockholm Conference.[307] I must observe
that I am writing all this letter personally, as from myself,
since I have had no chance either to ask the C.C. or even
communicate with it. Therefore, in replying to me with
particular detail, append to your letter your official,
detailed, business-like, documentary report (of the whole
Bureau) to the Central Committee, and I will send it on.

So, I am absolutely against participating in the Stockholm
Conference. I consider Kamenev's statement[308] (have you
seen *Novaya Zhizn*? you ought to subscribe to it) the height
of stupidity, if not of baseness, and have already written
about this to the Central Committee and for the press.
Luckily Kamenev was speaking only for himself, and was
disavowed by another Bolshevik.

I consider participation in the Stockholm Conference, or
in any other, with the Ministers (and scoundrels) Chernov,
Tsereteli, Skobelev and their parties, to be direct betrayal,
and will state this opinion in the press against all and sundry. If in the "Zimmerwald Commission" (judging by the
report of the social-chauvinist Rozanov) it proved possible
almost to reject Stockholm, or to half-reject it, this is very
good. But "almost" and "half" are of no use at all, and
all this "half"-social-chauvinist Zimmerwald Commission,
which depends on the Italians and the Ledebourites, who desire "unity" with the social-chauvinists, is a most harmful
institution.

(6) We are making the very greatest and unforgivable
mistake in delaying or postponing the convening of a con-

ference of the Left to found a Third International. It is just now, when Zimmerwald is so shamefully wavering or obliged to be inactive, just now *while* there *still* is in Russia a legal (almost legal) internationalist party with more than 200,000 (240,000) members* (which does not exist anywhere else in the world in wartime), it is just now that we are in duty bound to call a conference of the Left, and we shall really be criminals if we are *late* in doing so (the Bolshevik Party in Russia is being driven more and more underground day by day).

Money for the conference will be found. It is possible to issue several numbers of its *Bulletin*. There is a centre for it in Stockholm. There is a French "foothold" (*Demain*) and an English one (the "Socialist *Labour* Party" of America; its delegate Reinstein** was recently in Petrograd and will probably be in Stockholm) —though by the way *in addition* to the S.L.P. (the "Socialist *Labour* Party" of America) there is also an English foothold, Tom Mann in Britain, the minorities within the British Socialist Party, the Scottish socialists and *The International* in America.

It would be simply criminal to postpone now the calling of a conference of the Left.

It would be immeasurably stupid to "wait" for a "large" number of participants, and to be "embarrassed" by the fact that at present there are "few". For just now such a conference will be a *moral* force, independently of the number of participants, while later it may be *hushed up*.

The Bolsheviks, the P.S.D., the Dutch, *Arbeiterpolitik*, *Demain*—there is already a sufficient *nucleus*. They will certainly be joined, if energetic action is taken, by part of the Danes (Trier and others, who have left the party of the scoundrel Stauning), part of the Swedish Young (against whom *we* are sinning, in not *leading* them, because they *must be led*), some of the Bulgarians, the Lefts in Austria ("Franz"[309]), some of the friends of Loriot in France, part of the Lefts in Switzerland (*Youth International*) and in

---

* Seventeen daily papers; 1,415,000 copies weekly altogether; 320,000 daily.

** I have no idea what sort of a bird this is. According to the press, he greeted the "Unity Congress" of the Mensheviks!! That means he's a suspect bird.

Italy, and then the elements in the Anglo-American movement which I have already mentioned.

The resolutions of the conference of .the Bolsheviks (April 24-29, 1917) and of their congress (July 1917; see the resolutions in *Novaya Zhizn*),[310] the draft new programme of the same Party—there is a sufficient *ideological basis* (adding *Vorbote*, *Tribune*, *Arbeiterpolitik* and others) to be able to present the whole world with clear answers to the questions raised by imperialism, and to accuse the social-chauvinists and the Kautskians.

Such a conference must be called *at once*, *its* provisional *Bureau* must be set up, and its manifesto and draft resolutions printed in three languages for passing on to the parties. I repeat once again: I am profoundly convinced that, if we do not do this *now*, we shall make this work terribly difficult for ourselves in the future, and will terribly facilitate an "amnesty" for the traitors to socialism.

(7) The ministerialism of the Russian Menshevik- "Zimmerwaldists" must be specially utilised to put an ultimatum to Zimmerwald in general: either a break with the Brantings, Huysmans and Co., or we walk out immediately. By the way: is *Arbeiterpolitik* making a campaign against Zetkin and against the Braunschweiger *Volksfreund* for the way these scoundrels, pursuing their intrigues, have been whitewashing and supporting the Russian Mensheviks, Chkheidze and Co., who have proved ministerial swine, just like Sembat, Renaudel, Thomas and Co.?

Has Mehring, too, still not understood to this day the utter baseness of Chkheidze, Tsereteli, Skobelev and Co.?

(8) You must get your letters sent on here—I hope to receive immediately *just* as detailed a letter as mine (otherwise I do not agree to correspond)—and literature as well: files from the middle of June, at the very least, of *Arbeiterpolitik*, *Demain*, *Kampf* (Duisburg), *Weekly People* (S.L.P.), *Leipziger Volkszeitung*, *Neue Zeit*, *The Call* and others. *Spartacus*, the publications of Loriot and his friends, *Avanti!*, etc., etc. As a beginning, you might at least send cuttings.

(9) You should send here, if possible every week, first, articles for the provincial and Petrograd Party press (reviews of the Left-wing movement abroad, facts, facts, facts);

secondly, leaflets (4-8-16 small pages) for publication as booklets. Summaries of *facts* about the collapse of the International, the disgrace of the social-chauvinists, the disgrace of the Kautskians, the growth of the movement of the Left: at least 4 booklets on each of these subjects, 16-32 small pages each. *Facts* and *facts*. There is a hope of publishing this. Reply at once whether you can take it on. When sending it on by our method (there can be no question now of sending it legally) I think it is *all the same* which language it is written in.

(10) I hope you have the file of *Pravda*, and are subscribing to *Novaya Zhizn*. If you have not received *Rabochy i Soldat* (closed down), *Proletarskoye Dyelo* (Kronstadt) and *Sotsial-Demokrat* (Moscow), write at once, and I will send them as soon as the new method, being tested for the first time by this letter, is organised satisfactorily.

P.S. August 18. I have just received Nos. 1, 2, 4 of the new paper *Proletary*, the Central Organ[311]—of course, they will soon close it down. I will try and send it to you. I am sending Nos. *1-7*.

August 20. I have still not succeeded in sending off my letter, and probably won't succeed for some time. So this is becoming something like a diary instead of a letter! It can't be helped. You must have a lot of patience and determination, if you want to communicate at all with internationalists in the "most free" imperialist republic. Today I have learned from *Izvestia* that *News of the Stockholm Information Bureau of the Soviet of Workers' and Soldiers' Deputies* is being published weekly in Stockholm. Try to send *files* of all Stockholm publications. *We see nothing*.

August 25 (September 7). It looks as though tomorrow it will be possible to send this letter. Make *every* effort to organise delivery from your end. Reply without fail *at once*, if only briefly, to the address (within *your* country) which the comrade delivering this letter (or his friend) communicates to you. He will also pass on a cipher; as an experiment I am writing a few words in this cipher, and please reply to them in the same cipher.*

---

* A few lines are in cipher here.—*Ed.*

P.S. Write one more pamphlet, 16-32 small pages, about the secret diplomatic treaties of Russia: brief, precise, facts, facts. Such-and-such a treaty of such-and-such a date, month, year, content so-and-so. A list of the treaties. A summary. As brief and factual as possible. Reply whether you undertake to do it, and when you will send it.

I conclude: for God's sake, a conference of the Left immediately, a bureau of the Left, a bulletin of the bureau, and decide on a *second* conference in 2 (1$^{1}/_{2}$) months.

Greetings!

Lenin

Sent from Helsingfors to Stockholm

First published in 1930   Printed from the original
in *Lenin Miscellany XIII*

138

TO THE FINNISH COMRADES[312]
Manner, Sirola, Kuusinen, Valpas and Viiku

Dear Comrades,

With the greatest happiness I have heard from my Finnish friends that you are at the head of the revolutionary wing of the Finnish Social-Democratic Labour Party and are carrying on a struggle for the cause of the proletarian socialist revolution. I can state with confidence on behalf of the revolutionary proletariat of Russia that the great organising talent of the Finnish workers, their high level of development and their prolonged political schooling in democratic institutions will help them successfully to effect the socialist reorganisation of Finland. We count on the fraternal aid of the revolutionary Social-Democrats of Finland.

Long live the international socialist revolution!

With best greetings,

November 11, 1917   *N. Lenin*

Written in German

First published in Russian
in *Pravda* No. 21,
January 21, 1931

Printed from the original

139

TELEGRAM
TO THE PRESIDIUM OF THE MOSCOW SOVIET OF WORKERS' AND SOLDIERS' DEPUTIES[313]

All power is in the hands of the Soviets. Confirmations are unnecessary. Your dismissal of the one and appointment of the other is law.

Written on November 19
(December 2), 1917

First published
in *Rabochaya Moskva* No. 255,
November 7, 1927

Printed from the original

140

TELEGRAM TO THE CHAIRMAN
OF THE OSTROGOZHSK SOVIET[314]

Draw up a precise inventory of the valuables, put them away in a secure place, you are responsible for their safe-keeping. The estates are the property of the people. Prosecute for looting. Inform us of the sentences of the court.

Lenin

Written on December 6 (19), 1917

First published in 1933
in *Lenin Miscellany XXI*

Printed from the original

1918

141

TELEGRAM TO G. K. ORJONIKIDZE

People's Secretariat
For Commissar Orjonikidze
Kharkov

I have received your telegram of January 20, 1918. Hearty thanks for your energetic measures regarding food. Go on trying for God's sake as hard as you can to secure foodstuffs, press on with collection and delivery of grain, so as to arrange supply before the spring floods. All hopes are on you, otherwise famine by the spring is inevitable.

I have talked, and will talk, with Pyatakov about sending money. A hundred millions have been sent, fifty will be sent to Kharkov. Take measures for triple defence of the railway line from Petrograd to Kharkov. I am sure that your relations with the Central Executive Committee in Kharkov will as before be entirely friendly. Greetings and best wishes.

Lenin

Written on January 22
(February 4), 1918

First published in 1931
in *Lenin Miscellany XVIII*

Printed from the original

142

TELEGRAM TO THE CHAIRMAN
OF THE DRISSA TOWN SOVIET[315]

To Urban, Chairman of the Drissa Soviet of Deputies

Offer resistance where it is possible. Evacuate all valuables and foodstuffs. Destroy all the rest. Leave nothing to the enemy. Take up the railway lines—two versts out of every ten. Blow up the bridges.

Lenin

Written on February 19, 1918

First published in 1945
in *Lenin Miscellany XXXV*

Printed from the text
of N. P. Gorbunov's notes

143

TO THE PEOPLE'S COMMISSARIAT FOR WAR

April 22, 1918

On April 22 at 11 p.m. the Council of People's Commissars resolved that the War Commissariat be requested to take immediately all steps within its power to defend the eastern boundary of Kharkov Gubernia, especially Chertkovo station, which the Germans and haidamaks are trying to occupy in order to interrupt railway communication with Rostov.

Details to be discussed with Stalin.

V. Ulyanov (*Lenin*)
Chairman, Council of People's Commissars

First published in 1931
in *Lenin Miscellany XVIII*

Printed from the typewritten
original signed by V. I. Lenin

144

TO D. I. KURSKY[316]

It is essential *immediately*, with demonstrative speed, to introduce a Bill stating that the penalty for bribery (extortion, graft, acting as an agent for bribery, *and the like*) shall be

not less than

ten years' imprisonment and, in addition, ten years of compulsory labour.[317]

Written on May 4, 1918

First published
in *Krasnaya Gazeta* No. 260,
November 7, 1928

Printed from the original

145

TO S. G. SHAHUMYAN

Dear Comrade Shahumyan,

Many thanks for your letter. We are delighted with your firm and resolute policy. Be capable of combining with it the most cautious diplomacy, unquestionably required by the present most difficult situation—and we shall be victorious.

The difficulties are immeasurable. *So far* we are being saved *only* by the contradictions and conflicts and struggles among the imperialists. Be capable of making use of these conflicts: *for the time being* we have to learn diplomacy. [318]

Best greetings and wishes, and greetings to all friends.

Yours,

Lenin

Written on May 14, 1918

Sent to Baku

Published in *Bulletins of the Dictatorship of the Tsentrokaspy and the Presidium of the Provisional Executive Committee* No. 33, September 8, 1918

Printed from the *Bulletins* text

146

TO V. D. BONCH-BRUYEVICH

May 23, 1918

Vladimir Dmitriyevich Bonch-Bruyevich,
Office Manager, Council of People's Commissars

In view of your failure to fulfil my insistent request to point out to me the justification for raising my salary as from March 1, 1918, from 500 to 800 rubles a month, and in view of the obvious illegality of this increase, carried out by you arbitrarily by agreement with the secretary of the Council, Nikolai Petrovich Gorbunov, and in direct infringement of the decree of the Council of People's Commissars of November 23, 1917, I give you a severe reprimand. [319]

V. Ulyanov (Lenin)
Chairman, Council of People's Commissars

First published in 1933
in *Lenin Miscellany XXI*

Printed from the typewritten
original signed by V. I. Lenin

147

TELEPHONE MESSAGE TO THE PETROGRAD SOVIET

To be telephoned to the Smolny, Petrograd*:

In view of the cutting of the Siberian Railway by the Czechoslovaks and the tremendous threat to transport, in view of interrupted communications the very greatest peril menaces the food supply.

Comrade Vladimirov insists, and I support him, that Petrograd should urgently send its best food supply personnel to Moscow. These personnel, together with strong detachments of selected workers, may save the situation.

Don't delay. Don't wait for help from outside. Strain every effort for extraordinary measures by the Petrograd workers.

Lenin

Written on June 2, 1918

First published in 1931
in *Lenin Miscellany XVIII*

Printed from the original

---

* At the top of this document Lenin wrote: "If this cannot be telephoned immediately to Petrograd, it should be sent by direct line."—*Ed.*

148

TELEGRAM TO NIZHNI-RIVERSIDE

Urgent. Nizhni-Riverside.
Copies to Saratov, Tsaritsyn

You are instructed to carry out immediately and without question all orders and instructions of People's Commissar Stalin, extraordinary plenipotentiary of the Council of People's Commissars.

Transmit to Stalin: copies of all his orders and instructions must be sent immediately to Nizhni-Riverside, Volga Regional Authority.

Contents of this telegram to be passed on at once to all districts.

Lenin
Chairman, Council of People's Commissars

Written on June 8, 1918

First published in 1931
in *Lenin Miscellany XVIII*

Printed from a text
written in an unknown hand
corrected and signed
by V. I. Lenin

149

TO G. Y. ZINOVIEV

June 26, 1918

Also to Lashevich and other members of the C.C.

Comrade Zinoviev,

Only today we have heard at the C.C. that in Petrograd the *workers* wanted to reply to the murder of Volodarsky by mass terror and that you (not you personally, but the Petrograd Central Committee members, or Petrograd Committee members) restrained them.[320]

I protest most emphatically!

We are discrediting ourselves: we threaten mass terror, even in resolutions of the Soviet of Deputies, yet when it comes to action we *obstruct* the revolutionary initiative of the masses, a *quite* correct one.

This is im-poss-ible!

The terrorists will consider us old women. This is wartime above all. We must encourage the energy and mass character of the terror against the counter-revolutionaries, and particularly in Petrograd, the example of which is *decisive*.

Greetings!

Lenin

P.S. Detachments and still more detachments: make use of your victory at the elections. If the Petrograders move 10-20 thousand into *Tambov* Gubernia, the Urals, etc., they will save both themselves and the whole revolution, *completely and for certain*. The harvest is a giant one, we have to hang on only a few weeks more.

First published in part
in *Pravda* No. 17, January 21, 1925

Published in full in 1931
in *Lenin Miscellany XVIII*

Printed from the original

150

TELEGRAM TO A. M. YURIEV

If you are still disinclined to understand Soviet policy, which is equally hostile both to the British and to the Germans, you will have only yourself to blame. Natsarenus is on his way.

We shall fight the British if they continue their policy of plunder.[321]

Lenin

Written on June 26, 1918
    Sent to Murmansk

First published in *Pravda*
No. 51, February 21, 1935

Printed from the original

151

TO S. G. SHAHUMYAN

June 29, 1918

Dear Comrade Shahumyan,

I send my best greetings and wishes.

Stalin is in Tsaritsyn. Better send your letters through Stalin.

Greetings.

Yours,
Lenin

Sent to Baku
First published in 1938

Printed from the original

152

TELEGRAM TO CHIEFS OF REQUISITIONING DETACHMENTS ON ALL RAILWAYS[322]

The Council of People's Commissars has been informed of quite intolerable behaviour, damaging to Soviet power, by some requisitioning detachments. The detachments have been sent for responsible service on the railways, for the struggle against actual profiteering. Chiefs of detachments are instructed to maintain the most stringent discipline in their detachments, for the absence of which, as for all offences by the detachments, the chiefs will be held to strict account before the merciless judgement of the Revolutionary Tribunal. Detachments should be informed that the Council of People's Commissars is convinced that class-conscious workers will not tolerate any breach of the strictest proletarian discipline, and will treat with the greatest severity those who by their behaviour are disgracing Soviet power. But if obvious hooligans have found their way into the detachments, and refuse to obey the instructions of the central authorities and their chiefs, or disgrace the Soviet Republic by taking bribes from grain speculators, they must be immediately arrested by their chiefs and the local Soviets of Deputies, and delivered under guard to Moscow for committal to most severe judgement by the Revolutionary Tribunal.

Ulyanov (Lenin)
Chairman, Council of People's Commissars

Written on July 1, 1918

First published in 1931
in *Lenin Miscellany XVIII*

Printed from the typewritten
original corrected, amended
and signed by V. I. Lenin

22*

153

TO ALL DISTRICT COMMITTEES OF THE R.C.P., ALL DISTRICT SOVIETS OF DEPUTIES, ALL STAFFS OF THE RED ARMY

Two bombs were thrown in the German Embassy about 3 p.m. today, severely wounding Mirbach. This is an obvious act of the monarchists or of those provocateurs who want to drag Russia into war in the interests of the Anglo-French capitalists, who have also bribed the Czechoslovaks. Mobilise all forces, put everyone on guard immediately to catch the criminals. *All* cars are to be detained and held for a triple check.[323]

V. Ulyanov (Lenin)

Chairman, Council of People's Commissars

Written on July 6, 1918

Published on July 7 (June 24), 1918
in *Pravda* No. 138 and
Izvestia No. 140

Printed from the original

154

TELEPHONE MESSAGE TO THE MOSCOW SOVIET

To be transmitted to all volost, village and uyezd Soviets of Moscow Gubernia.*

The defeated bands of Left Socialist-Revolutionaries who revolted against Soviet power are scattering through the surrounding districts. The leaders of this whole adventure are fleeing. Take all steps to capture and detain those who had the insolence to rise against Soviet power. Detain all cars. Lower barriers over the highways everywhere. Concentrate near them armed detachments of the local workers and peasants. There is information that one armoured car, which the rebels possessed, has got out of the city. Take all steps to detain this armoured car.

Lenin
Chairman, Council of People's Commissars

Written on July 7, 1918

Published on July 8 (June 25), 1918
in *Pravda* No. 139 and
Izvestia No. 141

Printed from the text
written in an unknown hand
and signed by V. I. Lenin

----

* *Gubernia, uyezd, volost*—Russian administrative-territorial units. The largest of these was the gubernia, which had its subdivisions in uyezds, which in turn were subdivided into volosts. This system continued under Soviet power until the introduction of the new system of administrative-territorial division in 1929-30.—*Ed.*

155

RADIO MESSAGE TO S. G. SHAHUMYAN

July 22, 1918

Shahumyan
Soviet of Deputies
Baku

I can only support in full Stalin's telegram against the Narodnik faction of the Baku Soviet and concerning the will of the Fifth Congress of Soviets.[324]

Lenin
Chairman, Council of People's Commissars

First published
in *Bakinsky Rabochy* No. 221,
September 24, 1933

Printed from the original

156

TO CLARA ZETKIN

July 26, 1918

Esteemed Comrade Zetkin,

Many warm thanks for your letter of June 27, which was brought me by Comrade Hertha Hordon. I will do all I can to help Comrade Hordon.

We are all extremely glad that you, Comrade Mehring and the other "Spartacus comrades" in Germany are with us, "head and heart".[325] This gives us confidence that the best elements of the West-European working class—in spite of all difficulties—will nevertheless come to our assistance.

We here are now living through perhaps the most difficult weeks of the whole revolution. The class struggle and the civil war have penetrated deep among the population: everywhere there is a split in the villages—the poor are for us, the kulaks are furiously against us. The Entente has bought the Czechoslovaks, a counter-revolutionary revolt is raging, the bourgeoisie is making every effort to overthrow us. Nevertheless, we firmly believe that we shall escape this "usual" (as in 1794 and 1849) course of the revolution, and will conquer the bourgeoisie.

With great gratitude, very best greetings and sincere respect,

Yours,
Lenin

P.S. My wife asks me to give you her special greetings. To Comrade Hoschka (we have translated his speech, as we have your article) and to all, all friends the very best greetings.

P. S. I have just been brought our new State Seal. Here is the impression. The inscription reads: Russian Socialist Federative Soviet Republic. Workers of all countries, unite![326]

Written in German

First published in Russian
in *Pravda* No. 21, January 21, 1933

Printed from the original

157

TELEGRAM TO S. G. SHAHUMYAN[327]

July 29

Astrakhan
For Shahumyan in Baku

Any actions by the Dashnaks against the decision of the Fifth Congress of Soviets and the central Soviet power will be considered insurrection and treason. As regards sending troops we shall take steps, but cannot promise for certain.

Lenin

Written on July 29, 1918

First published in 1938
in the magazine *Krasny Arkhiv*
No. 4-5

Printed from the original

158

TO A. D. TSYURUPA[328]

In view of the critical food situation, we must not scatter our forces. We must concentrate them in one place, where it is *possible* to secure *a lot* of grain.

I suggest that forces be concentrated in Yelets Uyezd where, according to a number of reports and on the evidence of the People's Commissar for the Interior Pravdin, who inspected this area, the state of affairs, in the sense of the throttling of the kulaks and the organisation of the poor peasants, is a model one.

Send immediately, with the maximum speed, *all* the food, harvesting and harvest-requisitioning detachments to Yelets Uyezd, with the maximum number of threshers and attachments (if possible) for rapid drying of the grain, etc.

Give them the task of *clearing* the uyezd of grain *surpluses completely*.

Probably this will yield several million poods of grain (in my opinion, more than 6 million poods).

First send the maximum forces to those 12 (out of 21) volosts of the uyezd where, according to the local people, the organisation of the poor peasants is best, and particularly to the former landed estates which have been registered.

Don't be *niggardly* with bonuses for rapid harvesting and delivery of grain, assign for this purpose *up to 30 million* rubles immediately (grant bonuses to volosts and villages in the shape of machinery, grants for schools and hospitals and, in general, mainly for such purposes). The maximum bonuses must be given for delivery of *all* surpluses of grain, medium bonuses for big deliveries in general, and so forth.

Among the workers of the famine-stricken gubernias (and among the famine-stricken peasants there also) develop mass agitation: crusade for grain to Yelets Uyezd!

Written on August 5, 1918

First published in 1931   Printed from the origina
in *Lenin Miscellany XVIII*

159

TELEGRAM TO N. A. ANISIMOV

Anisimov
Astrakhan

The situation in Baku is still not clear to me.
Who is in power?
Where is Shahumyan?
Inquire of Stalin, and act in the light of all the circumstances; you know that I have complete confidence in Shahumyan. The situation cannot be understood from here, and there is no possibility of giving speedy help.[329]

Lenin

Written on August 9, 1918

First published in 1938
in *Krasny Arkhiv* No. 4-5

Printed from the original

160

TO G. F. FYODOROV

August 9, 1918

Comrade Fyodorov,

It is obvious that a whiteguard insurrection is being prepared in Nizhni. You must strain every effort, appoint three men with dictatorial powers (yourself, Markin and one other), organise *immediately* mass terror, *shoot and deport the hundreds* of prostitutes who are making drunkards of the soldiers, former officers and the like.

Not a minute of delay.

I can't understand how Romanov could leave at a time like this!

I do not know the bearer. His name is Alexei Nikolayevich Bobrov. He says he worked in Vyborgskaya Storona District in Petrograd (from 1916).... Previously worked in Nizhni in 1905.

Judging by his credentials, he can be trusted. Check up on this and set him to work.

Peters, Chairman of the Extraordinary Commission, says that they also have *reliable* people in Nizhni.

You must act with all energy. Mass searches. Execution for concealing arms. Mass deportation of Mensheviks and unreliables. Change the guards at warehouses, put in reliable people.

They say Raskolnikov and Danishevsky are on their way to see you from Kazan.

Read this letter to the friends and reply by telegraph or telephone.

Yours,
Lenin

Sent to Nizhni-Novgorod
First published, but not
in full, in 1938
in *Bolshevik* No. 2

Printed in full from a
photo-copy of the original

161

TELEGRAM TO V. V. KURAYEV

August 10, 1918

Kurayev
Gubernia Executive Committee
Penza

Have received your telegram, passed it on to Sverdlov and reached agreement with him.

All measures will be taken.

Essential to crush the kulak rising with the greatest energy, speed and ruthlessness, drawing part of the troops from Penza, confiscating all the property of the rebel kulaks and all their grain. Telegraph more frequently how this is going.

Lenin

Chairman, Council of People's Commissars

First published in 1931
in *Lenin Miscellany XVIII*

Printed from the original

162

TELEGRAM TO V. V. KURAYEV

Kurayev
Gubernia Executive Committee
Penza

Extremely important to gather and publish facts of participation of Left Socialist-Revolutionaries in the kulak rising. Inform us in as much detail as possible what steps you are proposing to take against the Left S.R.s. I have cabled the rest to Minkin and Bosh.

Lenin
Chairman, Council of People's Commissars

Written on August 12, 1918

First published in 1931
in *Lenin Miscellany XVIII*

Printed from the original

163

TELEGRAM TO A. Y. MINKIN

August 14, 1918

Minkin
Gubernia Executive Committee
Penza

I have received two complaints against you: the first, that you are showing softness in crushing the kulaks. If this is true, you are committing a great crime against the revolution. The second complaint is that you are cutting down agitation, reducing the circulation of leaflets, complaining of lack of money. We shall not grudge hundreds of thousands for agitation. Demand money urgently from the Central Executive Committee, there will be no lack of money. We shall not accept such excuses.

Lenin

Chairman, Council of People's Commissars

First published in 1931
in *Lenin Miscellany XVIII*

Printed from the original

164

TELEGRAM TO M. F. BOLDYREV

August 17, 1918

Boldyrev
Executive Committee
Zadonsk

Act in the most resolute way against the kulaks and the Left Socialist-Revolutionary scoundrels who have made common cause with them. Issue appeals to the poor peasants. Organise them. Ask for help from Yelets. Essential to suppress the kulak extortioners mercilessly. Telegraph.

Lenin
Chairman, Council of People's Commissars

First published in 1927
in the magazine
Revolutsia i Kultura No. 2

Printed from the original

165

TELEGRAM
TO THE ZDOROVETS EXECUTIVE COMMITTEE, OREL GUBERNIA

Burov, Pereyaslavtsev
Zdorovets, Orel Gubernia

Copy to the Orel Gubernia Soviet of Deputies

Essential to combine ruthless suppression of the kulak Left Socialist-Revolutionary rising with confiscation of all the grain from the kulaks and exemplary clearing out in full of grain surpluses, distributing part of the grain free to the poor peasants. Telegraph fulfilment.

Lenin
Chairman, Council of People's Commissars

Written on August 19, 1918

First published in 1931
in *Lenin Miscellany XVIII*

Printed from the original

166

TELEGRAM
TO THE LIVNY EXECUTIVE COMMITTEE

August 20, 1918

Executive Committee
Livny

Copy to Military Commissar Semashko and Communist Organisation

Congratulations on energetic suppression of the kulaks and whiteguards in the uyezd. Essential to strike while the iron is hot and, without losing a minute, organise the poor peasants in the uyezd, confiscate all the grain and all the property of the rebel kulaks, hang the kulak ring-leaders, mobilise and arm the poor peasants under reliable leaders drawn from our detachment, arrest hostages from among the rich peasants and hold them so long as all surpluses of grain have not been gathered and delivered in their volosts. Telegraph fulfilment. Send part of the model Iron Regiment at once to Penza.

Lenin
Chairman, Council of People's Commissars

First published in 1931
in *Lenin Miscellany XVIII*

Printed from the original

167

TELEGRAM TO THE ASTRAKHAN GUBERNIA EXECUTIVE COMMITTEE

August 21, 1918

Gubernia Executive Committee
Astrakhan
Copy to Gubernia Communist Organisation

Can it really be true that in Astrakhan there is already talk about evacuation?

If it is true, it is essential to take ruthless measures against the cowards, and immediately appoint the most reliable and resolute people to organise the defence of Astrakhan and to pursue the most firm policy of struggle to the bitter end in the event of an offensive by the British.

Telegraph detailed reply.

Lenin
Chairman, Council of People's Commissars

First published in 1938
in *Bolshevik* No. 2

Printed from the original

168

TO PEOPLE'S COMMISSARS

August 29, 1918

I allow myself to express the following wishes on the question of fulfilment of the Council of People's Commissars' resolution of August 29, on the submission of *reports* within *one week*:

In the reports, which must be *as popular as possible*, it is particularly necessary to note

(a) improvement in the position of the masses (raising of wages for the *workers*, school-teachers, etc.),

(b) participation of the workers in administration (personally outstanding workers, workers' organisations likewise, etc.),

(c) participation of the poor peasants and their help to Soviet power in the struggle against the kulaks,

(d) expropriation of the landowners, capitalists, traders, financiers, etc.

The main task is to demonstrate *concretely*, with facts, *exactly how* Soviet power has made definite steps (*the first*) towards socialism.

Lenin

First published in 1928
in *Lenin Miscellany VIII*

Printed from the original

169

TO M. S. KEDROV[330]

August 29, 1918

Comrade Kedrov,

You are giving us too little factual information. Send reports *with every messenger*.

How much fortification work has been done?

Along what line?

At what points on the railway have sappers been *provided*, so that in the event of an advance in force by the Anglo-French we can blow up and *seriously* damage *such-and-such a number* (how many, there must be a full report, and where precisely) of bridges, versts of the railway, passages through the marshes, etc., etc.

Have you taken sufficient measures to safeguard Vologda against the whiteguard peril? It will be unforgivable if you display weakness or carelessness in this regard.

Greetings!

Lenin

Sent to Vologda

First published
in *Krasnaya Gazeta* No. 17,
January 21, 1927

Printed from the original

170

TELEGRAM TO L. D. TROTSKY

Trotsky, Sviyazhsk

Copy to Kayurov and Chugurin
Staff of 5th Army

Thanks. Recovery proceeding excellently.[331] Am sure that the crushing of the Kazan Czechs and whiteguards, as well as of the kulak extortioners supporting them, will be exemplarily ruthless.

Best greetings.

Lenin

Written on September 7, 1918

First published in *Pravda*
No. 201, August 30, 1928

Printed from the original

171

TELEGRAM TO A. V. LUNACHARSKY

September 18, 1918

People's Commissar Lunacharsky
Petrograd

Copy to Pokrovsky, 53 Ostozhenka, Moscow

I have heard today Vinogradov's report on the busts and monuments, and am utterly outraged; nothing has been done for months; to this day there is not a single bust, the disappearance of the bust of Radishchev is a farce. There is no bust of Marx on public display, nothing has been done in the way of propaganda by putting up inscriptions in the streets. I reprimand you for this criminal and lackadaisical attitude, and demand that the names of all responsible persons should be sent me for prosecution. Shame on the saboteurs and thoughtless loafers.

Lenin
Chairman, Council of People's Commissars

First published in 1933
in *Lenin Miscellany XXI*

Printed from the original

172

TO RAILWAYMEN COMRADES
ON THE MOSCOW-KIEV-VORONEZH RAILWAY

I thank you with all my heart for your greetings and good wishes and, for my part, wish you every success in the cause of building socialism. The proletarian mass of railwaymen and clerks must overcome not only sabotage but also syndicalist strivings and inclinations, and I am sure it will overcome them.

With communist greetings,

V. Ulyanov (Lenin)

Moscow, September 20, 1918

Published on October 15, 1918
in the magazine *Vestnik Glavnogo
Voyenno-Revolutsionnogo Komiteta
Moskovsko-Kievo-Voronezhskoi
Zheleznoi Dorogi* (Kursk) No. 33

Printed from the original

173

TO Y. A. BERZIN, V. V. VOROVSKY
AND A. A. JOFFE

September 20, 1918

Dear Comrades,

Today's *Pravda* has quoted extracts from Kautsky's article against Bolshevism (from *Sozialistische Auslandspolitik*).[332]

Kautsky's disgraceful rubbish, childish babble and shallowest opportunism impel me to ask: why do we do nothing to fight the *theoretical* vulgarisation of Marxism by Kautsky?

Can we tolerate that even such people as Mehring and Zetkin keep away from Kautsky more "morally" (if one may put it so) than *theoretically*.... Kautsky has found nothing better to do now than to write against the Bolsheviks, they say.

Is that an argument? Can one really so weaken one's own position? Why, that is only putting a weapon into Kautsky's hands!!

And this instead of writing:

Kautsky has *absolutely* failed to understand and has distorted in a purely opportunist way

the teaching of Marx on the state

      "   "   "   "   *on the dictatorship* of the proletariat

      "   "   "   "   on bourgeois democracy

      "   "   "   "   on parliamentarism

      "   "   "   "   on the role and significance of the Commune, etc.

We ought to take these measures:

(1) have a detailed talk with the Left (Spartacists and others), stimulating them to make a statement *of principle*,

of *theory*, in the press, that on the question of dictatorship Kautsky is producing philistine Bernsteinism, not Marxism;

(2) publish as soon as possible in German my *The State and Revolution*;

(3) provide it with at least a *publisher's* foreword, as for example:

"The publisher considers the appearance of this booklet particularly essential at the present moment, in view of the complete distortion of Marxism, precisely on these questions, in the latest works of Kautsky, who is replacing the viewpoint of the dictatorship of the proletariat by philistine social-liberalism in the spirit of Bernstein and other opportunists."

(4) If it is impossible to publish the booklet quickly, then get a note similar to the "publisher's foreword" in the *newspapers* (of the Left).

I would very much ask you to send (especially addressed to me) Kautsky's pamphlet (about the Bolsheviks, dictatorship, etc.) as soon as it appears—[333]

—and then to collect for me *all* Kautsky's articles about the Bolsheviks ("Democracy and Dictatorship", the end of 1917 or the beginning of 1918; then the article from *Sozialistische Auslandspolitik*, August 1918) *and other articles, if there were any.*

Very best greetings!

Lenin

Sent to Berne, Stockholm and Berlin

First published, but not in full, in *Pravda* No. 17, January 21, 1925

Published in full in 1932 in the second and third editions of Lenin's *Collected Works*, Vol. XXIX

Printed from the original

174

TO Y. M. SVERDLOV AND L. D. TROTSKY

October 1, 1918

Comrades *Sverdlov and Trotsky*

Things have so "accelerated" in Germany that we must not fall behind either. But today we are already behind.

We should call *tomorrow* a joint session of the

      Central Executive Committee

      Moscow Soviet

      District Soviets

      Trade unions, etc., etc.

A *number* of reports must be made on *the beginning of the revolution in Germany.*

      (Victory of *our* tactics of struggle against

      German imperialism. And so forth.)

A resolution to be adopted.

The international revolution has come so close in *one week* that it has to be reckoned with as an event of the *next few days.*

No alliances either with the government of Wilhelm, or with the government of Wilhelm II+Ebert and the other scoundrels.

But for the German worker masses, the German working people in their millions, once they have begun with their spirit of revolt (so far *only* a spirit), we

are beginning to prepare

a fraternal alliance, *bread*, military aid.

We are all ready to die to help the German workers advance the revolution which has begun in Germany.

The conclusion: (1) ten times more effort to secure grain (clean out *all* stocks both for ourselves *and for the German* workers).

(2) Ten times more *enrolments* for the army. We must have *by the spring* an army of three millions to help the international workers' revolution.

This resolution should go out to the whole world by cable on Wednesday night.

Appoint the meeting for 2 p.m. on Wednesday. We shall begin at *4*, give me the platform for 1/4 hour of introduction, I shall drive up and leave immediately afterwards. Send the car for me tomorrow morning (but by telephone say only: *agreed*).[334]

Greetings!

Lenin

First published in 1933
in *Lenin Miscellany XXI*   Printed from the original

175

TELEGRAM ON THE OCCASION OF THE CAPTURE OF SAMARA

Samara has been captured. The Volga is free. It would be criminal not to make use of the few days remaining before navigation closes. It is essential to strain every effort to deliver the maximum quantity of oil and food cargoes to the upper reaches of the Volga. This task cannot be performed without the strictest centralisation of all measures, and the precise fulfilment in the localities of orders from the centre. Taking this into account, the Council of People's Commissars resolves, and orders the fulfilment without fail:

(1) All vessels, rafts, etc., commandeered by various organisations shall be returned immediately to the *Central Inland Waterways Board* and the *Central Oil Board* respectively. (This does not apply to the vessels and floating transport already included in the Volga Military Flotilla.)

(2) The right of requisitioning vessels, rafts, etc., on the Volga, previously granted to various organisations, institutions and individuals, is annulled. The requisitioning of floating means of transport required for military purposes shall henceforth take place on each occasion only by special permission of the Revolutionary Military Council of the Republic.

(3) All Commanders of Fronts, Extraordinary Commissions and Soviets shall immediately take the most stringent measures to ensure the unhindered movement of vessels and the protection of cargoes against any seizures and delays whatsoever.

(4) The control of the entire Volga tanker fleet and all oil cargoes on the Volga is vested exclusively in the Central Oil Board. (Telegraphic address: *Glavkoneft*, Moscow.) All authorities, including the military and Front Commanders, are instructed to carry out without question all decisions of the *Central Oil Board* concerning the movement of oil cargoes, and decisions of the *Central Inland Waterways Board* concerning vessels.

(5) The direct control of oil cargoes along the whole Volga is vested in Comrade *Tarvid, member of the Collegium of the Central Oil Board*. All his instructions, and likewise those of his agents, regarding oil are absolutely binding on all authorities.

(6) All decisions as to requisitioning or prohibition of dispatch of oil, etc., published up to this day, remain in force only insofar as they do not contradict the instructions of the *Central Oil Board*.

(7) Most strictly confirming the aforesaid, the *Council of People's Commissars* has decided to prosecute before military-revolutionary courts all who infringe the present decision, without regard to their posts or their Party membership. Agents of the *Central Oil Board, the Central Inland Waterways Board and the Commissariat of Food* in the localities are instructed to report to Moscow urgently all actions by local authorities which interfere with the planned work of these centres. Extraordinary Commissions will be dispatched immediately to try the guilty and carry out the sentences.

(8) The content of the present decision of the *Council of People's Commissars* is to be made known to all local executive bodies and persons in official positions.

Lenin
Chairman, Council of People's Commissars

Kremlin, Moscow
October 9, 1918

Published in *Izvestia* No. 223, October 13, 1918

Printed from the typewritten original signed by V. I. Lenin, collated with the newspaper text

176

TO THE PRESIDIUM OF THE MOSCOW SOVIET OF WORKERS' AND RED ARMY DEPUTIES[335]

Dear Comrades,

I have received your paper numbered 24962 with an extract from the resolution of the Presidium of October 7.

In all conscience I must say that this resolution is so *politically* illiterate and so stupid that it makes one sick. "...The Presidium is obliged to disclaim responsibility...." That is how capricious young ladies behave, not grown-up politicians. You will not free yourselves of responsibility, but increase it threefold.

If the Commissariat of Public Education does not reply to you and does not fulfil its duty towards you, then you are obliged to *complain*, and with documents. You are not children, are you, that you can't understand this?

When did you complain? Where is the copy? Where are the documents and the proofs?

Both the whole Presidium and Vinogradov, in my opinion, ought to be sent to prison for a week for inactivity.

If the Commissariat of Public Education "does not produce the busts" (when did you demand them? From whom? The copy and the document? When did you complain?), you should have *fought for your rights*. But "to disclaim responsibility" is the way of capricious young ladies and stupid Russian intellectuals.

Forgive this frank expression of my opinion, and accept communist greetings from one who hopes that you will get your lesson in prison for inaction in authority, and from one who is profoundly indignant at your behaviour.

October 12, 1918   *Lenin*

First published in 1933
in *Lenin Miscellany XXI*

Printed from the original

V. I. Lenin in the Kremlin courtyard during convalescence after the attempt on his life. *October 1918*

177

TO THE MEMBERS OF THE SPARTACUS GROUP[336]

October 18, 1918

Dear Comrades,

We have had news today that the Spartacus group, together with the Bremen Left Radicals,[337] has taken the most energetic steps to promote the setting up of Workers' and Soldiers' Councils throughout Germany. I take this opportunity to send our best wishes to the German revolutionary internationalist Social-Democrats. The work of the German Spartacus group, which has carried on systematic revolutionary propaganda in the most difficult conditions, has really saved the honour of German socialism and the German proletariat. Now the decisive hour is at hand: the rapidly maturing German revolution calls on the Spartacus group to play the most important role, and we all firmly hope that before long the German socialist proletarian republic will inflict a decisive blow on world imperialism.

I hope that the book by the renegade Kautsky against the dictatorship of the proletariat will also bring certain benefits. It will prove the correctness of what the Spartacus group always said against the Kautskians, and the masses will the more quickly be freed from the corrupting influence of Mr. Kautsky and Co.

With best greetings and firm hopes that in the very near future it will be possible to hail the victory of the proletarian revolution in Germany.

Yours,

N. Lenin

Sent to Berlin

First published in 1929
in German in *Illustrierte Geschichte der Deutschen Revolution* No. 6, Berlin

First published in Russian
in *Pravda* No. 308,
November 7, 1930

Printed from a photo-copy
of the original

Translated from the German

178

TELEGRAM TO I. I. VATSETIS

October 20, 1918

Vatsetis
Arzamas

Extremely surprised and concerned at the delay in taking the Izhevsk and Votkinsk Works. Please adopt the most energetic measures to hasten this. Telegraph what precisely you have undertaken.[338]

Lenin
Chairman, Council of People's Commissars*

First published in 1934
in *Proletarskaya Revolutsia* No. 3

Printed from the original

---

* The telegram is also signed by Y. M. Sverdlov, Chairman of the All-Russia C.E.C.—*Ed.*

179

TELEPHONE MESSAGE TO A. A. JOFFE

Russian Ambassador Joffe
Berlin

Immediately transmit our very warmest greetings to Karl Liebknecht. The liberation from prison of the representative of the revolutionary workers of Germany is the portent of a new era, the era of victorious socialism, which is now opening up both for Germany and for the whole world.

On behalf of the Central Committee of the Russian Communist Party (Bolsheviks),

*Lenin**

Written on October 23, 1918

Published in *Pravda* No. 231 and *Izvestia* No. 233, October 25, 1918

Printed from the original

---

* The names of Sverdlov and Stalin are also appended, in Lenin's handwriting.—*Ed.*

180

TELEGRAM TO THE OREL AND KURSK GUBERNIA EXECUTIVE COMMITTEES AND GUBERNIA PARTY COMMITTEES

Secret
Urgent, top priority
November 9, 1918

2 addresses:

Orel, Gubernia E.C. and Gubernia Communist Party Committee

Kursk, Gubernia E.C. and Gubernia Communist Party Committee

A radio message has just been received from Kiel, addressed to the international proletariat and stating that power in Germany has passed into the hands of the workers and soldiers.

This radio message is signed by the Council of Sailors' Deputies of Kiel.

In addition, German soldiers at the front have arrested a peace delegation from Wilhelm, and have themselves begun negotiations for peace direct with the French soldiers.

Wilhelm has abdicated.

It is essential to make every effort to communicate this as soon as possible to the German soldiers in the Ukraine, and to advise them to attack the troops of Krasnov, because then we shall together win tens of millions of poods of grain for the German workers, and beat off an invasion by the British, whose squadron is now approaching Novorossiisk.

Telegraph receipt and fulfilment.

Lenin
Chairman, Council of People's Commissars

First published in 1933
in *Lenin Miscellany XXI*

Printed from the original

181

TELEGRAM TO IVANOV,
CHAIRMAN OF THE UNECHA R.C.P.(B.)
ORGANISATION[339]

November 13, 1918

Ivanov, Chairman of the Unecha R.C.P
Unecha

I thank everyone for the greetings. Am particularly touched by the greetings from the revolutionary soldiers of Germany. It is now extremely important that the revolutionary soldiers of Germany should take an immediate and active part in liberating the Ukraine. First of all, the whiteguards and the Ukrainian authorities must be arrested and, secondly, delegates from the revolutionary troops of Germany must be sent to all German military units in the Ukraine, so that they may take rapid and common action to liberate the Ukraine. There is no time to lose. Not an hour must be wasted. Telegraph immediately whether the revolutionary soldiers of Germany are accepting this proposal.

Lenin
Chairman, Council of People's Commissars

N.B. *Urgent.*
Top priority.
Report to me at what time Unecha *received* this.

First published, but not in full, in 1937 in the book: Y. Gerasimov and M. Erlikh, *Nikolai Alexandrovich Shchors. Boyevoi Put*, Moscow

Published in full in the Fourth (Russian) Edition of the *Collected Works*

Printed from the original

182

TELEGRAM TO THE OREL GUBERNIA COMMITTEE OF THE R.C.P.(B.)

November 13, 1918

Gubernia Committee of the R.C.P. of Bolsheviks
For the Ukrainians
Orel

I have just received from Unecha greetings from the revolutionary soldiers of Germany. I consider it extremely important that you should inform all posts on the Ukrainian border of this by telegraph and, replying on my behalf with gratitude for the greetings of the revolutionary soldiers of Germany, you should appeal to them to help by rapid and resolute action in the liberation of the Ukraine. Let the revolutionary soldiers of Germany complete the glorious German revolution they have begun by arresting the whiteguards in the Ukraine and liberating it.

Long live the revolutionary soldiers of Germany in the Ukraine!

Long live the fraternal alliance between the German Soviet Republic and the Ukrainian Soviet Republic!

Lenin
Chairman, Council of People's Commissars

First published in 1942
in *Lenin Miscellany XXXIV*

Printed from the original

183

TELEPHONE MESSAGE TO I. I. VATSETIS

Commander-in-Chief Vatsetis
Serpukhov

The Defence Council inquires:
(1) Is it true that during the battles in the Balashov area about two weeks ago our units in the course of two or three days surrendered 25-30 guns to the enemy and, if this is true, what have you done to bring those guilty to trial and to avert similar happenings?
(2) Is it true that a fortnight ago you gave an order for the capture of Orenburg and, if it is true, why is the order not being carried out?
(3) What has been done to stabilise the position of our units in the Perm area who are demanding urgent help from the Centre?
The Defence Council awaits a reply from you to these questions.

V. Ulyanov (Lenin)
Chairman, Defence Council

Written on December 23, 1918

First published in *Pravda* No. 44,
February 23, 1927

Printed from the typewritten
text amended by J. V. Stalin
and signed by V. I. Lenin

184

TELEGRAM TO THE SOVIET OF COMMUNES
OF THE NORTHERN REGION

Zinoviev, Smolny, Petrograd

Northern Region Food Committee, Economic Council, Petrokomprod

Gubernia Food Committee, Optosoyuz

Copies to Trudosoyuz, Gubernia Food Committees

Olonets, Cherepovets, Novgorod, Pskov Economic Councils

According to information received, notwithstanding the decree of November 21, local co-operatives are being nationalised and closed, their goods requisitioned and no help is being given in restoring their legitimate activity.[340] All this causes dislocation of supply and upsets the organisation of the Soviet Republic's rear. The present is an instruction immediately to cease attempts to infringe and evade the decree of November 21, to restore the closed and nationalised co-operatives, to return their goods, and without fail to include the co-operatives in the distributive system, on an equal footing with state shops. The co-operative machinery should be made use of in all possible ways in the business of purchasing supplies and distribution, and representatives of the co-operative movement should be drawn into co-operative commissions of the food supply organisations. Infringement and evasion of the decree will be punished. This telegram is to be communicated for information and action to all Executive Committees and food supply organisations of the Northern Region. To be published in the local newspapers.

Ulyanov (Lenin)
Chairman, Defence Council

Written on December 25, 1918

Published in *Petrogradshaya Pravda* No. 285, December 27, 1918

Printed from a typewritten copy

1919

185

TELEGRAM TO L. D. TROTSKY

Urgent

Trotsky, Chairman of the Revolutionary Military Council
   of the Republic
Kursk (or present whereabouts)

The operations report of the Chief of Staff of the Caucasus Front No. 4873 shows that the Krasnov troops have
occupied Raigorod, on the banks of the Volga south of
Sarepta, threatening in the first place our military freight
moving from Vladimirovka to Tsaritsyn, and secondly
the safety of the line from Astrakhan to Saratov. Please
take steps. The same operations report shows that a British
fleet of four vessels bombarded Staroterechnaya, south of
Astrakhan, set fire to two of our barges and withdrew to sea
unscathed, seizing our hospital ship *Alesker* with medical
staff on board. Where is our fleet and what is it doing?

Lenin
Chairman, Council of People's Commissars

Written on January 2 or 3, 1919

First published in *Pravda* No. 21,
   January 21, 1937

Printed from the text
written by J. V. Stalin
and signed by V. I. Lenin

186

TELEGRAM TO G. Y. SOKOLNIKOV

In code

Sokolnikov

I am extremely worried by the slowing down of operations against the Donets coalfields and Rostov. There must be a speed-up but, of course, only with substantial forces. Work out practical directives for this purpose, and we shall get them adopted by the Central Committee for the Ukrainians, and equally for our own people. It is a crying scandal that the suppression of the Cossack rising is dragging on.[341] Reply in as much detail as you can.

Lenin

Written on April 20, 1919

First published
in *Proletarskaya Revolutsia*
No. 3, 1934

Printed from the original

187

TELEGRAM TO V. A. ANTONOV-OVSEYENKO

In code

Antonov, Kiev
Copies to *Podvoisky and Rakovsky*

Sokolnikov cables me that Denikin has magnificently taken advantage of the interlude in the Donets coalfields, fortified himself and gathered fresher forces than ours. The peril is a tremendous one. The Ukraine is bound to recognise the Donets Basin Front as unquestionably the most important Ukrainian front, and at all costs to begin immediately carrying out the directive of the Commander-in-Chief to provide solid reinforcements for the sector Donets-Mariupol. From Podvoisky's information I see that there is a mass of war matériel in the Ukraine, even without counting Odessa. It should not be hoarded, and both Donets workers and new units should be formed to take Taganrog and Rostov. Have you mobilised all the officers in the Ukraine? At all costs the forces against Denikin must be rapidly and considerably increased. Cable in as much detail as possible, and make your cipher clerks do their ciphering more carefully, so that everything can be understood.

Lenin

April 22, 1919

First published
in *Krasnaya Zvezda* No. 17,
January 20, 1929

Printed from the original

188

TELEGRAM TO K. A. MEKHONOSHIN

Military
Top priority
In code

April 24, 1919

Mekhonoshin
Astrakhan

Extremely strange that you are sending only boastful telegrams about future victories. Discuss immediately:

first—is it not possible to accelerate the capture of Petrovsk in order to get oil out of Grozny?

secondly—cannot the mouth of the Ural and Guriev be captured, in order to take oil from there? The need for oil is desperate.

Bend all your efforts to the most rapid securing of oil, and telegraph in detail.

Lenin

First published, but not in full,
in 1930 in the book *Grazhdanskaya
voina. 1918-21,* Vol. III

Published in full
in the Fourth (Russian) Edition
of the *Collected Works*

Printed from the original

189

TELEGRAM TO K. G. RAKOVSKY, V. A. ANTONOV-OVSEYENKO, N. I. PODVOISKY, L. B. KAMENEV

Rakovsky, Antonov, Podvoisky, Kamenev
Kiev

At all costs, using all your strength and as rapidly as possible, help us to finish off the Cossacks and take Rostov, even at the price of a temporary weakening in the west of the Ukraine, since otherwise we are threatened with destruction.

Lenin

Written on April 24, 1919

First published in 1934
in *Proletarskaya Revolutsia* No. 3

Printed from the original

190

TELEGRAM TO THE COMMANDER-IN-CHIEF AND THE REVOLUTIONARY MILITARY COUNCIL OF THE WESTERN FRONT

In code

Commander-in-Chief, Serpukhov
Revolutionary Military Council, Western Front

With the loss of Vilna the Entente has become still more insolent. It is essential to develop the maximum speed in regaining Vilna in the shortest possible time, so as not to give the Whites the opportunity of bringing up their forces and consolidating. Speed up the reinforcements which are on the way and act as energetically as you can. The Field Staff is to increase its supervision of the operation in this direction in every possible way.

Lenin
Chairman, Defence Council

Written on April 24, 1919

First published in 1942
in *Lenin Miscellany XXXIV*

Printed from the text
written by E. M. Sklyansky
and signed by V. I. Lenin

191

TELEGRAM TO V. A. ANTONOV-OVSEYENKO

In code

Antonov, Kiev
Copy to Rakovsky, Podvoisky, Kamenev

I have received your code message, and also your scheme for dividing the Southern Front and the Ukrainian Front. For the first I thank you, for the second I rebuke you for playing at independence.[342] Send the Ukrainian units to capture Taganrog without fail, immediately and at all costs. Telegraph.

Lenin

Written on April 25, 1919

First published in 1942
in *Lenin Miscellany XXXIV*

Printed from the original

192

TO N. I. BUKHARIN

Comrade Bukharin,

Print this with a *circumstantial* and calm analysis, demonstrating *in detail* that *such* waverings of the Socialist-Revolutionaries in the direction of the kulak and of separation from Russia, i.e., of *fragmentation* of our forces in face of Kolchak and Denikin, *objectively* lead to *helping* the bourgeoisie and Kolchak.[343]

Lenin

April 25

First published in 1945
in *Lenin Miscellany XXXV*

Printed from the original

193

TO THE STAFF OF THE 2nd UKRAINIAN SOVIET ARMY AND ALL COMRADES OF THAT ARMY

May 2, 1919

I express my very deepest gratitude and appreciation to the comrades of the 2nd Ukrainian Soviet Army for the tank sent as a present.[344]

This gift is dear to all of us, dear to the workers and peasants of Russia, as evidence of the heroism of their Ukrainian brothers, and is dear also because it bears witness to the complete collapse of the Entente which seemed so strong.

Best greetings and the warmest good wishes for success to the workers and peasants of the Ukraine and the Ukrainian Red Army.

V. Ulyanov (Lenin)
Chairman, Defence Council

First published in 1926
in Voyenny Vestnik No. 3

Printed from the original

194

TELEGRAM TO K. G. RAKOVSKY,
V. A. ANTONOV-OVSEYENKO,
N. I. PODVOISKY

In code

May 5, 1919

Rakovsky, Antonov, Podvoisky
Kiev

Up till now there has not been a single precise factual reply from you as to what units have been moved into the Donets Basin, how many rifles, sabres, guns, at what station the advanced trains are. The capture of Lugansk proves that those who accuse you of leaning to independence and turning your eyes to Rumania are right. Understand that you will be responsible for a disaster if you are late with serious help to the Donets Basin.

Lenin

Please return to me with a note: sent in code—hours—minutes.

Urgent

Lenin

May 5

First published
in *Proletarskaya Revolutsia*
No. 3, 1934

Printed from the original

195

TELEGRAM TO G. Y. SOKOLNIKOV
AND A. L. KOLEGAYEV

In code

May 6, 1919

Sokolnikov and Kolegayev
Revolutionary Military Council, Southern Front
Kozlov

The delay in suppressing the revolt is simply outrageous. I have seen a report today that the suppression is getting no further. It is essential to take the most energetic steps and root out this tardiness. Should we not send you reinforcements of Cheka men?[345] Telegraph in detail. The delay over this revolt is intolerable.

Lenin

First published, but not in full, in 1938 in *Bolshevik* No. 2

Published in full in the Fourth (Russian) Edition of the *Collected Works*

Printed from the original

196

TELEGRAM TO I. N. SMIRNOV

May 12, 1919

Ivan Nikitich Smirnov,
  Member of the Revolutionary Military Council
Revolutionary Military Council 5

Do you guarantee that the reports attributed to you, concerning the demoralisation of Kolchak's forces and their mass desertion to our side, are not exaggerated? If you do, what steps have you taken, first, to accelerate the offensive and consolidate the victory and, secondly, to dispatch to all units of both the Eastern and Southern Fronts deserters from Kolchak who have experienced his atrocities and are capable of raising the spirit of our army?

Lenin
Chairman, Defence Council

First published in 1942
in *Lenin Miscellany XXXIV*

Printed from the original

197

TELEGRAM
TO THE PETROGRAD DEFENCE COMMITTEE[346]

Zinoviev, Defence Committee, Petrograd

With the object of ascertaining the situation in Petrograd, the Defence Council requests you to give an exhaustive reply: on what considerations was it decided to evacuate several factories from Petrograd and the neighbourhood, by whom and why was an instruction given to sink ships, the total numbers of workers mobilised and remaining in the factories, are all those who have been mobilised really being used for defence requirements, for what reasons were Commissars appointed to the state factories, was there an indiscriminate call-up of citizens or was the decision of the central authority observed. The Defence Council, while leaving in force for the time being the state of siege in Petrograd, notifies you that measures taken by the Petrograd Defence Committee must be applied with the knowledge of, and in appropriate cases by agreement with, the central authority. [347]

Lenin
Chairman, Defence Council

Written on May 13, 1919

First published, but not
in full, in *Pravda* No. 165,
June 16, 1939

Published in full in 1941
in the book *Dokumenty o geroicheskoi
oborone Petrograda v 1919*, Moscow

Printed from the typewritten
text signed by V. I. Lenin

198

TELEGRAM TO G. Y. SOKOLNIKOV

Urgent

In code

Sokolnikov,
  Member, Revolutionary Military Council, Southern Front
Boguchar

The offensive against Petrograd multiplies tenfold the peril, and the extreme necessity of suppressing the revolt immediately, at all costs. Telegraph how things are going—has the division which was landed got to work at last, are the Voronezh and Tambov Communists who were sent you arriving, do you need more reinforcements, and of what sort?—in as much detail and as frequently as possible. Delays are extraordinarily dangerous.

Lenin
Chairman, Council of People's Commissars

Written on May 19, 1919

First published in 1934   Printed from the original
in *Proletarskaya Revolutsia* No. 3

199

TELEGRAM TO A. L. KOLEGAYEV

In code
May 21, 1919

Kolegayev
Revolutionary Military Council, Southern Front
Kozlov
Copy to Sokolnikov, Member, Revolutionary Military
   Council
Boguchar
Copy to Khvesin and Beloborodov,
   Staff of the Commander of the Expeditionary Forces

From Beloborodov's telegram of the 20th I learn monstrous news, that orders reach units several days late, while
armoured cars have no fuel. I am putting pressure on here,
pull things together in your own area. The Military Commissar at Tambov telegraphs that he has sent you 669
Communists to Boguchar and Ust-Medveditskaya. I am
surprised that, having them, plus 2,000 Red Army cadets,
plus a division, you are slow to take resolute action to crush
the revolt, which must be done immediately. Telegraph
in as much detail as possible.

Lenin
Chairman, Council of People's Commissars

First published in 1934
in *Proletarskaya Revolutsia* No. 3

Printed from the original

200

TELEGRAM TO K. G. RAKOVSKY
AND V. I. MEZHLAUK

In code

May 26, 1919

Rakovsky, Council of People's Commissars
Kiev
Mezhlauk, Deputy People's Commissar for War
Kharkov

I repeat my request that you telegraph me twice a week about your actual help to the Donets Basin. I insist on the fulfilment of this request. Don't lose a moment of your victory over Grigoryev, don't release a single soldier who has been fighting Grigoryev.[348] Decree and put into effect the complete disarmament of the population, shoot on the spot without mercy for every concealed rifle. The whole problem of the moment is a rapid victory in the Donets Basin, the collection of all rifles from the villages, the creation of a stable army. Concentrate all forces on this task, don't relax your energies, mobilise the workers en masse. Read this telegram to all prominent Bolsheviks.

Lenin

Sent to Kiev

First published in 1933
in *Lenin Miscellany XXIV*

Printed from the original

201

TELEGRAM TO S. I. GUSEV, M. M. LASHEVICH, K. K. YURENEV

In code

May 29, 1919

Gusev, Lashevich, Yurenev
Revolutionary Military Council, Eastern Front
Simbirsk

On your insistence Kamenev* has been appointed again. If we don't win the Urals before the winter, I consider that the revolution will inevitably perish. Strain all your energies. Telegraph me in code and in good time about every friction between Kamenev and the Staff. Watch over reinforcements more attentively; mobilise the front-line population en masse; keep your eye on political work. Telegraph me results weekly in code. Read this telegram to Muralov, Smirnov, Rozengolts and all prominent Communists and Petrograd workers. Notify receipt. Pay particular attention to mobilisation of the Orenburg Cossacks. You are responsible for seeing that units do not get demoralised or depressed. Don't get carried away by the operations side.

Lenin

First published, but not in full, in 1930 in *Grazhdanskaya voina*, *1918-21*, Vol. III Published in full in the Fourth (Russian) Edition of the *Collected Works*

Printed from the original

* Reference is to S. S. Kamenev, Commander-in-Chief of the Eastern Front.—*Ed.*

202

TELEGRAM TO D. I. YEFREMOV

May 30, 1919

Yefremov
Revolutionary Military Council 10

Immediately select a group of the most responsible and energetic Tsaritsyn workers who took part in carrying out the measures ordered by Stalin in the defence of Tsaritsyn, and instruct them to begin carrying out all these measures with the same energy. Telegraph the names of those responsible.

Lenin
Chairman, Defence Council

Sent to Tsaritsyn

First published in 1934
in *Proletarskaya Revolutsia* No. 3

Printed from the original

203

TELEGRAM
TO THE REVOLUTIONARY MILITARY COUNCIL OF THE EASTERN FRONT

> The same directive
> to be issued through
> the Central Committee

Lashevich, Yurenev, Gusev, Rozengolts,
Smirnov, Muralov

Revolutionary Military Council, Eastern Front

Serious worsening of the situation near Petrograd and the break-through in the South oblige us again and again to take troops from your front. We cannot do otherwise. You must go over to more revolutionary forms of military work, cutting through the usual methods. Mobilise in the front-line area everyone between 18 and 45 en masse, give them the task of capturing the nearest big works like Moto-vilikha, Minyar, promising to let them go when they have captured these places, assigning two or three men per rifle, calling on them to drive Kolchak out of the Urals. Mobilise 75 per cent of members of the Party and the trade unions. There is no other way out, you must go over to revolutionary methods. Discuss in part with Kamenev how to carry this out, and reply what you are undertaking.

Lenin

Written on June 9, 1919

First published in *Pravda* No. 21,
January 21, 1937

Printed from the original

204

TO E. M. SKLYANSKY

Comrade Sklyansky,

(1) Without fail at once appoint (and carry through to the end) an investigation into *who* misinformed you, *minimising* the disaster.* After all, this is *treachery*.

(2) *All* measures must be taken and *special attention given* to the rapid movement of the 6 regiments from the Eastern Front.

For really it is *you, Comrade Sklyansky, who have proved to be responsible for the delay*!![349]

Reply to me *what exactly you have done* on both points.

Lenin

Written on June 10, 1919

First published in 1945
in *Lenin Miscellany XXXV*

Printed from the original

---

* Reference is to the critical situation in Petrograd.—*Ed.*

205

TELEGRAM TO S. I. GUSEV AND M. M. LASHEVICH

Gusev, Lashevich

We have to take the division in view of the bad and almost catastrophic situation near Petrograd and in the South. No help for it. We shall hope that, in view of the capture of Ufa, the 5th Army will be able to give up the division without yielding the Belaya River, and that by doubling and redoubling our Party energy we shall together cope with the problem of not letting things go as far as defeat on the Eastern Front.

Lenin

Written on June 11, 1919

First published in *Pravda* No. 53, February 23, 1938

Printed from the original

206

TELEGRAM TO O. I. SOMOV AND D. I. YEFREMOV

In code
June 14, 1919

Somov, Yefremov
Revolutionary Military Council 10
Tsaritsyn
Copy to Raskolnikov

It is essential to retain Tsaritsyn, it has withstood a siege more than once. Strain every effort, inform us in more detail, more often, we are taking steps. Hasten the evacuation of anything not absolutely essential, and valuables. Mobilise en masse. Don't weaken the political work. Mind you keep in touch with us.

Lenin

First published in *Pravda* No. 53,
February 23, 1938

Printed from the original

207

TELEGRAM
TO THE REVOLUTIONARY MILITARY COUNCIL OF THE SOUTHERN FRONT

In code

June 14, 1919

Revolutionary Military Council, Southern Front
Kozlov

Are you taking all steps to support Tsaritsyn? They are asking for 15,000 infantry and 4,000 cavalry. It is essential to retain Tsaritsyn. Report what has been done and what is being done.

Lenin

First published in 1942
in *Lenin Miscellany XXXIV*

Printed from the original

208

TELEGRAM TO M. V. FRUNZE AND S. Z. ELIAVA

Top priority
June 16, 1919

Frunze-Mikhailov, Commander of the Southern Group
Samara (or the present whereabouts of the Staff
  of the Southern Group)
Eliava, Member of the Revolutionary Military Council

Please convey to the Uralsk comrades my warm greetings for the heroes of the fifty days' defence of besieged Uralsk, and my request not to get down-hearted, and to hold out just a few more weeks. The heroic defence of Uralsk will be crowned with success. [350]

Lenin
Chairman, Defence Council

First published (facsimile)
in 1927 in *Krasnoarmeyets* No. 2 (95)

Printed from the original

209

TELEGRAM
TO THE EXECUTIVE COMMITTEES OF SOVIETS
OF THE FRONT-LINE DISTRICTS

June 16, 1919

Gubernia Executive, Voronezh
Uyezd Executive, Novokhopyorsk, Voronezh Gubernia
Uyezd Executive, Borisoglebsk, Tambov Gubernia
Uyezd Executive, Balashov, Saratov Gubernia
Uyezd Executive, Atkarsk, Saratov Gubernia
Uyezd Executive, Kamyshin, Saratov Gubernia
Gubernia Executive, Tambov
Gubernia Executive, Saratov

Immediately take all steps for compulsory conscription of all the able-bodied population and requisitioning of carts for the work of strengthening the positions which is being carried on by military field engineering units. Appoint a member of the Executive Committee, personally responsible for fulfilment of work, to each sector. Urgently telegraph fulfilment, on your responsibility under war-time law. Name all the responsible members of the Executive Committees. The Gubernia Executive Committees answer for immediate fulfilment.

Lenin
Chairman, Defence Council

First published in 1940
in *Proletarskaya Revolutsia* No. 1

Printed from the original

210

TELEGRAM
TO THE REVOLUTIONARY MILITARY COUNCIL OF THE 10th ARMY AND THE TSARITSYN GUBERNIA EXECUTIVE COMMITTEE

June 18, 1919

Revolutionary Military Council 10
Chairman of the Gubernia Executive Committee
Tsaritsyn
Copy to Revolutionary Military Council, Southern Front
Kozlov

I have been watching with joy the heroism of the 10th Army and the Tsaritsyn proletariat in the defence of Tsaritsyn. I am sure that Red Tsaritsyn, which has withstood winter sieges lasting many months, will withstand all trials now as well. Greetings to the defenders of Red Tsaritsyn! The promised reinforcements are on the way.

Lenin
Chairman, Council of People's Commissars

Published in *Kommunist* (Astrakhan) No. 136, June 25, 1919

Printed from the original

211

TELEGRAM
TO M. M. LASHEVICH AND K. K. YURENEV

In code

June 20, 1919

Lashevich, Yurenev
Revolutionary Military Council, Eastern Front
Simbirsk

There are reports, first, of a considerable decrease in the number of political workers in the armies of the Eastern Front, because they are leaving for local administrative work in the areas liberated from the enemy; and, secondly, of the fatigue of some divisions. The most serious attention must be given to this. Political workers and all others, whoever they may be, should be absolutely forbidden to leave the army before the Urals have been occupied, and before they have been replaced by double the number of Urals workers; and then at all costs you should *secure* mobilisation en masse in the front-line area and replace the tired units by fresh forces, if only for a temporary rest, because the *offensive* against the Urals must not be weakened, it must definitely be intensified, speeded up, strengthened with reinforcements. *Telegraph what measures you are taking. Pay attention* to the rising near Samara and on the Irgiz.[351] Your silence about this is suspicious.

Lenin

Chairman, Defence Council

First published in 1934
in *Proletarskaya Revolutsia* No. 3

Printed from the original

212

TELEGRAM
TO THE REVOLUTIONARY MILITARY COUNCIL
OF THE EASTERN FRONT

July 1, 1919

Revolutionary Military Council, Eastern Front
Simbirsk
Copy to Staff of Army 3

I congratulate the heroic Red troops who have captured Perm and Kungur. Warm greetings to the liberators of the Urals. At all costs complete victory must be rapidly achieved. It is extremely necessary to mobilise, immediately and to a man, the workers of the Urals factories that are being liberated. New revolutionary methods must be found for at once incorporating these workers in the army, in order to provide a rest for those who are tired and to transfer troops for the South. Inform the regiments of the first part of this telegram.

Lenin
Chairman, Defence Council

First published in *Pravda* No. 17
and *Izvestia* No. 17,
January 21, 1927

Printed from the original

213

TELEGRAM TO V. V. KURAYEV,
V. A. RADUS-ZENKOVICH, K. I. PLAKSIN

July 2, 1919

Kurayev, Member of the Revolutionary Military Council 4
Zenkovich, Chairman of the Gubernia Executive Committee
Plaksin, Chairman of the Gubernia Party Committee
Saratov

All attention to cleansing the garrison and strengthening
the rear. Mercilessly root out the whiteguards in town and
country. Personally check up on the political work and
organisation in the garrison. Everyone to switch to war work!
Make everyone pull himself together and be disciplined.
Telegraph results. Fortify Rtishchevo particularly.

Lenin

Chairman, Defence Council

First published in 1934
in *Proletarskaya Revolutsia* No. 3

Printed from the original

214

TELEGRAM TO V. A. RADUS-ZENKOVICH

July 8, 1919

Zenkovich, Chairman of the Gubernia Executive Committee Saratov
Copy to Kurayev,
  Member of the Revolutionary Military Council 4
Copy to Plaksin, Chairman of the Gubernia Party Committee
Copy to Krylenko
Copy to Yaroslavsky

Telegraph as precisely as possible, if necessary in code, what practical successes you have achieved, and whether there is a change of mood in the garrison. It is essential that special detachments should go round all the volosts of the front-line area and work them over—organising the poor peasants, removing the kulaks, taking hostages from among them, suppressing the "Greens",[352] returning deserters to duty. Particular attention to Atkarsk Uyezd and Rtishchevo. I await a detailed factual reply.

Lenin

Chairman, Defence Council

First published (facsimile) in 1930 in *Grazhdanskaya voina. 1918-21*, Vol. III

Printed from the original

215

TELEGRAM
TO THE TULA METALWORKERS' CONGRESS

Presidium of the *Metalworkers' Congress*, Tula
(Copy to be sent to Melnichansky)

I welcome with all my heart the decision of the Tula Metalworkers' Congress to increase tenfold the output of arms, etc.[353] Please inform me monthly, by post or by messenger, exactly what actual successes are being achieved on all your decisions.

Lenin

Written on July 11, 1919
First published in *Pravda* No. 53,
February 23, 1933

Printed from the original

216

TELEGRAM TO M. M. LASHEVICH AND K. K. YURENEV

July 17, 1919

Lashevich, Yurenev
Revolutionary Military Council, Eastern Front
Simbirsk

Congratulations on your victories.[354]

Special measures should be taken: first, to prevent the Urals workers from pilfering arms, so that they don't get involved in harmful guerrilla warfare and, secondly, to prevent the Siberian partisan spirit from demoralising our troops.

Telegraph your opinion, also inform me *whether you are working well with the new Commander of the Front*, and in more detail about Bashkir affairs.[355]

Lenin

First published in 1942
in *Lenin Miscellany XXXIV*

Printed from the original

217

TO MAXIM GORKY

July 18, 1919

Dear A. M.,

Come here for a rest—I often go away for two days to the country, where I can put you up splendidly for either a short or a longer time.

Do come!

Telegraph *when*; we shall arrange a compartment for you, so that you can travel in comfort. Really, you need a little change of air. I await your reply.

Yours,
Lenin

Sent from Moscow to Petrograd

First published in *Pravda* No. 75
and *Izvestia* No. 75,
March 29, 1928

Printed from the original

218

TO MAXIM GORKY

July 31, 1919

Dear Alexei Maximych,

The more I read over your letter, and the more I think of the connection between its conclusions and what it sets forth (and what you described at our meetings), the more I arrive at the conviction that the letter, and your conclusions, and all your impressions, are quite sick.

Petrograd has been one of the sickest places in recent times. This is quite understandable, since its population has suffered most of all, the workers have given up more of their best forces than anyone else, the food shortage is grave, and the military danger too. Obviously your nerves can't stand it. That is not surprising. Yet you won't listen when you are told that you ought to change your abode, because to let oneself flog the nerves to a state of sickness is very unwise, unwise even from the plain common-sense point of view, not to speak of other points of view.

Just as in your conversations, there is in your letter a sum of sick impressions, leading you to sick conclusions.

You begin with dysentery and cholera, and immediately a kind of sick resentment comes over you: "fraternity, equality". Unconscious, but the result is something like communism being responsible for the privations, poverty and diseases of a besieged city!!

Then follow some bitter witticisms, which I don't understand, against "hoarding" literature (which? why connected with Kalinin?). And the conclusion that a "wretched remainder of the intelligent workers" say that they have been "betrayed" into "captivity to the muzhik".

That, now, has no sense in it at all. Is it Kalinin who is being accused of betraying the workers to the muzhik? That is what it amounts to.

This might be invented by workers who are either quite green, stupid, with a "Left" phrase instead of a brain, or else by those who are overwrought, exhausted, hungry, sick, or else by the "remainder of the aristocracy" who have a splendid ability to distort everything, a splendid gift for picking on every trifle to vent their frenzied hatred of Soviet power. You yourself mention this remainder at the same point in your letter. Their state of mind is having an unhealthy influence on you.

You write that you see "people of the most varied sections of society". It's one thing to see them, another thing to feel daily contact with them, in all aspects of one's life. What you mainly experience is from the "remainder"—if only by virtue of your profession, which obliges you to "receive" dozens of embittered bourgeois intellectuals, and also by virtue of your general circumstances.

As though the "remainder" cherish "something bordering on sympathy for Soviet power", while "the majority of the workers" produce thieves, "Communists" who have jumped on the band-waggon, etc.! And you talk yourself into the "conclusion" that a revolution cannot be made with the help of thieves, cannot be made without the intelligentsia.

This is a completely sick psychology, acutely aggravated in the environment of embittered bourgeois intellectuals.

Everything is being done to draw the intelligentsia (the non-whiteguard intelligentsia) into the struggle against the thieves. And *month by month* the Soviet Republic acquires a *growing* percentage of bourgeois intellectuals who are *sincerely* helping the workers and peasants, not merely grumbling and spitting fury. This cannot be "seen" in Petrograd, because Petrograd is a city with an exceptionally large number of bourgeois people (and "intelligentsia") who have lost their place in life (and their heads), but for all Russia this is an unquestionable fact.

In Petrograd, or from Petrograd, one can only become convinced of this if one is exceptionally well informed

politically and has a specially wide political experienc‹
This you haven't got. And you are engaged, not in politic
and not in observing the *work* of political construction, bu‹
in a particular profession, which surrounds you wit‹
embittered bourgeois intellectuals, who have understoo‹
nothing, forgotten nothing, learned nothing and *at best*—
very rare best—have lost their bearings, are in despai‹
moaning, repeating old prejudices, have been frightene‹
to death or are frightening themselves to death.

If you want to *observe*, you must observe from below‹
where it is possible to *survey* the work of building a ne‹
life, in a workers' settlement in the provinces or in the coun‹
tryside. There one does not have to make a political sum‹
ming-up of extremely complex data, there one need onl‹
observe. Instead of this, you have put yourself in the posi‹
tion of a professional editor of translations, etc., a posi‹
tion in which it is impossible to observe the new buildin‹
of a new life, a position in which all your strength is frit‹
tered away on the sick grumbling of a sick intelligentsia‹
on observing the "former" capital* in conditions of des‹
perate military peril and fierce privations.

You have put yourself in a position in which you *canno‹*
directly observe the new features in the life of the worker‹
and peasants, i.e., nine-tenths of the population of Russia‹
in which you are compelled to observe the fragments of lif‹
of a former capital, from where the flower of the worker‹
has gone to the fronts and to the countryside, and wher‹
there remain a disproportionately large number of intellec‹
tuals without a place in life and without jobs, who *speciall‹*
"besiege" you. Counsels to go away you stubbornly reject‹

Quite understandably, you have reduced yourself to ‹
condition of sickness: you write that you find life not onl‹
hard, but also "extremely revolting"!!! I should say so‹
At such a time to chain oneself to the sickest of places a‹
an editor of translated literature (the most suitable occu‹
pation for observing people, for an artist!). As an artist‹
you *cannot* see and study anything there that is new—in‹
the army, in the countryside, in the factory. You hav‹

---

* Petrograd. In March 1918 the capital was transferred to Moscow.—*Ed.*

deprived yourself of any opportunity of doing what would satisfy the artist: in Petrograd a politician can work, but you are not a politician. Today it's windows being broken for no reason at all, tomorrow it's shots and screams from prison, then snatches of oratory by the most weary of the non-workers who have remained in Petrograd, then millions of impressions from the intelligentsia, the intelligentsia of a capital which is no longer a capital, then hundreds of complaints from those who have been wronged, *inability* to see any building of the new life in the time you have left after editing (the building goes on in a particular way, and least of all in Petrograd)—how could you fail to reduce yourself to a point when it is extremely revolting to go on living?

The country is living in a feverish struggle against the bourgeoisie of the whole world, which is taking a frenzied revenge for its overthrow. Naturally. For the first Soviet Republic, the first blows *from everywhere*. Naturally. Here one must live either as an active politician or (if one's heart does not draw one to politics), as an artist, observe how people are building life anew somewhere that is not, as the capital is, the centre of furious attack, of a furious struggle against conspiracies, of the furious anger of the capital's intelligentsia—somewhere in the countryside, or in a provincial factory (or at the front). There it is easy, merely by observing, to distinguish the decomposition of the old from the first shoots of the new.

Life has become revolting, the "divergence" from communism "is deepening". Where the divergence lies, it is impossible to tell. Not a shadow of an indication of a divergence in politics or in ideas. There is a divergence of *mood*—between people who are engaged in politics or are absorbed in a struggle of the most furious kind, and the mood of a man who has artificially driven himself into a situation where he can't observe the new life, while his impressions of the decay of a vast bourgeois capital are getting the better of him.

I have expressed my thoughts to you frankly on the subject of your letter. From my conversations (with you) I have long been approaching the same ideas, but your letter gave shape and conclusion, it rounded off the sum total of the impressions I have gained from these conversations. I don't want to thrust my advice on you, but I cannot help saying: change your circumstances radically, your environment, your abode, your occupation—otherwise life may disgust you for good.

All the best.

Yours,

Lenin

Sent to Petrograd

First published in 1925   Printed from the original
in *Krasnaya Letopis* No. 1

219

TELEGRAM TO A. P. ROZENGOLTS

Address:

Rozengolts
Revolutionary Military Council 7

All in code

Has every measure been taken to hold Petrograd at all costs? We are pushing ahead with the promised reinforcements, but it will take time for them to arrive. Make an exceptional effort.

Lenin

Written on August 1, 1919

First published in 1942
in *Lenin Miscellany XXXIV*

Printed from the text
written by E. M. Sklyansky
and amended and signed
by V. I. Lenin

220

TELEGRAM TO L. D. TROTSKY

In code

Trotsky
Copy to Rakovsky

The Political Bureau of the Central Committee requests that the Central Committee's directive be communicated to all responsible workers: to hold out to the last, defending Odessa and Kiev, the communications between them and their communications with us to the last drop of blood. This is a question of the fate of the whole revolution. Remember that our help is not far off.

For the Political Bureau of the Central Committee,
Lenin

Written on August 9, 1919

First published in 1942
in *Lenin Miscellany XXXIV*

Printed from the original

221

TO E. M. SKLYANSKY

Comrade Sklyansky,

I am not well, I have had to go to bed.

Therefore *reply by messenger.*

The delaying of the offensive in the Voronezh direction (*from August 1* to *10*!!!) is monstrous. The successes of Denikin are enormous.

What's wrong? Sokolnikov said that there (on the approaches to Voronezh) our forces were *four* to one.

So what is wrong? How could we miss the boat in this way?

Tell the Commander-in-Chief *that this won't do. Serious* attention is required.

Should I not send the following telegram to the Revolutionary Military Council of the Southern Front (copy to Smilga):

In code

To be late with the offensive is quite intolerable, because this delay will yield the whole Ukraine to Denikin and will ruin us. You answer for every day and even hour that the offensive is held up unnecessarily. Inform us at once of your explanations, and the date when at last you will begin a resolute offensive.

Lenin

Chairman, Defence Council

Written on August 10, 1919

First published in 1942 in *Lenin Miscellany XXXIV*

Printed from the original

222

INSTRUCTION TO A SECRETARY
AND NOTE TO E. M. SKLYANSKY

Secret. Take *2 copies*, and send one to Comrade *Sklyansky* with this note:

Comrade Sklyansky,

It is clear from this that they are trying to shift responsibility. Probably *there isn't a single battle-worthy* unit against Mamontov: this is an absolute disgrace, and complete negligence on the part of the Revolutionary Military Council, or *complete failure to use an opportunity.*

As energetic measures as possible must be taken!

Lenin

To Sklyansky. See to it yourself that all this is kept *secret.*

Addition: The railway people say that our units that have been sent against Mamontov *are afraid to leave their trucks.*

By sending such units, the Revolutionary Military Council of the Republic *disgraces itself.*

Written at the end of August 1919

First published in 1942   Printed from the original
in *Lenin Miscellany XXXIV*

223

TELEGRAM
TO THE BASHKIR REVOLUTIONARY COMMITTEE

Bashkir Revolutionary Committee
Ufa
Copy to Comrade *Validov*

Now that the decisive victories of the Red Army in the East have assured the free development of the Bashkir people, the decision of the Revolutionary Military Council of the Republic to transfer some Bashkir units to Petrògrad acquires exceptional political importance. The predatory imperialists will see that the awakened peoples of the East have risen to defend the centres of the proletarian revolution. At the same time close contact between the armed Bashkirs and the workers of Petrograd will ensure close ties and mutual respect in the spirit of communism. I express my profound conviction that the Revolutionary Committee of the Bashkir Republic, and all advanced Bashkir comrades, will make every effort to ensure that the transfer of the Bashkir units takes place in the shortest possible time and with the least possible burdening of the railways. Please transmit fraternal greetings to the Bashkir Red Army men.

Lenin
Chairman, Council of People's Commissars

Written on September 5, 1919

First published in 1932
in *Grazhdanskaya voina v Bashkirii*.
Vospominania uchastnikov. Ufa

Printed from the typewritten text
signed by V. I. Lenin

224

TO S. I. GUSEV[356]

Comrade Gusev,

Thinking over the letter from Sklyansky (about the situation on September 15) and the sum total of the operations reports, I am becoming convinced that our Revolutionary Military Council of the Republic is working badly.

To keep on with reassuring reports is bad tactics. It becomes "a game of reassurance".

But in reality, we have stagnation, almost collapse.

At the Siberian Front they have put some blackguard Olderogge and the old woman Pozern in charge, and "reassured themselves". An absolute disgrace! And now we are beginning to get beaten! We shall make the R.M.C.R. responsible for this, if *energetic* steps are not taken! To let victory slip out of our hands is a disgrace.

Inaction against Mamontov. Evidently, there has been one delay after another. The troops marching on Voronezh from the North were late. We were late in transferring the 21st Division to the South. We were late with the armoured cars. Late with communications. Whether it was the Commander-in-Chief alone who visited Orel, or whether he went with you, is all one: the job was not done. Communications with Selivachov were not established, supervision of him was not established, in spite of the *long-standing* and *direct* demand of the Central Committee.

As a result, inaction against Mamontov and inaction with Selivachov (instead of the "victories" promised from day to day in childish little drawings—do you remember how you showed me these little drawings, and how I said: they've forgotten the enemy?!).

If Selivachov deserts, or his divisional commanders betray us, the guilty party will be the R.M.C.R., because it slept, and sent us soothing messages, but didn't do its job. We must send the best, *most energetic* commissars to the South, not sleepy owls.

We are late, too, with new formations. We are letting the autumn go by—and Denikin will triple his forces, get tanks, etc., etc. This can't go on. The *sleepy* tempo of work must be made into a *lively* one.

Reply (through Lydia Alexandrovna Fotiyeva).

Lenin

September 16

Apparently our R.M.C.R. "gives orders", without being interested in or able to follow up *fulfilment*. This may be our common vice, but in military affairs it simply means destruction.

Written on September 16, 1919

First published in *Pravda* No. 63,
      March 5, 1933   Printed from the original

225

TO E. M. SKLYANSKY

October 15, 1919

Comrade Sklyansky,

Cavalry radio stations, and also light mobile field stations, of which there are large quantities in the stores of the Central Military Engineers' Board, are absolutely essential for the Southern Front. Give immediate instructions for the urgent transfer to the Southern Front of 50 of each type. This is demanded by Stalin, who complains very much of lack of communications.

Write me what exactly you have done, and incidentally order for me from the C.M.E.B. a brief summary of the total number of radio stations they possess, and their distribution among the forces.

V. Ulyanov (*Lenin*)
Chairman, Defence Council

First published in *Pravda* No. 53. February 23, 1933

Printed from the original

226

NOTE ON A LETTER FROM G. K. ORJONIKIDZE[357]

In the opinion both of Unshlikht and of Stalin, Sergo is a most reliable *military* worker. That he is a most loyal and *most practical* revolutionary, I know from my own experience of over 10 years.

Written not earlier than October 15,1919

First published in *Pravda* No. 298, October 28, 1936

Printed from the original

227

TO G. N. KAMINSKY, D. P. OSKIN, V. I. MEZHLAUK

October 20, 1919

Comrades Kaminsky, Oskin and Mezhlauk
Tula

Comrades,

Tula is just now of exceptional importance—and generally speaking, even independently of the enemy being close at hand, Tula is of vast importance to the Republic.

Therefore you must exert *all* your energy to achieve *co-ordinated* work, concentrating *everything* on military affairs and military supplies.

I regret very much the friction between yourselves and Zelikman on one side and Peters (he is an important and extremely dedicated person) on the other, and I think that this is Zelikman's fault because, if some unevenness was noticeable, it should have been immediately put right (and this was not difficult to do), without letting matters reach a conflict. The slightest *unevenness* must in future be settled, reporting to the centre *in time*, not allowing it to develop into a conflict.

Every effort must be made to improve the work in Tula; it must be placed *entirely* on a *war footing*. A decree reducing the civil administration will be published in a few days. Not only must it be observed; it must be applied with supreme conscientiousness and zeal.[358] In Tula *the masses* are far from being on our side. Hence the necessity for *particularly* intensive work among the troops, among the reservists, among the working men and women.

If you are short of personnel, write: we shall send you help from Moscow.

Check up on the defence work unremittingly. Are strong points being put up? Is the work weakening? Are there enough materials, and workers? Are the Red Army men being trained? Are supplies for them in order? All these and similar questions must be *assigned* for special *supervision* to practical people and comrades devoted to the Party. You bear full responsibility for the *success* of this work and for any negligence (if you do not complain in time and do not appeal to the centre). The formation of army units is of *exceptional* importance.

If we take Orel,[359] the effort should not be reduced, but multiplied *tenfold*, since without this we shall not conquer, and an interruption in the offensive means death for us.

Read this letter to *all* responsible workers and Party members and *regularly*, *very briefly*, keep me informed of what *in fact* is being done.

      With communist greetings,

                       V. Ulyanov (Lenin)

First published in 1931 in the book: Printed from the original
   D. Oskin, *Zapiski Voyenkoma*,
     Moscow

228

INSTRUCTIONS
TO THE DEPUTY PEOPLE'S COMMISSAR FOR WAR

October 24, 1919

From *Stalin*
(*To be settled urgently*)

(1) The mobilised Letts to be sent to the reserve battalions of the Lettish Division
(hurry up Peterson; repeat the order to him).
(2) The Turkestan Cavalry Brigade, promised by the Commander-in-Chief, to be moved to Kozlov.
To be checked up. Hurry him up.
(3) Eight battalions for the 8th Army, promised by the Commander-in-Chief. Hurry him up.
Appoint a responsible person.
(4) The Commander-in-Chief promised reinforcements from Kaluga for the 45th Division.
Check this. Hurry him up.
Appoint a responsible person.

Lenin

First published in *Pravda* No. 53,
February 23, 1938

Printed from the original

229

TO V. V. VOROVSKY[360]

October 24, 1919

Comrade V. V. Vorovsky
State Publishing House

Having looked through the pamphlet *Third International,
March 6-7, 1919*, brought out by the State Publishing House,
Moscow, 1919 (price 8 rubles), 99 pages, I impose a *severe
reprimand* for such a publication, and demand that all
members of the collegium of the State Publishing House
should read my present letter, and should work out serious
measures to guarantee that such an outrage is not repeated.

The pamphlet is a horrible piece of work. A slovenly
mess. No table of contents. Some idiot or sloven, evidently
an illiterate, has lumped together, as though he were drunk,
all the "material", little articles, speeches, and printed
them *out of sequence*.

No preface, no minutes, no exact text of the decisions,
no separation of decisions from speeches, articles, notes,
nothing at all! An unheard-of disgrace!

A great historic event has been disgraced by such a pamphlet.

I demand:

(1) Correction by *pasting in*. (The guilty persons to
be sent to prison and obliged to *paste in* the additions in
every copy.)

That I should be informed:

(2a) How many copies were printed?

(2b) How many have been sold?

(3) Reprinting in a *decent* form. *Proofs to be shown to me.*

(4) Establishment of a rule that *one definite person* should be responsible for *each* publication (a register of responsible persons to be started).

(5) Other measures for introducing order; they are to be worked out and sent to me.

V. Ulyanov (Lenin)

Chairman, Council of People's Commissars

First published in 1933   Printed from the original
in *Lenin Miscellany XXIV*

230

TO G. Y. ZINOVIEV

Comrade Zinoviev,

(1) It is said that the combustible slate near Veimarn is not deep down. If two or three sazhens of earth are removed, an excavator can be used to break up the slate and extract it.

We must make an effort; mobilise the bourgeoisie for this (they can live in dug-outs for the time being); work three shifts of eight hours; rouse the Petrograd workers for this job;

mobilise the peasants (four hours a day for two weeks, *as a beginning and so on*).

(2) It is said that Zhuk (the one who was killed) was making sugar out of sawdust?

Is that true? If it is true, you absolutely must *find his assistants*, in order to continue the job. *The importance is tremendous*.

Greetings!

Lenin

Written later than October 25, 1919

First published in 1925
in the book *K godovshchine
smerti V. I. Lenina 1924 g.—
21 yanvarya 1925 g.*
Moscow-Leningrad

Printed from the original

231

TO G. M. KRZHIZHANOVSKY

Gleb Maximilianych,

I was very interested in your report on peat.

Wouldn't you write an article about it in *Ekonomicheskaya Zhizn* (and then republish as a pamphlet, or in some journal)?[361]

The question must be discussed in the press.

Here, you should say, are reserves of peat—milliards.

Its heat efficiency.

Its location—near Moscow; *Moscow Region.*

Near Petrograd—as exactly as possible.

Easy to secure (in comparison with coal, combustible slate, etc.).

Use of the labour of the *local* workers and peasants (*even if only four hours a day for a start*).

Here, you say, is the basis for electrification, increasing output *so many times* by using *existing* power stations.

Here is the *most rapid* and *most certain* basis for the restoration of industry—

—organisation of labour in socialist fashion (agriculture + industry);

—a way out of the fuel crisis (we shall release *so many* millions of cubic metres of timber for transport).

Put in the *conclusions* of your report; add a peat map; brief and general calculations. The possibility of building peat machines quickly, etc., etc. Briefly, the essence of the economic programme.

The question must be brought up *immediately* in the press.

Yours,
Lenin

December 26

P.S. In case of necessity, get Winter on the job, but provide the article as soon as you can.

First published
in *Ekonomicheskaya Zhizn* No. 18,
January 22, 1925

Printed from the original

232

TELEGRAM TO M. M. LITVINOV

To Litvinov from Lenin

It is extremely important for us to have all the documents, resolutions, pamphlets, newspaper articles and speeches dealing with the ideological trends in Left-wing socialism and communism, especially anarcho-syndicalist distortions of communism or attacks on communism. Collect all this carefully in all languages, make clippings, send, or bring, them in three or four copies, especially the German "Independents", their congress and after their congress,[362] and the German Communists.

Lenin

Written on December 28, 1919
Sent to Copenhagen

First published in 1945
in *Lenin Miscellany XXXV*

Printed from the original

V. I. Lenin
1920

1920

233

TO THE ALL-RUSSIA CENTRAL COUNCIL OF TRADE UNIONS[363]

January 16, 1920

To Comrade Tomsky, with a request to bring this before
  the All-Russia C.C.T.U.
  and the Communist group in the All-Russia C.C.T.U.

Dear Comrades,

I send you herewith a report on the astonishing *red tape*,
carelessness, bureaucracy and helplessness displayed in a
most important *practical* matter.

I have never doubted that there is still very much bureaucracy in our Commissariats, in all of them.

But I did not expect that there would be *no less* bureaucracy in the trade unions.

This is the greatest disgrace. I very much ask you to
read all these documents in the Communist group of the
All-Russia C.C.T.U., and to work out *practical* measures
for combating bureaucracy, red tape, idleness and helplessness.

Please be good enough to let me know the results.

Melnichansky *himself* rang me up about these 10,000
metalworkers. I made a fuss at the People's Commissariat
of Railways, and now Comrade Melnichansky has let me
down....

With communist greetings,
V. Ulyanov (Lenin)

First published in *Trud* No. 18,
  January 22, 1925

Printed from the original

234

TO A. V. LUNACHARSKY

January 18, 1920

Comrade Lunacharsky,

Recently I had occasion—to my regret and shame, for the first time—to look through the famous Dahl dictionary.[364]

It's a magnificent thing, but then .it's a dictionary of *regional* terms, and out of date. Is it not time to produce a dictionary of the *real* Russian language, a dictionary, say, of words used *nowadays* and by the *classics*, from Pushkin to Gorky?

What if 30 scholars were set to work at this, and provided with Red Army rations?

What would be your attitude to this idea?

A dictionary of the classical Russian language?

Without making a noise about it, have a talk with people who know the subject, if it's not too much trouble, and let me know your opinion.

Yours,
Lenin

First published in *Pravda* No. 21,
January 21, 1940

Printed from the original

235

TO G. M. KRZHIZHANOVSKY

Gleb Maximilianovich,

I have received and read the article.[365]

Magnificent.

We need *several* such articles. Then we shall publish them as a pamphlet.[366] What we lack is specialists with a wide horizon and "an eye for the future".

It is necessary (1) *for the time being* to cut out the footnotes or reduce them. There are too many of them for a newspaper (I will have a talk with the editor tomorrow).

(2) Would it not be possible to add a *plan*, not a technical one (this, of course, is a job for *many* people, and not to be done in a hurry), but a political or state plan, i.e., a task for the proletariat?

Approximately as follows: in 10 (5?) years let us build *20-30* (30-50?) power stations, in order to cover the whole country with a network of centres of 400 (or 200, if we can't manage more) versts radius; using peat, water, combustible slate, coal, oil (*for example*, make a survey of the whole of Russia, giving *rough* approximations). Let's begin at once buying the necessary machines and models, you say. In 10 (20?) years we'll make Russia "electrical".

I think you could produce such a "plan"—I repeat, not a technical one but a state one—a draft plan.

It must be provided right away, in a visual, popular form, for the masses, so as to carry them forward with a clear and vivid perspective (entirely *scientific* at its foundations): let's set to work, and in 10-20 years we shall make all Russia, both industrial and agricultural, *electrical*. We shall set ourselves the target of having *so many* (thousands or millions of horse-power or kilowatts?? devil knows what) mechanical slaves and so on.

Could there also be a *tentative* map of Russia with centres and their areas? Or is that not yet possible?

I repeat, we must carry away the *mass* of workers and politically-conscious peasants with a *great* programme for the next 10-20 years.

Let's have a talk on the telephone.

Yours,
Lenin

January 23

P.S. Krasin says that electrification of the railways is impossible for us. Is that true? And if it is, perhaps it will be possible in 5-10 years? Maybe it is possible in the Urals?

Could not a special article be written about a "state plan" for a network of power stations, with a map, or with the approximate list (number) of them, with the prospects of centralising the power of the whole country?

Ring me up on the telephone, please, when you get this letter, and we shall have a talk.

Written on January 23, 1920

First published in *Ekonomicheskaya*
  Zhizn No. 18, January 22, 1925   Printed from the original

236

TO M. A. BONCH-BRUYEVICH

February 5, 1920

Mikhail Alexandrovich,

Comrade Nikolayev has given me your letter and told me the essence of the thing. I made inquiries of Dzerzhinsky, and immediately sent off both the telegrams for which you asked.

I take this opportunity of expressing to you my deep gratitude and sympathy for the great work of radio inventions which you are carrying on. The newspaper without paper and "without distances" which you are bringing into being will be a great achievement. I promise to assist you in any and every possible way in this and similar work.

With best wishes,

V. Ulyanov (Lenin)

First published in 1924
in the magazine *Telegrafiya
i telefoniya bez provodov*
(Nizhni-Novgorod) No. 23

Printed from the original

237

TELEGRAM TO L. D. TROTSKY

All in code
February 27, 1920

Trotsky

Of course, the Defence Council will not object to the disbanding of the army clerical staff.[367] All the symptoms are that Poland will present us with absolutely unreasonable, even arrogant terms. All attention must be directed to preparing, strengthening the Western Front. I should think extraordinary measures essential for rapid transportation of everything possible to the Western Front from Siberia and from the Urals. I am afraid we have been in a little too much of a hurry with the labour armies,[368] if we don't use them entirely to accelerate deliveries to the Western Front. We have to give out the watchword of being ready for war with Poland.

Lenin

First published in full in 1945
in *Lenin Miscellany XXXV*

Printed from the original

238

TELEGRAM TO I. T. SMILGA AND G. K. ORJONIKIDZE

All in code

March 11, 1920

Smilga and Orjonikidze
R.M.C., Caucasus Front
Copy to Stalin
R.M.C., South-Western Front

I am very glad of your report that you expect the complete defeat of Denikin soon, but I am afraid of your excessive optimism. The Poles evidently are going to make war with them inevitable. Therefore the main problem now is not the Caucasus Labour Army, but preparations for the speediest possible transfer of the maximum troops to the Western Front. Concentrate all your efforts on this problem. Make use of prisoners most energetically for the same purpose.

Lenin

First published in 1934 in the
magazine *Voina i revolutsia* No. 1

Printed from the original

239

TO G. M. KRZHIZHANOVSKY

March 14

Gleb Maximilianovich,

After looking through the statement by the *GOELRO*[369] and thinking over yesterday's talk, I have come to the conclusion that it is *dry*.

It is not enough.

Can't you write, or commission an article from Krug (or someone else) of such a kind as to

prove

or, at any rate, illustrate

a) the tremendous advantage,

b) the *necessity* of electrification.

For example:

I. Transport. To restore in the old way—

we need α millions (at pre-war prices)

or α fuel $+ \beta$ working days.

But to restore it on the basis of electrification

α minus x million rubles

α minus y fuel $+ (\beta$ minus $z)$ working days.

Or *also* $\frac{\alpha}{\alpha + \beta}$, but with an effect so many times greater than the previous one.

II. Steam power. If industry is restored in the old way, we must spend *more* than for restoring it on the basis of electrification.

III. Agriculture.

To restore, say, $+ 5$ million ploughs and teams of horses.

The cost of doing this in the old way, and with electrification?

This is a *rough idea*. I think an intelligent specialist will do this work in a couple of days (if he wants to do it conscientiously), taking either the figures of pre-war statistics (a few, really a few, summary figures), or a *rough and approximate* calculation ("as a first approximation"[370] *towards a first approximation*).

Commission this. Perhaps you will commission somebody to collect the *material* for you and write the article yourself or *give an interview*. I will send an interviewer. Then we shall have the *warp* for propaganda. And that is important.

After reading this, ring me up on the telephone.

Yours,
Lenin

Written on March 14, 1920

First published in *Ekonomicheskaya Zhizn* No. 18, January 22, 1925

Printed from the original

240

TO E. M. SKLYANSKY

March 15, 1920

Comrade Sklyansky,

A decision of the R.M.C. is required:

to turn particular attention to the *mistake* that has obviously been *made* with the Crimea (sufficient forces were not moved in time)[371];

—all efforts should be exerted to correct the mistake (events in Germany[372] render *extremely* acute the question of *hastening* Denikin's final defeat);

—in particular, prepare naval equipment (mines, submarines, etc.) and a possible advance from Taman into the Crimea (I seem to remember that Mikhail Dmitriyevich Bonch-Bruyevich told me this would be easy).

A number of most precise and most energetic decisions by the R.M.C. on this are *essential immediately*.

Send me a copy.

Lenin

First published (facsimile) in 1930 in *Grazhdanskaya voina. 1918-21*, Vol. III

Printed from the original

241

TELEGRAM TO I. T. SMILGA AND G. K. ORJONIKIDZE

In code

March 17, 1920

Smilga and Orjonikidze
R.M.C., Caucasus Front

It is extremely, extremely necessary for us to take Baku. Devote all your efforts to this, and in your statements you must be particularly diplomatic and make maximum sure that a firm local Soviet authority is ready. The same applies to Georgia, though I advise you to be even more careful there. Come to an understanding with the Commander-in-Chief about transfer of troops.

Lenin

First published in 1942
in *Lenin Miscellany XXXIV*

Printed from the original

242

TO V. V. ADORATSKY[373]

April 6, 1920

Comrade Adoratsky,

I have passed on to Comrade Khodorovsky a request to help you as regards rations, wood fuel, etc.

He has promised to do this.

Write to me when someone is coming this way (better through the military)

(1) has anything been done to help you? in rations? in fuel?

(2) do you need anything more?

(3) can you collect material for the *history of the Civil War*

and the *history of the Soviet Republic*?

Can you collect any of this material in Kazan? Can I be of assistance?

Files of *Izvestia* and *Pravda*? Is a lot missing?

Can I help in getting what is missing?

Please write to me, and *give your address*.

Best greetings.

Yours,
Lenin

Sent to Kazan

First published in 1924
in *Proletarskaya Revolutsia* No. 3

Printed from the original

243

TO K. A. TIMIRYAZEV[374]

April 27, 1920

Dear Klimenty Arkadyevich,

Many thanks to you for your book and kind words.[375] I was simply delighted to read your remarks against the bourgeoisie and for Soviet power. I shake your hand very warmly and with all my heart wish you health, health and health again!

Yours,

V. Ulyanov (Lenin)

First published in 1923
in *Ogonyok* No. 35

Printed from the original

244

TELEGRAM TO G. K. ORJONIKIDZE

Orjonikidze,
Member of the R.M.C., Caucasus Front
Baku via Rostov

To be delivered through responsible persons, and on delivery inform Sklyansky, Revolutionary Military Council of the Republic.

The Central Committee instructs you to withdraw your units from the territory of Georgia to the frontier, and to refrain from an advance into Georgia.

After the conversations with Tiflis it is clear that peace with Georgia is not ruled out.

Let us know immediately all most precise details about the insurgents.

By instruction of the Political Bureau of the Central Committee,

*Lenin**

Written on May 4, 1920

First published in 1942
in *Lenin Miscellany XXXIV*

Printed from a copy
written in an unknown hand

---

* The telegram was also signed by J. V. Stalin.—*Ed.*

245

TO M. N. POKROVSKY[376]

May 5, 1920

Comrade Pokrovsky,

Some time ago it happened that I talked with Comrade Lunacharsky about the necessity of publishing a good dictionary of the Russian language.* Not like Dahl, but a dictionary for use (and study) by all, a dictionary, so to speak, of the classical, contemporary Russian language (for example, from Pushkin to Gorky, perhaps). Provide about 30 scholars, or as many as are needed, with rations, taking, of course, those who are not suitable for any other work—and let them do the job.

Lunacharsky said that he had been thinking about this already, and that it was either being done or would be done.

Be so kind as to find out whether it is being done, and drop me a line.

Yours,
Lenin

First published in 1942
in *Lenin Miscellany XXXIV*

Printed from the original

---

* See Letter 234.—*Ed.*

246

TO A. S. SERAFIMOVICH[377]

May 21, 1920

To Comrade Serafimovich

Dear Comrade,

My sister has just told me of the terrible misfortune which has overtaken you. Allow me to give you the very warmest handshake, and to wish you courage and firmness of spirit. I very much regret that I have not been able to fulfil my desire to see you more often and to become better acquainted. But your books, and what my sister has often told me, have aroused a profound affection for you in me, and I very much want to say to you how *necessary* your work is for the workers and for all of us, and how essential it is now for you to be firm, in order to overcome your grief and *force* yourself to return to work. Forgive me for writing in a hurry. Once again, I shake you very warmly by the hand.

Yours,
Lenin

First published in 1924
in the book: V. Veshnev,
A. Serafimovich kak khudozhnik slova

Printed from the original

247

TO D. I. KURSKY[378]

Have measures been taken for the *immediate* (1) setting up of *Soviet power* in the liberated areas; (2) holding of *congresses* of Soviets; (3) expulsion of the *landowners*, distribution of *part* of their lands among the poor peasants and the remainder among *Soviets* of agricultural labourers?

Written early in July 1920

First published in 1945   Printed from the original
in *Lenin Miscellany XXXV*

248

TO THE EXECUTIVE COMMITTEE
OF THE COMMUNIST INTERNATIONAL

Theses should also be written for the Second Congress of the Third International on the international economic and political situation.

Could not Radek, or *Lapinsky*, who has more time, or *someone else*, whom they would advise, be given the job of making a *preliminary draft of these theses, approximately* on the following *lines*[379]:

(1) The division of the whole world (both in the sense of the spheres of influence of banking and finance capital, and in the sense of international syndicates and cartels, and equally in the sense of the seizure of colonies and semi-colonies) is the basic fact of imperialism, of the economy of the twentieth century.

(2) Hence imperialist wars are inevitable in general, and particularly the first imperialist war of 1914-18.

(3) Results of this war:

(a) *reduction* in the number of states that are world powers, *increase* in the number of weak, dependent states which are being plundered and divided;

(b) the tremendous sharpening of *all* capitalist contradictions, both within all the capitalist countries and among the countries themselves;

(c) in particular, the sharpening, on a world scale, of both poles of capitalism:

increase of luxury among a tiny number of capitalist magnates;

increase of need, poverty, ruin, famine, unemployment, extreme insecurity of existence;

(d) intensification of militarism, more intense and accelerated preparation for new imperialist wars, economically inevitable; a growth in the number of wars throughout the world, particularly of revolutionary wars;

(e) complete bankruptcy of the League of Nations, exposure of its falseness; the collapse of "Wilsonism". The bankruptcy of bourgeois *democracy*.

(4) Explanation, in the briefest way, by characterising (cf. the report by P. Levi, April 14, 1920[380]):

Britain and America

France

Japan

the other, neutral countries of Europe and America

the defeated countries (principally Russia and Germany)

the colonies

the semi-colonies (Persia, Turkey, China).

(5) Raw material—its exhaustion

industry—its weakening (fuel, etc.)

currencies—their collapse. Debts. Devaluation.

"Dislocation", *break-up* of the whole system of world economy.

(6) The result=a world revolutionary crisis. The communist movement and Soviet power.

Written earlier than July 19, 1920

First published in 1942   Printed from the original
in *Lenin Miscellany XXXIV*

249

TO G. V. CHICHERIN[381]

July 22, 1920

To Comrade Chicherin

My proposal:

1) Directives to be given to Kopp through the People's Commissariat of Foreign Affairs in the spirit of Comrade Chicherin's proposal (only trade negotiations).

2) Gukovsky to be answered.

3) Curzon to be replied to *in two days* (not earlier; why spoil them), after asking Kamenev and the Consul once again: why haven't we received the original in English?

The reply to be extra polite on the following lines if *Britain* (+ France +? +?) wants a general, i.e., a *real* peace, *we* have long been *for it*. In that case *remove Wrangel*, since he is *your man*, kept by you, and then we begin negotiations at once.

If Poland wants peace, we are *for*; we've said it clearly and we repeat it, let her make an offer.

If you interrupt *trade* negotiations, we are very sorry, but you expose *yourselves* as departing from the truth, because you began these negotiations *during* Poland's war and *promised an armistice*. Calmly and precisely expose their contradictions.

The draft reply to be approved by telephone through the members of the Political Bureau on Friday or Saturday, July 23 or 24.

Lenin

Comrade Chicherin,

If you agree, inform Comrade Krestinsky (he agrees in principle), then draft the reply.

Yours,
Lenin

Published for the first time
in the Fourth (Russian) Edition
of the *Collected Works*

Printed from the original

250

TO THE LIBRARY OF THE RUMYANTSEV MUSEUM

If, according to the rules, reference publications are not issued for home use, could not one get them for an evening, for the night, when the Library is closed. *I will return them by the morning*.

For reference for *one* day:

I. The two *best*, fullest, dictionaries of the *Greek* language, Greek-*German*, -French, -Russian or -English.

II. The best *philosophical* dictionaries, dictionaries of philosophical terms: the German, I think, is Eisler; the English, I think, is Baldwin; the French, I think, is Frank (if there is nothing newer); the Russian, the latest you have.

III. A history of Greek philosophy

1) *Zeller*, the complete and latest edition.

2) *Gomperz* (the Vienna philosopher): *Griechische Denker*.

Written on September 1, 1920

First published in 1929
in *Ogonyok* No. 3

Printed from the original

251

TELEGRAM TO G. K. ORJONIKIDZE

In code

September 9, 1920

Orjonikidze
R.M.C., Caucasus Front

The most rapid and complete elimination of all bands and remnants of the whiteguards in the Caucasus and the Kuban area is a matter of absolute importance to the whole state. Inform me more frequently and more precisely on how matters stand.

Lenin

First published in *Pravda* No. 298,
October 28, 1936

Printed from the original

252

TO THE CHEREMKHOVO COAL MINERS

September 15, 1920

To the Chief Board of Management of the Coal Mines
of Eastern Siberia
For the workers in the mines and also
for their technical personnel

Dear Comrades,

I thank you with all my heart for your greetings of August 2, 1920, transmitted through Comrade Ivan Yakovlevich Ilyin. My talk with Comrade Ilyin about the energetic work being done in the Siberian mines and his report of the gradual growth of conscious discipline among the workers (who are now working not for the capitalists but for themselves) gave me tremendous pleasure.

Particularly precious in your greetings, comrades, was the feeling of the deepest conviction in the final and complete victory of Soviet power over the landowners, capitalists and all kinds of exploiters, and also your unswerving firmness and determination to overcome all obstacles and difficulties. It is from this firmness of the working class and toiling masses that, like every other Communist, I draw my confidence in the inevitable world victory of the workers and the workers' cause.

With communist greetings, and wishes for your speediest success,

Devotedly yours,

V. Ulyanov (Lenin)

Petrogradskaya Pravda No. 253,
November 11, 1920

Printed from the original

253

TELEGRAM
TO THE REVOLUTIONARY MILITARY COUNCIL OF THE 1st CAVALRY ARMY[382]

By direct line (in code)

R.M.C., 1st Cavalry Army

It is extremely important to accelerate to the utmost the transfer of your Army to the Southern Front. Please take all steps for this purpose, not hesitating at the heroic. Telegraph what precisely you are doing.

Lenin
Chairman, Defence Council

October 4

First published in *Pravda* No. 53, February 23, 1933

Printed from a typewritten copy

254

TELEGRAM TO M. V. FRUNZE

In code

Secret

Frunze, R.M.C., Southern Front[383]

Having received the exultant telegrams from Gusev and yourself, I am afraid of excessive optimism. Remember that at all costs you must enter the Crimea on the heels of the enemy. Prepare as carefully as possible, and check whether all the fords for taking the Crimea[384] have been studied.

Lenin

October 16, 1920

First published in 1935
in *Krasny Arkhiv* No. 5

Printed from a typewritten copy

255

TO THE TULA COMRADES

Dear Comrades,

As *you* have set it forth, I am in agreement with you, but if you want to make use of my opinion against your "opposition", *give* them both your letter to me and my reply.[385] Then they will be informed, and will be in a position to give me *their* version: and then I will *not* be informed one-sidedly.

On the substance of the matter, this briefly is my view. Until we have *completely* beaten Wrangel, until we have captured the entire Crimea, military tasks come *first*. That is absolutely unquestionable.

Furthermore, *for* Tula, in view of its armaments and ammunition works, *it may very well be* that for a certain time *even after victory* over Wrangel it will still be a task of first priority to go throught with producing rifles and ammunition, *because the Army must be made ready* by the spring.

Excuse my brevity, and please inform me whether you have shown the "opposition" this letter of mine and your letter to me.

With communist greetings,
Lenin

Written on October 20, 1920

First published in 1942
in *Lenin Miscellany XXXIV*

Printed from a typewritten copy

256

TO THE PRESIDIUM OF THE PETROGRAD SOVIET[386]

Dear Comrades,

In my opinion, to provide scientists with an extra room for a study, and for a laboratory, in Petrograd (a city exceptionally well off as regards apartments) is really and truly no sin. You should even have taken the initiative yourselves.

I strongly request you to get this thing moving and, if you disagree with me, to be kind enough to drop me a few words immediately, so that I see where the obstacle is.

With communist greetings,

V. Ulyanov (Lenin)

October 21

First published
in *Leningradskaya Pravda* No. 209,
September 13, 1924

Printed from the original

257

TELEGRAM
TO THE REVOLUTIONARY MILITARY COUNCIL OF THE 1st CAVALRY ARMY

R.M.C., 1st Cavalry Army
Copy to the Southern Front
Copy to L. B. Kamenev

Wrangel is obviously withdrawing his forces. Possibly he is already trying to take refuge in the Crimea. To let him give you the slip would be the greatest crime. The success of the impending blow depends to a considerable degree on the 1st Cavalry Army. We request the R.M.C. of the 1st Cavalry Army to adopt the most heroic measures to accelerate the concentration of this Army.

*Lenin**
Chairman, Council of People's Commissars

October 24, 1920

·First published in 1940
in *Voyenno-istorichesky zhurnal*
No. 10

Printed from a typewritten copy

* The telegram is also signed by L. D. Trotsky, Chairman of the Revolutionary Military Council.—*Ed.*

258

TO R. E. KLASSON[387]

November 2, 1920

Comrade Klasson,

I fear that you—excuse my frankness—will not be up to making use of the decision of the Council of People's Commissars on Hydropeat.[388] I fear this because you, evidently, have spent too much time on "senseless dreams" about the restoration of capitalism, and have not been sufficiently attentive to the extremely specific features of the transitional period from capitalism to socialism. But I say this not in order to reproach you, and not only because I remembered the theoretical arguments I had with you in 1894-95, but with a narrowly practical object.

In order to make proper use of the decision of the C.P.C. you must

1) complain with ruthless strictness and in good time of any breaches of this decision, checking up very closely on its fulfilment and, of course, selecting for complaint only those cases which come under the rule, "few but to the point";

2) from time to time—again following the same rule— write to me (N.B. *mark the envelope*: *PERSONAL*, from *so-and-so*, on such-and-such a question):

please send a reminder or inquiry
such-and-such (draft text on a separate sheet)
to such-and-such a person or institution, on such-and-such a question, in view of the recognition of the works undertaken by Hydropeat as being of state importance.

If you don't let me down, i.e., if your reminders and inquiries are strictly business-like (without departmental squabbles or polemics), I will sign such reminders and inquiries in two minutes, and they will sometimes be of practical value.

Wishing you rapid and great success with your invention.

Greetings,

V. Ulyanov (*Lenin*)

First published in 1929
in the magazine *Izobretatel* No. 2

Printed from the original

259

TO G. M. KRZHIZHANOVSKY

November 6

G. M.,

This is a very important thing. Our Commission[389] (to which surely you have been invited? by the previous decision?) will meet *tomorrow* (or November 8 in the morning).

The (attached) draft of the subcommission must be attentively discussed beforehand.

GOELRO* has not been included at all!

In my opinion this is not right: what is any "plan" worth (or any "planning commission" or "planning programme") *without a plan of electrification*? It is worth nothing.

Strictly speaking, it is GOELRO which should be the single planning organ of the Council of People's Commissars; but so simply and brutally this will not be accepted, and it would be wrong. We must think over (urgently, before tomorrow) how the question should be put.

Perhaps (1) the chairman of GOELRO should be given a consultative vote in the *economic department* of the Narrow Council of People's Commissars[390]?

(2) GOELRO should be made a *standing* commission of the *C.P.C.*, since it prepares *and carries out*, or should carry out, electrification for the Supreme Economic Council, for the People's Commissariat of Agriculture, for the People's Commissariat of Railways, *etc.*

---

* See Note 369.—*Ed.*

(3) *All* planning commissions of all People's Commissariats should be linked and co-ordinated with GOELRO. But how?

By setting up yet one more commission *attached* to GOELRO, composed of the chairmen of *all* the separate planning commissions? Or how otherwise?

Ring me up when you have read this.

And *return me the minutes* (*of the subcommission of November 5*) *today*, *not later than 10* p.m.

Yours,
Lenin

Written on November 6, 1920

First published in 1924 in the book:
G. M. Krzhizhanovsky, *Tovaroobmen i planovaya rabota*, MOSCOW

Printed from the original

260

TO THE STATE PUBLISHING HOUSE

Please inform me (1) whether there exists in the State Publishing House a general practice under which, when any book or pamphlet without exception is published, there is recorded in writing:

(a) the signature of the member of the Board of the Publishing House who is responsible for editorial supervision of the publication in question;

(b) the signature of the actual editor of the text;

(c) the signature of the responsible proof-reader or publisher or printer.

(2) If not, what objections are there to such a system? What are the present means of supervision?

(3) Information under § 1 about the pamphlet:

On Concessions. Decree of the Council of People's Commissars, November 23, 1920. Text of the Decree. Units for Concession. Maps. State Publishing House. 1920.[391] State Printing Works (former Sytin), 71 Pyatnitskaya, Moscow, 1920.

Written on December 11, 1920

First published in 1921
in the magazine *Zhizn* No. 1

Printed from the original

261

TO G. M. KRZHIZHANOVSKY

G. M.,

The following idea has come into my head.

There must be propaganda for electricity. How? Not only in words but by example.

What does this mean? The most important thing is to make it popular. For this we have, here and now, to work out a *plan* for lighting up *every house* in the R.S.F.S.R. by electricity.

This is a long-term affair, because neither 20,000,000 (-40,000,000?) bulbs, nor wire, etc., shall we have *for a long time*.

But all the same a plan is needed *now*, if only to cover a number of years.

That comes first.

And secondly, we must work out right away a *shorter* plan, and then thirdly—and this is most important—we must be able to arouse both *competition* and *initiative among the masses*, so that they set about the job *straightaway*.

Would it not be possible for this purpose immediately to work out such a plan (for example):

(1) All volosts (10-15 thousand) to be supplied with electric lighting in *one* year.

(2) All settlements ($^1/_2$-1 million, probably not more than $^3/_4$ million) in *two* years.

(3) Priority for the reading-room and the Soviet (two light bulbs).

(4) Get the poles ready *at once* in such-and-such a way.

(5) Prepare the insulators *at once yourselves* (ceramics

works, I believe, are local and small affairs?). Make them *in such-and-such a way.*

(6) *Copper* for the wires? *Collect it yourselves* in your uyezd and volosts (a gentle hint at church bells, etc.).

(7) Organise training in electricity in such-and-such a way.

Could not something *of this kind* be considered, worked out and *decreed*?

Yours,
Lenin

Written in December 1920

First published
in *Economicheskaya Zhizn* No. 18,
January 22, 1925

Printed from the original

262

TO G. M. KRZHIZHANOVSKY

Comrade Krzhizhanovsky

Would it not be possible to develop (not at once, but *straightaway* after the Congress, [392] for the Council of Labour and Defence) a practical plan for an electrification campaign:

Etwas*:

(1) in *each* uyezd *urgently* to set up at least one power station;

(2) make it obligatory for this centre to become a *training*, lecture, demonstration, etc., centre, and *take the entire* population through these courses (beginning with the young people, or by volosts, etc.);

(3) immediately assign tasks among the population as to what they can now make a start on (we need $2^1/_2$ million poods of copper—so let us at once assign tasks for bringing in 25 million poods, let people *voluntarily* begin to collect church bells, door handles, etc.; then *poles*, etc.);

(4) begin preparatory *navvying* work *at once*, assigning tasks among the uyezds;

(5) mobilise *all* engineers, electricians, all who have done courses at physico-mathematical faculties, etc., without exception. Their obligation will be to deliver not less than two (four?) lectures a week, to teach *not less than* (10-50?) people about electricity. If they fulfil this—a bonus. If they don't—gaol.

(6) Write *urgently* a few popular pamphlets (some to

---

* Something like this.—*Ed.*

be translated from *German*) and adapt the "book" (yours) into a number of more popular articles, for teaching in the schools and reading to the peasants.

And then a number of detailed measures on the following two groups:

aa) propaganda and training

bb) first steps towards putting this into practice at once, and from all angles.

Lenin

Written late in December 1920

First published in 1942
in *Lenin Miscellany XXXIV*

Printed from the original

1921

263

TO THE BAKURY VOLOST ORGANISATION
OF THE R.C.P.(B.)

Bakury Volost Organisation of the R.C.P.,
Bakury Volost, Serdobsk Uyezd, Saratov Gubernia
Copy to the Saratov Gubernia Party Committee
 and the Gubernia Executive Committee

Dear Comrades,

The secretary of your organisation, Comrade *Turunen*, has informed me in writing that, at the request of the peasants, you have passed a decision to bring to my knowledge through him the counter-revolutionary activities of certain food-supply workers in your volost who are ill-treating poor peasants, robbing them for personal gain, encouraging illicit distilling, getting drunk, raping women, provoking attacks on Soviet power, etc. You ask me to take steps from here in Moscow to put an end to these counter-revolutionary actions. But to fight on the spot, with all your strength against counter-revolution is one of the most important tasks of local Party organisations, including yours. Your bounden duty is, by getting into touch with the Uyezd Party Committee, and—if that does not help—with the Gubernia Party Committee, to secure the arrest and prosecution before the Revolutionary Tribunal of counter-revolutionaries and scoundrels like those about whom you are reporting.

What have you done in this direction?

In the second part of his letter, Comrade *Turunen* sets out your view that Soviet power, in order to overcome economic break-down, must for some time lean on the peasantry as it would on a crutch. This is quite true. This has been said in our Party Programme, and in the resolutions of Party Congresses. At the last, Eighth All-Russia Congress of Soviets, the question of reviving agriculture was considered in detail and very carefully, and the Congress adopted important practical decisions, which you will have to apply on the spot, as directed by the Gubernia authorities.

These decisions have been published in the newspapers. In addition, Comrade *Turunen* will bring you some supplementary material which he will have received at the People's Commissariat of Agriculture, where he was sent on my recommendation.

With communist greetings,

V. Ulyanov (Lenin)

Chairman, Council of People's Commissars

Written on January 21, 1921

First published in *Izvestia* No. 31.
February 8, 1927

Printed from the typewritten
text signed by V. I. Lenin

264

TO N. P. GORBUNOV

Comrade Gorbunov,

This Bonch-Bruyevich (no relation, only has the same surname as V. D. Bonch-Bruyevich) is by all accounts a *very outstanding* inventor. The matter is *of immense importance* (a newspaper without paper and without wires, for with a loudspeaker and with the receiver which Bonch-Bruyevich has developed in such a way that it will be easy for us to produce *hundreds* of receivers, all Russia will be able to hear a newspaper read in Moscow).

I particularly ask you:

(1) to follow up this matter specially, *calling in Ostrya-kov* and *telephoning Nizhni*,

(2) to get the attached draft decree *speedily* through the Narrow Council. If unanimity cannot be reached quickly, be sure to prepare it for the Full Council of People's Commissars for Tuesday,

(3) to inform me twice a month on the *progress* of the work. [393]

Lenin

January 26

First published in *Pravda* No. 92,
April 22, 1926

Printed from the original

265

TO E. M. SKLYANSKY

February 6, 1921

Comrade Sklyansky,

I attach one more "warning".

Our military command has failed disgracefully by allowing Makhno to get away (in spite of an immense superiority of forces and strict orders to catch him), and is now failing still more disgracefully by proving unable to crush a handful of bandits.

Order a *brief* report for me from the Commander-in-Chief (with a brief sketch showing the disposition of bands and troops) about what is being done.

How is the wholly reliable cavalry being used?

—the armoured trains? (Are they rationally distributed? Are they not moving *wastefully*, requisitioning grain?)

—armoured cars?

—aeroplanes?

How, and how many are in use?

Both grain and wood fuel, everything is being lost because of the bands, while we have a million-strong army. You must do all you can to brace up the Commander-in-Chief.

Lenin

First published, but not
in full, in 1938
in *Bolshevik* No. 2

Published in full
in the Fourth (Russian) Edition
of the *Collected Works*

Printed from the original

266

TO G. M. KRZHIZHANOVSKY

Secret

G. M.,

Look at this and note it. Return it at once secretly.

Milyutin is writing nonsense about the plan.[394] The greatest danger is that the work of planning the state economy may be bureaucratised.

This danger is a great one. Milyutin does not see it.

I am very much afraid that with your different approach to the question *you do not see it either*.

We are beggars. Hungry, ruined beggars.

A complete, integrated, real plan for us at present= "a bureaucratic utopia".

Don't chase it.

At once, without delaying a day or an hour, bit by bit single out *the most important*, the minimum number of enterprises, and *put them on their feet*.

Let's talk about this personally before your report. *Think it over*.

Lenin

Written on February 19, 1921

First published, but not in full, in 1924 in the book: G. M. Krzhizhanovsky, *Tovaroobmen i planovaya rabota*, Moscow

Published in full in 1928 in *Zapiski Instituta Lenina*, Vol. III

Printed from the original

267

TO G. M. KRZHIZHANOVSKY

February 25

Comrade Krzhizhanovsky,

On the question of the General Planning Commission.[395]

(1) On its composition in general we shall come to an agreement after your arrival. This will not be difficult.

(2) The Central Committee has decided to leave in Larin for the time being. The danger from him is a very great one, because it is in his character to disorganise any work, *seize power*, overthrow all chairmen, *drive specialists away*, speak (*without a shadow of right to do so*) in the name "of the Party", etc.

On you falls the *heavy* task of subordinating, disciplining, moderating Larin. Remember: directly he "begins" to go beyond limits, rush to me (or send me a letter). Otherwise Larin will upset the *whole* General Planning Commission.

(3) You have to set up within the *General Planning* Commission a *super-firm* presidium (it must be *without* Larin), so that organisers and strong people (capable of giving a complete rebuff to Larin, and *steadily* going ahead with this difficult work) should *help* you and *relieve you* of *administrative* work (it was pointed out at the Central Committee that you are, strictly speaking, not an administrator). The Presidium, perhaps, could consist of two of your assistants, one secretary, and so forth. You must be the "leading spirit" of the work and the *ideological* guide (in particular, kick out, get rid of *tactless* Communists

who may drive out the specialists).... Your task is to catch, select, *put on the job* capable organisers, administrators (like Osadchy, etc.)—to *provide the Central Committee of the R.C.P. with the opportunity, the data, the material, for evaluating them.* ‖‖N.B

(4) The "GOELRO" *as a* GOELRO, you must restore as a *subcommission* of the General Planning Commission. You will be chairman of this subcommission too.

(5) You will have to set up quite a number of subcommissions: we must have a talk about this, when you have a plan for them.

(6) What will be exceptionally important is the subcommission on

> study,
> checking
> and
> "tying up", co-ordination,
> making proposals
> for altering

current economic plans (for 1921 at the present moment). Larin must without fail be made a member of this subcommission but (1) not as chairman and not as vice-chairman and not as secretary; (2) counterbalancing *him*, say, with Sereda, as a model of balanced mind, non-fantasy, non-harrassment.

(7) I suggest that you think over the following plan (I consider it most important): to oblige *a few persons*, members of the *General Planning Commission*, systematically to present either to the Commission or to the *subcommission under § 6 reports* and *articles* on the fulfilment by various departments (and by various gubernias, uyezds, groups of factories, individual factories, etc.) of current economic plans and on the comparison of this fulfilment with various years and for printing in *Ekonomicheskaya Zhizn*. (I consider it most important that *Larin* without fail, and also Sereda, Popov, Strumilin, should be *formally* obliged to follow with the greatest attention the facts and figures of the *real* fulfilment of our economic plans, and should *print* regular notes in *Ekonomicheskaya Zhizn* for public criticism and checking. *Two* or *three* specialists could also be set to work on this. It is essential that each should answer

individually for the study and the checking; and that on each part of this work there should be *two* persons, independent of one another, for mutual checking and for testing various methods of analysis, summarising, etc.).

Think about all this and let's have a talk *more than once* after your arrival.

Greetings!

Lenin

Written on February 25, 1921

First published, but not in full, in 1924 in the book: G. M. Krzhizhanovsky, *Tovaroobmen i planovaya rabota*, Moscow

Published in full in 1928 in *Zapiski Instituta Lenina*, Vol. III

Printed from the original

268

TELEGRAM
TO THE REVOLUTIONARY MILITARY COUNCIL
OF THE 11th ARMY

Copy to R.M.C., Caucasus Front
Copy to the Revolutionary Committee of Georgia
Copy to Comrade Orjonikidze

In view of the fact that units of the 11th Army are on the territory of Georgia, you are instructed to establish complete contact with the Revolutionary Committee of Georgia and to abide strictly by the directives of the Revolutionary Committee, undertaking no measures which might affect the interests of the local population, without co-ordinating them with the Georgian Revolutionary Committee; to observe particular respect for the sovereign bodies of Georgia; to display particular attention and caution in regard to the Georgian population. Issue the appropriate directive at once to all army institutions, including the Special Department. Hold to account all who infringe this directive. Inform us of every case of such infringement, or of even the least friction and misunderstanding with the local population.

Lenin

Chairman, Defence Council

Written on March 10, 1921

Pravda Gruzii No. 13,
March 17, 1921

Printed from the newspaper text
collated with a typewritten copy

269

TO G. M. KRZHIZHANOVSKY

G. M.,

I return your speech.[396]

Its main defect: too much about electrification, too little about *current* economic plans.

The main emphasis is not laid where it should be.

When I had before me the communist "wiseheads" who had not read the book *The Electrification Plan*[397] and had not understood its importance and were chattering and writing nonsense about the plan in general, I had to push their noses into this book, because there is no other serious plan and there cannot be.*

If I had before me the people who *wrote* that book, I should push their *noses* not into the book but *away from it*—into the problems of *current* economic plans.

Get down to those problems now, Messrs. Professors! Your electrification is *in allen Ehren.*** Honour to it indeed. You've written the first edition. We'll make improvements and publish a second. The specialists in such-and-such a subcommission will write a dozen decrees and resolutions on teaching electricity and the electrification plan, and so forth. We shall endorse them.

But the general state planning commission should now busy itself *not* with this, but immediately, with all its strength, set about the *current* economic plans.

Fuel *today*. For 1921. Now, this spring.

---

* See present edition, Vol. 32, pp. 137-41.—*Ed.*
** In great esteem.—*Ed.*

V. I. Lenin
1921

The gathering of refuse, of scrap, of dead materials. Making use of them *for the purpose of* exchange for grain.

And the like.

This is what *"their"* noses have to be pushed into. This is what they should be set to work at. Now. Today.

1-2 subcommissions on electrification.

9-8 subcommissions on current economic plans.

That is how the forces should be allocated for the year 1921.

Yours,
Lenin

Written later than April 5, 1921

First published in
Trud No. 120, May 29, 1924

Printed from the original

270

TO A. V. LUNACHARSKY, M. N. POKROVSKY AND Y. A. LITKENS[398]

April 8, 1921

Comrades *Lunacharsky, Pokrovsky and Litkens*

Signs are increasing that, as regards systematic and planned work, affairs in the People's Commissariat of Education are not improving, in spite of the directives of the Central Committee and the special instructions of the Central Committee when the People's Commissariat of Education was being reorganised.

When will the main plan of work be drawn up? What questions will be included in this plan? Such questions as the writing of textbooks—the library network and its use—model schools—accountability of the teachers—programmes for training courses, lectures, classes in schools—supervision over the degree of effective fulfilment of programmes and the progress of class studies?

Or other questions? Which?

What questions have been recognised as most important and urgent?

Are there decisions on this subject? What measures are being taken for systematic supervision of their fulfilment?

I request a brief reply.

V. Ulyanov (Lenin)
Chairman, Council of People's Commissars

First published in 1932
in *Lenin Miscellany XX*

Printed from the typewritten
text signed by V. I. Lenin

271

TELEGRAM TO G. K. ORJONIKIDZE

Cipher what is marked in blue pencil*

Orjonikidze

I have received your cipher message about the desperate food situation in Transcaucasia. We have taken a number of steps, given a little gold to Armenia, confirmed all kinds of instructions to the Commissariat of Food. But I must warn you that we are in great need here, and will not be able to help. I urgently require that you should set up a regional economic body for the whole of Transcaucasia, make the utmost effort with concessions, especially in Georgia; try and buy seed, even if it be abroad, and push forward irrigation in Azerbaijan with the help of the resources of Baku, in order to expand agriculture and cattle-breeding, and also try and develop commodity exchange with the North Caucasus. Have you and the Georgian comrades grasped the significance of our new policy in connection with the tax in kind[399]? Read this to them and keep me more frequently informed; read my letter to Serebrovsky in Baku.

Lenin

Written on April 9, 1921

First published in 1925
in the book: M. D. Orakhelashvili,
Lenin i Z.S.F.S.R. (Documents), Tiflis

Printed from the original

---

* Lenin marked the following passages: "about the desperate food situation ... will not be able to help" and "with concessions, especially in Georgia".—*Ed.*

272

TO A. V. LUNACHARSKY

Anatoly Vasilyevich *Lunacharsky*
Copy to the Central Peat Board

In order to expand the output of peat, there must be a large-scale development of propaganda—leaflets, pamphlets, mobile exhibitions, films, publication of textbooks; teaching about the peat industry to be introduced as a compulsory subject in schools and higher technical colleges; textbooks must be written; study groups must be sent abroad annually.

Specifically it is necessary (1) to instruct the State Publishing House to print by April 15, 100,000 copies of *Peat*, a pamphlet of $1^1/_2$ signatures, delivered by the Central Peat Board on February 8 this year to Comrade Mordvinkin at the Agitation Department, and to accept from the Central Peat Board another three pamphlets and leaflets, for publication by May 1; 15,000 copies of the pamphlets to be issued to the Central Peat Board for distribution.

(2) To instruct the Film Department to make 12 films in the course of May—under the direction of the Central Peat Board—showing how peat is secured (for Russia, the Ukraine, the Urals, Byelorussia and Siberia).

(3) To instruct the Central Board for Vocational Training to draw up by June 1, together with the Central Peat Board, a draft course of compulsory lessons in schools and higher educational establishments on the peat industry.

Please send me copies of your instructions, and the replies of the institutions and persons concerned, with an indication of the dates.

V. Ulyanov (Lenin)

Chairman, Council of People's Commissars

Written on April 9, 1921

First published in 1932
in *Lenin Miscellany XX*

Printed from the typewritten
text amended and signed
by V. I. Lenin

273

TO G. M. KRZHIZHANOVSKY

April 12

G. M.,

Yesterday I talked with Smilga. He should be having a talk with you today.

The question of the main features of the state plan, not as an institution but as a *plan*, cannot be put off.

You now know the tax in kind and other decrees. There is the policy for you. And you make as careful a calculation as possible (taking into account harvests of various sizes) how much this can produce.

Immeasurably still more urgent is fuel. Timber-floating has broken down. The bad harvest resulting from such a spring will thwart deliveries.

Let Ramzin and Co. within two days provide me with *brief* summaries: *three* figures (wood fuel, coal, oil)

by half-years	1918???
	1919
	1920
particularly	*1921*
and the plan for	1922
the fuel plan for	1920

four figures: laid down?
     secured?
     how was the quantity laid down to be distrib-
      uted (only the main headings)?
     how was the quantity secured distributed?

By Thursday morning. On this will depend my decision regarding foreign trade. Order it today. We shall have a talk tomorrow.

Greetings!

Lenin

Written on April 12, 1921

First published, but not in full, in 1924 in the book: G. M. Krzhizhanovsky, *Tovaroobmen i planovaya rabota,* Moscow

Published in full in 1933 in the second and third editions of Lenin's *Collected Works*, Vol. XXIX

Printed from the original

274

TO G. M. KRZHIZHANOVSKY

G. M.,

Is the instruction clear?

We must presume that we shall have in 1921-22
the same, or even worse,

      harvest failure

      fuel shortage (on account of lack of food and fodder
        for the horses).

From this point of view there should be calculated what
purchases are needed abroad in order *at all costs* to overcome our most dire shortages, i.e., to procure without fail
the foodstuffs that are lacking (by direct purchase of provisions abroad, and by exchange of goods for grain in the out-
lying regions of Russia) and to secure the necessary additional minimum of fuel.

Only those requirements can and must be justified which
are essential *from this point of view*.

Not all electrical requirements come under this heading.
It is not enough to demonstrate that electricity economises
fuel.

It must be demonstrated in addition that this expenditure
is essential for 1921-22, given maximum shortage of grain
and fuel.

Lenin

Written on April 13, 1921

First published in 1924 in the book:
G. M. Krzhizhanovsky, *Tovaroobmen
i planovaya rabota*, Moscow

Printed from the original

275

TO Y. A. LITKENS

Comrade Litkens,

I forgot when we met to ask you to check how matters stand with the committee of scholars who are drawing up a dictionary (brief) of the *contemporary* (from Pushkin to Gorky) Russian language.

I long ago, and many times, made arrangements for this with Pokrovsky and Lunacharsky.

Is it being done? What precisely? Find out and send me exact details.

With communist greetings,

Lenin

May 6

First published in 1932
in *Lenin Miscellany* XX

Printed from the original

276

TO THE EDITORIAL BOARDS
OF *PRAVDA* AND *IZVESTIA*

May 9, 1921

I request you to pay particular attention to the article in *Posledniye Novosti*[400] (Paris) No. 309:

"Milyukov and Avksentyev among the Americans".

It is essential *systematically* to record *such* articles and paragraphs; there is a mass of them; they should be *summarised*, impressing on our departments and on the reading public among the workers and peasants

that the more intelligent whiteguard bourgeoisie understands perfectly well the importance of concessions and foreign trade to Soviet power and therefore makes it its *main* task now to thwart trade agreements between the R.S.F.S.R. and foreign states, to frustrate the policy of concessions.

Please drop me a line on this question.

With communist greetings,
Lenin

First published in 1924
in *Zhizn* No. 1

Printed from the original

277

TO M. F. SOKOLOV

May 16

Comrade *M. Sokolov*, Secretary of the Department
for Management of Property Evacuated from Poland

Dear Comrade,

I have received and read your draft report for May 18.[401]
You write that I have "slipped up". On the one hand, you
say, by leasing forests, land, etc., we are introducing *state
capitalism*, and on the other hand, he (Lenin) "talks" about
"expropriating the landowners".

This seems to you a contradiction.

You are mistaken. Expropriation means *deprivation
of property*. A lessee is *not* a property-owner. That
means there is no contradiction.

The introduction of capitalism *(in moderation* and skilfully, as I say more than once in my pamphlet*) is possible
without restoring the landowners' property. A lease is a
contract *for a period*. Both ownership and control remain
with us, the workers' state.

"What fool of a lessee will spend money on model organisation," you write, "if he *is pursued by the thought of
possible expropriation...*"

Expropriation is a *fact*, not a *possibility*. That makes
a big difference. *Before* actual expropriation not a single
capitalist would have entered our service as a lessee. Where-
as now "they", the capitalists, have fought three years,

---

* See "The Tax in Kind" (present edition, Vol. 3   pp. 329-65).—
Ed.

and wasted *hundreds of millions of rubles in gold* of their own (and those of the Anglo-French, the biggest *moneybags* in the world) on war with us. Now they are having a bad time abroad. What choice have they? Why should they not accept an agreement? For 10 years you get not a bad income, otherwise ... you die of hunger abroad. Many will hesitate. Even if only five out of 100 try the experiment, it won't be too bad.

You write:

"Independent mass activity is *possible* only when we *wipe off* the face of the earth that ulcer which is called the bureaucratic chief administrations and central boards."

Although I have not been out in the provinces, I know this bureaucracy and all the harm it does. Your mistake is to think that it can be destroyed all at once, like an ulcer, that it can be "wiped off the face of the earth".

This is a mistake. You can throw out the tsar, throw out the landowners, throw out the capitalists. We have done this. But you cannot "throw out" bureaucracy in a peasant country, you cannot "wipe it off the face of the earth". You can only. *reduce* it by slow and stubborn effort.

To "throw off" the "bureaucratic ulcer", as you put it in another place, is wrong in its very formulation. It means you don't understand the question. To "throw off" an ulcer of this kind is *impossible*. It can only be *healed*. Surgery in *this* case is an absurdity, an *impossibility*; only a *slow cure*—all the rest is charlatanry or naïveté.

You are naïve, that's just what it is, excuse my frankness. But you yourself write about your youth.

It's naïve to wave aside a healing process by referring to the fact that you have 2-3 times tried to fight the bureaucrats and suffered defeat. First of all, I reply to this, your unsuccessful experiment, you have to try, not 2-3 times, but 20-30 times—repeat your attempts, start over again.

Secondly, where is the evidence that you fought correctly, skilfully? Bureaucrats are smart fellows, many scoundrels among them are extremely cunning. You won't catch them with your bare hands. Did you fight correctly? Did you *encircle* the "enemy" according to all the rules of the art of war? I don't know.

It's no use your quoting Engels.[402] Was it not some

"intellectual" who suggested that quotation to you? A futile quotation, if not something worse. It smells of the doctrinaire. It resembles despair. But for us to despair is either ridiculous or disgraceful.

The struggle against bureaucracy in a peasant and absolutely exhausted country is a long job, and this struggle must be carried on persistently, without losing heart at the first reverse.

"*Throw off*" the "chief administrations"? Nonsense. What will you set up *instead*? You don't know. You must not *throw them off*, but cleanse them, heal them, heal and cleanse them ten times and a hundred times. And not lóse heart.

If you give your lecture (I have absolutely no objection to this), read out my letter to you as well, please.

I shake your hand, and beg you not to tolerate the "spirit of dejection" in yourself.

Lenin

Written on May 16, 1921

First published in *Pravda* No. 1,   Printed from the original
      January 1, 1924

278

TO Y. A. LITKENS

May 19

Take advantage of Pokrovsky's holiday to begin work on the compiling of a dictionary of the Russian language without burdening him with administrative functions.

(1) Appoint a committee of 3-5 of the best philologists. They should within two weeks draw up a plan and the composition of the final committee (to [define]* the work, its nature, time limits, etc.).

(2) The task is a brief dictionary of the Russian language, from Pushkin to Gorky (the *small* "Larousse" as a model). Model, and contemporary. With the new orthography.

(3) On the basis of their report (of the 3-5), some *scientific academic* centre must *endorse* the plan. Then we shall begin by the autumn.

Written on May 19, 1921

First published in 1932
in *Lenin Miscellany XX*

Printed from the original

---

* This word is not clear in the original.—*Ed.*

279

TO G. M. KRZHIZHANOVSKY

May 25

Comrade Krzhizhanovsky,

You should have been sent the *draft* "Instructions of the Council of Labour and Defence".*

Think it over yourself (and the Presidium too—and all members of the State Planning Commission should be informed) from two points of view:

(a) it includes problems concerning your "department": electrification and the local bodies of the State Planning Commission. What is needed in this case is a detailed analysis and study by all of you, in order to *verify* and *supplement* (*resp.* alter) the list of detailed *problems*;

(b) the remainder does not come under the jurisdiction of the State Planning Commission, but *much of it* in essence affects the Commission. The opinion of the latter is desirable (not obligatory).

Lenin

P.S. Do you not think that it will be necessary to appoint a group of members of the State Planning Commission to study the uyezd reports, and all economic reports in general? Or should all members of the Commission be given several reports each, with the *obligation* to read *and study* them?

By the way: the study of current economic plans (for 1921) must definitely be *individualised*. Each member of

---

* See present edition, Vol. 32, pp. 375-98.—*Ed.*

the State Planning Commission answers for *such-and-such* a side or part of this work. And vice versa: for *every* side or part of economic activities in 1921, from the point of view of the current plan, so-and-so answers, in the sense of studying the results. Send this to me without fail.

Written on May 25, 1921

First published, but not   Printed from the original
in full, in 1924 in the book:
G. M. Krzhizhanovsky,
Tovaroobmen   i   planovaya   rabota,
Moscow
Published in full in 1928
in *Zapiski Instituta Lenina,* Vol. III

280

TO G. M. KRZHIZHANOVSKY

May 26, 1921

Comrade Krzhizhanovsky,

I think it is necessary for the State Planning Commission to work out two things:

(1) through the statistical subcommission, to draw up a kind of index-number.

A monthly summary of the chief data of our economic life (figures and a curve). Approximately:

Output of fuel
"   ore
"   iron.

The main data about other branches of industry:

% of workers engaged in production;

% of under-fulfilment of sowing plan;

state of agricultural production;

% of locomotives out of action;

absolute number of pood-versts;

timber, wood fuel, etc.;

supplies of foodstuffs, etc.;

electrification likewise

(in each case a comparison with the previous year and with pre-war).

Without this we shall not have a survey of economic life.

This is one of the fundamentals for the work of the State Planning Commission.

(2) A subcommission of *economic* statistics.

The Central Statistical Board should be made into an organisation that does analysis for us, *current*, not "scientific" analysis. For example:

How many superfluous people fed?

How many superfluous factories?

How should raw materials be redistributed? And labour-power?

The economic work of the army?

Statisticians must be our *practical assistants*, not engage in scholastics.

Think over this, and drop me a line about the results.

Yours,
Lenin

First published in 1924
in the book: G. M. Krzhizhanovsky,
Tovaroobmen i planovaya rabota,
MOSCOW

Printed from the original

281

TELEGRAM TO F. E. DZERZHINSKY[403]

Urgent

Dzerzhinsky, Chairman, All-Russia Extraordinary
  Commission
Southern Area (or present whereabouts)
Copy to *Voinov*, trio for combating the break-up of transport, Moscow

All the Ukrainian comrades most pressingly insist on intensification of the struggle against profiteering in the Ukraine, which threatens to disorganise the purchases of grain for the famine-stricken centres of the Republic, purchases which have begun and are already showing good results. Please devote particular attention, and inform me whether emergency measures are being taken, what measures in particular and what their results are.

Lenin
Chairman, Council of Labour and Defence

Written on May 27, 1921

First published in 1933
in *Lenin Miscellany XXIII*

Printed from the original

282

TO I. T. SMILGA

Comrade Smilga
Copy to the Central Oil Board
Copy to Comrade *Gubkin*

Both the press and reports from people on the spot show more and more frequently that things are getting worse in Baku.

Care for and attention to Baku must be increased.

Please bring before the *Council of Labour and Defence* a programme of systematic measures to aid Baku, making use of purchases abroad.

Constant "observation" must be established of what is happening at Baku and *how we are helping*.

Brief summaries should be drawn up on both items, (a) *what they have*, (b) *what we have provided*, and supervise continuously.

Lenin

Chairman, Council of Labour and Defence

Written on May 27, 1921

First published in 1932
in *Lenin Miscellany XX*   Printed from the original

283

TO M. P. PAVLOVICH[404]

Comrade Pavlovich
People's Commissariat of Nationalities

May 31, 1921

Comrade Pavlovich,

I have arranged for publication of a school atlas (in Petrograd).[405]

It would be extremely important to include maps of imperialism.

Would you not undertake this?

For example:

(1) colonial possessions 1876-1914-1921, adding or specially shading off semi-colonial countries (Turkey, Persia, China, and so forth).

(2) Brief statistics of colonies and semi-colonies.

(3) Map of financial dependencies. For example, for each country $\pm$ with a figure (millions or milliards of francs) of how much this country owes, and how much it is owed; also comparatively for 1876-1914-1921

(if 1876 be taken as the culminating point of pre-monopoly capitalism).

(4) Railways of the world, with a note, in each country, showing to whom most of them belong (British, French, North America, etc.).

Will this prove too much of a mixture? Convenient forms can be found, with what matters, what predominates noted very briefly.

(5) The main sources of those raw materials over which there is a struggle (oil, ores, etc.)—also with notes (% or millions of francs belong to such-and-such a country).

We must without fail include maps of this kind *in the textbooks*, of course with a brief explanatory text.

A statistical assistant can be given you for the auxiliary work.

Please reply whether you undertake this, how and when.

With communist greetings,

V. Ulyanov (Lenin)

Chairman, Council of People's Commissars

First published in 1923
in the magazine
Prozhektor No. 21

Printed from the original

———————

284

TO Y. A. LITKENS

Comrade Litkens,

So let us agree on the question of the dictionary as follows:

(1) Approximately within a month (in the absence of Pokrovsky) adopt a *formal* decision and appoint a *responsible person* or *persons*.

(2) On the basis of this decision draw up a *plan* of work, indicating not only the persons responsible but also the expenditure and rations required.

The plan should provide for the work to begin in August or September.

Lenin

Written late in May 1921

First published in 1932
in *Lenin Miscellany XX*

Printed from the original

285

TO V. A. AVANESOV[406]

June 1

Comrade Avanesov,

You should draw up a circular to all local bodies of the Workers' and Peasants' Inspection[407] on the subject of local economic conferences.

(1) You should require a *personal* list of all representatives of the Workers' and Peasants' Inspection in all economic conferences.

(2) You should be immediately informed of every change in the list.

(3) You should demand that, whether they are Communists or non-Party people, they should be *specially and personally* recommended for their reliability and honesty.

(4) You should demand that they be strictly accountable, *particularly* as regards drawing non-Party people into the work and as regards reports to *them*, the non-Party people, on the work of the economic councils.

All this should be brought before the Presidium of the All-Russia Central Executive Committee and adopted, so that the local bodies conform to it.

Lenin

Written on June 1, 1921

First published in 1928
in *Lenin Miscellany VIII*

Printed from the original

286

TO I. M. GUBKIN

June 3, 1921

Comrade Gubkin
Central Oil Board

Looking through the journal *Neftyanoye i Slantsevoye Khozyaistvo*, I came across a note (p. 199), in No. 1-4 (1921), "On the Replacement of Metal Tubes by Cement Solution in the Drilling of Oil Wells".

It turns out that this can be applied in rotary drilling, which we have in Baku, as I have read in the report of the Baku comrades.

We are ruining ourselves and ruining Baku because of insufficient drilling.

It is *possible* to replace iron tubes with cement, etc., which after all is easier to come by than iron tubes, and which costs, as your own journal points out, a "quite insignificant" sum!

And this kind of information you bury in a tiny note in a super-learned journal, which perhaps one person in 1,000,000 in the R.S.F.S.R. is capable of understanding.

Why didn't you sound the big bells? Why didn't you publish it in the general press? Or appoint a committee of practical experts? Or get the Council of Labour and Defence to adopt incentives?

V. Ulyanov (Lenin)

Chairman, Council of Labour and Defence

First published in 1932
in *Lenin Miscellany* XX

Printed from the original

287

TO G. M. KRZHIZHANOVSKY

Comrade Krzhizhanovsky,

I don't know whether everything has been done to acquaint members of the Third Congress of the Communist International with the electrification plan.

If not, it must be done *without fail* in one-two weeks.

There should be set out (in the lobbies of the Congress)

(1) a map of electrification, with a brief text in *three* languages

(2) similarly, regional maps

(3) the electrification balance-sheet

$$\left\{\begin{array}{l}\text{370 million working days,}\\ \text{bricks,}\\ \text{copper, etc.}\end{array}\right.$$

(4) a map of the most important local, small, new stations.

There must be a *brief* (16-24 pp.) pamphlet in *three languages*, a summary of the *Electrification Plan*.

I shall not be able to attend the Council of People's Commissars on Tuesday, June 7.

If the question of the Committee for Utilisation arises, be prepared *yourself* for a serious battle and make *precise* proposals, so that, if the circumstances require, you can complain to the Central Committee and the All-Russia Central Executive Committee.[408]

Yours,
Lenin

In confidence:

A new plot has been discovered in Petrograd. Intellectuals were participating. Some are professors not very remote from Osadchy. This has led to a lot of his friends having their houses searched, *and quite right too.*

Caution!!!

Written on June 5, 1921

First published, but not in full,   Printed from the original
in *Pravda* No. 21, January 21, 1931

Published in full in 1932
in *Lenin Miscellany XX*

288

TELEGRAM TO G. K. ORJONIKIDZE

Orjonikidze

I am surprised that you are interfering with Stalin's holiday. Stalin ought still to rest for not less than four or six weeks. Get a written opinion from good doctors.

Let me know what you are doing for Baku and for the development of foreign trade. Your silence about this makes me suspicious.

Lenin

Written on July 4, 1921
Sent to Tiflis

First published in 1942
in *Lenin Miscellany XXXIV*

Printed from the original

289

TO N. P. BRYUKHANOV

July 10

Comrade Bryukhanov,

I have received a letter from Lobachov dated July 9, indicating a sharp deterioration in the supply situation in Petrograd and Moscow. He asks for instructions.

In my opinion, you should draw up measures to intensify the work. I propose

(1) that you should press *immediately*, in particularly urgent, accelerated, *revolutionary* fashion for *collection of the tax* in Moscow Gubernia (the rye has already been harvested). Moscow workers, in particular, should be mobilised for this, *to assist* the food supply organisations.

(2) In general, mobilise more workers for food supply, *plundering* the People's Commissariats, in accordance with *yesterday's* decision of the Political Bureau[409] (take a copy of it).

(3) Once more send precise orders to the Ukrainian and Siberian People's Commissariats of Food.

(4) Delegate *an emergency* expedition (together with the Central Union of Consumers' Co-operative Societies) to *Podolsk* Gubernia where, they say, there are masses of grain and it costs *6,000* rubles a pood in Soviet currency.

(In general, my impression is that, as regards purchases and barter, the People's Commissariat of Food is *asleep*, and *lagging behind* disgracefully. No initiative. No bold work.)

With communist greetings,
Lenin

Please reply to me on July 11.

Written on July 10, 1921
First published in 1932
in *Lenin Miscellany XX*

Printed from the original

290

TELEPHONE MESSAGE TO G. K. ORJONIKIDZE

In code

First: please inform me of the state of Stalin's health, and the doctors' opinion on this. Secondly, it would be extremely important for us to get a concession from the Turks for the copper mines, south of Batum, which were ceded to them. Inform me whether any steps have been taken, and which. Thirdly, Krasin is in Moscow, and this should be taken advantage of in order to clear up the position of the Transcaucasian Commissariat of Foreign Trade. Fourthly, inform me of the state of Reske's health, and when his treatment will be completed.

Lenin

Dictated by telephone
on July 17, 1921

First published in 1932
in *Lenin Miscellany XX*

Printed from a typewritten text

291

TO A. A. KOROSTELEV

Comrade Korostelev,

The work of your commission[410] is exceptionally important, responsible and difficult.

You must strain all your energies to see that you have fewer reverses; and not lose heart because of the reverses, but insistently and patiently resume the work, again and again. In Moscow it is much more difficult to work than in the provinces—there is more bureaucracy, there are more corrupted and spoiled "top" people, etc.

But, in return, the work in Moscow will have tremendous demonstrative and *political* importance.

In my belief, your commission should try and adapt its work to the "Instructions of the Council of Labour and Defence".

The main thing is not to scatter your forces. It is better to take *a few establishments*, not very big tasks, set yourselves, at first, modest aims—but pursue them stubbornly, not forgetting what you have begun, not dropping the work half-way, but going on with it to the end.

Gradually, but without fail, draw in *non-Party* people from amongst *workers* well known for their honesty, and respected in every district. Time and effort should not be spared in discovering them and getting to know them.

They should little by little, and carefully, be *introduced* to the work, and you must try to find an occupation *entirely suited* to each one, and appropriate to his capacities.

The main thing is to get the workers and the population used to the commission, in the sense that they should *see help* coming from it; the main thing is to *win the confidence* of the masses, the non-Party people, the rank-and-file workers, the ordinary men in the street.

For you of all people, as chairman of the commission and as a man from the centre, a member of the collegium of the *unpopular* Workers' and Peasants' *Inspection*, this will not be easy. But this is the whole essence of the thing.

You must in every possible way, and in all possible respects, show that you are able to give, and actually give, *help*, real help, even if on a small scale. Only on this basis can you go on further.

Please write to me or, if you don't like writing, ring me up on the telephone—I can talk to you from my study, where it is quieter, so that we can exchange ideas on the work of your commission.

Show this letter to the other members of the commission, if you think it timely.

With communist greetings,
Lenin

July 26

P.S. The main task of the commission is to improve our economy, improve management, secure *real personal responsibility*. For this purpose a few more institutions should be selected: a canteen, baths, a laundry, a hostel, etc.

Written on July 26, 1921

First published in 1924   Printed from the original
in *Bolshevik* No. 1

292

TO L. M. KHINCHUK

July 29

Comrade Khinchuk,

They say you are leaving? For how many months? Before your departure it is essential that you should both officially get your *"deputy"* appointed and, unofficially, should let me know to which of the Communists who are *fully* experienced people (2-3 of them) in the Central Union of Consumers' Co-operative Societies I can address myself.

Then before your departure you must tell me, *very briefly*, when the machinery of the co-operative movement will begin working at last.

What I mean is this:

(1) In how many *volosts* (of *such-and-such* gubernias) are there shops (co-operatives) and, consequently, your trading agents, and in how many are there none? How many per volost?

(2) How many of the shops (agents) reply promptly to all the questions of the centre, and render reports? Once a week? Once a fortnight?

(3) How many volost shops have received goods, and which (even the briefest replies)? Salt? Kerosene? Textiles? *etc.*

(4) How many replies are there about the amount of surpluses and raw materials held by the peasants (which can be acquired in exchange for *this or that*)?

grain?

other foodstuffs?

industrial raw materials? etc.

(5) How much have you exchanged during the period under review? Of what, for what?

In my opinion, so long as there are no such reports, *there is nothing*. Only talk.

I await your reply.

With communist greetings,

Lenin

Written on July 29, 1921

First published
in *Soyuz Potrebitelei* No. 5,
May 1924

Printed from the original

293

TELEPHONE MESSAGE TO THE CHAIRMAN OF THE MOSCOW GUBERNIA COMMUNE

Copy to the Presidium of the Moscow Soviet
    "   to the People's Commissariat of Education

Comrade Smolyaninov has informed me that a workers' and peasants' delegation from Stavropol Gubernia has delivered to Moscow, addressed to me, a railway wagon of food for the hungry workers, as a gift. Please, in the first place, take over this wagon as rapidly as possible, without any red tape; secondly, dispatch it to the most needy Moscow workers, notifying them without fail that this is a present from the Stavropol workers and peasants; thirdly, see to it that the delegation is looked after, both in the sense of its being put up properly and of its receiving thanks from the Moscow Soviet, and, finally, that they are supplied with literature and given the opportunity of seeing the institutions in Moscow which interest them.

Please report fulfilment to me, immediately and precisely.

Lenin

Dictated by telephone
on July 30, 1921

First published in 1932   Printed from a typewritten text
in *Lenin Miscellany XX*

294

TO V. V. ADORATSKY

August 2

Comrade Adoratsky,

I have looked through the introduction. It's difficult to judge, because it's unfinished. It looks as though it should be cut down, and expressed much more clearly, with closer attention to the formulations.[411]

The *really* outstanding quotations from the letters should be combined with *other* works of Marx and with *Capital* (for example, on the question of "equality" *what matters most* is in *Capital*[412]). If you take question x, then on *this* question there is so-and-so in the letters, so-and-so in other works of Marx, so-and-so in *Capital*.

I could only glance at the letters. Of course, you will still have to cut them down considerably, link them up, arrange them properly; think over each one two or three times, and then *briefly* comment. Evidently there is more work involved than it seemed at first.

The chronological order (very likely you are right) is probably more convenient.

With communist greetings,

Lenin

P.S. I am on holiday. Unwell. Can't make appointments. If you have finished the "textbook", you should start pushing it.[413] Probably the quickest way is through M. N. Pokrovsky.

Written on August 2, 1921

First published, but not in full, in 1924 in *Proletarskaya Revolutsia* No. 3

Published in full in 1932 in the second and third editions of Lenin's *Collected Works*, Vol. XXIX

Printed from the original

295

TO THE PEOPLE'S COMMISSARIAT OF AGRICULTURE AND THE STATE PUBLISHING HOUSE

Comrade Teodorovich (P.C.A.) and
the State Publishing House

August 7

Among the new books I have received from the State Publishing House is

Semyon Maslov: "The Peasant Economy". 1921. *5th* ed.! (or *4th* ed.).

Looking it through, I see that it is a dirty bourgeois little book from beginning to end, stuffing up the mind of the muzhik with sham bourgeois "scientific" lies.

Nearly 400 pages, and nothing about the Soviet system and its policy, about our laws and measures for transition to socialism, etc.

Only a fool or a malicious saboteur could have passed this book.

Please investigate and send me the names of *all* those responsible for editing and publishing it.

V. Ulyanov (*Lenin*)

Chairman, Council of People's Commissars

Written on August 7, 1921

First published in 1924
in *Zhizn* No. 1

Printed from the original

296

TO G. I. SAFAROV

August 7

Comrade Safarov,

Thank you very much for the pamphlet[414] and other material.

We are sending Joffe to make an attempt to *combine* your line and Tomsky's.

That *must* be done.

Unquestionably grain and meat to Moscow, *first and foremost*.

For this purpose, both the "New Economic Policy" in general and a *number* of concessions and bonuses to the merchants.

At the same time, systematic and maximum concern for the Moslem poor, for their organisation and education.

Such a policy can and must be worked out and *fixed* (in a number of the *most precise* directives).

It must be a model for the *whole* East.

Best greetings.

Yours,
Lenin

P.S. After the line has been worked out, you, too, will probably be granted leave.

Written on August 7, 1921

Sent to Tashkent

First published, but not
in full, in the Fourth
(Russian) Edition
of the *Collected Works*

Printed from the original

297

LETTER TO V. S. DOVGALEVSKY
AND INSTRUCTION TO A SECRETARY

To the People's Commissar for Posts and Telegraphs

Typed copies to $\begin{cases} \text{(1) addressee} \\ \text{(2) me} \\ \text{(3) N. P. Gorbunov} \end{cases}$

Comrade Dovgalevsky,

Please let me have information about the state of wireless telephony in our country.

1) Is the Central Moscow Station working? If so, how many hours a day, and over what distance in versts?

If not, what is lacking?

2) Are we manufacturing (and how many?) receivers, installations capable of voice reception from Moscow?

3) How do matters stand with loudspeakers, installations which enable a whole hall (or square) to hear Moscow? Etc.

I am very much afraid that this business has once again "gone to sleep" (in the damnable manner of the Russian Oblomovs, [415] putting everyone and everything to *sleep*).

It has been "promised" many times, and all time limits have long ago expired!

The importance of this affair for us (for propaganda in the East especially) is *exceptional*. Delay and negligence here are criminal.

All this already exists abroad; what is lacking can and

must be bought. In all probability, there is criminal negligence somewhere.

V. Ulyanov (Lenin)

Chairman, Council of People's Commissars

September 2, 1921

First published, but not in full, in 1932 in *Radiofront* No. 3

Published in full in 1933 in *Lenin Miscellany XXIII*

Printed from the original

298

LETTER TO D. I. KURSKY
AND INSTRUCTION TO A SECRETARY

September 3

Comrade Kursky, *People's Commissar for Justice*,
 and his deputy, and also all the members of the Collegium

Typed on *headed notepaper* to (1) the addressee

copies to { (2) me
(3) Avanesov
(4) Gorbunov and Smolyaninov

 I have sent you through the Office Manager of the Council of People's Commissars a statement from Professor Graftio with astonishing documents about red tape.[416]
 This red tape is just what is to be expected, especially in the Moscow and central institutions. But all the more attention should be given to fighting it.
 My impression is that the People's Commissariat of Justice is purely formal, i.e., radically wrong, in its attitude to this question.
 What is needed is:
 (1) to bring this matter before the courts;
 (2) to secure the disgrace of those guilty, both in the press and by strict punishment;
 (3) to stiffen up the judges through the Central Committee, so that they punish red tape more severely;
 (4) to arrange a conference of the Moscow People's Judges, members of tribunals, etc., to work out *effective* measures for fighting red tape;

(5) without fail, this autumn and winter of 1921-22, to bring up for trial in Moscow 4-6 cases of Moscow red tape, selecting the more "vivid" cases, and making each trial a *political* affair;

(6) to find some, if only 2-3, sensible "experts" on questions of red tape, among the more fierce and militant Communists (get hold of Sosnovsky), so as to train people to *hound out* red tape;

(7) to publish a *good*, intelligent, non-bureaucratic *letter* (a circular of the People's Commissariat of Justice) on the struggle against red tape.

I impose this most important task on the People's Commissar and his deputy, on their *personal* responsibility, and request that I be given *regular* information as to its fulfilment.

Lenin

Chairman, Council of People's Commissars

Written on September 3, 1921

First published in *Pravda* No. 30,   Printed from the original
      February 6, 1927

299

TO I. K. YEZHOV

September 27, 1921

Comrade *Yezhov*, Head of Central Stores Board,
Supreme Economic Council

Comrade Yezhov,

I have received and looked through the papers about the store.

Transfer to the Supreme Economic Council has now been decided.[417]

I will expect you to let me have *brief* but precise reports on whether *in practice* any improvement in the stores business is being achieved, how the struggle against pilfering is going, as regards this store and other stores.

I am obliged to charge you, too, with red tape: "We've been shouting for three years", "I took the matter through to the end nearly ten times, *it seemed*", you write. But the whole trouble is that *not once* did you take the matter through to the end, without any "it seemed".

You know the Constitution of the R.S.F.S.R. and the Rules of the R.C.P. "To the end" means up to the session of the All-Russia Central Executive Committee (if there is no Congress of Soviets). In the Party line, it means the plenary meeting of the Central Committee.

You have not once taken the matter through to the end.

(1) A brief, "telegraphic", but clear and precise statement to members of the C.C. and members of the Presidium of the All-Russia Central Executive Committee;

(2) an article in the press;

(3) an initiative by the local or neighbouring unit of the R.C.P., its opinion, its question asked at the Moscow Soviet

—these are *three* measures which are obligatory in the struggle against red tape.

This is a difficult struggle, that goes without saying. But the difficult is not the impossible.

You gave up in despair, you did not fight, you did not exhaust all the means of fighting.

The stores business requires much more insistence in the struggle against red tape—checking "from below" and "by those below"—publicity in the press—checking again and again—etc.

I should like to hope that, having now had a painful and melancholy but useful experience, you will set about this battle with red tape in such a way as to really take the matter through "to the end".

From time to time one must know the results of this struggle.

With communist greetings,

Lenin

P.S. Will you not send on some occasion, together with *brief*, quite brief information about the course of the struggle (with red tape), *brief* data about your staff (the number of people, how many of them are Communists, their qualifications; responsible, purely executive, office workers, etc.) and a *brief* plan of your work?

Write briefly, in cablese, separating out special points, if necessary. I won't read a long document at all, that's certain.

If there are *practical* proposals, put them down on a separate sheet, extremely brief, *like a telegram*, with a copy to my secretary.

Lenin

First published, but not in full,   Printed from the original
in *Ekonomicheskaya Zhizn* No. 95,
        January 25, 1924

Published in full in *Pravda* No. 30,
        February 6, 1927

300

TO N. P. GORBUNOV

October 13, 1921

Comrade Gorbunov,

Please get a decision, after the necessary agreement with the Chairman of the Narrow Council of People's Commissars (and clearing the matter with the secretaries), that the system for summoning rapporteurs (both to the Full and the Narrow Council of People's Commissars) should be altered.

At present those who have to report get a general summons to the meeting and wait for hours.

This is outrageous and barbarous.

You must see to it that they are told to come at *one particular time*.

Provided there is a *double* check by telephone, whether rapporteurs are needed, and which; provided there is a *correct* distribution of the agenda of the given meeting (business requiring rapporteurs, business not requiring them), we can and must see to it that rapporteurs *do not wait more than 15 minutes*.

Please, work out such a system without delay, considering it carefully, and let me have a decision on the subject, adopted by the Narrow Council of People's Commissars.

V. Ulyanov (*Lenin*)

Chairman, Council of People's Commissars

First published in *Pravda* No. 17,
January 21, 1925

Printed from the original

301

TO SIDNEY HILLMAN

October 13, 1921

Comrade Hillman,

I thank you with all my heart for your help. Thanks to you an agreement was rapidly achieved on organisation of help for Soviet Russia by the American workers. Particularly important is the fact that the organisation of this aid has now been arranged in respect also of those workers who are *not* Communists. Throughout the world, and particularly in the most advanced capitalist countries, millions of workers do not at the present time share the views of the Communists, but nonetheless are ready to help Soviet Russia, to help and feed the starving, if only some of them, and to help the cause of restoring the economy of the Russian Socialist Federative Soviet Republic. Such workers repeat with complete conviction the words—and what is more important not only repeat the words but give them practical expression in life—of the leaders of the Amsterdam Trade Union International (unquestionably hostile to communism), namely, that any victory of the international bourgeoisie over Soviet Russia would mean the greatest possible victory of world reaction over the working class in general.

Soviet Russia is exerting all her strength to overcome starvation, ruin and dislocation. The financial aid of the workers of the whole world is infinitely important for us in this respect, side by side with moral help and political help. America, naturally, is at the head of the states where the workers can help us, are already helping us and will help—I am profoundly convinced—on a far greater scale.

Devoted to the cause, the energetic advanced workers of America will be taking the lead of all the workers of a number of industrial countries who are bringing Soviet Russia their technical knowledge, and their determination to make sacrifices in order to help the Workers' and Peasants' Republic to restore its economy. Among the peaceful means of struggle against the yoke of international finance capital, against international reaction, there is no other means with such rapid and certain promise of victory as aid in the restoration of the economy of Soviet Russia.

With best greetings to all workers who are bringing aid, in one form or another, to Soviet Russia.

N. Lenin

First published in 1930
in the second and third editions
of Lenin's *Collected Works*, Vol. XXVII

Printed from the original

302

TO N. A. SEMASHKO

October 24, 1921

Comrade Semashko,

After signing today the decision of the Narrow Council of People's Commissars on the 2,000 millions (I think that is the figure?[418] I don't remember it exactly) for cleaning up Moscow, and after reading the "Regulations" of the People's Commissariat of Health for the week of housing sanitation (*Izvestia* of *July 12*), I have come to the conclusion that my suspicions (about the complete inadequacy of the organisation of the whole business) are increasing.

The thousand millions will be taken, stolen and pilfered but the job won't be done.

We must secure model (or at least, as a beginning, *tolerable*) cleanliness in Moscow, for one cannot even imagine a greater scandal than "Soviet" dirt in the "first" Soviet houses. What then is to be expected in houses which are *not* first?

Please send me the most brief but precise, business-like, factual report on what has been achieved by the week of sanitation, and where? Is there any gubernia where something has been done without muddle?

Further. What is being done (and what has been done?) in Moscow? Who answers for this work? Is it only "officials" with a pompous Soviet title, who don't understand a thing, who don't know the business and only sign papers? Or are there *business-like* people in charge? Who in particular?

V. I. Lenin watches the trials of the first Soviet electric plough at the training and experimental farm of the Moscow Zootechnics Institute. *October 22, 1921*

The most important thing is to secure personal responsibility.

What has been done to secure personal responsibility? Checking is done by whom?

By inspectors? How many are there? Who are they?

By youth detachments (Young Communist League)? Do such exist? How many? Where and how have they given examples of their work?

What other methods for *real* checking are there?

Is money being spent on buying valuable articles (carbolic? cleaning equipment? how much has been bought?) or is it being spent on maintaining new "official" loafers?

V. Ulyanov (Lenin)
Chairman, Council of People's Commissars

First published, but not in full, in *Izvestia* No. 18, January 22, 1927,

Published in full in 1933 in *Lenin Miscellany XXIII*

Printed from the original

303

TO G. M. KRZHIZHANOVSKY

G. M.,

I have read it, and approve *very, very much.*[419] Get it ready *as soon as possible*, dictate it.

One addition, in my opinion, is essential: about the New Economic Policy. I think it would be better to insert it (*throwing light* from different points of view on the place, the significance, the *role in the general framework* of the New Economic Policy) in the separate chapters. Almost in every chapter you can (and should, in my belief) add a page or two about the fact that the New Economic Policy *does not change* the single state economic plan, and *does not go beyond* its framework, but alters the *approach* to its realisation.

Your opinion?

Greetings,
Lenin

Written on November 16, 1921

First published in 1924
in the book: G. M. Krzhizhanovsky,
Tovaroobmen i planovaya rabota,
Moscow

Printed from the original

304

TO A. S. YENUKIDZE

Comrade Yenukidze,

Cannot the vacating of the apartment, promised to Stalin, be speeded up?

I ask you particularly to do this and *to ring me up* (the telephone is a good one; through the upper switchboard) whether you are being successful, or whether there are obstacles.

Yours,
Lenin

Written in November 1921

First published in 1942
in *Lenin Miscellany XXXIV*

Printed from the original

305

TO LYDIA FOTIYEVA

Remind me tomorrow that I must see Stalin, and before this put me through on the telephone to *Obukh* (the doctor) about Stalin.

Written on December 28, 1921

First published in full in 1933
in *Lenin Miscellany XXIII*

Printed from the original

1922

306

TO D. I. KURSKY

Comrade *Kursky*
People's Commissariat of Justice

I have received two communications from the People's Commissariat of Justice—of November 14 and December 20—on the "fulfilment" of my instruction to organise a systematic campaign against red tape.

In the first communication you write:

"It involves a great deal of labour to single out the processes in which this organisational defect (viz., the ponderousness and bureaucratic complexity of our apparatus, inter-departmental relations, friction, etc.) does not have such a decisive effect, and red tape is the result of the activity of persons, and not an objective consequence of the insufficiently smooth working of our apparatus."

With such an approach, of course, nothing will come of the struggle against red tape. It is the responsible persons who are to blame for these "organisational defects"; these, and no others, are the ones we must learn to prosecute and punish with exemplary severity. You will never catch a saboteur engaged in red tape.

The second communication from the People's Commissariat of Justice, signed by Krasikov, and the attached reports of the investigators of "exceptionally important cases"—Vyukov, Roizman and Kedrov, a member of the staff of the Workers' and Peasants' Inspection—truly discover America. These reports, in a pretty illiterate form, set forth standard platitudes about bureaucracy, complexity of apparatus, etc., etc.

In a word, it is obvious that the struggle against red tape has not moved ahead one iota.

In essence, I have not received an exhaustive reply to a single one of the five tasks which I laid down.

I suggest that you once again examine the question and organise the struggle against red tape in business-like fashion, according to all the rules of war.

I ask you by the 20th of each month, without any preliminary reminders, to send me a report on the course of the campaign.

V. Ulyanov (Lenin)

Chairman, Council of People's Commissars

Written on January 17, 1922

First published in 1928
in *Lenin Miscellany VIII*

Printed from the typewritten
text signed by V. I. Lenin

307

TO A. D. TSYURUPA[420]

1

NEW ARRANGEMENTS FOR THE WORK
OF THE COUNCIL OF PEOPLE'S COMMISSARS
AND THE COUNCIL OF LABOUR AND DEFENCE

January 24, 1922

Comrade Tsyurupa,

In connection with our telephone conversation yesterday,
and your promise to observe a strict regime, we need to have
a detailed talk on the whole system of work, and to think it
over thoroughly.

The most radical defect of the C.P.C. and the C.L.D.
is the absence of any checking-up on fulfilment. *We are
being sucked down* by the rotten bureaucratic swamp into
writing papers, jawing about decrees, drawing up decrees—
and in this sea of paper live work is being drowned.

Clever saboteurs are deliberately luring us into this paper
swamp. Most of the People's Commissars and other grandees
are, quite unconsciously, "sticking their heads into the
noose".

The strict medical regime laid down for you must be used
at all costs to break away from turmoil and commotion,
commissions, talking and writing of papers—to break away,
to *think over* the system of work and *radically reform it*.

The centre of gravity of your activities must be just this
refashioning of our disgustingly bureaucratic way of work,
the struggle against bureaucracy and red tape, the *checking-
up on fulfilment*.

The checking-up on fulfilment, the checking-up on what

happens in practice—this is your main and principal task. You should set up for this a little staff (four-six persons) of particularly tried and tested assistants (an office manager, his assistants, a secretary and such like).

For this purpose, in my opinion, it is essential:

(1) to relieve the *C.P.C.* and the *C.L.D.* of unnecessary burdens, transferring all petty questions to the Narrow Council of People's Commissars and the procedural meetings of the *C.L.D.*

This has begun. But it will "come apart" in two weeks, given our damned Oblomov ways, if it is not followed up, chased up, checked up, flogged along with three knouts.

The office manager must be taught (just as the Secretariat of the *C.P.C.* and the *C.L.D.* should be) to watch very closely to see that petty questions are not brought before the C.P.C. and the C.L.D., and that all questions in general first go through a triple filter (an inquiry to the appropriate People's Commissariats; their urgent reply; the same from the Codification Department, etc., etc.).

You and Gorbunov* must together work out written *regulations* for the bringing forward and consideration of questions, and check *not less than* once a month, *you personally*, whether the regulations are being observed and whether they are achieving their object, i.e., reduction of paper work, red tape, more forethought, more sense of responsibility on the part of the People's Commissars, *replacement of half-baked decrees by careful, prolonged, businesslike checking-up on fulfilment* and by *checking of experience*, establishment of personal responsibility (in effect, we have complete irresponsibility at the top, in the People's Commissariats and in their departments, and the saboteurs make magnificent use of this: as a result we have an Oblomov situation which wrecks all business).

I know that this is *extraordinarily* difficult. But just because it is difficult, you must devote yourself *entirely* to this matter.

Hence

(2) a minimum of sessions. The standard should be once a week for the Council of People's Commissars+once a week for the Council of Labour and Defence, two hours each.

---

* +a codifier+1 from the Narrow Council of People's Commissars.

(3) The Supreme Economic Commission. Close down *all* its subcommissions as rapidly as possible, and replace them by demanding of the People's Commissars that each of them should have *responsible* people to write drafts, that the People's Commissar should endorse them, and that he himself should get them co-ordinated in the *briefest* possible time with all "interested" People's Commissars and at the C.L.D. or the C.P.C.

The Supreme Economic Commission should exist *only* for co-ordination (*codification*) and the most rapid checking (*stamping*) by yourself plus Kamenev.

Only for this.

Not for talk.

Not for discussion.

(4) You are not to become a member of a single commission, not one, except the Supreme Economic Commission.

(5) To fight the outrageous abundance of commissions, replacing them by a formal demand for *a written opinion* in the shortest possible time.

(6) You must in this way set yourself free from commotion and turmoil, which are *killing all of us*, and make it possible for you to think calmly about the work *as a whole*—

—and particularly to concentrate on checking-up on fulfilment, on fighting bureaucracy and red tape.

I beg you to think over this whole question, and to write to me.

With communist greetings,

Lenin

First published, but not in full, in *Krasnaya Gazeta* No. 14, January 16, 1927

First published in full in 1928 in *Lenin Miscellany VIII*

Printed from the original

308

2

A PROGRAMME FOR WORK ON NEW LINES

February 20

Comrade Tsyurupa,

More on the subject of work on new lines.

I will try to formulate its programme in this way:

(1) the C.P.C. and the C.L.D. to be made ten times more compact, in the sense that the People's Commissars should not dare to bring trivial matters before them, but should decide them themselves and *answer* for them themselves;

(2) the staff of the Managing Department of the C.P.C. (at present three-quarters idle) should be made responsible for this, for putting this into effect;

(3) the same applies to the Narrow Council of People's Commissars, plus its *especial* reduction in size;

(4) some of the members of the Narrow Council and its staff, and also the staff of the Managing Department of the C.P.C., to be taken by you under your personal command in order to *check up on effective fulfilment* (you instruct so-and-so: take a journey down there, look, read, check up, you will answer for any bungling through gullibility).

(5) You (and Rykov) must devote *first and foremost* one hour, or if your health permits, two, every day, to personal checking-up on the work: you summon to your office (or visit) not grandees, but members of Collegiums *and lower*, practical workers of the People's Commissariat of X, Y, Z—and check up on their work, get down to rock-bottom, school them, teach them, give them a proper trouncing. Study people, search for *able* workers. This is now the essence;

all orders and decisions without this are dirty bits of paper.

Reply to me. We shall think it over, consult with members of the Central Committee, and as rapidly as possible *fix* such a (or some other) programme.

Yours,
Lenin

P.S. A. Bryukhanov is not suitable. Someone else must be found. For the time being you had better set up a "trio" there, something pretty strong.

Written on February 20, 1922

First published in 1928
in *Lenin Miscellany VIII*

Printed from the original

309

3

PROPOSAL FOR THE DRAFT DIRECTIVE
TO THE NARROW COUNCIL OF PEOPLE'S COMMISSARS

Comrade Tsyurupa,

I send you my addition. My advice is to get *brief* comments from *all* People's Commissars and *all* members of the Narrow Council of People's Commissars.

Yours,
Lenin

A special supplementary decision should lay down:

The principal task of the Narrow Council of People's Commissars must be strict watchfulness that the People's Commissariats (1) observe the laws, (2) do not evade responsibility by needlessly transferring a mass of unnecessary questions to the Narrow Council for decision, but should decide the questions themselves, on their own responsibility or by agreement between two or more People's Commissariats under ordinary procedure; (3) checking the legality, expediency and rapidity of individual instructions and acts of the People's Commissariats; the struggle against bureaucracy and red tape by such checking, and by persistent reduction of the number of officials.

Written on February 20-21, 1922

First published in 1928
in *Lenin Miscellany VIII*

Printed from the original

310

4

DRAFT DIRECTIVE REGARDING THE WORK OF THE COUNCIL OF LABOUR AND DEFENCE, THE COUNCIL OF PEOPLE'S COMMISSARS AND ALSO THE NARROW COUNCIL OF PEOPLE'S COMMISSARS

The chief defect of these institutions is that they are over-burdened with trivial matters. As a result, they are floundering in bureaucracy instead of fighting it.

The causes of this evil are: (1) the weakness of the Managing Department, (2) the inability of the People's Commissars to climb out of the mire of trivialities and bureaucratic details, (3) the desire of the People's Commissars (and still more that of their departmental bureaucrats who egg them on) to shift responsibility on to the C.P.C., (4) last and most important—the fact that responsible workers do not realise that the order of the day now is to fight the sea of paper and show distrust of it and of the eternal "reorganisations", that the first task of the moment is not decrees, not reorganisations but *selection of people*; establishment of *individual responsibility for what is being done*; *checking-up on work actually performed*. Otherwise we shall not climb out of the bureaucracy and red tape which are throttling us.

The Narrow Council of People's Commissars, the C.L.D. and the C.P.C. must go all out to get rid of trivialities, teaching the People's Commissariats to settle minor matters themselves and to answer for them more strictly.

The staff of the Managing Department of the C.P.C. must regard as its main task the practical realisation of the following: to reduce the number of matters coming before the

Narrow C.P.C., the C.L.D. and the C.P.C., and to ensure that the People's Commissars (severally and jointly) should decide more themselves and answer for it; to shift the centre of gravity to checking up on effective fulfilment.

For the same purpose, the Deputy Chairmen of the C.P.C., Comrades Rykov and Tsyurupa, must go all out to free themselves of trivial matters and commissions, fight against attempts to drag them (the deputies) into matters which should be settled by the People's Commissars; devote two or three hours a day, as a minimum, to making the personal acquaintance of the responsible workers (not the grandees) of the most important (and later, all) People's Commissariats, in order to check up and select people; make use of the staff of the Managing Department of the C.P.C. and some of the members of the Narrow Council, and also the Workers' and Peasants' Inspection, to check up on the work actually done and what success it has had; in short, they should become practical instructors in administrative work, such as we lack most of all.

Distrust of decrees, of institutions, of "reorganisations" and of grandees, especially among Communists; struggle against the mire of bureaucracy and red tape by checking up on people and on the actual work done; merciless expulsion of unnecessary officials, reduction of staff, replacement of Communists who don't study the art of management seriously—such must be the line of the People's Commissars and the C.P.C., of its Chairman and his Deputy Chairmen.

Lenin

February 27

First published in 1928   Printed from the original
in *Lenin Miscellany VIII*

311

TO V. A. KARPINSKY

January 26, 1922

Comrade Karpinsky,

Would you not write to me briefly (two-three pages maximum)

how many letters come from the peasants to *Bednota*[421]?

what is important (particularly important) and new in these letters?

Their moods?

The topical subjects?

Could I not *once in two months* receive such letters (the next by March 15, 1922)? α) average number of letters

β) moods

γ) most important topical subjects.

With communist greetings,

Lenin

First published in *Pravda* No. 19,
January 24, 1924 Printed from the facsimile

312

TO G. M. KRZHIZHANOVSKY

January 28, 1922

G. M.,

I have read Gorev's work[422] and return it.

I expected more. A former Bolshevik, who captivated you so, and who in your opinion had once again become a real Bolshevik, should have produced impressive, vivid, powerful, popular propaganda, a defence of communism for France, starting from her electrification.

But Gorev's work has turned out "professorial".

I offer the following plan for your consideration:

(1) send it to be set *at once*, in order to publish it soon in *any* case;

(2) suggest to Gorev—*if you agree*—that he should write in addition a preface or an afterword, in which he should in very clear and popular form and a little more freely (prescribe for him to this end three grammes of extract of Larinism: they say it has appeared on sale in Moscow) attack French capitalism, and say to the French workers and peasants: you could become in three-five years three times as rich, and work not more than six hours a day (approximately), if there were a Soviet government in France putting electrification into effect;

(3) if in your (or Gorev's) opinion, Gorev will do this badly or unwillingly, then think over whether someone should not be asked to do this work separately (a *brief* "Ballod"[423] for France);

(4) send me Gorev's article, as soon as you can, once it is set up (to be published as a pamphlet or in some journal, whichever you choose). *Perhaps* I will write an introduction.[424]

Greetings,

Yours,

Lenin

Published for the first time
in the Fourth (Russian) Edition
of the *Collected Works*

Printed from the original

313

TO G. Y. SOKOLNIKOV

Top secret

Comrade Sokolnikov
Copy to Comrade Tsyurupa and Comrade Krzhizhanovsky

You said to me that some of our trusts may, in the immediate future, find themselves without any money and ask us in an ultimatum to nationalise them. I think that trusts and factories have been founded on a self-supporting basis precisely in order that they themselves should be responsible and, moreover, fully responsible, for their enterprises working without a deficit. If it turns out that they have not achieved this, then in my opinion they must be prosecuted and punished, as regards all the members of their boards of management, by prolonged terms of imprisonment (perhaps applying conditional release after a certain time), confiscation of all their property, etc.

If, after setting up trusts and enterprises on a self-supporting basis, we do not prove able by business-like, mercantile methods fully to protect our interests, we shall turn out to be complete idiots.

The Supreme Economic Council must watch over this, but still more the People's Commissariat of Finance through the State Bank and through special inspectors, since it is precisely the People's Commissariat of Finance which, not being directly interested, is obliged to establish effective and real control and supervision.

Lenin

Dictated by telephone on
February 1, 1922

First published in *Pravda* No. 79,
March 21, 1931

Printed from a typewritten copy

314

TO G. Y. SOKOLNIKOV

February 15, 1922

Copy to Comrade Tsyurupa and Comrade Kamenev

Comrade Sokolnikov,

Should not the main attention be directed to the development of trade, and to supervision of it through the Trade Department of the State Bank?

Should we not organise this matter so as to find two or three dozen (or even less, if our damned bureaucratic machine cannot cope with such a "difficult" task) representatives of the Trade Department of the State Bank, and so that these representatives should receive bonuses in proportion to the growth of commercial turnover in those enterprises or territorial regions which have been "entrusted" to them?

It would seem to me that this would be more realistic than setting up special commissions or institutions which, given our rotten customs (with pretensions to "true communism"), will *inevitably* degenerate into bureaucratic stupidity. Meanwhile the Trade Department of the State Bank must be given a clear *practical* task—to develop internal trade and take it under its own control. And for the development of operations let both the representatives and the members of the board (if there are members of the board in the Trade Department of the State Bank) receive their bonuses—but only for the development of operations.

Judging by what Gorbunov has told me about the results of his "troubles" over the Belov and GUM[425] affair, it is clear that the Trade Department of the State Bank is *at fault* here. They slept in, they missed the bus, they waited, like real jack-in-office scoundrels, for an *order* "from above". I think the Trade Department should be punished at once for this, where it hurts most, with the warning: one more such yawn, one more such display of sleepiness—and it means *prison*.

Another practical means, it would seem to me, is the registration of private commercial deals and a tax on them, by means of a stamp duty or something similar. How does this question stand? *Cannot* private trade be placed in *such* a way (or begin to be placed) under the control of the People's Commissariat of Finance and the State Bank?

I think that the success of the work of the entire People's Commissariat of Finance should be measured 99 per cent by *the development of state trade* and of the *Trade Department of the State Bank* (in the granting of credit to private trade). Everything else counts only 1 per cent.

With communist greetings,
Lenin

First published in 1949   Printed from the original
in *Bolshevik* No. 1

315

TO G. Y. SOKOLNIKOV

February 22

Comrade Sokolnikov,

The question is not just of GUM alone. All the work of all our economic bodies suffers most of all from bureaucracy. Communists have become bureaucrats. If anything will destroy us, it is this. And for the State Bank it is most dangerous of all to be bureaucratic. We are still thinking in terms of decrees, of institutions. This is the mistake. The whole essence now is practical men and practice. To find people who are *men of business* (1 out of 100; 1 out of 1,000 Communists, and that only with God's help); to transform our decrees out of dirty paper (it's all the same whether they are bad or good decrees) into living practice—that is the *essence*.

Whether the State Bank itself should trade, or through subordinate firms, through its agents, or through its client debtors, etc.—I don't know. I don't take it upon myself to judge, because I am not sufficiently acquainted with the technique of currency circulation and banking business. But what I do know firmly is that the whole problem now is the rapid development of state trade (in all its varieties: co-operation, clients of the State Bank, mixed companies, factors, agents, etc., etc.).

February 28

On account of my illness I did not finish and send away this letter. You speak (in your interview) about replacing state trusts by mixed companies. There will be no practical results. The clever capitalists will draw stupid (most honest and most virtuous) Communists into the mixed companies, and swindle us as they are swindling us now. The problem now is not one of institutions but of people, and of checking up on practical experience. *One by one* we must discover people who know how to trade, and step by step use their experience, their labour, to *clean out* the..., expelling the virtuous Communists from boards of management, shutting down sleepy (and strictly communist) enterprises, shutting them down, separating out the one per cent which are worth while. Either the People's Commissariat of Finance will prove *able* to go over to *such* work, or the entire People's Commissariat of Finance=0.

Yours,
Lenin

Written on February 22 and 28, 1922

First published in 1949   Printed from the original
in *Bolshevik* No. 1

316

TO G. M. KRZHIZHANOVSKY

April 6, 1922

G. M.,

Yesterday Martens[426] told me that the existence of an unheard-of wealth of iron deposits in Kursk Gubernia has been "proved" (you said "nearly").

If that is so, should we not *already this spring*—

(1) put down the necessary narrow-gauge lines there?

(2) Prepare the nearest peatbog (or bogs?) for exploitation, so that an electric power station can be put up there?

If this does not seem to you unnecessary, write to Martens about it (and two words to me).

Martens wants to go there in three weeks' time. I have written to Rykov and Tsyurupa that he should also be given an engineer from the State Planning Commission.

This business must be pushed ahead with *particular* energy. I am very much afraid that without triple checks it will go to sleep. When I leave, don't forget that Rykov and Tsyurupa have my letter about it.

Yours,
Lenin

First published
in *Ekonomicheskaya Zhizn* No. 17,
January 21, 1925

Printed from the original

317

TO CHARLES P. STEINMETZ

Moscow. April 10, 1922

Dear Mr. Steinmetz,

I thank you cordially for your friendly letter of February 16, 1922. I must admit to my shame that I heard your name for the first time only a few months ago from Comrade Krzhizhanovsky, who was the Chairman of our State Commission for Working out a Plan for the Electrification of Russia and is now Chairman of the State General Planning Commission. He told me of the outstanding position which you have gained among the electrical engineers of the whole world.

Comrade Martens has now made me better acquainted by his accounts of you. I have seen from these accounts that your sympathies with Soviet Russia have been aroused, on the one hand, by your social and political views. On the other hand, as a representative of electrical engineering and particularly in one of the technically advanced countries, you have become convinced of the necessity and inevitability of the replacement of capitalism by a new social order, which will establish the planned regulation of economy and ensure the welfare of the entire mass of the people on the basis of the electrification of entire countries. In all the countries of the world there is growing—more slowly than one would like, but irresistibly and unswervingly—the number of representatives of science, technology, art, who are becoming convinced of the necessity of replacing capitalism by a different socio-economic system, and whom the "terrible difficulties"* of the struggle of Soviet Russia against the

---

* These words were written by Lenin in English.—*Ed.*

entire capitalist world do not repel, do not frighten away but, on the contrary, lead to an understanding of the inevitability of the struggle and the necessity of taking what part in it they can, helping the new to overcome the old.

In particular, I want to thank you for your offer to help Russia with your advice, suggestions, etc. As the absence of official and legally recognised relations between Soviet Russia and the United States makes the practical realisation of your offer extremely difficult both for us and for you, I will allow myself to publish both your letter and my reply, in the hope that many persons who live in America, or in countries connected by commercial treaties both with the United States and with Russia, will then help you (by information, by translations from Russian into English, etc.) to give effect to your intention of helping the Soviet Republic.

With very best greetings,

Yours fraternally,

Lenin

Sent to New York

Published in *Pravda* No. 85, April 19, 1922

Printed from the typewritten text corrected by V. I. Lenin

318

TO N. I. BUKHARIN

Comrade Bukharin,

I send you today's *Pravda*. Now, why print stupidities in the guise of the article by Pletnyov,[427] who puts on pompous airs with all the learned and fashionable words he can? I have marked two stupidities and put a number of question marks. The author has to learn not "proletarian" science, but simply to learn. Can it be that the editorial board of *Pravda* is not going to explain the author's mistakes to him? Why, this is *falsification* of historical materialism! Playing at historical materialism!

Yours,
Lenin

Written on September 27, 1922

Published for the first time
in the Fourth (Russian) Edition
of the *Collected Works*

Printed from the original

319

TO THE PRESIDIUM OF THE SUPREME ECONOMIC COUNCIL

Comrade Bogdanov,
   Presidium of the Supreme Economic Council
Copies:
   to *Comrades Krzhizhanovsky and Pyatakov*, State
      Planning Commission
   " *Comrade Vladimirov*, People's Commissariat of
      Finance
   " Presidium of the All-Russia Central Execu-
      tive Committee
   " *Comrade Kamenev*, Deputy Chairman of the
      Council of People's Commissars and
   " Comrade *L. B. Krasin*

Comrade Krasin has sent me a letter in which he tells
me of the very great successes of a group of engineers, headed by Comrade Gubkin, who, with stubbornness bordering
on the heroic, and with insignificant support by state organisations, have not only developed from zero the detailed
scientific investigation of combustible slates and sapropelite,
but have also learned in practice to produce out of these
minerals various useful products, such as ichthyol, black
varnish, various soaps, paraffins, ammonium sulphate, etc.
   In view of the fact that this work, as Comrade Krasin
testifies, represents a firm foundation for an industry which
in ten or twenty years will produce hundreds of millions for
Russia, I propose that:
   (1) the further development of this work be immediately
guaranteed in the financial sense;

(2) all obstacles retarding it be eliminated, now and henceforth;

(3) this group of engineers be awarded the Order of the Red Banner of Labour and a large sum of money.

Please inform me of further developments in writing through Comrade Gorbunov, Office Manager of the C.P.C. In the event of any obstacles arising, inform me immediately through the same channel.

V. Ulyanov (Lenin)
Chairman, Council of People's Commissars
and Council of Labour and Defence

Written on October 16, 1922

First published in *Izvestia*
No. 20, January 20, 1930

Printed from the typewritten
copy signed by V. I. Lenin

320

TO I. I. SKVORTSOV-STEPANOV

Dear Ivan Ivanovich,

I have read your article about specialists.[428]
I don't agree. Two points.

The first is at the beginning (the third column from the beginning): "The proletarian dictatorship will collapse if, in the first place...*" (this is correct) "and secondly, if these specialists are not our own specialists, *such as see their aim to be the consolidation and development of the dictatorship of the proletariat.*"

What I have underlined is incorrect. We shall not have such specialists for a long time, until the *bourgeois* specialists, the *petty-bourgeois* specialists have disappeared, until *all* the specialists have become *Communists*. Yet the proletarian dictatorship must certainly not "*collapse*" in the meantime. A *lesser* condition will be enough—namely, the *first*. The second does not imperil our existence. It is sufficient to "have at our disposal".

For a long time yet there will be doubts, uncertainty, intrigues, betrayals, etc. The second condition will last until the *end* of the dictatorship, and therefore *is not a condition of the dictatorship.*

Now the second point, at the end of the article, the third and second paragraphs *from the end*.

"The class struggle ... no more abnormal than the relations which it expresses".[429]

---

* Lenin refers to the following passage: "...in the first place, it does not have at its disposal well-qualified specialists of the most diverse categories".—*Ed.*

Untrue. It is *untrue*, and not merely abnormal. It is worse than abnormal: it is *scientifically untrue*. This is *not* the class struggle.

Further. "The scientific laboratory is a united collective, acting co-ordinately, concertedly *and consciously in all* its elements."

Untrue. This cannot be the case before the *abolition of classes*.

This is not scientific but sentimental: *before* classes have been abolished, *"share and share alike"* in everything. Wrong. It will degenerate into the practices of 1918: medical assistants demand that doctors should "share and share alike" in everything (*scientific*).

This is both wrong and practically harmful.

An example: the Political Bureau and its *girl secretaries*. "Share and share alike" in everything (*scientific*)? You yourself will not insist on that. You have been carried away.

Best greetings!

Yours,
Lenin

Written on November 15, 1922

First published in 1929
in *Proletarskaya Revolutsia* No. 10

Printed from the original

321

TO COMRADE MÜNZENBERG, SECRETARY OF THE INTERNATIONAL WORKERS' AID[430]

Supplementing your report at the Fourth Congress of the Comintern, I should like in a few words to point out the significance of the organisation of aid.

The assistance given to the starving by the international working class helped Soviet Russia in considerable measure to endure the painful days of last year's famine and to overcome it. At the present time we have to heal the wounds inflicted by the famine, provide in the first place for many thousands of orphaned children, and restore our agriculture and industry which have suffered heavily as a result of the famine.

In this sphere, too, the fraternal aid of the international working class has already begun to operate. The American tractor column near Perm, the agricultural groups of the American Technical Aid, the agricultural and industrial undertakings of the International Workers' Aid, the allocation of and subscriptions to the first proletarian loan, through the Workers' Aid to Soviet Russia—all these are very promising beginnings in the cause of workers' fraternal aid to promote the economic restoration of Soviet Russia.

The work of economic assistance, so happily begun by the International Workers' Aid to Soviet Russia, should be supported in every possible way by the workers and toilers of the whole world. Side by side with the continuing strong political pressure on the governments of the bourgeois countries over the demand for recognition of the Soviet government, widespread economic aid by the world proletariat is at present the best and most practical support of Soviet Russia in her difficult economic war against the imperialist concerns, and the best support for her work of building a socialist economy.

Vl. Ulyanov (Lenin)

Moscow, December 2, 1922

First published in 1924
in the book *Tri goda mezhdunarodnoi rabochei pomoshchi. 1921-24*,
Moscow, Mezhrabpom Publishers

Printed from the Russian translation
of the German original
signed by Lenin

NOTES

[1] Reference is to the resolutions passed by the Sixth (Prague) All-Russia Conference of the R.S.D.L.P. of 1912. The resolutions and "Announcement" concerning the Conference were published in booklet form in Paris in February 1912 by the C.C. of the R.S.D.L.P.   p. 23

[2] *Liquidationism*—an opportunist trend in the R.S.D.L.P. that emerged in the period of reaction following the defeat of the 1905-07 revolution. The liquidators demanded liquidation of the illegal revolutionary party of the working class and tried to subordinate the working-class movement to bourgeois interests. The Sixth (Prague) All-Russia Conference of the R.S.D.L.P. expelled the liquidators from the Party.   p. 23

[3] *Zvezda* (The Star)—legal Bolshevik newspaper (December 1910-May 5, 1912). In 1911 and 1912 it published seven stories by Gorky from his *Tales of Italy* series.   p. 23

[4] *Sovremennik* (The Contemporary)—literary and political monthly published in St. Petersburg from 1911 to 1915. It was a rallying point for Menshevik liquidators, Socialist-Revolutionaries, Popular Socialists and Left-wing liberals.   p. 23

[5] *Zhivoye Dyelo* (Vital Cause)—Menshevik liquidationist legal weekly, published in St. Petersburg from January to April 1912. Sixteen issues appeared. Its contributors included L. Martov, F. Dan and P. Axelrod.   p. 24

[6] The daily newspaper for the workers that succeeded *Zvezda* was *Pravda* (Truth), the first issue of which appeared on May 5, 1912.
                                                                                p. 24

[7] Reference is to Gorky's work for the magazine *Zavety* (Behests), to which V. Chernov, a Socialist-Revolutionary leader, contributed, and for the magazine *Sovremennik*, which in 1911 was run by A. Amfiteatrov.   p. 24

[8] Znaniye (Knowledge)—a book-publishing firm founded in St. Petersburg in 1898 by a group of writers. Gorky joined the firm

later and virtually became its leading spirit. The managing
director was K. P. Pyatnitsky.   p. 24

[9] *Irkutskoye Slovo* (Irkutsk Word)—weekly newspaper with a
Menshevik-liquidationist orientation (1911-12). Its publisher,
Rozhkov, a member of the R.S.D.L.P. since 1905, had in the
years of reaction become one of the ideologists of liquidationism;
N. Chuzhak (N. F. Nasimovich) was a literary critic.   p. 24

[10] *M. F.*—Maria Fyodorovna Andreyeva—Gorky's wife.   p. 24

[11] Lenin refers to reports on the Sixth (Prague) All-Russia Conference of the R.S.D.L.P. (January 1912). G. L. Shklovsky
made reports on the Conference in Berne and Lausanne, but his
tour of all Switzerland did not take place.   p. 25

[12] *Vperyod* group—an anti-Party group of otzovists, ultimatumists
and god-builders (see Notes 73 and 77); was organised in December 1909 on the initiative of A. Bogdanov and G. Alexinsky. It
had its own organ called *Vperyod* (Forward). Lacking the support
of the workers, the group had virtually collapsed by 1913. Its
complete and formal dissolution occurred in 1917, after the February bourgeois-democratic revolution.   p. 25

[13] *Trotsky (Bronstein), L. D.* (1879-1940)—joined the R.S.D.L.P.
in 1897, became a Menshevik. During the years of reaction (1907-
10) and the subsequent revolutionary revival, though ostensibly
an advocate of "non-factionalism", he in fact adopted the position of the liquidators. In 1912, he was the organiser of the anti-
Party August bloc. During the first world war he took up a Centrist stand. Returning from emigration after the February bourgeois-democratic revolution of 1917, he joined the Inter-District
Organisation and together with its other members was admitted to
the Bolshevik Party at the Sixth Congress of the R.S.D.L.P.(B.).
After the October Socialist Revolution Trotsky held a number of
government posts. In 1918 he was opposed to the Brest Peace
Treaty, in 1920-21 he led the opposition in the discussion on the
trade unions, and from 1923 conducted a bitter factional struggle
against the Party's general line, against Lenin's programme of
building socialism, and preached the impossibility of the victory
of socialism in the U.S.S.R. In 1927 Trotsky was expelled from the
Party. For anti-Soviet activities he was deported from the U.S.S.R.
in 1929, and in 1932 deprived of Soviet citizenship.
  Plekhanov, G. V. (1856-1918)—outstanding figure in the Russian
and international working-class movement, the first propagandist
of Marxism in Russia. In 1883 he set up in Geneva the first Russian
Marxist organisation, the Emancipation of Labour group. An
opponent of Narodism, Plekhanov also opposed revisionism in the
international working-class movement. He wrote a number of
works that played a big part in defending and propagating mate-
rialist philosophy. After the Second Congress of the R.S.D.L.P.

(1903) Plekhanov took up a position of reconciliation with opportunism and later joined the Mensheviks. In the years of reaction (1907-10) and during the subsequent revolutionary revival Plekhanov came out against the Machist revision of Marxism and against liquidationism. During the first world war he became a social-chauvinist. After the February bourgeois-democratic revolution he returned to Russia from emigration, and opposed the Bolsheviks and the socialist revolution on the grounds that Russia was not ripe for socialism. When the October Socialist Revolution occurred, his attitude to it was negative, but he took no part in the struggle against Soviet power.   p. 25

[14] *Bund* (General Jewish Workers' Union of Lithuania, Poland and Russia) was organised in 1897; it spread nationalism and separatism in the working-class movement in Russia. It disbanded in March 1921.   p. 26

[15] Lenin has in mind the resolution of November 26, 1910, passed at a meeting of the so-called Party Social-Democratic Club in Vienna (mainly composed of Trotskyists) and aimed against *Rabochaya Gazeta* (Workers' Gazette) (see Note 29).   p. 26

[16] The delegates which the Social-Democratic group in the Third Duma sent to the Prague Party Conference were N. G. Poletayev and V. Y. Shurkanov (the latter was subsequently exposed as an *agent provocateur*). They arrived late at the Conference. Lenin met them in Leipzig.   p. 26

[17] *Golos* group—Mensheviks associated with the liquidators' paper *Golos Sotsial-Demokrata* (Voice of the Social-Democrat) published first in Geneva and then in Paris.   p. 27

[18] *International Socialist Bureau* (I.S.B.)—permanent executive and information body of the Second International. The decision to set up the Bureau was taken at the Paris Congress of the Second International in 1900. From 1905 to 1912 Lenin represented the R.S.D.L.P. in the Bureau. With the outbreak of the world war the I.S.B. became an obedient tool in the hands of the social-chauvinists.   p. 27

[19] In Paris, on March 12, 1912, a meeting of representatives of the Bund Committee Abroad, the *Vperyod* group, *Golos Sotsial-Demokrata*, Trotsky's Vienna *Pravda*, the pro-Party Mensheviks and the conciliators passed a slanderous anti-Party resolution aimed against the Sixth (Prague) All-Russia Conference of the R.S.D.L.P. and its decisions. As representative of the C.C. of the R.S.D.L.P. in the International Socialist Bureau, Lenin wrote two letters concerning this resolution to the Bureau Secretary Camille Huysmans (see present edition, Vol. 17, pp. 547-50, and this volume, pp. 31-32).   p. 27

[20] Reference is to Plekhanov's article "Vechnaya Pamyat" (Eternal Memory) published in Supplement 2 to No. 15 of *Dnevnik Sotsial-Demokrata* (Diary of a Social-Democrat), which Plekhanov brought out at intervals between March 1905 and April 1912 in Geneva. Sixteen numbers were issued. Publication was resumed in 1916 in Petrograd, but only one issue appeared.   p. 27

[21] *Nasha Zarya* (Our Dawn), *Zhivoye Dyelo* (Vital Cause) and *Golos Sotsial-Demokrata* (Voice of the Social-Democrat) were organs of the Menshevik liquidators.   p. 27

[22] At the Sixth (Prague) All-Russia Conference of the R.S.D.L.P., G. K. Orjonikidze and S. S. Spandaryan were elected to the Central Committee and the Bureau of the C.C. of the R.S.D.L.P. in Russia. Yelena Stasova was elected a candidate for membership of the Central Committee.   p. 28

[23] *Savka's town*—Ekaterinoslav, where Y. D. Zevin, who used the pseudonym "Savka", was working.   p. 28

[24] *Vorwärts* (Forward)—daily newspaper, central organ of the German Social-Democratic Party, started in Berlin in 1891. In the late nineties, after the death of Engels, the editorship of the paper fell into the hands of the Party's Right wing and regularly published articles by opportunists.

In the issue for March 26, 1912, *Vorwärts* carried an anonymous slanderous article written by Trotsky against the Sixth (Prague) All-Russia Conference of the R.S.D.L.P. and its decisions. The German opportunists on *Vorwärts* refused to publish Lenin's reply to Trotsky. In order to give the German workers a true picture of the Prague Conference, *Sotsial-Demokrat* printed Lenin's reply in German and published it as a separate pamphlet *Der Anonymus aus dem "Vorwärts" und die Sachlage in der Sozialdemokratischen Arbeiterpartei Russlands* (The Anonymous Writer in *Vorwärts* and the State of Affairs in the R.S.D.L.P.).

The pamphlet was sent out to 600 German addresses—editorial boards of Social-Democratic publications, local committees, and libraries.   p. 29

[25] *Huysmans, Camille* (b. 1871)—veteran of the Belgian working-class movement; professor of philology and journalist. From 1904 to 1919 he was Secretary of the International Socialist Bureau of the Second International. During the world imperialist war of 1914-18 he adopted a Centrist position.   p. 31

[26] Lenin refers to the slanderous resolution passed by the meeting of anti-Party groups in Paris on March 12, 1912 (see Note 19). p. 31

[27] Reference is to the resolutions of the Prague Party Conference of 1912 on "Liquidationism and the Group of Liquidators" and "The Party Organisation Abroad" (see present edition, Vol. 17, pp. 480-81, 484).   p. 31

[28] *Caucasian Regional Committee*—factional centre of the Caucasian Menshevik liquidators. It joined the anti-Party August bloc organised by Trotsky.   p. 33

[29] *Rabochaya Gazeta* (Workers' Gazette)—illegal popular organ of the Bolsheviks, published irregularly in Paris between 1910 and 1912.
Reference is to the article "What Should the People Be Taught about the Election Campaign?" published in *Rabochaya Gazeta* No. 8, March 17 (30), 1912.   p. 33

[30] *Izvestia* (News)—the projected publication did not take place.
                                                                         p. 33

[31] Reference is to the resolution "Elections to the Fourth Duma", adopted by the Sixth (Prague) All-Russia Conference of the R.S.D.L.P. in 1912.   p. 34

[32] *Novoye Vremya* (New Times)—daily newspaper published in St. Petersburg from 1868 to 1917. At first moderate-liberal in tone, it became an organ of reactionary aristocratic circles and official-dom after it was taken over by A. S. Suvorin in 1876. From 1905 onwards it was an organ of the Black Hundreds. It was closed down by the Revolutionary Military Committee of the Petrograd Soviet on October 26 (November 8), 1917.   p. 37

[33] Lenin refers to the Bolshevik legal daily paper *Pravda* that was being prepared for publication.   p. 37

[34] *Knipovich, B. N.* (1880-1924)—economist and statistician, participated in the Social-Democratic movement, arrested in 1911 and deported. His first scientific work *A Contribution to the Problem of Differentiation of the Russian Peasantry* appeared in 1912. p. 38

[35] *Maslov, P. P.* (1867-1946)—economist, Social-Democrat, wrote a number of books on the agrarian problem in which he attempted to revise Marxism.   p. 39

[36] The expression recalls the summer of 1907, when Lenin for conspiratorial purposes and to restore his health was living at Knipovich's country house in Stjernsund (Finland). To get water for their flowers the Knipovich family had to pull a water-cart from a well that was situated a long way from the garden. When he saw members of the family setting out for water, Lenin came out of the house and helped them pull the cart.   p. 39

[37] *Pravda* (Truth)—the first legal mass workers' daily in Russia. The first issue appeared in St. Petersburg on May 5, 1912.
Pravda played a key role in the history of the Bolshevik Party and the revolution. It was a collective propagandist, agitator and organiser in the struggle to put the Party's policy into practice.

As a centre of the campaign for Party principles, it fought resolutely against the Menshevik liquidators, otzovists and Trotskyists
and opposed international opportunism. *Pravda* helped to build a
firm foundation for a mass Bolshevik party.

Lenin guided the policy of *Pravda*, which published 270 of his
articles. The paper was closed down eight times by the tsarist
government but continued to appear under fresh names: *Rabochaya
Pravda* (Workers' Truth), *Severnaya Pravda* (Northern Truth),
Pravda Truda (Truth of Labour), *Za Pravdu* (For Truth), *Proletarskaya Pravda* (Proletarian Truth), *Put Pravdy* (Path of Truth),
Rabochy (The Worker), and *Trudovaya Pravda* (Labour Truth).
Before the outbreak of the first world war, on July 21, 1914, the
paper was banned and did not recommence publication until
after the February bourgeois-democratic revolution of 1917.

On March 18, 1917, *Pravda* began appearing as the organ of the
Central and Petrograd Committees of the R.S.D.L.P. On April 18,
upon his return from abroad, Lenin joined the editorial board and
became its leading spirit. Between July and October 1917, the paper was persecuted by the bourgeois Provisional Government and
had frequently to change its name, appearing as *Listok Pravdy*
(*Pravda*'s News Sheet), *Proletary* (The Proletarian), *Rabochy* (The
Worker) and *Rabochy Put* (Workers' Path). After the victory of
the October Socialist Revolution, on November 9, 1917, the Party's
Central Organ began appearing under its original name *Pravda*.
p. 40

[38] *Rech* (Speech)—daily newspaper, central organ of the Constitutional-Democratic Party; appeared in St. Petersburg from February 1906 to October 1917. p. 41

[39] *Wiener Arbeiter-Zeitung* (Vienna Workers' Newspaper)—daily
newspaper, central organ of the Austrian Social-Democratic Party,
founded by Victor Adler in Vienna in 1889. Banned in 1934, it
resumed publication in 1945 as the central organ of the Socialist
Party of Austria. p. 41

[40] *Nevskaya Zvezda* (Neva Star)—legal Bolshevik newspaper published in St. Petersburg from February to October 1912. Lenin
directed the paper's policy from abroad. It was constantly persecuted by the government. Of the 27 numbers that appeared
9 were confiscated, and for 2 the editors were fined. The editors
were frequently prosecuted. p. 42

[41] The articles Lenin mentions here, "Petty Artifices (A Reply to
Blank)" and "Unquenchable Hopes", have not been discovered
to this day. p. 42

[42] The liquidators' paper *Nevsky Golos* (Neva Voice) No. 6, for July
5, 1912, carried a report on meetings held in St. Petersburg by
representatives of various Social-Democratic trends (allegedly
including supporters of *Pravda* and *Nevskaya Zvezda*) to discuss the
Fourth Duma election campaign. The editors of *Nevskaya Zvezda*

and *Pravda* denied any participation by their representatives in
these meetings.   p. 43

[43] *Axelrod, P. B.* (1850-1928)—a Menshevik leader. During the years
of reaction and the subsequent revolutionary revival, he was one
of the leaders of the liquidators and a member of the editorial board
of the Menshevik liquidators' newspaper *Golos Sotsial-Demokrata*.
During the first world war he maintained a position of social-chauvinism under cover of Centrist phrases. He was hostile to the October Socialist Revolution.   p. 43

[44] The article Lenin refers to was "On Current Themes (From P. B.
Axelrod's Letters to Friends)", published in *Nevsky Golos* No. 6
on July 5, 1912, and in *Nasha Zarya* No. 6 for 1912. Lenin criticises the article in his work *How P. B. Axelrod Exposes the Liquidators* (see present edition, Vol. 18, pp. 175-86).   p. 43

[45] This article, which Lenin sent to *Pravda* in July 1912, was not
published and has never been discovered.   p. 45

[46] Lenin's article about November 9 (the reply of a correspondent)
has hever been found.   p. 48

[47] No report on the subject suggested by Lenin was published in
Pravda.   p. 49

[48] The publications mentioned here—*Pochin* (Beginning), *Izvestia
zagranichnoi oblastnoi organizatsii* (Journal of the Regional Organisation Abroad), *Revolutsionnaya Mysl* (Revolutionary Thought) and
Revolutsionnaya Rossiya (Revolutionary Russia)—were run by
various groups and trends in the Socialist-Revolutionary Party.
                                                                  p. 50

[49] Reference is to the novels by V. Ropshin (B. Savinkov), one of the
leaders of the Socialist-Revolutionary Party: *Kon bledny* (The
Pale Horse), published in the magazine *Russkaya Mysl* No. 1
for 1909, and *To chego ne bylo* (What Never Happened),
published in the magazine *Zavety* Nos. 1-8, April-November
1912, and in No. 1 for January 1913.   p. 50

[50] *Vekhi* (Landmarks)—a symposium published by the Constitutional-
Democrats in Moscow in the spring of 1909. Its articles devoted
to the Russian intelligentsia cast a slur on the revolutionary-demo-
cratic traditions of the liberation movement in Russia, and the
views and activities of the outstanding revolutionary democrats
of the nineteenth century V. G. Belinsky, N. A. Dobrolyubov,
N. G. Chernyshevsky and D. I. Pisarev. The contributors to the
symposium vilified the revolutionary movement of 1905 and
thanked the tsarist government for protecting the privileged
classes "with its bayonets and jails" from "the fury of the people".
                                                                  p. 50

[51] *Milyukov, P. N.* (1859-1943)—leader of the Constitutional-Democratic (Cadet) Party, prominent ideologist of the Russian imperialist bourgeoisie. One of the men who in October 1905 founded the Cadet Party, he became chairman of its Central Committee and editor of its central organ, the newspaper *Rech* (Speech). He was a member of the Third and Fourth Dumas. After the February bourgeois-democratic revolution of 1917 he became Minister for Foreign Affairs in the bourgeois Provisional Government, and after the October Socialist Revolution helped to organise the foreign military intervention against Soviet Russia. Later he was active among the White émigrés.

Gredeskul, N. A. (b. 1864)—professor of law, publicist, Constitutional-Democrat; deputy to the First Duma. Worked on Cadet *Rech* and a number of other bourgeois-liberal papers. In 1916 he left the Constitutional-Democratic Party. After the October Socialist Revolution taught as a professor in Leningrad.

p. 50

[52] *Socialist-Revolutionary Party* (S.R.s)—a petty-bourgeois party in Russia; emerged at the end of 1901 and the beginning of 1902 as a result of the union of various Narodnik groups and circles. The S.R.s did not recognise the class differences between the proletariat and the small owners. They glossed over the class differentiation and contradictions within the peasantry and denied the leading role of the proletariat in the revolution. The tactics of individual terrorism which the S.R.s advocated as the main form of struggle against the autocracy did great harm to the revolutionary movement and made it more difficult to organise the masses for revolutionary struggle.

The Bolshevik Party exposed the S.R.s' attempts to masquerade as socialists, waged a determined struggle against them for influence over the peasantry, and exposed the harm caused to the working-class movement by their tactics of individual terrorism. At the same time the Bolsheviks, under certain conditions, made temporary agreements with the S.R.s in the struggle against tsarism.

The heterogeneity of the peasantry as a class determined the political and ideological instability and organisational disunity of the Socialist-Revolutionaries and their constant wavering between the liberal bourgeoisie and the proletariat. In the period of reaction (1907-10) the S.R.s suffered complete ideological and organisational collapse. During the first world war the majority of them became social-chauvinists.

After the victory of the February bourgeois-democratic revolution in 1917, the S.R.s together with the Mensheviks and the Cadets were the mainstay of the counter-revolutionary bourgeois-landowner Provisional Government, and their leaders (Kerensky, Avksentyev, Chernov) were members of it. The S.R. Party refused to support the peasant demand for abolition of the landed estates and came out in favour of landed proprietorship. The S.R.

ministers in the Provisional Government sent punitive expeditions against peasants who had seized the landowners' estates.

At the end of November 1917, the Left wing of the party formed the independent party of Left S.R.s. In an attempt to preserve their influence over the mass of the peasants, the Left S.R.s formally recognised Soviet power and came to an agreement with the Bolsheviks, but soon joined the struggle against Soviet power.

During the years of foreign intervention and civil war, the S.R.s engaged in counter-revolutionary subversion, actively supported the interventionists and whiteguards, participated in counter-revolutionary conspiracies, and organised terrorist acts against leaders of the Soviet state and the Communist Party. After the Civil War the S.R.s continued their hostile activities against the Soviet state.   p. 50

[53] *Trudovik group* (Trudoviks)—group of petty-bourgeois democrats in the Duma, consisting of peasants and intellectuals with a Narodnik orientation.

Their politics were the class politics of the small peasant farmer and the Trudoviks in the Duma wavered between the Cadets and Social-Democrats. Since the Trudoviks did to some extent represent the peasant masses, the Bolsheviks in the Duma adopted tactics of co-operating with them, in certain fields, for the sake of the common struggle against tsarist autocracy and the Cadets.
                                                                        p. 50

[54] *Bezzaglavtsi*—semi-Cadet, semi-Menshevik group of the Russian bourgeois intelligentsia, formed when the revolution of 1905-07 was on the wane. It took its name from the political weekly *Bez Zaglaviya* (Without a Title) published in St. Petersburg between January and May 1906. Under cover of their formal non-attachment to any party, the Bezzaglavtsi advocated bourgeois-liberal and opportunist ideas, and supported the revisionists in the Russian and international Social-Democratic movement.   p. 50

[55] *Cadets*—members of the Constitutional-Democratic Party, the leading party of the liberal-monarchist bourgeoisie in `Russia. Founded in October 1905, it represented the bourgeoisie, landowners and bourgeois intellectuals. The Cadets wanted to make a deal with tsarism. They advocated a constitutional monarchy, opposed the slogan of a republic and insisted on preservation of the landed estates. During the world war of 1914-18 they became ideologists of imperialism and supported the expansionist policy of tsarism.

After the victory of the October Socialist Revolution the Cadets took an active part in all armed counter-revolutionary actions and in the interventionist campaigns against Soviet Russia. p. 50

[56] *Dnevnitsky (Tsederbaum, F. O.)* (b. 1883)—Social-Democrat, Menshevik, publicist. From 1909 onwards he lived abroad, became associated with the pro-Party Mensheviks, worked for

Plekhanov's *Dnevnik Sotsial-Demokrata* (Diary of a Social-Democrat) and the Bolshevik newspapers *Zvezda* and *Pravda*. p. 52

[57] *Zaprosy Zhizni* (Demands of Life)—magazine run by Cadets, Popular Socialists and Menshevik liquidators. Appeared in St. Petersburg 1909-12.

Prokopovich, S. N. (1871-1955)—bourgeois economist and publicist. One of the first advocates of Bernsteinism in Russia. In 1906 he became a member of the Central Committee of the Cadet Party, and in 1917 was Minister for Food in the bourgeois Provisional Government.

Blank, R. M. (b. 1866)—bourgeois publicist. At one time editor of *Zaprosy Zhizni*. p. 52

[58] Reference seems to be to L. B. Kamenev's article "Ob obyazanno-styakh demokrata (otvet V. Chernovu)" ("On the Duties of a Democrat [A Reply to V. Chernov]"), published in No. 8-9 of *Prosveshcheniye* in July-August 1912. p. 54

[59] Reference is to the liquidators' so-called August Conference, which was held in Vienna in August 1912. This conference was responsible for the forming of the anti-Party August bloc, organised by Trotsky. p. 55

[60] Lenin has in mind the newspaper *Warsaw Latest News*, published from July 13 to August 19, 1912 under the editorship of V. N. Chudovskaya. A. Amfiteatrov was a contributor. p. 55

[61] Reference is to the article "Kulturniye lyudi i nechistaya sovest" ("Cultured People and a Sullied Conscience") by M. S. Olminsky (A. Vitimsky), published in *Pravda* No. 98, August 23, 1912. p. 57

[62] Lenin refers to the elections to the Fourth State Duma, which ended on November 7 (20), 1912. p. 58

[63] *Luch* (Ray)—legal daily newspaper put out by Menshevik liquidators in St. Petersburg from September 1912 to July 1913. In all, 237 issues appeared. The newspaper existed mainly on the liberals' donations. Its policy was controlled by P. B. Axelrod, F. I. Dan, L. Martov and A. S. Martynov. p. 58

[64] *Dyen* (The Day)—liberal-bourgeois daily paper, published in St. Petersburg from 1912 until it was closed down on October 26 (November 8), 1917. Its contributors were Menshevik liquidators, who took over the paper completely after the February bourgeois-democratic revolution of 1917. p. 58

[65] *Witte, S. Y.* (1849-1915)—statesman of tsarist Russia, a convinced supporter of the autocracy, who sought to preserve the

monarchy by means of small concessions and promises to the liberal bourgeoisie and harsh repressive measures against the people. He was Prime Minister (1905-06).   p. 58

[66] *Krugozor* (Horizon)—literary-political monthly with a bourgeois-liberal orientation. Two numbers were published in St. Petersburg in January and February 1913. Maxim Gorky was listed among the contributors but actually did not take part.   p. 60

[67] This mandate was adopted at meetings of workers of the larger enterprises in St. Petersburg and at a congress of workers' representatives on October 17 (30), 1912.   p. 63

[68] Lenin refers to No. 166 of *Pravda*, which appeared on November 11 (24), 1912, the day the Extraordinary International Socialist Congress of the Second International opened in Basle.

The telegram from A. Y. Badayev and other deputies, greeting the Basle Congress and protesting against war, was published in *Pravda* No. 167, on November 13 (26), 1912.   p. 65

[69] *Baturin* (*Zamyatin, N. I.*) (1877-1927)—one of the editors of *Pravda*.   p. 65

[70] *Zavety* (Behests)—legal literary-political monthly with a Socialist-Revolutionary orientation; appeared in St. Petersburg, April 1912 to July 1914.   p. 68

[71] *Malinovsky* was subsequently exposed as an *agent provocateur*.
                                                                         p. 69

[72] Reference is to the Party school at Poronin, which the C.C. of the R.S.D.L.P. planned to organise in 1913, during the Duma's summer recess, for members of the Social-Democratic group in the Duma, workers and Party activists. Lenin intended giving an important series of lectures on political economy, the theory and practice of socialism in Russia, and on the agrarian and nationalities problems. Difficulties, such as lack of funds, etc., prevented the school from being organised.   p. 69

[73] *Machism, or empirio-criticism*—a reactionary subjective-idealist philosophical trend which became widespread in Western Europe at the end of the nineteenth and the beginning of the twentieth centuries. Its founders were the Austrian physicist and philosopher Ernst Mach and the German philosopher Richard Avenarius. In Russia, during the years of reaction, the influence of Machism made itself felt among some intellectuals of the R.S.D.L.P., particularly Menshevik intellectuals (N. Valentinov, P. Yushkevich and others). Some literary men among the Bolsheviks also adopted Machist positions (V. Bazarov, A. Bogdanov and others). Though they claimed to advocate Marxism, the Russian Machists

were trying to revise the fundamental principles of Marxist philosophy. In his book *Materialism and Empirio-criticism* Lenin revealed the reactionary essence of Machism, defended Marxist philosophy from revisionist attacks and in the new historical conditions obtaining at the time pushed forward the development of dialectical and historical materialism in all respects. The defeat of Machism was a crippling blow to the ideology of Menshevism, otzovism and god-building.

God-building—a religious-philosophical trend hostile to Marxism. It arose during the period of reaction among certain Party intellectuals who departed from Marxism after the defeat of the 1905-07 revolution. The god-builders (A. V. Lunacharsky, V. Bazarov and others) advocated a new "socialist" religion and tried to reconcile Marxism with religion. Maxim Gorky was at one time associated with them.   p. 70

[74] *Bogdanov, A. (Malinovsky, A. A.; Maximov, N.)* (1873-1928)—Social-Democrat, philosopher, sociologist, economist; by training, a doctor. After the Second Congress of the R.S.D.L.P. he joined the Bolsheviks and was elected a member of the Central Committee. He was on the editorial boards of the Bolshevik newspapers *Vperyod* and *Proletary*, and worked as an editor of the Bolshevik newspaper *Novaya Zhizn*. In the years of reaction (1907-10) and the subsequent revolutionary revival he headed the otzovists, and the *Vperyod* anti-Party group. In philosophy he tried to create his own system of "empirio-monism" (a variety of subjective-idealist philosophy), which Lenin criticised sharply in his *Materialism and Empirio-criticism*. At a meeting of the enlarged editorial board of the newspaper *Proletary* in June 1909 Bogdanov was expelled from the Bolshevik Party. After the October Socialist Revolution he became one of the organisers and leaders of the Proletcult (Proletarian Culture Organisation). From 1926 onwards he was director of the Blood-Transfusion Institute which he had founded.

Bazarov, V. (real name Rudnev, V. A.) (1874-1939)—philosopher and economist, joined the Social-Democratic movement in 1896. Between 1905 and 1907 he contributed to a number of Bolshevik publications, gave up Bolshevism in the years of reaction, and became one of the main representatives of the Machist revision of Marxism.

Lunacharsky, A. V. (1875-1933)—professional revolutionary, prominent Soviet statesman.
Having entered the revolutionary movement in the early nineties, he became a Bolshevik after the Second Congress of the R.S.D.L.P. During the years of reaction he turned away from Marxism, took part in the anti-Party *Vperyod* group, and called for the merging of religion and Marxism.   p. 70

[75] Lenin visited Capri for a few days at Gorky's request in April 1908. During his stay he told A. Bogdanov, V. Bazarov and

A. V. Lunacharsky that he definitely disagreed with them in
matters of philosophy. p. 70

[76] *Alexinsky, G. A.* (b. 1879)—started his political career as a Social-
Democrat. An otzovist and one of the organisers of the anti-Party
Vperyod group in the years of reaction, he became a social-
chauvinist during the world war and worked for a number
of bourgeois papers. In July 1917 he made slanderous allegations
against Lenin and the Bolsheviks. In April 1918 he fled the
country. p. 71

[77] *Otzovism* (from the Russian "otozvat"—to recall)—opportunist
trend among the Bolsheviks, which was led by A. Bogdanov.
Under cover of revolutionary phrases the otzovists (besides Bogdanov the group included G. A. Alexinsky, S. Volsky, A. V. Lunacharsky and M. N. Lyadov) demanded the recall of the Social-
Democratic deputies from the Third Duma. They also refused
to work in legal organisations. Declaring that under conditions
of reaction the Party should conduct only illegal work, the otzovists refused to participate in the Duma, the trade unions, the
co-operatives or any mass legal and semi-legal organisations.
A variety of otzovism was ultimatumism. The ultimatumists
proposed that the Social-Democratic deputies in the Duma should
be presented with an ultimatum demanding implicit obedience
to the decisions of the Party Central Committee and, if they
rejected it, that they should be recalled. Ultimatumism was
actually a masked form of otzovism. Lenin called the ultimatumists "bashful otzovists".
The otzovists caused great harm to the Party. Their policy
would have isolated the Party from the masses and converted
it into a sectarian organisation. p. 71

[78] Reference is to the Conference of the C.C. of the R.S.D.L.P.
with Party workers, known for conspiratorial purposes as the
"February Conference". It took place in Cracow on December 26,
1912, lasting till January 1, 1913 (January 8-14, 1913). p. 72

[79] Lenin refers to his article "On Bolshevism", which was written
for the second volume of N. A. Rubakin's book *Sredi Knig* (Among
Books) (see present edition, Vol. 18, pp. 485-86).
On January 10 (N.S.), 1913, Rubakin wrote Lenin a letter
asking him for a "brief *exposé* (not more than one sheet of notepaper) .... of the very *essence* of Bolshevism and to indicate the
books where this essence is expounded". Lenin's article in the
second volume of *Sredi Knig* was published without alterations.
p. 73

[80] Reference is to the newspaper *Nash Put* (Our Path). Lenin had
pointed out the necessity for a legal workers' newspaper in Moscow
in the summer of 1912. But the fund-collecting campaign for the

Moscow newspaper did not begin until November 1912. *Pravda* No. 176 for November 24 (O.S.), 1912 published a "Letter from a Group of Moscow Workers", which indicated that it would be possible and opportune to start a workers' newspaper in Moscow. The call to make collections for the paper was enthusiastically supported by the workers, but its appearance was delayed by the arrest, in February 1913, of the group of Bolsheviks who were starting it.

The first number of *Nash Put* appeared on August 25 (September 7), 1913. Lenin was active on the paper. Its contributors included Maxim Gorky, Demyan Bedny, M. S. Olminsky, I. I. Skvortsov-Stepanov, and also the Bolshevik deputies to the Fourth Duma. *Nash Put* was very popular among the workers and received donations from 395 workers' groups. When the paper was banned on September 12 (25), 1913, after only 16 issues had appeared, the Moscow workers staged a protest strike but did not succeed in getting the ban lifted.   p. 74

[81] *Skvortsov-Stepanov, I. I.* (1870-1928)—one of the oldest participants in the Russian revolutionary movement. He joined the R.S.D.L.P. in 1896, becoming a Bolshevik and Marxist writer towards the end of 1904. On several occasions between 1907 and 1911 he was nominated by the Bolsheviks as a candidate for the Duma. In the period of reaction he held incorrect views on the agrarian problem and adopted a conciliatory attitude to the anti-Party *Vperyod* group, but under Lenin's influence overcame his mistakes.   p. 75

[82] *Larin, Y. (Lurye, M. A.)* (1882-1932)—Social-Democrat, Menshevik. After the defeat of the 1905-07 revolution he became an active supporter of liquidationism, but in August 1917 was admitted to the Bolshevik Party. After the October Socialist Revolution he held various administrative and managerial posts.
                                                                         p. 75

[83] *Novaya Sibir* (New Siberia)—socio-political and literary daily newspaper with a liberal orientation. It was published in Irkutsk from December 1912 to February 1913. The liquidator N. Rozhkov was, in practice, its editor.   p. 75

[84] *Prosveshcheniye* (Enlightenment)—legal Bolshevik socio-political and literary monthly; began publication in St. Petersburg in December 1911. Maxim Gorky was editor of the fiction section. The magazine was banned by the tsarist government on the eve of the first world war, in June 1914. One further issue (a double one) appeared in the autumn of 1917.   p. 76

[85] Reference is probably to rumours of the possibility of a rising in Turkish Armenia under the leadership of the Armenian bourgeois-nationalist Dashnaktsutyun Party. This was suggested in

an article "Turkish Armenians and Russia" in the newspaper *Russkoye Slovo* (Russian Word) No. 7, January 9, 1913.   p. 76

[86] Reference is to the resolutions of the Cracow Conference of the C.C. of the R.S.D.L.P. and Party workers (January 8-14, 1913).
                                                                                  p. 77

[87] This letter deals with the state of affairs in the *Pravda* editorial office at the end of 1912 and the beginning of 1913. The "February" Conference of the C.C. of the R.S.D.L.P. and Party workers in Cracow in 1913 prescribed measures for improving the editors' work.   p. 78

[88] Members of the Bolshevik group in the Fourth Duma were referred to by their "numbers" for purposes of secrecy. No. 1 was A. Y. Badayev, No. 3—R. Malinovsky, and No. 6—G. I. Petrovsky. p. 78

[89] *Dyen* (The Day)—cover name for *Pravda*.   p. 78

[90] Lenin refers to a leading article "The Working Masses and the Underground" published in the Menshevik liquidators' paper *Luch* No. 15 (101), January 19, 1913. It was aimed against the Party's illegal work. This liquidationist sally was exposed by Lenin in his article "To the Social-Democrats", published as a hectographed leaflet in Cracow (see present edition, Vol. 18, pp. 529-31).   p. 79

[91] Lenin refers to Bogdanov's letter to *Pravda* protesting at the refusal of *Pravda* supporters to co-operate with the liquidators in the nomination of a workers' deputy to the Fourth Duma. In a note to the letter the editors confined themselves to stating that agreement had not been reached through the fault of the liquidators.   p. 81

[92] *The enquiry from the Riga workers* of January 19, 1913 was printed in No. 24 of *Pravda*, January 30, 1913. The authors of the enquiry, who signed themselves "A group of Narodnik workers and Social-Democrat Readers of *Pravda*" asked the editors to state their opinion on the question of "uniting with the Left Narodniks". Lenin's article "On Narodism", with which he wanted to link up this enquiry, had been published in Nos. 16 and 17 of *Pravda* on January 20 and 22, 1913 (see present edition, Vol. 18, pp. 524-28).   p. 81

[93] See Note 89.   p. 82

[94] See Note 88.   p. 82

[95] Reference is to the letters from the Bolshevik deputies in the Fourth Duma that were published in *Pravda* in January-

February 1913 under the heading "Local Impressions of the Deputies of the Social-Democratic Group".   p. 82

[96] Lenin refers to *V. I. Khaustov* (b. 1884)—a Social-Democrat, Menshevik, and one of the deputies to the Fourth Duma who belonged to the Social-Democratic group.   p. 82

[97] *Vechernaya Pochta* (Evening Post)—cover name for the Menshevik liquidators' paper *Luch*.   p. 82

[98] Lenin refers to the following letter from the Bolshevik deputies in the Fourth Duma—A. Y. Badayev, G. I. Petrovsky, F. N. Samoilov and N. R. Shagov—on their resignation from the liquidators' newspaper *Luch*: "On December 18, 1912, we, in accordance with the wishes of the Social-Democratic group of December 15, accepted the proposal of the newspaper *Luch* that we should be included among its contributors.

"Since then more than a month has passed. In all this time *Luch* has acted in constant and rabid opposition to anti-liquidationism. We consider its advocacy of an 'open' workers' party and its attacks on the underground, in the present conditions of Russian life, impermissible and harmful.

"Since we find it impossible to allow our names to be used as a cover for the liquidationist views advocated by *Luch* we request the editors to remove us from the list of its contributors" (*Luch* No. 24, January 30, 1913).   p. 84

[99] Lenin refers to J. V. Stalin's writing of the article "The Nationalities Problem and Social-Democracy".   p. 84

[100] Gorky suspected dishonesty on the part of K. P. Pyatnitsky, the managing director of the St. Petersburg publishing firm Znaniye (Knowledge). The matter was never actually taken to court.   p. 85

[101] Lenin's articles "A Reply to Mayevsky", "Bulgakov on the Peasants" and two other articles on morality, mentioned in this letter, have never been found.   p. 86

[102] *Russkaya Molva* (Russian Tidings)—daily newspaper of the Progressist Party; appeared in St. Petersburg from December 1912 to August 1913.   p. 86

[103] On March 1 (14), 1913, the thirtieth anniversary of the death of Karl Marx, *Pravda* published Lenin's article "The Historical Destiny of the Doctrine of Karl Marx" (see present edition, Vol. 18, pp. 582-85). The issue of *Pravda* dedicated to the anniversary appeared on March 3 (16), 1913.   p. 87

[104] Lenin's article criticising boycottism, which he mentions in this letter, has not been found.   p. 88

[105] *Sotsial-Demokrat* (Social-Democrat)—Central Organ of the R.S.D.L.P., an illegal paper published abroad from February 1908 to January 1917. Lenin was virtually in charge of the paper, which printed more than 80 of his articles and short items. During the period of reaction (1907-10) and the subsequent revolutionary revival *Sotsial-Demokrat* was of enormous significance in the Bolsheviks' campaign against the liquidators, Trotskyists and otzovists, for the preservation of the illegal Marxist party and strengthening of its ties with the masses. p. 90

[106] The "Manifesto" referred to is the amnesty decree promulgated in connection with the 300th anniversary of the House of the Romanovs. p. 92

[107] Reference is to a school on Capri organised by the *Vperyod* group in 1909 with Gorky's participation. p. 92

[108] *Mayevsky, Y. (Gutovsky, V. A.)* (1875-1918)—Social-Democrat, Menshevik. He contributed to the magazine *Nasha Zarya*, the newspaper *Luch* and other Menshevik liquidators' organs. p. 94

[109] In March and April 1913 Lenin was working on an article to be called "Rosa Luxemburg's Unsuccessful Addition to Marxist Theory". He drew up a plan of the article, compiled statistical tables and copied quotations from Marx's *Capital*, but the article was never published. p. 94

[110] Lenin refers to the resolution "The Attitude to Liquidationism, and Unity" passed at the "February" Conference of the C.C. of the R.S.D.L.P. and Party workers held in Cracow from December 26, 1912 to January 1, 1913 (January 8-14, 1913) (see present edition, Vol. 18, pp. 463-65). p. 95

[111] *The Seven* were the seven Menshevik liquidator deputies who belonged to the Social-Democratic group in the Fourth Duma. p. 95

[112] Reference is to the resolution of the Petersburg Committee of the R.S.D.L.P. passed in February 1913. The resolution noted the correctness of the political line maintained by the Bolshevik deputies in the Fourth Duma and condemned the conduct of the Menshevik deputies supporting the liquidators' paper *Luch*. p. 96

[113] At a meeting in February 1913 the Petersburg Committee took a decision to publish *Izvestia P.K. R.S.D.R.P.* (News of the P.C. of the R.S.D.L.P.) and planned the first issue. The project did not materialise. p. 96

[114] In the May 1913 issue of *Prosveshcheniye* there are no works by Gorky, but the June issue contains his story *Krazha* (The Theft). p. 97

[115] *Bedny, Demyan (Pridvorov, Y. A.)* (1883-1945)—outstanding Soviet poet, joined the Bolshevik Party in 1912. In 1911 he had begun contributing to the Bolshevik newspapers *Zvezda* and *Pravda*. His poems and fables were fired with the spirit of the class struggle against the capitalist system and its defenders. During the period of foreign intervention and civil war Bedny went to the front as a poet-agitator. p. 97

[116] The elections of the Board of the Petersburg Metalworkers' Union took place on April 21 (May 4), 1913. The meeting was attended by nearly 800 people and another 400 were unable to get in because there was no room. The Bolsheviks submitted a list of candidates for the Board that had been published in *Pravda* No. 91 and was distributed among those present. Despite the liquidators' demand that candidates should be elected "irrespective of trend", the majority of the meeting voted for the *Pravda* list; 10 out of the 14 successful candidates for the Board were *Pravda* nominees. p. 98

[117] Reference is to *Pravda* No. 92, April 23, 1913, which contained Lenin's articles "Anniversary of *Pravda*" and "A Few Words on Results and Facts". p. 98

[118] Lenin refers to the article by M. S. Olminsky (A. Vitimsky) "Kto s kem?" ("Who Is on Whose Side?"), published in *Pravda* No. 106, May 10, 1913. The article was part of the polemic with *Luch* concerning the conference between the editors of bourgeois publications and representatives of the workers' press. The conference was called for the purpose of protesting at the introduction of harsher laws against the press. The chairman of the conference did not allow a vote on the draft resolution submitted by the *Pravda* representatives. They and representatives of a number of trade union papers refused to sign the liberal editors' resolution. Besides the representatives of *Rech*, *Russkaya Molva*, *Sovremennoye Slovo* and *Dyen*, etc., only the representatives of *Luch* and *Nasha Zarya* signed the resolution, thus acting against the workers' papers represented at the conference. p. 100

[119] On Lenin's insistence A. A. Bogdanov's article "Ideology" (from the "Dictionary of Foreign Words" series) was rejected by *Pravda* as anti-Marxist. Concerning the statement which Bogdanov then sent to *Pravda* announcing his resignation from the paper, Lenin wrote a "Letter to the Editor" which was published in the newspaper *Put Pravdy* No. 9, January 31, 1914 (see present edition, Vol. 20, pp. 93-94). p. 100

[120] *Fyodor* (Feodora)—cover name for the Menshevik section of the Social-Democratic group in the Fourth Duma. p. 101

[121] Lenin means a report on the activity of the Social-Democratic group in the Fourth Duma. No such report had been published. p. 101

[122] "The co-operative" was the cover name for the Social-Democratic group in the Fourth Duma. p. 101

[123] Lenin refers to the controversy over the right of J. I. Jagiello, the deputy to the Fourth Duma for Warsaw, to belong to the Social-Democratic group. p. 102

[124] *Octobrists* or *Union of October Seventeen*—counter-revolutionary party of the big industrial bourgeoisie and big landowners who ran their estates on capitalist lines. It was founded after publication of the tsar's manifesto of October 17, 1905, in which the tsar, frightened by the revolution, promised the people "civil rights" and a constitution. The Octobrists unreservedly supported the home and foreign policy of the tsarist government. Their leaders were A. Guchkov, the powerful industrialist, and M. Rodzyanko, who owned huge estates. p. 102

[125] *The Black Hundreds*—bands of monarchists organised by the tsarist police to fight the revolutionary movement. These bands murdered revolutionaries, attacked progressive intellectuals and staged pogroms against the Jews. p. 102

[126] Reference is to the arrest of Y. M. Sverdlov and K. T. Novgorodtseva (Sverdlova) at the apartment of G. I. Petrovsky, a member of the Fourth Duma, on February 10 (23), 1913. They were given away to the police by the *agent provocateur* R. V. Malinovsky. p. 102

[127] Lenin refers to accommodation for the Party school which the C.C. of the R.S.D.L.P. was planning to organise at Poronin. p. 102

[128] Gorky had been a delegate to the Fifth (London) Congress of the R.S.D.L.P., which took place from April 30 to May 19 (May 13 to June 1), 1907. p. 105

[129] The conflict was between the Fourth Duma and the government, in connection with a speech by the Black Hundred deputy Markov II, who had said with reference to a representative of the Ministry of Finance "there must be no stealing". The Duma had not reacted in any way to the statement. The Cabinet, considering this an insult to the whole government, insisted that Markov II should be prosecuted for slander and demanded that Rodzyanko, Chairman of the Fourth Duma, should make a public statement condemning Markov's speech. p. 105

[130] *Pravda* was banned on July 5 (18), 1913 by decree of the St. Petersburg Chamber of Justice on the proposal of N. A. Maklakov, Minister of the Interior. On July 13 (26) of the same year it resumed publication under the new name of *Rabochaya Pravda* (Workers' Truth). p. 106

[131] *Shahumyan, S. G.* (1878-1918)—outstanding figure in the Communist Party and the Soviet state. Joined the R.S.D.L.P. in 1900. From 1904 to 1910 he was one of the leaders of Party work in the Transcaucasus and one of the organisers and editors of Bolshevik legal and illegal publications. An active opponent of the Mensheviks. He was co-opted as an alternative member for the Central Committee by the Central Committee which had been elected by the Sixth (Prague) Conference of the R.S.D.L.P. While exiled to Astrakhan (1911-14), he wrote, on Lenin's instructions, the work *National-Cultural Autonomy*, in which he upheld the principles of proletarian internationalism. On his return from exile in 1914 he became leader of the Baku Bolshevik organisation.
p. 110

[132] In reply to this letter Lenin received a letter from S. G. Shahumyan written on September 7, 1913 in Astrakhan. Shahumyan wrote that later he would send statistics of nationalities in the Caucasus, and gave the following provisional figures—5 million Moslems, 2 million Armenians and 2 million Georgians. Concerning the distribution of nationalities in uyezds, gubernias and the cities—Tiflis, Baku, Batum, Elisavetpol, etc., he suggested using the *Caucasian Calendar*. He also sent the pamphlet he had promised and a translation of two reports on Armenian affairs.
p. 110

[133] *Pravda Truda* (Truth of Labour)—Bolshevik daily which appeared in St. Petersburg from September 11 (24) to October 9 (22), 1913 instead of *Severnaya Pravda* (Northern Truth) that had been banned on September 7 (20). Only 20 numbers of *Pravda Truda* appeared.
p. 111

[134] *Novaya Rabochaya Gazeta* (New Workers' Newspaper)—Menshevik liquidators' daily published in St. Petersburg from August 1913 to January 1914.

Nash Put (Our Path) was a Moscow Bolshevik paper published in September 1913 (see Note 80).
p. 111

[135] Lenin refers to a telegram sent by Maxim Gorky from Rimini to the Central Committee of the R.S.D.L.P. about the death of August Bebel. It was published in *Severnaya Pravda* No. 4, August 4, 1913.
p. 112

[136] *Za Pravdu* (For Truth)—one of the names under which the Bolshevik paper *Pravda* appeared from October 1 (14) to December 5 (18), 1913. Altogether 52 issues appeared; 21 were confiscated and for 2 the editors were fined.
The financial report referred to in the letter was printed in No. 9 of *Za Pravdu*, October 13.
p. 114

[137] In October 1913 *Za Pravdu* published a statement by the Bolshevik deputies (the Six) demanding that the Menshevik section of the Social-Democratic group in the Fourth Duma (the Seven)

should recognise the equality of the Six and the Seven to decide all questions in the Social-Democratic group in the Duma. In the same month the Bolshevik deputies announced in *Za Pravdu* the refusal of the Menshevik liquidators to acknowledge the equality of the Six and the Seven in the group and stated that it was necessary to form an independent Bolshevik workers' group in the Duma.

p. 115

[138] Lenin refers to the article "A Threat to the Unity of the Social-Democratic Group", which was published in the liquidators' *Novaya Rabochaya Gazeta* No. 60, October 18, 1913.   p. 115

[139] Reference is to the resolution "The Social-Democratic Group in the Duma", passed at the Poronin Conference of the C.C. of the R.S.D.L.P. and Party workers. It was published in *Za Pravdu* No. 12, October 17, 1913 (see present edition, Vol. 19, pp. 425-26).

p. 119

[140] The resolutions passed by St. Petersburg workers and published in *Za Pravdu* beginning from October 22 (November 4). They are summed up in Lenin's "How the Workers Responded to the Formation of the Russian Social-Democratic Labour Group in the Duma" (see present edition, Vol. 20, pp. 536-43).   p. 119

[141] The Bolshevik deputies' statement ("Reply to the Seven Deputies") on the setting up of an independent Russian Social-Democratic Labour group in the Fourth Duma was published in No. 22 of *Za Pravdu*, October 29, 1913.   p. 120

[142] Lenin's letter was prompted by the appearance in *Russkoye Slovo* (Russian Word) No. 219, September 22, 1913, of an article by Gorky "On the Karamazov Attitude", protesting against the Moscow Art Theatre's staging of Dostoyevsky's reactionary novel *The Possessed*. The bourgeois press came to the defence of the play and Gorky replied with another article "Once Again on the Karamazov Attitude", which was published in No. 248 of *Russkoye Slovo*, October 27, 1913.

Large sections of the article, but without the concluding paragraph, were reprinted on October 28 (November 10) in *Rech* No. 295. The next day Gorky's article, including the final paragraph, which Lenin quotes in full in his letter, was reprinted in the liquidators' *Novaya Rabochaya Gazeta* No. 69.   p. 121

[143] *Russkaya Mysl* (Russian Thought)—literary-political magazine that was published in Moscow 1880-1918. After the 1905 revolution it became the organ of the Right wing of the Constitutional-Democratic (Cadet) Party. *Izgoyev, A. S.*, a bourgeois journalist, was one of the ideologists of this party.   p. 123

[144] Lenin's article "Material on the Conflict Within the Social-Democratic Duma Group", first published in *Za Pravdu* No. 22,

October 29, 1913 (see present edition, Vol. 19, pp. 458-74), was not reprinted in the newspaper. In 1914 it was reprinted in the symposium *Marxism and Liquidationism* under the title "Material on the History of the Formation of the Russian Social-Democratic Labour Group in the Duma".

Issue No. 22 of *Za Pravdu* was confiscated because of its leading article "Beilis Acquitted".   p. 125

[145] *Purishkevich, V. M.* (1870-1920)—big landowner, monarchist, leader of the Black Hundreds, notorious for his anti-semitic speeches in the Duma.

Struve, P. B. (1870-1944)—bourgeois economist and publicist, a leader of the Constitutional-Democratic (Cadet) Party. In the nineties he was a prominent representative of "legal Marxism" and tried to adapt Marxism and the working-class movement to the interests of the bourgeoisie.   p. 128

[146] *Armand, Inessa* (1875-1920)—outstanding figure in the international women's working-class and communist movement. She became a member of the Bolshevik Party in 1904 and took an active part in the 1905-07 revolution and in the Great October Socialist Revolution of 1917.   p. 130

[147] Reference is to Kautsky's speech at the meeting of the International Socialist Bureau on December 14, 1913. It was criticised severely by Lenin in his articles "A Good Resolution and a Bad Speech" and "Kautsky's Unpardonable Error" (see present edition, Vol. 19, pp. 528-31, and 546-48).   p. 130

[148] *Trusted agents*—workers chosen to maintain constant contact between the Central Committee and the local Social-Democratic groups, and to evolve flexible forms of leadership for local activities in the big working-class centres. The system of trusted agents was initiated by the Cracow Conference of the C.C. of the R.S.D.L.P. of 1913 and the need for it was confirmed by the Poronin Conference.   p. 131

[149] *Sputnik Rabochego* (Worker's Handbook) *for 1914*—a pocket calendar put out by the Party Priboi publishers in December 1913. The whole edition was sold in one day. In February 1914 a second, revised edition was produced.

The calendar included Lenin's article "Strikes in Russia" (see present edition, Vol. 19, pp. 534-38).   p. 132

[150] Lenin refers to the preparation for the publication of the magazine *Rabotnitsa* (Working Woman), the first issue of which appeared in St. Petersburg on February 23 (March 8), 1914.   p. 132

[151] *Bremer Bürger-Zeitung*—Social-Democratic daily published 1890-1919. Until 1916 it was under the influence of the Bremen Left

Social-Democrats, but later fell into the hands of the social-chauvinists. p. 133

[152] *Shakhtyorsky Listok* (Miners' Leaflet)—appeared on March 16,
1914 as a supplement to No. 38 of *Put Pravdy*. It was published
on the initiative of the miners themselves and on funds which
they collected. The second *Shakhtyorsky Listok* came out in No. 77
of *Put Pravdy*, May 4, 1914.

The *Appeal to the Ukrainian Workers* was printed in Ukrainian
in No. 28 of *Trudovaya Pravda* on June 29, 1914 over the signature
of Ocksen Lola. The MS. of Lenin's draft appeal has not been preserved. The contents of the document published in *Trudovaya
Pravda* justify the assumption that it was Lenin's work.

The "Editorial Comment on Ocksen Lola's 'Appeal to the Ukrainian Workers'" was written by Lenin (see present edition, Vol. 20,
p. 494). p. 135

[153] *Lola, O. N.* (Stepanyuk) (1884-1919)—Ukrainian worker and Bolshevik. Persecuted for his revolutionary activities, he emigrated
after the 1905-07 revolution to Galicia, then to Paris. p. 135

[154] Lenin sent Inessa Armand O. Lola's (Stepanyuk's) letter of April
22 (N.S.), 1914, in which Lola wrote that he was entirely in
agreement with the "Appeal to the Ukrainian Workers", but that
it should be printed on behalf of the *Pravda* editorial board and
not over his signature. p. 137

[155] The "important affair" was the preparation for the next Party
Congress, which was to be held in accordance with the decision
of the "August" (sometimes called "Summer") 1913 Conference
of the C.C. of the R.S.D.L.P. and Party workers. The outbreak
of the first world war prevented this. p. 137

[156] *The Programme and Rules of the Russian Social-Democratic Labour
Party*, with amendments to the Rules made by the Sixth (Prague)
All-Russia Conference of the R.S.D.L.P. of 1912, were published
by the C.C. of the R.S.D.L.P. in Paris in 1914. p. 138

[157] Lenin's letter is an addendum to a letter from G. Y. Zinoviev
to the editorial board of the magazine *Dzvin*, in which Zinoviev
reported on his talks with a member of the editorial board, L. Yurkevich, on the conditions under which the Bolsheviks might work
for the magazine.

The statements in favour of splitting off the Ukrainian workers
into a separate Social-Democratic organisation which roused
Lenin's indignation had been made in Yurkevich's preface to
a book by Levinsky *Ocherk razvitiya ukrainskogo rabochego dvizhe-
niya v Galitsii* (Outline of the Development of the Ukrainian Working-Class Movement in Galicia) (Kiev, 1914). Lenin sharply criticised the views of the bourgeois nationalist Yurkevich on the
problem of nationalities in his article "The Right of Nations to
Self-Determination" (see present edition, Vol. 20, pp. 448-49).

Dzvin (The Bell)—legal nationalist monthly with a Menshevik orientation; published in Ukrainian in Kiev from January 1913 to the middle of 1914. p. 139

[158] *Nakoryakov, N. N.* (b. 1881)—began his revolutionary activity in 1901, worked in the R.S.D.L.P. committees in Kazan and Samara and was a delegate to the Fourth Congress of the R.S.D.L.P. In 1911 he emigrated to America, where he edited the Menshevik-orientated newspaper *Novy Mir*, published by Russian émigrés. In 1917 he returned to Russia and in 1925.joined the R.C.P.(B.). p. 140

[159] *Novy Mir* (New World)—Menshevik-orientated newspaper published by a group of Russian émigrés in New York in 1911-17. From 1912 to 1916 the paper was edited by J. Ellert (whose real name was N. N. Nakoryakov. See Note 158.). p. 140

[160] The date "May 19" was crossed out by N. K. Krupskaya and replaced by the date when the letter was sent "June 4". In the margin is written: "For ... [one word heavily deleted.—*Ed.*] *urgent*". The letter has an addendum by N. K. Krupskaya: "Because of the Bill the letter remained unposted for two weeks. Have you received the previous letter sent to the same address? Why don't you reply? Warmest greetings!" p. 142

[161] Reference is to Shahumyan's pamphlet *National-Cultural Autonomy*, which he wrote in Armenian in 1913. The pamphlet was a reply to articles by the Armenian bourgeois nationalist D. Ananun (An) "The Problem of Nationalities and Democracy".

No communication from the author about the contents of the pamphlet was published in *Prosveshcheniye*. p. 142

[162] The outlines of the Bill given in this letter formed the basis of Lenin's "Bill on the Equality of Nations and the Safeguarding of the Rights of National Minorities" (see present edition, Vol. 20, pp. 281-83). The Bill was to be brought into the Fourth Duma by the Bolshevik group, but this was not achieved. p. 142

[163] Lenin refers to the novel *Paternal Testaments* by the Ukrainian writer V. Vinnichenko, a bourgeois nationalist. p. 144

[164] Reference is to the report of the C.C. of the R.S.D.L.P., drawn up by Lenin for the Brussels "Unity" Conference. On Lenin's instructions the report was delivered at the conference by Inessa Armand (see present edition, Vol. 20, pp. 495-535). p. 146

[165] *Yedinstvo* (Unity)—newspaper uniting the extreme Right-wing group of the Menshevik defencists led by Plekhanov. It was published in Petrograd. Four issues came out in May-June 1914. It appeared daily from March to November 1917. From December

1917 to January 1918, it was published under the title *Nashe Yedin-stvo* (Our Unity).   p. 146

[166] Kautsky's letter against Rosa Luxemburg concerning the report on the meeting of the I.S.B. was published in *Vorwärts*, central organ of the German Social-Democrats, No. 339, December 24, 1913 and reprinted in *Proletarskaya Pravda* No. 12, December 20 (O.S.), 1913 with a postscript by Lenin (see present edition, Vol. 20, pp. 63-64). Kautsky's letter was a reply to Rosa Luxemburg's letter to the editorial board of *Vorwärts*.   p. 148

[167] Lenin has in mind the resolution "Property in the Hands of the Former Trustee, and Financial Reports", passed by the Prague Party Conference of 1912. The Conference declared that in view of the liquidators' infringement of agreement and in view of the trustees' refusal to arbitrate, the Bolsheviks' representatives had every formal right to use the Party property in the hands of the former trustee C. Zetkin.   p. 149

[168] This refers to G. V. Plekhanov's articles "Under a.Hail of Bullets (Passing Notes)", published in *Pravda*, April-June 1913.   p. 149

[169] Reference is to the Fourth Congress of the Social-Democrats of the Lettish Region, which was held from January 26 to February 8 (N.S.), 1914 in Brussels.   p. 150

[170] *Trudovaya Pravda* No. 32, July 4, 1914, published a resolution "On the Current Situation and Unity" over the signature of the "Leading Institution of the Social-Democrats of the Lettish Region" (C.C. of the S.D.L.R.). Stressing the "need for unity of forces and activity of the working class", the resolution stipulated the following as the basis of unity: (1) "uncurtailed demands"; (2) recognition of the underground; (3) unity from below; (4) "recognition of the democratic majority and not the federation"; (5) struggle "against the liquidators both on the right and on the left".   p. 150

[171] The resolution was on "The Absence of Delegates from the Non-Russian National Centres at the General Party Conference" passed by the Sixth (Prague) All-Russia Conference of the R.S.D.L.P.   p. 150

[172] Reference is to the "Draft Terms of the Amalgamation of the Lettish Social-Democratic Labour Party with the R.S.D.L.P.", passed at the Fourth (Unity) Congress of the R.S.D.L.P., April-May 1906, in Stockholm.   p. 151

[173] The paper was the Menshevik liquidators' *Nasha Rabochaya Gazeta*, which came out in St. Petersburg from May to July 1914.   p. 151

[174] The Polish opposition, which at the earlier sessions of the Brussels Conference had been unanimous with the Bolsheviks and the Lettish Social-Democrats, voted at the last session in favour of the resolution of the International Socialist Bureau drawn up by Kautsky. p. 152

[175] Reference is to the conditions of "unity" proposed by the Bolsheviks at the Brussels "Unity" Conference (see present edition, Vol. 20, pp. 515-27). p. 152

[176] Lenin managed to finish his article on Marx in November 1914 (see present edition, Vol. 21, pp. 43-91).

In its reply to Lenin's letter the Granat Bros. Publishing House wrote on July 12 (O.S.), 1914: "Since with this particular article we connect a whole series of factors of great importance to the entire character of the Dictionary, we are unable to resign ourselves to having an indifferent, average interpretation of this subject. We have all along wanted to get a scientifically serious and forceful interpretation.... Though we have considered foreign as well as Russian names, we cannot find an author. We request you most earnestly, therefore, to go ahead with the article.... We are prepared ... to grant a considerable postponement—till August 15.... We request you most insistently, again and again, not to give it up and to share with us the view that this article would be a valuable and necessary undertaking." (Central Party Archives of the Institute of Marxism-Leninism of the C.C. of the C.P.S.U.) p. 153

[177] Lenin refers to the plans for publishing the Central Organ of the R.S.D.L.P., *Sotsial-Demokrat* (see Note 105), and illegal Bolshevik literature. p. 155

[178] Lenin was to lecture on "The European War and Socialism". He did so in Geneva on October 15, 1914. p. 155

[179] Reference is to the theses "The Tasks of Revolutionary Social-Democracy in the European War", known as "The Theses on War", and to the Manifesto of the C.C. of the R.S.D.L.P. "The War and Russian Social-Democracy" (see present edition, Vol. 21, pp. 15-19, 25-34). p. 156

[180] The *Committee of Organisations Abroad* was elected at a conference of the groups of the R.S.D.L.P. abroad in Paris in December 1911. Its composition changed several times. At the conference of R.S.D.L.P. groups abroad held in Berne, February 27 to March 4, 1915, N. K. Krupskaya, I. F. Armand, G. L. Shklovsky and V. M. Kasparov were elected to the Committee. During the war the Committee was based in Switzerland and worked under Lenin's immediate guidance. It did much to co-ordinate the activities of the R.S.D.L.P. sections abroad, campaigned against the social-chauvinists, and worked for unity of the Left-wing internationalists among the Social-Democrats of various countries. p. 157

[181] Plekhanov's lecture "On the Socialists' Attitude to the War" was organised by the local group of Mensheviks in Lausanne, October 11, 1914.

Only Lenin spoke in the discussion of the lecture. Some brief notes by Lenin on Plekhanov's lecture and reply to the discussion, and also the rough plan of Lenin's speech on the lecture, have been preserved. A newspaper report of Lenin's speech was printed in *Golos* No. 33, October 21, 1914. A report on the meeting, containing the text of Plekhanov's lecture, was published in the same paper. p. 158

[182] Lenin lectured on "The Proletariat and the War" in Lausanne on October 14, 1914, and on "The European War and Socialism" in Geneva on October 15. p. 158

[183] This refers to the Bolsheviks' reply to Emile Vandervelde's telegram, which he sent to the Social-Democratic group in the Duma, appealing for support of the Russian Government in the war against Germany. The reply, which was published over the joint signature of the C.C. of the R.S.D.L.P. in *Sotsial-Demokrat* No. 33, November 1, 1914, stated that in the interests of democracy and socialism the Bolsheviks considered it an urgent task of the revolutionary proletarian party in the period of the imperialist war to extend and consolidate the class organisations of the proletariat and to develop the class struggle against the imperialist bourgeoisie and its governments. p. 159

[184] The Central Organ of the R.S.D.L.P. *Sotsial-Demokrat* was revived by Lenin after it had been silent for almost a year. No. 33 appeared in Geneva on November 1 (14), 1914. p. 159

[185] *Golos* (Voice)—a Menshevik daily; came out in Paris from September 1914 to January 1915. p. 159

[186] During the imperialist world war Shlyapnikov was sent to Stockholm by the Petersburg Committee of the R.S.D.L.P. and the Bolshevik group in the Duma and was for a time the connecting link between Lenin and the Russian section of the C.C. of the R.S.D.L.P. and the Petersburg Committee. p. 161

[187] Lenin refers to P. Maslov's letter to the editors of *Russkiye Vedomosti*, which was published under the heading "War and Commercial Agreements" in No. 207 of the paper for September 10 (23), 1914, to the article by Y. Smirnov (Gurevich) "The War and European Democracy", published in No. 202 of *Russkiye Vedomosti*, September 3 (16), 1914, and to the appeal by writers, artists and actors "Concerning the War", published in *Russkoye Slovo* No. 223, September 28 (October 11), 1914. p. 161

[188] At the beginning of the war part of the Committee of R.S.D.L.P. Organisations Abroad, which was in Paris, and some members

of the Paris section of the Bolsheviks—N. I. Sapozhkov (Kuznetsov), A. V. Britman (Antonov) and others—together with the Mensheviks and Socialist-Revolutionaries approved a declaration on behalf of the "Russian Socialists", published it in the French press, and then went to the front.   p. 161

189 Lenin refers to the Brussels "Unity" Conference of July 16-18, 1914, convened by the Executive Committee of the International Socialist Bureau "for an exchange of opinion" about the possibility of restoring the unity of the R.S.D.L.P. Represented at the conference were the C.C. of the R.S.D.L.P. (Bolsheviks), the Organising Committee (Mensheviks), the Plekhanov *Yedinstvo* group, the *Vperyod* group, the Bund, the Social-Democratic Party of the Lettish Region, the Social-Democrats of Lithuania, the Polish Social-Democrats, the Polish Social-Democratic opposition and the P.P.S. (Left wing). The Executive Committee of the International Socialist Bureau was represented by Emile Vandervelde, Camille Huysmans, Karl Kautsky, A. Nemets and others. Well in advance of the Conference, the leaders of the I.S.B. reached a secret agreement with the liquidators for joint action against the Bolsheviks. The Bolsheviks, led by Lenin, refused to submit to the decisions of the Brussels Conference and exposed before the international proletariat the true aims of the "unifiers".   p. 162

190 *Die Neue Zeit* (New Times)—theoretical journal of the German Social-Democratic Party. It was published in Stuttgart from 1883 to 1923. Up to October 1917 it was edited by Karl Kautsky, and afterwards by Heinrich Cunow. During the first world war the journal took up a Centrist position and virtually supported the social-chauvinists.   p. 162

191 Reference is to the manifesto on the war passed by the Extraordinary International Socialist Congress held in Basle, November 24-25, 1912. The manifesto recommended that in the event of an imperialist war socialists should use the economic and political crisis evoked by the war to fight for a socialist revolution. p. 164

192 Lenin refers to the third session of the Fourth State Duma, which opened on January 27 (O.S.), 1915.   p. 165

193 Reference is to the Russian Social-Democratic Labour group in the Fourth Duma, consisting of the Bolshevik deputies A. Y. Badayev, G. I. Petrovsky, M. K. Muranov, F. N. Samoilov, N. R. Shagov and R. V. Malinovsky (Malinovsky was subsequently exposed as an *agent provocateur*). Working under the direct supervision and control of the Central Committee, the Bolshevik group in the Duma acted on behalf of the Party and the majority of class-conscious workers.   p. 165

194 When he speaks of the creation of a "German" International Socialist Bureau, Lenin has in mind the German social-chauvin-

ists' proposal to move the headquarters of the I.S.B. Executive Committee from Brussels to Amsterdam. p. 166

[195] This apparently refers to L. B. Kamenev's note to Lenin. The note was passed on to Lenin by A. G. Shlyapnikov, who called on Kamenev at Mustamäki on his way abroad. p. 166

[196] Shlyapnikov's letter to Lenin contained news of the workers' strikes and demonstrations in protest against the imperialist war. They had occurred in Nevskaya Zastava District, Vyborgskaya Storona District and other working-class districts of Petrograd on August 1 (July 19), 1914 when general mobilisation began. p. 167

[197] *Kollontai, Alexandra* (1872-1952)—member of the Social-Democratic movement from the 1890s, took part in the revolution of 1905-07. Between 1906 and 1915 she was associated with the Mensheviks. In 1915 she became a member of the Bolshevik Party, having adopted a revolutionary-internationalist stand at the outbreak of war. After the October Socialist Revolution she held responsible posts. p. 167

[198] At the end of October 1914 Shlyapnikov talked with Pieter Troelstra, leader of the Dutch Social-Democratic movement, who had come to Stockholm on behalf of the opportunist leaders of German Social-Democracy to get an agreement on the transfer of the International Socialist Bureau (I.S.B.) to Amsterdam for the duration of the war, and to influence the Scandinavian Social-Democrats towards justifying the treacherous position taken up by the leaders of German Social-Democracy. During his meeting with Troelstra, which took place in the presence of a representative of the Organising Committee, Y. Larin, the Menshevik Dalin, Alexandra Kollontai and others, Shlyapnikov handed him the manifesto of the C.C. of the R.S.D.L.P., and the reply of the Bolshevik group in the Duma to Emile Vandervelde, and later, at his request, sent him letters explaining the Bolsheviks' attitude to the war.

p. 168

[199] Reference is to Anton Pannekoek's article "Der Zusammenbruch der Internationale" ("The Collapse of the International"), printed in *Berner Tagwacht*, the organ of the Swiss Social-Democratic Party, Nos. 245, 246 and 247, for October 20, 21 and 22, 1914. p. 168

[200] Lenin refers to the conference of socialists of the neutral countries proposed by Pieter Troelstra and Thorvald Stauning. The conference took place in Copenhagen on January 17-18, 1915. It was attended by representatives of the socialist parties of Sweden, Denmark, Norway and Holland. The conference approved a resolution calling on the Social-Democratic parties of the neutral countries to urge their governments to mediate between the belligerent countries and thereby help to restore peace. Some of the

Social-Democratic parties placed before the conference declarations on their attitude to the war. From the C.C. of the R.S.D.L.P. the conference received No. 33 of *Sotsial-Demokrat* containing the manifesto "The War and Russian Social-Democracy", and an official report of the arrest of the Bolshevik deputies to the Duma. p. 169

201 To improve connections with Party organisations in Russia Lenin tried to find out through some of the comrades whether it would be possible for him to move from Switzerland to Sweden or Norway. The move did not take place. p. 171

202 The proclamation "From Writers, Artists and Actors" was written in a spirit of bourgeois patriotism and justification of tsarist Russia's participation in the war. It appeared over the signatures of several prominent figures in the world of letters and the arts, including Maxim Gorky. p. 171

203 Reference is to Lenin's article "Karl Marx (A Brief Biographical Sketch with an Exposition of Marxism)", which he wrote for the Granat Bros. Publishing House. It appeared in abridged form in Vol. 28 of the Encyclopaedic Dictionary, over the signature of V. Ilyin. The full text of the article was printed in 1925 (see present edition, Vol. 21, pp. 43-91). p. 173

204 This was Lenin's personal library, which he left in Cracow during the imperialist world war (1914-18). Much of it was lost. p. 174

205 *Branting, Karl Hjalmar* (1860-1925)—leader of the Social-Democratic Party of Sweden, and one of the leaders of the Second International. He adopted opportunist positions. p. 175

206 Five Bolshevik deputies in the R.S.D.L.P. group in the Fourth Duma were denounced by an informer and arrested on November 5 (18), 1914, the day after the Bolsheviks' conference on the war. The tsarist government accused the Bolshevik deputies of "high treason", and all the deputies were sentenced to deprivation of their rights and exile to Eastern Siberia. p. 175

207 The Mensheviks' Organising Committee declared its intention of publishing its own paper *Otkliki* (Echoes), but the project was never realised.

Mysl (Thought)—daily paper of the Socialist-Revolutionaries. Edited by M. Natanson and V. Chernov, it appeared in Paris from November 1914 to March 1915, when it was closed down by the French Government. p. 176

208 The enclosure was a letter from Shaw Desmond, correspondent of the British Social-Democratic paper *The Labour Leader*, which he wrote on November 29, 1914 asking for information on the

attitude of the R.S.D.L.P. to the questions of war and peace. Lenin wrote his reply on Shaw Desmond's letter and in this letter. p. 177

209 *Hamburger Echo*—daily newspaper, organ of the Hamburg organisation of the German Social-Democratic Party.
    Lenin refers to the article by Haenisch "Der deutsche 'Verrat' an der Internationale" ("The German 'Betrayal' of the International"), published in *Hamburger Echo* No. 286, December 8, 1914. p. 177

210 This letter was written in reply to a letter from Basok (M. I. Melenevsky), one of the leaders of the bourgeois-nationalist Alliance for the Emancipation of the Ukraine, proposing co-operation (see Lenin's article "Slanderers", present edition, Vol. 25, pp. 283-84). p. 179

211 Reference is to the plan of a pamphlet for working-class women that Inessa Armand intended to write. The pamphlet did not appear in print. p. 180

212 *Key, Ellen* (1849-1926)—Swedish writer, author of a much talked of pedagogical book *The Century of the Child* (1900). Her views on pedagogics were considerably influenced by mysticism and individualism. p. 184

213 An attempt was being made by the Baugy group (N. I. Bukharin, E. F. Rozmirovich, N. V. Krylenko) to publish a newspaper independently of the Central Organ. The group took its name from the town of Baugy in Switzerland, where it had its headquarters. Lenin learned of the project by chance, from a letter which the group sent to Inessa Armand suggesting that she should contribute to the paper. Lenin was against the publication of such small papers and the question "The C.O. and a new newspaper" was placed before the conference of R.S.D.L.P. organisations abroad, held in Berne, February 27 to March 4, 1915. The conference adopted a resolution confirming the correctness of Lenin's line. p. 185

214 Reference is to Plekhanov's pamphlet *The War. A Reply to Comrade Z. P.*, Paris, 1914. p. 186

215 *The Conference of the Socialists of the Triple Entente* was held in London on February 14, 1915. See Lenin's articles "The London Conference" and "On the London Conference" (present edition, Vol. 21, pp. 132-34, 178-80). p. 186

216 *Dan (Gurevich), F. I.* (1871-1947)—a Menshevik leader. During the years of reaction and the subsequent revolutionary revival he headed a group of liquidators abroad. His position during the world war was that of a social-chauvinist. After the October Socialist Revolution he fought against Soviet power. p. 187

²¹⁷ *Organising Committee*—the Mensheviks' leading centre, was formed in 1912 at the August Conference of Menshevik liquidators, Trotskyists and other anti-Party groups and trends.   p. 187

²¹⁸ The magazine *Kommunist* was organised by Lenin and published by the editorial board of the newspaper *Sotsial-Demokrat* in cooperation with G. L. Pyatakov and E. B. Bosh, who both financed the publication. N. I. Bukharin was also on the editorial board. Only one (double) issue appeared, in 1915.

Lenin had intended making *Kommunist* the organ of the Left Social-Democrats but serious difficulties soon arose between the editorial board of *Sotsial-Demokrat* and Bukharin, Pyatakov and Bosh. These difficulties became more acute after the double issue had appeared.

This issue contained Alexandra Kollontai's article "Why Was the German Proletariat Silent in the July Days?"

Nashe Slovo (Our Word) printed a number of articles by Kollontai.   p. 189

²¹⁹ Lenin criticises the incorrect position of Carl Zeth Höglund and the Swedish, Norwegian and Swiss Left Social-Democrats, in his articles "The Military Programme of the Proletarian Revolution" and "The 'Disarmament' Slogan" (see present edition, Vol. 23, pp. 77-87; 94-104).   p. 189

²²⁰ Reference is to Eduard David's book *Die Sozialdemokratie im Weltkrieg* (Social-Democracy in the World War) published in Berlin in 1917. For a criticism of this book see Lenin's article "The Main German Opportunist Work on the War" (see present edition, Vol. 21, pp. 270-74).   p. 190

²²¹ On August 4, 1914 the Social-Democratic group in the German Reichstag voted for war credits.   p. 191

²²² *Vorkonferenz*—preparatory conference for the first International Socialist Conference (Zimmerwald) held in Berne July 11, 1915.   p. 193

²²³ The Menshevik group in the Fourth Duma.   p. 193

²²⁴ *The International Women's Socialist Conference* concerning the attitude to be adopted towards the war was held March 26-28, 1915 in Berne. See Lenin's article "On the Struggle Against Social-Chauvinism" (present edition, Vol. 21, pp. 199-203). p. 194

²²⁵ Reference is to Anton Pannekoek's article "Der Jahreskongress der S.D.P. in Holland" ("The S.D.P. Congress in Holland"), pub-, lished in the supplement to *Berner Tagwacht* No. 170, July 24, 1915.   p. 195

[226] *Internationale Korrespondenz* (International Bulletin)—German social-chauvinist weekly, appeared in Berlin from the end of September 1914 to October 1, 1918.   p. 196

[227] Lenin refers to the resolution on the nationalities problem passed by the "August" ("Summer") Conference of the C.C. of the R.S.D.L.P. with Party workers, held in Poronin, September 23 to October 1 (October 6-14), 1913 (see present edition, Vol. 19, pp. 427-29).   p. 197

[228] Reference is to the twelfth point in the Programme of the R.S.D.L.P. approved by the Second R.S.D.L.P. Congress. It was stated in the Programme that the Party set itself the immediate aim of overthrowing the tsarist autocracy and replacing it with a democratic republic, whose constitution would, as the twelfth point stipulated, ensure "replacement of the regular army by the general arming of the people".   p. 198

[229] This refers to the statement by the Norwegian Left Social-Democrats that, in principle, they agreed with the resolution Lenin had drafted for the Left Social-Democrats to present at the first International Socialist Conference. The Norwegian Lefts were later supported by the Swedish Lefts.   p. 200

[230] This was the resolution Radek drafted for the Left Social-Democrats to present at the forthcoming first International Socialist Conference.   p. 202

[231] Shlyapnikov was to make a journey to Russia.   p. 204

[232] In November 1915 the Zimmerwald Left published a pamphlet in German entitled *Internationale Flugblätter* No. 1 (*Die Zimmerwalder Linke über die Aufgaben der Arbeiterklasse*) (International Leaflets No. 1 [The Zimmerwald Left on the Tasks of the Working Class]).   p. 210

[233] The Parus (Sail) Publishing House was organised under the auspices of the magazine *Letopis* (Chronicle). Parus was to publish Lenin's *New Data on the Laws Governing the Development of Capitalism in Agriculture. Part One. Capitalism and Agriculture in the United States of America* (see present edition, Vol. 22, pp. 13-102).   p. 212

[234] *Sbornik Sotsial-Demokrata* (Social-Democratic Review) was published by the editorial board of the Central Organ of the R.S.D.L.P., the newspaper *Sotsial-Demokrat*, under Lenin's direct supervision. Two issues appeared: No. 1 in October, and No. 2 in December 1916.   p. 214

[235] Reference is to the conference of the R.S.D.L.P. sections abroad, which was held February 27 to March 4, 1915 in Berne (Switzerland).

38*

In his report to the conference on "The War and the Tasks of the Party" Lenin dealt with the most vital questions of Bolshevik strategy and tactics during the imperialist war.

Bukharin put forward theses in defence of anti-Marxist views, which Lenin characterised as a trend of "imperialist Economism".

The conference passed the resolutions written by Lenin on the character of the war, on the slogan "defence of the fatherland", on the slogans of revolutionary Social-Democracy, on the attitude to other parties and groups, etc. (see present edition, Vol. 21, pp. 158-64). p. 215

[236] Reference is to Lenin's reply to Bukharin, which criticised the theses "On the Self-Determination Slogan" that had been sent to the editors of *Sotsial-Demokrat* over the signatures of Bukharin, Pyatakov and Eugène Bosh in November 1915. Lenin also criticised these "theses" in his articles "The Nascent Trend of Imperialist Economism", "Reply to P. Kievsky (Y. Pyatakov)" and "A Caricature of Marxism and Imperialist Economism" (see present edition, Vol. 23). p. 215

[237] Reference is to the proposed publication of material on the position of Jews in Russia collected by Shlyapnikov during his trip. The project was never realised. p. 216

[238] Lenin is referring to the magazine *Vorbote* (Herald), the theoretical organ of the Zimmerwald Left. It appeared in German in Berne. Two issues were published: No. 1 in January and No. 2 in April 1916. Its official publishers were Henriette Roland-Holst and Anton Pannekoek. Lenin took an active part in the foundation of the magazine and, after the publication of No. 1, in organising its translation into French, so that it could be more widely distributed. p. 221

[239] The "Japanese" was a name for G. L. Pyatakov and Eugène Bosh, who emigrated from Russia to Switzerland through Japan. p. 224

[240] *Pokrovsky, M. N.* (1868-1932)—member of the Bolshevik Party from 1905, prominent Soviet statesman and historian.

From 1908 to 1917 he lived abroad. During the years of reaction he became associated with the otzovists and ultimatumists, and then with the anti-Party *Vperyod* group, with which he broke in 1911. During the imperialist world war he worked for the Centrist newspapers *Golos* and *Nashe Slovo*, returning to Russia in 1917. From November 1917 to March 1918, he was Chairman of the Moscow Soviet, from 1919, Deputy Commissar for Education of the R.S.F.S.R., and from 1929 onwards, a member of the Academy of Sciences. p. 226

[241] Reference is to *Letopis* (Chronicle), published by Maxim Gorky. p. 226

[242] For *Sbornik Sotsial-Demokrata* Bukharin wrote an article called "On the Theory of the Imperialist State", but because of its mistaken anti-Marxist propositions concerning the question of the state and the dictatorship of the proletariat the article was rejected by the editors. p. 228

[243] *Elimination of James* meant the arrest of Anna Yelizarova in Petrograd. p. 232

[244] Reference is to the split in the British Socialist Party at the Manchester Conference in April 1916, at which the Right, opportunist wing of the party, Hyndman and his supporters, were outvoted and left the party. The leadership of the British Socialist Party was then taken over by internationalist elements, which actively opposed the imperialist war. The British Socialist Party laid the foundation for the Communist Party of Great Britain, which was formed in 1920. p. 233

[245] *Potresov, A. N.* (1869-1934)—Menshevik leader. In the years of reaction and subsequent revolutionary revival he was an ideologist of liquidationism. During the first world war he became a social-chauvinist. p. 233

[246] *"Unifiers"*—members of the Inter-District Organisation of the united Social-Democrats, set up in St. Petersburg in 1913. It consisted of Trotskyists and some former Bolsheviks who had left the Party. During the first world war the "unifiers" took up a Centrist position and opposed the Bolsheviks. From August to November 1916 they published a legal magazine, *Rabochiye Vedomosti* (Workers' News), in Petrograd. In 1917 they declared themselves to be in agreement with the Bolshevik Party line and at the Sixth Congress of the R.S.D.L.P.(B.) were admitted to the Party. p. 234

[247] Reference is to the Volna (Wave) Publishing House, set up in Petrograd in 1916, whose organisers asked Lenin to contribute to its publications and send them articles. When he heard that one of the organisers of the publishing house was Chernomazov, who was suspected of being an *agent provocateur*, Lenin turned down the proposal. p. 236

[248] *Koritschoner, Franz (Nadin)* (1891-1942)—one of the men who founded the Austrian Communist Party in 1918, and a member of its Central Committee until 1927. He edited the party's Central Organ, *Die Rote Fahne* (The Red Banner). p. 237

[249] *Friedrich Adler,* one of the leaders of the Austrian Social-Democrats, had murdered the Austrian Prime Minister Karl Stürgkh. p. 237

[250] *Kiknadze, N. D.* (1885-1951)—member of the Bolshevik Party from 1903. Professional revolutionary; lived in emigration in Switzerland, 1906-17. p. 240

[251] In the discussion on the nationalities problem that developed after the publication of the first number of *Sbornik Sotsial-Demokrata* A. V. Lunacharsky and Bezrabotny (D. Z. Manuilsky) attacked Lenin's propositions on the defence of the fatherland and the right of nations to self-determination. Kiknadze opposed Lunacharsky and Manuilsky.   p. 240

[252] The article was "A Caricature of Marxism and Imperialist Econo-mism", which Lenin had intended to publish in No. 3 of *Sbornik Sotsial-Demokrata*. This number never appeared and the article was first published in 1924 (see present edition, Vol. 23, pp. 28-76).
                                                                  p. 240

[253] These theses of the *Internationale* group were published on Feb-ruary 29, 1916 in the *Bulletin of the International Socialist Commission in Berne* ("Bulletin" Internationale sozialistische Kommission zu Bern) No. 3. The fifth paragraph contains the assertion that national wars are impossible in the epoch of impe-rialism.   p. 242

[254] In the Declaration of the German and Austro-Hungarian Govern-ments published on November 5, 1916, Poland was proclaimed a constitutional monarchy under the protection of Germany and Austria-Hungary.   p. 244

[255] The views on the nationalities problem developed by Rosa Lu-xemburg in the magazine of the Polish Social-Democrats *Prze-glad Socjaldemokratyczny* (Social-Democratic Review), published in Cracow. (See Lenin's article "The Right of Nations to Self-Determination", present edition, Vol. 20, pp. 393-454).   p. 244

[256] This refers to a series of articles by Engels entitled "What Have the Working Classes to Do With Poland?" which was reprinted in 1916 in the *Archiv für die Geschichte des Sozialismus und der Arbeiterbewegung*, published by Grünberg.   p. 245

[257] Inessa Armand had translated into French the theses known as "Tasks of the Left Zimmerwaldists in the Swiss Social-Democratic Party" (see present edition, Vol. 23, pp. 137-48).   p. 246

[258] See Marx/Engels, *Werke*, Bd. 13, S. 267-68, Dietz Verlag, Berlin, 1964, and *Werke*, Bd. 22, S. 252-56.   p. 251

[259] The Congress of the Social-Democratic Party of Switzerland was held in Zurich, November 4-5, 1916.   p. 252

[260] The *Bulletin of the International Socialist Commission* No. 3, for February 29, 1916, published the draft programme of the Dutch Social-Democrats, which contained, among other points, the fol-lowing specific demands: democratisation of all representative institutions, the setting up of a republic, an eight-hour working day, abolition of militarism.   p. 254

[261] Reference is to *Sbornik Sotsial-Demokrata* (see Note 234).   p. 255

[262] *Schmid, Arthur* (b. 1889)—Swiss bourgeois economist.   p. 256

[263] The arguments Schmid advanced in his speech of November 30, 1916, at a meeting of Swiss Social-Democrats who supported the Zimmerwald Left. The meeting discussed the question of preparing a draft resolution for the forthcoming Extraordinary Congress of the Swiss Social-Democratic Party on the socialists' attitude to militarism and the war.   p. 256

[264] A decision taken by the Congress of the Swiss Social-Democratic Party (held in Aarau, November 20-21, 1915) on recognition of the mass revolutionary struggle against the war.   p. 257

[265] On August 15 (28), 1916 Guchkov wrote a letter to General Alexeyev, Chief of the General Staff of the Supreme Commander-in-Chief. The letter expressed the Russian bourgeoisie's fear of the mounting revolution and its dissatisfaction with the tsarist government, which was proving incapable of checking it. Guchkov's letter was published in *Sotsial-Demokrat* No. 57 for December 30, 1916.
                                                              p. 259

[266] *Lvov, G. Y.* (1861-1925)—prince, owner of large estates, Constitutional-Democrat, Chairman of the All-Russia Zemstvo Association during the first world war, subsequently one of the chairmen of the United Association of Zemstvos and Towns; both organisations represented the imperialist bourgeoisie and landowners.

Chelnokov, M. V. (b. 1863)—big industrialist and householder, one of the founders of the Constitutional-Democratic Party (Cadets). Deputy to the Second, Third and Fourth Dumas. Mayor of Moscow, 1914-17.   p. 259

[267] Reference is to Humbert-Droz's pamphlet *Guerre à la Guerre. A bas L'Armée. Plaidoirie complète devant le Tribunal Militaire à Neuchâtel le 26 août 1916* (War on War. Down with the Army. Full text of Counsel's Speech before the Military Tribunal at Neuchâtel on August 26, 1916). Humbert-Droz had been arrested for refusing to answer the call-up.   p. 260

[268] Lenin refers to Krupskaya's booklet *Public Education and Democracy*. It was published in 1917 by the Zhizn i Znaniye (Life and Knowledge) Publishing House.   p. 262

[269] The MS. of the book *Imperialism, the Highest Stage of Capitalism* was at this time in the Parus (Sail) Publishing House.   p. 262

[270] Reference is to Engels's Introduction to Marx's *The Class Struggles in France, 1848 to 1850* (see Marx and Engels, *Selected Works*, Vol. I, Moscow, 1962, pp. 118-38).   p. 269

[271] This apparently refers to what Engels said in a letter to F. A. Sorge dated April 8, 1891.   p. 269

[272] Lenin has in mind Kautsky's article "Einige Feststellungen über Marx und Engels" ("Some Facts about Marx and Engels") printed in *Die Neue Zeit*, 1908, No. 1, October 2, pp. 5-7. p. 272

[273] Inessa Armand gave her lecture on pacifism on January 21, 1917 (see Letter 119). p. 274

[274] The referendum was on the question of holding an extraordinary congress of the Swiss Social-Democratic Party to discuss the attitude to be adopted to militarism and war. The referendum was declared by the Swiss Left Social-Democrats in connection with the decision of the Executive of the Swiss Social-Democratic Party to postpone the congress indefinitely. p. 275

[275] See F. Engels, "The Housing Question" (Marx and Engels, *Selected Works*, Vol. I, Moscow, 1962, pp. 546-635). p. 281

[276] This refers to the resolution on peace proposed on behalf of Loriot, Rappoport and Saumoneau in December 1916, at the congress of the Seine Federation of the French Socialist Party. The resolution was voted down. p. 281

[277] Lenin intended publishing an article on the attitude of Marxism to the state in No. 3 of *Sbornik Sotsial-Demokrata*, but did not write it. The material he collected formed the basis of his book *The State and Revolution*. p. 286

[278] Lenin means the Lefts in the Swedish Social-Democratic movement, who looked for support in their struggle against the Right opportunists to the Social-Democratic Youth League. During the world war the Young joined the Zimmerwald Left. p. 287

[279] The Moscow Bureau's leaflet which Lenin mentions was not published in the Party's Central Organ *Sotsial-Demokrat*, because in January 1917, after the publication of No. 58, the paper closed down.

The Moscow Bureau of the Central Committee was at the time the leading body of the Moscow Regional Bolshevik Party organisation. Among the Bureau's members were Rozalia Zemlyachka, M. S. Olminsky and I. I. Skvortsov-Stepanov. p. 288

[280] The *Weekly People*—organ of the Socialist Labour Party of America, founded in New York in 1891. p. 288

[281] Reference is to Leaflet No. 1, "Gegen die Lüge der Vaterlandsverteidigung" ("Against the Lie about Defence of the Fatherland"), which was later published over the signature of the "Group of Zimmerwald Lefts in Switzerland". Lenin was closely concerned with the writing and editing of this leaflet. It included the

"Proposed Amendments to the Resolution on the War Issue" and a number of other writings by Lenin. p. 289

[282] The Congress of the Zurich Social-Democratic organisation in Töss was held February 11-12, 1917. It discussed the Social-Democratic attitude to militarism and war. Two draft resolutions were moved: (1) a resolution drafted by the Rights in a spirit of social-chauvinism and (2) a Centrist draft approved by the majority of the leaders of the Swiss Social-Democratic Party. The majority resolution was passed by 93 votes to 65. To prevent the social-chauvinist resolution being adopted, the Lefts voted for the majority resolution, but moved amendments drafted by Lenin (see present edition, Vol. 23, p. 282). The Lefts' motion containing these amendments received 32 votes. The materials of the Congress were published in the newspaper *Volksrecht*. p. 289

[283] *Milyukov, P. N.* (1859-1943). See Note 51.

Guchkov, A. I. (1862-1936)—big capitalist, organiser and leader of the Octobrists' party. After the bourgeois-democratic revolution of February 1917 he became Minister of Military and Naval Affairs in the first cabinet of the bourgeois Provisional Government.

Kerensky, A. F. (b. 1881)—Socialist-Revolutionary. After the bourgeois-democratic revolution of February 1917 he became first a minister, then Prime Minister of the bourgeois Provisional Government. p. 295

[284] *Shingaryov, A. I.* (1869-1918)—Constitutional-Democrat, deputy to the Second, Third and Fourth Dumas. After the February 1917 revolution, Minister of Agriculture in the first cabinet and Minister of Finance in the second cabinet of the bourgeois Provisional Government. p. 295

[285] *Konovalov, A. I.* (b. 1875)—big textile manufacturer; Minister of Trade and Industry in the bourgeois Provisional Government. p. 295

[286] *Chkhenkeli, A. I.* (1874-1959)—Menshevik, deputy to the Third and Fourth Dumas. During the first world war, a social-chauvinist. After the February revolution of 1917, representative of the bourgeois Provisional Government in the Transcaucasus. p. 295

[287] Reference is to the Bolshevik deputies in the Fourth Duma A. Y. Badayev, M. K. Muranov, G. I. Petrovsky, F. N. Samoilov and N. R. Shagov. (See Note 206.) p. 296

[288] *Gvozdyov, K. A.* (b. 1883)—Menshevik liquidator. Social-chauvinist during the imperialist world war. After the February bourgeois-democratic revolution of 1917 he became successively a member of the Executive Committee of the Petrograd Soviet, Deputy

Minister, and Minister of Labour in the bourgeois Provisional Government. p. 298

289 *Chkheidze*, *N. S.* (1864-1926)—one of the Menshevik leaders. During the imperialist world war, a Centrist. After the October Socialist Revolution he became Chairman of the Constituent Assembly of Georgia, a counter-revolutionary, Menshevik government. When Soviet power was established in Georgia in 1921, he emigrated to Paris. p. 298

290 *Nachalo* (The Beginning)—a Menshevik-Trotskyist paper, published in Paris from September 1916 to March 1917. p. 301

291 This letter was written in reply to a letter from A. V. Lunacharsky, who was to visit Zurich in March 1917 and had suggested to Lenin that there should be a joint conference of Bolsheviks and *Vperyod* supporters. Lenin turned down the proposal. p. 302

292 *Gvozdyov* (see also Note 288) was leader of the so-called "Workers' Group" under the Central War Industries Committee, set up by the Russian bourgeoisie in 1915. p. 302

293 This refers to the resolution adopted at a meeting of Russian and Swiss internationalists on March 22, 1917. p. 303

294 *Manifesto of Chkheidze*—an appeal by the Petrograd Soviet of Workers' and Soldiers' Deputies, which was dominated by Mensheviks and Socialist-Revolutionaries. It called for support of the Provisional Government. p. 304

295 *Hanecki*, *J. S.* (1879-1937)—prominent figure in the Polish and Russian revolutionary movements; in 1917, a member of the Bureau Abroad of the C.C. of the R.S.D.L.P.(B.). After the bourgeois-democratic revolution of February 1917 he took up residence in Stockholm. p. 308

296 *Die Glocke* (The Bell)—a fortnightly magazine published in Munich, and from 1915 to 1925 in Berlin, by Parvus (Helfand), a member of the German Social-Democratic Party, social-chauvinist, and agent of the German imperialists. p. 308

297 The pamphlet *Socialism and War* (*The Attitude of the R.S.D.L.P. Towards the War*) was published on the eve of the Zimmerwald Conference and distributed to the delegates.
In 1918 it was republished by the Petrograd Soviet of Workers' and Red Army Deputies (see present edition, Vol. 21, pp. 295-338). p. 310

298 Lenin stresses the responsibility borne by Kamenev because Kamenev, who had returned to Petrograd from exile on March 12, 1917, had become one of the editors of *Pravda* and a representative of the Bolshevik Party in the Petrograd Soviet.

Kamenev, however, adopted a semi-Menshevik position on certain vital aspects of Party policy. In articles published in *Pravda* he argued that the Bolsheviks should give the Provisional Government conditional support, while exerting pressure to make it open peace negotiations at once. In his assessment of the war Kamenev leaned towards defencism. Kamenev's position was sharply criticised by Lenin in his pamphlet *Letters on Tactics* (see present edition, Vol. 24, pp. 42-54).   p. 313

[299] Lenin refers to his speech of greeting on behalf of the C.C. of the R.S.D.L.P. at the Congress of the Swiss Social-Democratic Party in Zurich, November 4, 1916.   p. 315

[300] What is meant here is the "Conclusion" to Lenin's book *The Agrarian Programme of Social-Democracy in the First Russian Revolution, 1905-1907*. The book was written in November-December 1907 and printed in 1908, but while it was still at the print-shop it was confiscated by the police and destroyed.

While he was abroad, Lenin decided that when he returned to Russia he would get the book reprinted. This was done in 1917, but only part of the Conclusion appeared. The Conclusion was not published in full until 1924, in the magazine *Proletarskaya Revolutsia* (No. 5, pp. 166-72), after the discovery in the Geneva Party archives of Lenin's manuscript entitled "The Agrarian Problem during the First Russian Revolution (Towards a Revision of the Social-Democrats' Agrarian Programme)", which contained the full text of the Conclusion.   p. 316

[301] Reference is to the Seventh (April) All-Russia Conference of the R.S.D.L.P.(B.), held in Petrograd, April 24-29 (May 7-12), 1917 (see present edition, Vol. 24, pp. 225-313).   p. 317

[302] *Pravda* No. 88 for June 22 (July 5), 1917 published Hanecki's cable from Stockholm denying the slanderous statements made about him in the newspaper *Dyen* (Day). The same issue of *Pravda* also contained a telegram signed by Bronski, Orlovsky and Radek affirming Hanecki's innocence.   p. 318

[303] *Novaya Zhizn* (New Life) (Petrograd, 1917-18)—Menshevik-orientated daily, organ of a group of Social-Democrats known as the "Internationalists", which included Menshevik supporters of Martov and various semi-Menshevik intellectuals.

Reference is to Lunacharsky's letter to the editor published in *Novaya Zhizn* No. 60, June 28 (July 11), 1917.   p. 318

[304] *Bez Lishnikh Slov* (Without Wasting Words)—scurrilous weekly paper published by the Black-Hundred leader Alexinsky in Petrograd in July 1917.   p. 319

[305] Reference is to *Russische Korrespondenz "Pravda"* ("Pravda" Russian Bulletin), published by the R.S.D.L.P. Central Committee

Bureau Abroad in Stockholm in 1917. It was published in German; a French edition also appeared. p. 319

306 While Robert Grimm, Chairman of the International Socialist Commission (I.S.C.), was in Russia in the spring of 1917, he exchanged secret dispatches with the Swiss statesman Hoffmann concerning the German terms for conclusion of a separate peace treaty between Germany and Russia. When this became known, he was expelled from Russia. The investigation of the case was entrusted to a special commission nominated by the I.S.C., which declared Grimm's actions contradictory to the principles of the Zimmerwald movement. Grimm was removed from his post of Chairman of the I.S.C. and the commission's decision on the case was ratified by the third Zimmerwald Conference, held in Stockholm in September 1917. p. 320

307 Reference is to the International Socialist Conference, which was to take place in Stockholm in the summer of 1917. The Conference had been proposed by social-chauvinists of the neutral countries.
p. 320

308 On August 6 (19), 1917, at a meeting of the Central Executive Committee, held to discuss preparations for the Stockholm Conference, Kamenev spoke in favour of participation in the conference and revision of the Bolsheviks' decision on this question. The Bolshevik group in the C.E.C. dissociated itself from Kamenev's speech.

Lenin sent the editor of the newspaper *Proletary* an open letter called "Kamenev's Speech in the C.E.C. on the Stockholm Conference" (see present edition, Vol. 25, pp. 240-42). p. 320

309 Reference is to Franz Koritschoner. See Note 248. p. 321

310 Reference is to the resolutions passed at the Seventh (April) Conference and the Sixth Congress of the R.S.D.L.P.(B.) (see *KPSS v rezolyutsiyakh i resheniyakh syezdov, konferentsii i plenumov Tseka*, 7th ed., Part 1, 1954, pp. 335-53, and 372-89). p. 322

311 *Proletary* (The Proletarian)—daily paper, Central Organ of the Bolshevik Party; it appeared from August 13 (26) to August 24 (September 6), 1917 in place of *Pravda*, which had been banned by the Provisional Government. Ten issues were published.
p. 323

312 This letter was written in connection with the upswing of the revolutionary working-class movement in Finland sparked off by the October Socialist Revolution in Russia. p. 325

313 Lenin's telegram was sent in reply to a request from the Presidium of the Moscow Soviet of Workers' and Soldiers' Deputies that the Council of People's Commissars should confirm the appointment of

the newly elected Gubernia Commissar and the dismissal of the previous one.   p. 326

[314] This telegram was sent in reply to an inquiry from Y. Kryukov, Chairman of the Ostrogozhsk Soviet (Voronezh Gubernia), on what to do with the valuables collected during confiscation of the landed estates.   p. 327

[315] This telegram replies to an inquiry from Urban, Chairman of the Drissa Town Soviet, on what to do if German forces advanced on the town.   p. 329

[316] *Kursky, D. I.* (1874-1932)—member of the Bolshevik Party from 1904, People's Commissar for Justice of the R.S.F.S.R., 1918-28.
                                                              p. 331

[317] Lenin was prompted to write this letter by an incorrect decision taken by the Moscow Revolutionary Tribunal, which on May 2, 1918 heard the case against four members of the Moscow Commission of Investigation charged with bribery and blackmail and passed a sentence of only six months' imprisonment. On May 4 Lenin proposed to the C.C. of the R.C.P.(B.) that the judges who had passed such a lenient sentence should be expelled from the Party. Acting on the instructions given by Lenin in this letter, the Council of People's Commissars adopted a decision obliging the People's Commissariat of Justice "immediately" to draw up a Bill stipulating a "heavy minimum sentence for bribery and any connivance in bribery". The Commissariat of Justice's Bill was discussed by the C.P.C. on May 8 and amended by Lenin before it finally became law.   p. 331

[318] The defeat of the anti-Soviet revolt of the Mussavatists at the end of March 1918 consolidated Soviet power in Baku. A meeting of the Baku Soviet on April 25 set up the Baku Council of People's Commissars, which besides Bolsheviks included some Left Socialist-Revolutionaries. Shahumyan was made Chairman of the Baku Council of People's Commissars and Commissar for Foreign Affairs. The Council launched a number of socialist projects. In April and May 1918 Soviet power was established over a considerable part of Azerbaijan.

The Azerbaijan workers' and peasants' struggle for the victory of socialist revolution was waged in an extremely complex situation. The German-Turkish intervention had begun in the Transcaucasus and Turkish troops had invaded Azerbaijan. On the other hand, the British Command in Iran had made contact with the Baku Dashnaks, Socialist-Revolutionaries and Mensheviks, in the hope of using them to take over Baku and overthrow Soviet power in the city. Lenin therefore instructed the leaders of the Baku Council of People's Commissars to be extremely flexible in taking advantage of the contradictions within the imperialist camp and within the nationalist parties.   p. 332

[319] Lenin refers to the decision of the Council of People's Commissars, passed on November 18 (December 1), 1917, "On the Remuneration of People's Commissars, Senior Government Employees and Officials", which he had drafted. It set the maximum monthly salary for Commissars at 500 rubles with an allowance of 100 rubles for each member of the family unable to work.

Lenin also imposed a severe reprimand on N. P. Gorbunov, Secretary of the C.P.C.   p. 333

[320] *Volodarsky, V.*—a leader of the Petrograd Bolsheviks, editor of the Petrograd newspaper *Krasnaya Gazeta* (Red Gazette) and member of the Presidium of the Petrograd Soviet. He was murdered on June 20, 1918 by Socialist-Revolutionaries, who in direct collusion with whiteguards and foreign interventionists adopted terroristic tactics against the Bolsheviks.

On August 30, M. S. Uritsky, Chairman of the Petrograd Extraordinary Commission, was murdered by a Socialist-Revolutionary. The same day a villainous attempt to assassinate Lenin was made by the Socialist-Revolutionary terrorist Kaplan. Lenin was gravely wounded by two poisoned bullets.   p. 336

[321] This telegram was the last warning to A. M. Yuriev (Alexeyev), Chairman of the Murmansk Territory Soviet, where the Mensheviks and Socialist-Revolutionaries had a majority. On March 2, 1918 Yuriev had violated the instructions of the Soviet Government by entering into negotiations with representatives of the Entente and concluding a so-called "verbal agreement" with them, which virtually placed the Territory's military forces and economy in the hands of the "Allies" and enabled the imperialists of Britain, France and the United States to land troops in Murmansk. Despite several warnings from the Soviet Government Yuriev persisted in his criminal policy. On June 26 he sent Lenin a radio message demanding further concessions to the interventionists. Lenin's reply was the telegram published here.

Natsarenus, S. P. (1883-1938)—Military Commissar Extraordinary for the Murmansk-White Sea Territory in 1918; later Military Commissar for the Petrograd Military District. He was also at various times member of the Revolutionary Military Councils of the 7th, 14th and 15th armies.   p. 337

[322] This telegram followed a discussion by the Council of People's Commissars on July 1, 1918 concerning a report from V. I. Nevsky, People's Commissar for Railways, about protests received from railwaymen over the illegal activities of certain requisitioning detachments. Lenin drafted the telegram and submitted it to the meeting. A typewritten copy with corrections and amendments in Lenin's hand has been preserved.   p. 339

[323] The German Ambassador Mirbach was assassinated in the afternoon on July 6 by the Left Socialist-Revolutionaries Blyumkin and Andreyev, who got into the German Embassy with a forged

document for the alleged purpose of negotiating with the Ambassador and threw a bomb at him. The Left S.R.s hoped by this act to provoke a war with Germany and be able to overthrow Soviet power through the combined efforts of all the enemies of the revolution. The assassination of Mirbach marked the beginning of the Left S.R. counter-revolutionary revolt in Moscow, July 6-7, 1918, which was part of a general onslaught by internal counter-revolutionaries and the imperialists of the Entente against Soviet Russia; the rebels were secretly supported by foreign diplomatic missions.

The revolt occurred during the Fifth All-Russia Congress of Soviets, which instructed the Government to suppress the revolt at once. The group of Left S.R. delegates to the Congress was arrested. Thanks to the vigorous measures taken by the Soviet Government and the concerted action of Moscow workers and garrison, the revolt was put down.   p. 340

324 Reference is to the telegram that J. V. Stalin sent from Tsaritsyn to Shahumyan on July 20, 1918. In this telegram Stalin condemned the policy of the Mensheviks, Dashnaks and Socialist-Revolutionaries in the Baku Soviet, who, on the pretext of defending the city from the advancing Turkish army, advocated inviting the "assistance" of British troops. On behalf of the All-Russia Central Executive Committee and the Council of People's Commissars, Stalin demanded that the Baku Council of People's Commissars should unconditionally implement the decisions of the Fifth All-Russia Congress of Soviets on an independent foreign policy and resolute opposition to the agents of foreign capital.   p. 342

325 *Spartacists*—members of the Spartacus group, a revolutionary organisation of the German Left Social-Democrats, formed at the beginning of the first world war by Karl Liebknecht, Rosa Luxemburg, Franz Mehring, Clara Zetkin, Julian Marchlewski, Leon Jogiches (Tyszka) and Wilhelm Pieck. The group carried on revolutionary propaganda among the masses, organised anti-war demonstrations, led strikes, and exposed the imperialist nature of the war and the treachery of the opportunist Social-Democratic leaders. In April 1917, the group joined the centrist Independent Social-Democratic Party of Germany, while maintaining its organisational independence. In November 1918, during the revolution in Germany, the group renamed itself the Spartacus League; on December 14, 1918 it published its own programme and broke with the "Independents". At the Inaugural Congress held December 30, 1918 to January 1, 1919 the Spartacists founded the Communist Party of Germany.   p. 343

326 Lenin stamped the end of the letter with the State Seal of the R.S.F.S.R.   p. 344

327 This telegram was Lenin's reply to a telegram from Baku reporting the advance of the Turkish troops and the treacherous activities of

the Dashnaks, and also the Mensheviks and Socialist-Revolutionaries, who at an extraordinary meeting of the Baku Soviet on July 25, 1918, in spite of energetic protests by Bolshevik leaders of Soviet power in the city, had managed to gain an insignificant majority for a resolution inviting the British to give Baku military "assistance".

After the passing of this resolution, the Bolsheviks declared that they would resign their posts as People's Commissars. They continued, however, to fight for Soviet power. At an emergency meeting of the Executive Committee of the Baku Soviet on July 26, 1918 it was decided that until the question of power was finally settled all People's Commissars should remain at their posts. The All-Baku Conference of Bolsheviks held on July 27 resolved that emergency measures should be taken to defend Baku under the leadership of the C.P.C.; it also resolved to announce general mobilisation and call upon the workers to defend the city and Soviet power. The Baku C.P.C. undertook various measures to fulfil this decision.   p. 345

[328] *Tsyurupa, A. D.* (1870-1928)—professional revolutionary, prominent as a member of the Communist Party and government administrator. His posts included Deputy People's Commissar for Food (from November 1917), Commissar for Food (from 1918), Deputy Chairman of the Council of People's Commissars and of the Council of Labour and Defence (from 1921), People's Commissar for the Workers' and Peasants' Inspection (1922-23), Chairman of the State Planning Commission (1923-25) and People's Commissar for Home and Foreign Trade (1925); was elected member of the Party Central Committee at the 12th, 13th, 14th and 15th congresses of the Party.   p. 346

[329] On July 31, 1918 external pressure and various internal factors brought about the temporary collapse of Soviet power in Baku. On August 1, the Socialist-Revolutionaries, Mensheviks and Dashnaks organised a counter-revolutionary government known as the Dictatorship of the Central Caspian Area. Agents of the Entente, they immediately sent their representatives to Iran to fetch the British, and on August 4 a British force landed in Baku.

In these critical days the Baku Communists were with the masses, explaining the situation and exposing the treacherous policy of the Socialist-Revolutionaries, Mensheviks and Dashnaks; but the Baku Communists lacked the strength and opportunity to bring about any fundamental change in the political situation. On August 12, a Communist conference took the decision to withdraw temporarily to Astrakhan, taking as many arms and as much equipment as possible. A group of Communists was appointed to carry on Party work in Baku.

The plan of evacuation to Astrakhan did not succeed and the leaders of Soviet power in Baku were arrested.

In the middle of September 1918 the Turkish command launched an offensive on Baku. The troops of the Dictatorship of the

NOTES 609

Central Caspian Area and the British force withdrew, and on the morning of September 15 Turkish troops and Mussavatists entered the city. The previous day a group of Communists had managed to get the Commissars and other Bolsheviks out of prison. They escaped from the city aboard the steamer *Turkmen*, but on September 17 the crew, which had counter-revolutionary leanings, brought the ship into Krasnovodsk port, where the Socialist-Revolutionaries, Mensheviks and British interventionists were in command. All the members of the Baku Council of People's Commissars and other Party workers were immediately arrested. On the night of September 19, 1918, twenty-six leaders of the Baku Commune, who have since become known in history as the twenty-six Baku Commissars (S. G. Shahumyan, P. A. Japaridze, M. A. Azizbekov, I. T. Fioletov, Y. D. Zevin, G. N. Korganov, M. G. Vezirov and others), were brutally murdered in the Transcaspian desert by the British interventionists with the direct participation of the Socialist-Revolutionaries and the Mensheviks. p. 348

[330] *Kedrov, M. S.* (1878-1941)—joined the R.S.D.L.P. in 1901. After the October Socialist Revolution, member of the Collegium of the People's Commissariat for War, and Military Commissar for Demobilisation. In May 1918 he was sent to the North to organise defence. In March 1919 he became a member of the Collegium of the All-Russia Extraordinary Commission. p. 358

[331] Lenin refers to his recovery from wounds received when an attempt was made on his life by the Socialist-Revolutionary terrorist Fanny Kaplan on August 30, 1918.

His telegram was a reply to a telegram from the leaders of the Political Department of the 5th Army, wishing him a speedy recovery. p. 359

[332] Reference is to the article "Karl Kautsky and Henriette Roland-Holst on the Bolsheviks", published on September 20, 1918 in *Pravda*. The extracts mentioned by Lenin were taken from Kautsky's article "Democracy or Dictatorship" in No. 34 of the magazine *Sozialistische Auslandspolitik* (Socialist Foreign Policy) for August 1918. The magazine was the organ of the Kautskians. It was published in Berlin from 1915 to 1922 (after November 1918, under the title of *Der Sozialist*). p. 362

[333] Kautsky's pamphlet *The Dictatorship of the Proletariat* was published in Vienna in the autumn of 1918. It distorted the Marxist theory of the proletarian revolution and slandered the Soviet state. Lenin in his book *The Proletarian Revolution and the Renegade Kautsky* and other works of this period castigated the leaders of the Second International, particularly Kautsky, for their distortion of Marxist teaching on the socialist revolution and the dictatorship of the proletariat, and further developed Marxist theory on these vital questions. p. 363

[334] The joint meeting of the All-Russia C.E.C., the Moscow Soviet, the factory committees and the trade unions, proposed by Lenin, was held on Thursday, October 3, 1918. Lenin, who was convalescing at Gorki after being wounded, could not attend the meeting, but sent a letter that was read out. His main proposals were included in the resolution passed by the meeting, which on the same day was officially announced to the world by telegraph. p. 365

[335] Lenin was prompted to write this letter by the decision of the Presidium of the Moscow Soviet of October 7, 1918, in which the leaders of the Soviet attempted to avoid responsibility for not carrying out the decree of the Council of People's Commissars on setting up in Moscow monuments to outstanding figures in the revolutionary movement and the world of culture. p. 368

[336] See Note 325. p. 369

[337] Reference is to the Bremen group of German Left Social-Democrats; in 1919 the group joined the Communist Party of Germany. p. 369

[338] Reference is to the suppression of the whiteguard and S.R. revolt at the Izhevsk and Votkinsk Works (Vyatka Gubernia). The rebels took over Izhevsk and Votkinsk in August 1918. The two towns were liberated by Soviet troops on November 7 and 12, 1918. p. 370

[339] This telegram was Lenin's reply to the following telegram, which he received on November 13, 1918 from Unecha Station (Chernigov Gubernia): "The representatives of the revolutionary soldiers of Germany, delegates of the Lyshchichi Soviet of Soldiers' Deputies, together with the Unecha organisation of the R.C.P.(B.), welcome in your person the world revolution. Representatives of the revolutionary German troops of the village of Lyshchichi (signatures). Chairman of the Unecha organisation of the R.C.P.(B.) *Ivanov*. Revolutionary Commissar *Lind*. Commander of the Bogun Regiment *Shchors*." p. 373

[340] The decree "On Organisation of Supply", passed by the Council of People's Commissars on November 21, 1918, provided for development of the co-operative movement and the revival of nationalised and municipalised co-operative shops and stores. The decree made it incumbent on the Poor Peasants' Committees and the local Soviets to establish systematic supervision of the work of the co-operatives in order to prevent any attempts that might be made by kulaks and other counter-revolutionary elements to dominate them. p. 376

[341] Lenin refers to the whiteguard Cossack rising on the Don, in the Veshenskaya area, in the rear of the Southern Front. In a number of directives to the Revolutionary Military Council of the Republic and the Command of the Southern Front Lenin drew attention to the danger of the rebels' linking up with Denikin's

advancing troops, and the need to crush the rebellion with all speed (see this volume, pp. 381, 387, 390 and 391). p. 378

[342] Realising the tremendous significance of the struggle for the Donets coalfields, the Central Committee of the R.C.P.(B.) and Lenin repeatedly instructed the commanders of the Ukrainian Front and the Ukrainian Soviet Government to assist the Southern Front. But some of the military leaders of the Ukraine (N.I. Podvoisky, V. A. Antonov-Ovseyenko and others), prompted by narrow, local interests, held up the transfer of troops to the Donets sector. Antonov-Ovseyenko, Commander of the Ukrainian Front, demanded that the lines of demarcation between the Ukrainian Front and the Southern Front in the Donets Basin should be revised, and that the bulk of the forces operating in this area should be placed under his command, and refused to recognise the major importance of the Donets sector, claiming that the Ukrainian Front was confronted by more important tasks in the western and southern Ukraine. Lenin rejected his proposal. p. 383

[343] Reference is to the highly nationalistic resolution passed by the Ekaterinoslav organisation of the Ukrainian Socialist-Revolutionaries, who opposed the dictatorship of the proletariat, the policy of the Soviet Government, and the political, economic and military alliance between the Ukraine and Soviet Russia. p. 384

[344] The war trophies captured by the Red Army on the Southern Front included several French tanks. The Command of the 2nd Ukrainian Soviet Army sent one of them to Lenin as a gift, accompanying it with a letter of welcome. p. 385

[345] *Cheka* (All-Russia Extraordinary Commission to Combat Counter-Revolution and Sabotage)—a security organ set up by the Council of People's Commissars on December 7, 1917. In 1922 it was reorganised as the State Political Administration (G.P.U.). p. 387

[346] At the beginning of May 1919, the threat of an offensive by White Finnish troops made it necessary to mobilise the working people of Petrograd in defence of the city. Some of the Petrograd leaders, however, including G. Y. Zinoviev, Chairman of the city's Defence Committee, underestimated the strength and ability of the defenders. In a mood of panic they decided, without informing the Defence Council, to evacuate several factories, and were preparing to scuttle the Baltic Fleet. Workers were mobilised haphazardly with the result that many factories of great defence importance had to slow down. The telegram sent by Lenin was on behalf of the Defence Council. The draft of it was signed by L. B. Krasin and A. I. Rykov. p. 389

[347] The Defence Council took direct control over the organisation of the defence of Petrograd. On May 17, 1919 it decided not to announce and not to carry out any general evacuation of Petrograd

or the Petrograd area, but to set up a special commission with powers to state what should be moved out of the city, and how this should be done. p. 389

348 Reference is to the counter-revolutionary "ataman" Grigoryev, who in May 1919 had started an insurrection in the rear of the Red Army in the southern Ukraine (Elizavetgrad, Ekaterinoslav, Krivoi Rog and Kherson area). The insurrection was crushed at the end of May 1919. p. 392

349 Lenin refers to the criminal delay in fulfilling his instructions on the urgent dispatch of reinforcements to the Petrograd Front. p. 396

350 Besieged Uralsk was relieved by the Red Army on July 11, 1919. p. 400

351 During the decisive offensive actions of the Southern Group of the Forces of the Eastern Front against Kolchak, White Cossack and kulak risings occurred in a number of front-line areas (Samara and Orenburg gubernias, and the Urals Region). p. 403

352 Lenin refers to the counter-revolutionary bands marauding in the rear of the Soviet forces. p. 406

353 In its telegram to Lenin of July 11, 1919, the Presidium of the Tula Gubernia Metalworkers' Congress declared that the Congress had voted for a tenfold increase in arms output (underlined twice by Lenin), the military training of all workers and the forming of reserve workers' regiments that would be ready at any minute to go into action against the whiteguards. The Presidium asked Lenin to convey to the Council of People's Commissars "the metalworkers' socialist pledge to die or conquer all imperialists of this country and from abroad". p. 407

354 Lenin refers to the following decisive victories over the whiteguard forces in the struggle for the liberation of the Urals: the capture of the town of Zlatoust by the 5th Army (July 13, 1919), and the capture of the town of Ekaterinburg (now Sverdlovsk) by the 2nd Army on July 14, 1919.
The new Commander of the Forces of the Eastern Front appointed on July 13, 1919 was Mikhail Frunze. p. 408

355 Reference is evidently to the enlisting of the Bashkirs in the struggle against Kolchak, particularly the formation of Bashkir military units. p. 408

356 *Gusev, S. I.* (1874-1933)—joined the Party in 1896. On political work in the Red Army, 1918-20. Member of the Revolutionary Military Councils of the 5th and 2nd Armies of the Eastern, South-Eastern and Southern fronts. p. 420

[357] This was written on a letter from G. K. Orjonikidze (Sergo) of October 15, 1919, reporting disorder and criminal lack of discipline in the armies of the Southern Front.

Orjonikidze had written: "Something unbelievable, something bordering on treachery. A light-minded attitude to the work, an absolute failure to understand the seriousness of the situation. Not a sign of order at any of the headquarters. Front H.Q. is a riot.... Where is this order and discipline, where is Comrade Trotsky's regular army?! How could he have allowed such a collapse. This is beyond all bounds."   p. 423

[358] On October 15, 1919, the Political Bureau of the C.C. of the R.C.P.(B.) discussed the situation on the various fronts. In view of the grave military danger, the Bureau passed a decision that Soviet Russia should be turned into a veritable armed camp and that the maximum number of Communists and Communist sympathisers should be taken off general administrative work (except in the People's Commissariats of Railways and Food, and the Cheka). A commission consisting of Lenin, Trotsky, Kamenev and Krestinsky was instructed to draft a decree simplifying civil administration so as to release as many personnel as possible who were fit for military service. The draft decree "On Simplification of the Civil Apparatus of Soviet Power" was discussed by the C.P.C. on October 21 and 28, November 4, 21 and 25, and December 15. The decree was published in *Izvestia* No. 293, on December 28, 1919.   p. 424

[359] Orel was liberated by Soviet troops on October 20, 1919, the day Lenin wrote this letter.   p. 425

[360] *Vorovsky, V. V.* (1871-1923)—joined the Party in 1894. After the October Socialist Revolution he was the Soviet Republic's plenipotentiary in Scandinavia (1917-19), in charge of the State Publishing House (1919-20), then returned to diplomatic work, in Italy (1921-23).   p. 427

[361] Krzhizhanovsky's article was published in *Pravda* No. 5, on January 10, 1920, under the title "Torf i krizis topliva" ("Peat and the Fuel Crisis").   p. 430

[362] Lenin refers to the Independent Social-Democratic Party of Germany, a Centrist party founded in April 1917. The party held an emergency congress in Leipzig from November 30 to December 6, 1919, at which under pressure from Left-wing members of the party a programme of action recognising the idea of the dictatorship of the proletariat and the system of Soviets was adopted. The party's proletarian wing also proposed "immediate and unconditional joining of the Third International". In October 1920 at the Independent Social-Democratic Party's congress in Halle a split occurred, and in December 1920 a large section of the party joined the Communist Party of Germany. The Right-wing elements formed a separate

party, retaining the old title Independent Social-Democratic Party of Germany; this party existed until 1922. p. 432

[363] At the end of 1919, Lenin gave instructions that 10,000 qualified metalworkers should be sent to repair the railways. The leaders of the All-Russia Central Council of Trade Unions and the Moscow City Council of Trade Unions were slow in arranging the transfer of metalworkers to the Moscow railway system, and the delay prompted Lenin to write this letter. p. 433

[364] Reference is to *Tolkovy slovar zhivogo velikorusskogo yazyka* (Explanatory Dictionary of the Living Russian Language) by V. I. Dahl, published in four volumes, 1863-66.

In accordance with Lenin's instructions, the People's Commissariat of Education began work on compiling a new dictionary, but the project was not realised at that time. A new *Tolkovy slovar russkogo yazyka* (Explanatory Dictionary of the Russian Language) came out in 1935-40 in four volumes under the editorship of D. N. Ushakov. p. 434

[365] Lenin refers to Krzhizhanovsky's article "Zadachi elektrifikatsii promyshlennosti" ("Tasks of the Electrification of Industry"), a condensed version of which was published in *Pravda* No. 20 on January 30, 1920. p. 435

[366] Krzhizhanovsky had written a pamphlet *Osnovniye zadachi elektrifikatsii Rossii* (The Basic Tasks of the Electrification of Russia). It was published in February 1920. p. 435

[367] In his telegram of February 26, 1920 Trotsky wrote that it would be inexpedient to maintain the whole clerical staff of the 3rd Army, which had been transferred to labour service. The army had only one infantry and one cavalry division. The telegram further stated that the Field H.Q. had given its assent to the disbanding of the army clerical staffs and requested the opinion of the Defence Council. Lenin marked the telegram "Report to the Defence Council". p. 438

[368] Lenin refers to the transfer of certain Red Army units to labour service at the beginning of 1920, so that they could be used for purposes of reconstruction. The war with bourgeois-landowner Poland and Wrangel forced the Government to return the labour armies to the fighting line. p. 438

[369] Reference is to the programme of work of the State Commission for the Electrification of Russia (GOELRO) and the explanatory note to it, passed at a session of GOELRO on March 13, 1920. p. 440

[370] Krzhizhanovsky subsequently wrote that when Lenin used the words "as a first approximation" he was teasing him for his habit of prefacing any calculations or plans with this cautious formula. p. 441

[371] The task of taking the Crimea, where the remnants of Denikin's defeated army under the command of General Y. A. Slashchov had taken refuge, was given to the 13th Army of the South-Western Front. In January 1920, only the 46th Division of this army engaged Slashchov's forces, but it was unable to break through into the Crimea. Fresh attempts to take the Crimea in February and the first half of March 1920 were also unsuccessful.   p. 442

[372] Reference is to the events in Germany following the so-called "Kapp putsch". On March 13, 1920 Berlin was seized by counter-revolutionary officers of the Reichswehr, who aimed at restoring the monarchy and establishing a terroristic military dictatorship. The German working class replied to this attempted counter-revolutionary coup with a general strike, which spread all over the country. The putsch was defeated.   p. 442

[373] *Adoratsky, V. V.* (1878-1945)—professional revolutionary, Bolshevik. In 1920, he became assistant manager of the Central Archives Board, and in 1932 a member of the Academy of Sciences of the U.S.S.R. He wrote a number of works on the Marxist theory of the state and law, and on the philosophy and history of Marxism.   p. 444

[374] *Timiryazev, K. A.* (1843-1920)—Russian Darwinist, outstanding botanist and physiologist, gifted populariser and propagandist of scientific knowledge, Corresponding Member of the St. Petersburg Academy of Sciences. He was the first eminent scientist to welcome the October Socialist Revolution.   p. 445

[375] Reference is to Timiryazev's book *Nauka i Demokratiya. Sbornik statei 1904-1919* (Science and Democracy. Collected articles 1904-1919), Moscow, 1920.

On page IX of the book there is a gift inscription from the author that reads: "To deeply respected Vladimir Ilyich Lenin from K. Timiryazev, who counts it his good fortune to be Lenin's contemporary and a witness of his glorious work."   p. 445

[376] See Note 240.   p. 447

[377] The proletarian writer Serafimovich had lost his son during the Civil War.   p. 448

[378] This note was in response to information from Kursky that a communiqué had been received by the Revolutionary Military Council of the Republic from the Western Front, stating that the 15th Army's offensive was going well.   p. 449

[379] The plan of theses expounded in this letter formed the basis of Lenin's report on the international situation and the fundamental tasks of the Communist International which he made at the Second

Congress of the Comintern, held in Moscow from July 19 to August 7, 1920 (see present edition, Vol. 31, pp. 215-34). p. 450

[380] Reference is to Levi's report "The Political Situation and the Elections to Parliament" at the Congress of the Communist Party of Germany, which took place in Berlin, April 14-15, 1920. p. 451

[381] *Chicherin, G. V.* (1872-1936)—prominent Soviet statesman, People's Commissar for Foreign Affairs, 1918-30. p. 452

[382] This was written in connection with telegrams from Mikhail Frunze, who had asked Lenin to hasten the transfer of the 1st Cavalry Army to the Southern Front. p. 457

[383] *Frunze* was made Commander of the Forces of the Southern Front in September 1920. p. 458

[384] The Crimea was liberated by the Red Army in November 1920. p. 458

[385] In a letter addressed to Lenin certain members of the Presidium of the Tula Gubernia Committee of the R.C.P.(B.) asked for his advice on "which of the two positions in the situation at present experienced by Soviet Russia is correct—the position giving priority to peaceful construction, or the other position giving priority to the necessity of straining every effort to solve our military problems". The authors of the letter expressed misgivings that showing priority to economic and educational tasks, as certain members of the Tula Party organisation were trying to do, would weaken effort and discipline at the Tula munitions factories. p. 459

[386] This letter was written in response to Maxim Gorky's appeal to the All-Russia Commission for Improving Scientists' Living Conditions, in which he mentioned certain cases when scientific workers had been obliged to share too large a part of their flats with new tenants. Gorky was then chairman of the Petrograd branch of the Commission. p. 460

[387] *Klasson, R. E.* (1868-1926)—Soviet power engineer. He designed and directed the construction of a number of power stations in Moscow, Petrograd and in the Baku oilfields, and also the world's first peat-fuelled power station. He was one of the inventors of the hydraulic method of extracting peat. p. 462

[388] Lenin refers to the decision "On the Hydraulic Method of Extracting Peat", passed by the Council of People's Commissars on October 30, 1920. p. 462

[389] Reference is to the meeting of the preliminary conference on organisation of contact between all People's Commissariats concerned with the economy. The preliminary conference was set up by the

Council of People's Commissars on October 26, 1920; its chairman
was Lenin.   p. 464

[390] The *Narrow Council of People's Commissars* was organised in
December 1917. It had the rights of a commission of the Council of
People's Commissars and its task was to relieve the Council of
minor affairs. Its decisions, which had to be unanimous, were signed
by V. I. Lenin and acquired the force of decisions of the Council of
People's Commissars. If a difference of opinion arose the matter
was placed before the Council of People's Commissars.   p. 464

[391] This letter, a copy of which was sent to Y. A. Preobrazhensky,
was written apparently because Lenin had noticed omissions in
the proofs of the pamphlet *On Concessions. Decree of the Council
of People's Commissars of November 23, 1920. Text of the Decree.
Units for Concession. Maps*, which had been sent to him for inspection.   p. 466

[392] Lenin refers to the Eighth All-Russia Congress of Soviets, held
December 22-29, 1920, at which Krzhizhanovsky delivered a
report on the plan for the electrification of Russia. The resolution
on the electrification report was drafted by Lenin.   p. 469

[393] The letter was written on a memorandum which P. A. Ostryakov,
the construction chief of the first radio-telephone station in Moscow,
sent to Lenin on January 26, 1921. Ostryakov reported that he
was encountering difficulties and asked Lenin to help remove
them and endorse the decree Ostryakov had drafted.
On January 27, 1921 the C.P.C. passed a decree on organising
full-scale radio-telephone construction. It instructed the People's
Commissariat of Posts and Telegraphs to build stations for two-
way radio-telephone communication in Moscow and other centres.
Bonch-Bruyevich, M. A. (1888-1940)—outstanding Soviet
radio engineer. In 1916-19 he did research on electronic valves.
In 1918 he took charge of the Nizhni-Novgorod Radio Laboratory.
                                                                  p. 473

[394] Reference is to V. P. Milyutin's report "On Methods of Drawing
up an Integrated Economic Plan", which he delivered at the Socialist Academy on February 17, 1921. An account of the report and
its theses were published in the newspaper *Ekonomicheskaya Zhizn*
No. 37, on February 19, 1921. Lenin criticised Milyutin's theses in
his article "An Integrated Economic Plan" (see present edition,
Vol. 32, pp. 137-45).   p. 475

[395] Reference is to the State Planning Commission of the Council
of Labour and Defence of the R.S.F.S.R. It was organised on February 21, 1921.   p. 476

[396] The speech delivered by Krzhizhanovsky at the first session of
the State Planning Commission (Gosplan) on April 5, 1921.   p. 480

[397] This refers to the book *Plan elektrifikatsii R.S.F.S.R. Doklad vosmomu syezdu Sovetov Gosudarstvennoi Komissii po elektrifikatsii Rossii*" (Plan for the Electrification of the R.S.F.S.R. Report of the State Commission for the Electrification of Russia to the Eighth Congress of Soviets) published in December 1920.

Lenin spoke of the importance of this book in his report on the work of the Council of People's Commissars at the Eighth All-Russia Congress of Soviets (see present edition, Vol. 31, pp. 513-18) and in the article "An Integrated Economic Plan" (ibid., Vol. 32, pp. 137-41). p. 480

[398] *Litkens, Y. A.* (1888-1922)—member of the R.S.D.L.P. from 1904. In 1917 he was a member of the internationalist Mensheviks' Central Committee; in 1919 entered the R.C.P.(B.). Deputy Manager of the Chief Committee for Political Education, 1920; Deputy Commissar for Education of the R.S.F.S.R., from 1921 on. p. 482

[399] Reference is to *NEP* (New Economic Policy)—the policy of the proletarian state during the period of transition from capitalism to socialism. This policy was "new" in contrast to the economic policy which had been conducted in Soviet Russia in the period of foreign military intervention and the Civil War, known in history as the policy of War Communism (1918-20). The latter was made necessary by war-time conditions, and its characteristic features were extreme centralisation of production and distribution of goods, prohibition of free trading, and food requisitioning which compelled the peasants to turn in all surplus produce to the state.

When the New Economic Policy was adopted, commodity-money relations became the basic form of relations between socialist industry and the small-peasant economy. When food requisitioning was abolished and replaced by the tax in kind, the peasants were able to dispose of their surplus produce as they chose, i.e., sell them at the market, and through the market obtain the industrial goods they required.

The New Economic Policy was calculated to achieve a firm economic and political alliance between the working class and the peasantry for the building of socialism, for the development of the productive forces along socialist lines. It provided for a certain measure of capitalism while the basic economic positions remained in the hands of the proletarian state. It assumed the struggle of the socialist elements against the capitalist elements, the victory of the socialist elements, the elimination of the exploiting classes, and the building of socialism in the U.S.S.R. p. 483

[400] *Posledniye Novosti* (Latest News)—whiteguard émigré daily paper, organ of the counter-revolutionary Constitutional-Democratic Party (Cadets); published in Paris from April 1920 to July 1940. Its editor was P. N. Milyukov. p. 490

[401] Reference is to the co-report by Sokolov "On the Tax in Kind and the Change in the Policy of Soviet Power" at the general meeting

of the R.C.P.(B.) group at the People's Commissariat of Foreign Affairs, May 18, 1921. Sokolov sent it to Lenin, requesting him to read it and reply to a number of questions which it raised.
p. 491

402 In the draft of his co-report Sokolov quoted the following passage from Engels: "The worst thing that can befall a leader of an extreme party is to be compelled to take over a government at a time when society is not yet ripe for the domination of the class he represents and for the measures which that domination implies" (Engels, *The Peasant War in Germany*, Moscow, 1965, p. 112).
p. 492

403 *Dzerzhinsky, F. E.* (1877-1926)—Party member from 1895. After the October Socialist Revolution he became Chairman of the All-Russia Extraordinary Commission to Combat Counter-Revolution and Sabotage (known as the Cheka). In 1921 he was appointed People's Commissar for Railways, while remaining Chairman of the Cheka and People's Commissar for Internal Affairs. Member of the C.C. of the R.C.P.(B.).
p. 499

404 *Pavlovich, M. P. (Veltman, M. L.)* (1871-1929)—Social-Democrat, Menshevik. He became a Communist after 1917, and from 1921 was a member of the Collegium of the Commissariat for Affairs of Nationalities.
p. 501

405 Reference is to the preparations for the publication of the *Vsemirny geografichesky atlas* (Geographical Atlas of the World), launched on Lenin's initiative. The project was not realised.
p. 501

406 *Avanesov, V. A.* (1884-1930)—joined the Party in 1903. In 1917 he became a member of the Presidium of the All-Russia C.E.C.; in 1920-24, Deputy People's Commissar of the Workers' and Peasants' Inspection, member of the Collegium of the Cheka, and later Deputy People's Commissar for Foreign Trade.
p. 504

407 *Workers' and Peasants' Inspection (Rabkrin)* was set up in February 1920 on Lenin's initiative, on the basis of the reorganised People's Commissariat of State Control, which had been formed in the early months of Soviet power. Lenin attached great importance to control and verification at all levels. He worked out in detail the principles of organising control in the Soviet state, kept an eye on Rabkrin's activity, criticised its shortcomings and did his best to make it more efficient. In his last articles, "How We Should Reorganise the Workers' and Peasants' Inspection" and "Better Fewer, but Better", Lenin outlined a plan for reorganising Rabkrin. The basic principles of Lenin's plan were to merge Party and state control and to enlist more workers and peasants in its activities.
p. 504

[408] When the Regulations on the Council of Labour and Defence's
Commission for Utilising the Material Resources of the R.S.F.S.R.
were being drawn up, differences of opinion concerning
the functions of the commission arose between A. B. Khalatov
(People's Commissar for Food), G. M. Krzhizhanovsky (State
Planning Commission), P. A. Bogdanov (Supreme Economic
Council) and L. N. Kritsman (Commission for Utilising Material
Resources).

On June 14, 1921, the Council of People's Commissars endorsed
the amended draft Regulations drawn up by the State Planning
Commission. On June 29, the Regulations, which on the instructions of the Council of People's Commissars had been edited by
a commission composed of Bogdanov, Krzhizhanovsky, Kritsman and Khalatov, were signed by Lenin.   p. 506

[409] On July 9, 1921, the Political Bureau of the C.C. of the R.C.P.(B.)
passed a decision "On Intensifying Food Work". It stated: "The
Organising Bureau should confirm the need to take the maximum
number of Communists and, in exceptional cases, other particularly valuable comrades, from their present work and transfer
them to food work, even at the cost of causing a temporary clos-
ing-down of nine-tenths of departments in some institutions and
even whole People's Commissariats that are not absolutely essential."   p. 509

[410] Reference is to the commission for assisting economic bodies.
                                                            p. 511

[411] Reference is to the introduction Adoratsky wrote for the book
which Lenin had asked him to prepare, *K. Marks i F. Engels.
Pisma. Teoriya i politika v perepiske Marksa i Engelsa* (Letters.
Theory and Policy in the Correspondence of Marx and Engels).
The book appeared in 1922.   p. 516

[412] See Karl Marx, *Capital*, Vol. I, Moscow, pp. 59-60, 126-27. p. 516

[413] Adoratsky was preparing for the press the book *Programma
po osnovnym voprosam Marksizma* (Programme on the Basic
Problems of Marxism), published in 1922.   p. 516

[414] Reference is to Safarov's pamphlet *Ocheredniye voprosy natsional-
noi politiki* (Current Questions of the Nationalities Policy),
published in 1921.   p. 518

[415] *Oblomov*—landowner in Goncharov's novel of the same name,
personifying sluggishness, stagnation and inertia.   p. 519

[416] Professor G. O. Graftio, Chief Engineer at the Construction of
the Volkhov Hydro-Power Station, had stated that some institutions were taking a bureaucratic attitude to the project. p. 521

[417] Reference is apparently to the transfer of Store No. 11 from the People's Commissariat of Railways to the Supreme Economic Council.   p. 523

[418] This refers to the decision of the Narrow Council of People's Commissars on the allocation of 2,000 million rubles for repairing houses in Moscow, passed on October 21, 1921.   p. 528

[419] Reference is to Krzhizhanovsky's book *Khozyaistvenniye problemy R.S.F.S.R. i raboty Gosudarstvennoi obshcheplanovoi komissii (Gosplana)* (The Economic Problems of the R.S.F.S.R. and the Work of the State General Planning Commission [Gosplan]), Part I. The book appeared in December 1921 with the addition, of which Lenin writes in this letter.   p. 530

[420] On December 1, 1921, the Political Bureau of the C.C. of the R.C.P.(B.), having heard Lenin's report on the work of Tsyurupa, endorsed his appointment as Second Deputy Chairman of the Council of Labour and Defence. On December 5, by decision of the Political Bureau Tsyurupa was appointed Deputy Chairman of the Council of People's Commissars.   p. 535

[421] *Bednota* (The Poor)—daily peasant newspaper published in Moscow from March 27, 1918, to February 1, 1931, when it was merged with *Sotsialisticheskoye Zemledeliye* (Socialist Agriculture).   p. 543

[422] Reference is to Gorev's pamphlet *Elektrifikatsia Frantsii* (The Electrification of France). It was published in 1922.   p. 544

[423] Lenin refers to the book by Karl Ballod *Der Zukunftsstaat* (The State of the Future), a Russian translation of which appeared in 1920. Lenin writes of Ballod's book in his article "An Integrated Economic Plan" (see present edition, Vol. 32, p. 140).   p. 544

[424] The introduction to A. Gorev's pamphlet *Elektrifikatsia Frantsii* (The Electrification of France) was not written by Lenin.   p. 545

[425] *GUM*—a state department store in Moscow, of which Belov was director at the time.   p. 547

[426] *Martens, L. K.* (1875-1948)—Communist, technological engineer. In 1921 he was member of the Presidium of the Supreme Economic Council.   p. 551

[427] *Pletnyov, V. F.* (1886-1942)—one of the leaders of the Proletcult. He and A. Bogdanov spread anti-Marxist reactionary ideas on culture and art claiming that such ideas represented "proletarian culture". For a criticism of the views of the Proletcult supporters see present edition, Vol. 29, p. 336 and Vol. 31, pp. 316-17.   p. 554

[428] Lenin refers to the article by I. I. Skvortsov-Stepanov "Chto takoye spets i kak yego delayut" ("What a Specialist Is and How He Is Made"), published in *Pravda* No. 244, October 28, 1922.   p. 557

[429] Reference is to the following passage from the article by Skvortsov-Stepanov: "Here, too, the *class struggle* must develop, the struggle between socialism and 'capitalist craftsmanship' or 'craftsmen's capitalism', more likely the latter. After what has been said the reader will not be surprised by the abnormality of this phrase. It is no more abnormal than the real relations which it expresses."   p. 557

[430] *International Workers' Aid*—an international proletarian organisation, set up in 1921 to help the population of the parts of Soviet Russia which in 1921 were struck by famine because of the bad harvest. Its chairman was Clara Zetkin, and its General Secretary, Willi Münzenberg. International Workers' Aid was active in collecting money, provisions and medical supplies, organising children's homes, etc. In 1922 the I.W.A. launched a number of industrial and agricultural projects in Soviet Russia to promote her economic rehabilitation. The I.W.A. later grew into a powerful organisation, which rendered great assistance to the international working-class movement.   p. 559

IDENTIFICATION OF PSEUDONYMS, NICKNAMES AND INITIALS USED IN THE TEXT

A.,Alexander —Shlyapnikov, A.G.
A. M., Al. M., Al. Max.—
    Gorky, A. M.
A. M.—Kollontai, Alexandra
An—Ananun, D.
A. P.—Pannekoek, A.
Andrei—Sverdlov, Y. M.
Antonov—Popov, A. (Britman)

Bezrabotny—Manuilsky, D. Z.
Belenin—Shlyapnikov, A. G.
Bonch—Bonch-Bruyevich, V. D.

Chuzhak—Nasimovich, N. F.

Dnevnitsky—Tsederbaum, F. O.

E. B., Eug. B.—Bosh, Eugène

Foma-Piterests—Smirnov, A. P.
Franz—Koritschoner, F.
Frey—Lenin, V. I.
Friend—Chernomazov, M.

Galyorka—Olminsky, M. S.
Galina—Rozmirovich, E. F.
Grigory, Gr—y—Zinoviev, G. Y.
Grisha—Belenky, G.
Gylka, I.—Melenevsky, M.

Ilyin, V.—Lenin, V. I.
Inessa—Armand, Inessa
Isaac—Raskin
Ivanovich—Stalin, J. V.

J. K.—Marchlewski, Julian
James—Yelizarova, Anna

Jan—Savinov, I. T.
Junius—Luxemburg, Rosa

K., Kam.—Kamenev, L. B.
Kamsky—Vladimirsky, M. F.
Kievsky P., Kii—Pyatakov, G. L.
Koba—Stalin, J. V.
Kostrov—Jordania, N.
Kuba—Hanecki, J. S.

Lyudmila—Stahl, L. N.

M. F., Maria Fyodorovna—An-
    dreyeva, M. F.
Makar—Nogin, V. P.
Meshkovsky—Goldenberg, I. P.
Mikhalchi—Nakhimson, S. M.

N. I., N. Iv., Nik. Iv.
    —Bukharin, N. I.
N. K., Nadya,
Nadezhda Konstantinovna—
    Krupskaya, N. K.
Nik. Vas.—Kuznetsov, N. V.
    (Sapozhkov)
Nikolai—Orjonikidze, G. K.
Noah—Buachidze, S. G.
Nota Bene—Bukharin, N. I.

Olga—Ravich, S. N.

Pavel Vasilyevich,
    Pavlov—Berzin, Y.
Paragraph—Stučka, P. I.

Rosa—Luxemburg, R.

Ropshin—Savinkov, B. V.
Rude—Rudis-Gipslis, I.

S., Sergo—Orjonikidze, G. K.
Sima—Mikhailova, S. A.

Tria—Mgeladze, V. D.

V. I.—Lenin, V. I.
Varin—Fridolin, V.
Vasily—Stalin, J. V.
Vetrov—Savelyev, M. A.
Vitimsky—Olminsky, M. S.
Volsky—Sokolov, A. V.

Yuri—Pyatakov, G. L.

————